The Sign & Its Masters

"Hi! I assemble visual and verbal elements and package and market the result."

Drawing by Donald Reilly; © 1978 by The New Yorker Magazine, Inc.

The Sign & Its Masters

by Thomas A. Sebeok

University of Texas Press, Austin & London

For J. the Signifier & J. the Signified

The poem "Buffalo Bill" is reprinted from *Tulips and Chimneys* by E. E. Cummings with the permission of the Liveright Publishing Corporation. Copyright 1923, 1925, and renewed 1951, 1953 by E. E. Cummings. Copyright 1973, 1976 by Nancy T. Andrews. Copyright 1973, 1976 by George James Firmage.

Library of Congress Cataloging in Publication Data

Sebeok, Thomas Albert, 1920–
   The sign and its masters.

   Bibliography: p.
   Includes index.
   1. Semiotics.   I. Title.
P99.S34   001.5   78-12791
ISBN 0-292-77547-4

Copyright © 1979 by the University of Texas Press
All rights reserved
Printed in the United States of America

Contents

Introduction vii

PART ONE: THE SIGN

1. Semiosis in Nature and Culture 3
2. Semiotics and Ethology 27
3. Zoosemiotic Components of Human Communication 35
4. Ecumenicalism in Semiotics 61
5. Looking in the Destination for What Should Have Been Sought in the Source 84
6. Iconicity 107
7. Aboriginal Sign "Languages" from a Semiotic Point of View (with D. Jean Umiker-Sebeok) 128
8. The Two Sons of Croesus: A Myth about Communication in Herodotus (with Erika Brady) 168

PART TWO: THE MASTERS

9. The French Swiss Connection 183
10. Neglected Figures in the History of Semiotic Inquiry: Jakob von Uexküll 187
11. Gyula Laziczius 208
12. "Dialect" from a Zoosemiotic Perspective 216
13. Roman Jakobson's Teaching in America 221
14. John Lotz: A Personal Memoir 231

15. Parasitic Formations and Kindred Semiotic Sets: Notes on the Legacy of John Lotz 248

16. Marginalia to Greenberg's Conception of Semiotics and Zoosemiotics 253

APPENDICES

I. The Semiotic Self 263

II. Displaying the Symptoms 268

III. Teaching Semiotics: Report on a Pilot Program 272

Notes 281

References 297

Index of Names 327

Introduction

When two Budapest boulevardiers meet, one of them may confront the other with the first half of a familiar wry political two-liner: "This is a transitional year!" The other party is then most likely to rejoin, less with a peal of laughter than a rueful sigh: "Yes, it is decidedly worse than last year, but sure to be better than the next."

This is a transitional book. Its chapters, with a sporadic exception or two, were composed about midway between my *Contributions to the Doctrine of Signs*, which appeared in 1976, and *The Play of Musement: Further Essays over the Universe of Signs*, now half-finished toward early publication. I leave it to my reviewers to screen out of the several meanings of the polysemous lexeme *transitional* whatever most appeals to each critic, but I will attempt to pin down to my own satisfaction the sort of flux that I would prefer to convey.

Of the half dozen or so evaluations occasioned by my *Contributions*, I profited most from two lengthy, richly suggestive, and each in its way coruscatingly propaedeutic examinations by, respectively, John N. Deely ("What's in a Name?" *Semiotica* 22:151–181 [1978]) and Paul Bouissac ("A Compass for Semiotics," *Ars Semeiotica* [in press]). Along with this pair of innovative essays, Sanda Golopenția-Eretescu's tour de force design of a formal framework to accommodate all existing as well as all possible semiotics ("Contribution à la doctrine des sémiotiques," *Revue Roumaine de Linguistique* 22:117–130 [1977]) must surely be singled out in addition.

Deely (p. 152) visualized my role as that of a "midwife" who facilitated the entry of the *doctrina signorum* "into the learned world of today's academe," and quite rightly pointed out that I had deliberately selected *doctrine*—a scholastic term also used in a like context by both Locke and Peirce—because its burden is, first of all, a pedagogical one, as against, say, Saussure's *science* or Morris's *theory*, which both arrogate more than the field can as yet deliver (see also Golopenția-Eretescu, p. 117). Bouissac chooses to emphasize the "organizational" aspects of my activities on behalf of this doctrine, still full of caliginous corners and nooks, as having given "a viable direction for semiotics as a science and as a discipline." He, too, comments on my use of the notion of *doctrine* and all that this designation connotes and implies for him. From Bouissac's reading, it became even clearer to me than it was in the writing that four leitmotifs had indeed informed my book. These he succinctly summarized as follows: my "(1) ... critical assessment of the Saussurean tradition, (2) ... advocacy of biosemiotic research, (3) . . . efforts to build a taxonomy of signs, [and] (4) . . . insistence on the pertinence of R. Thom's topological theory for semiotics." Giulio Lepschy, in his instructive review of my *Contributions* (*Language* 54:661–663 [1978]), fastened on the first point, seemingly concurring with my strictures about "the limitations of Saussure's work on semiotics," yet disagreeing with what he refers to as my "undervaluation of contemporary French intellectual developments." This is surely an oversimplification of my position, which was influenced in decisive ways by the inspiring writings of Lévi-Strauss. It also ignores what Bouissac discerningly singles out under his fourth point, and which I develop further in this book, namely, that I regard the semiotic intimations of the French polymath Thom as pure nuggets of gold, in the aggregate containing the sole contemporary pointers toward the elevation of our doctrine to the status of a theory or a science. Ferdinand de Saussure and most adept epigones of his remind me of Georges Seurat and his neoimpressionist followers in late-nineteenth-century France who proficiently applied paint to their canvas in small dots and brush strokes so as to create a pleasing effect of blending and luminosity. But, surely, a pointillist painter's landscape or portrait is a mere retinal illusion of pure light through painting, a surface sensation of optical vibration. The perception of deep structure and its convincing delineation require creativity and bold inventiveness of a substantially higher order—in short, the authority of a Peirce, a von Uexküll, a René Thom.

In *The Sign & Its Masters*, all of the aforementioned themes—notably the second, which derives from my absolute conviction that semiotics begins and ends with biology and that the sign science and the life science ineluctably imply each the other—evidently all recur along, intertwined, with several others, but they are argued in an entirely different sort of situation than earlier, and are, I trust pregnantly, juxtaposed with novel topics, applications, and personalities. The title of my book obviously points to its two principal foci, and correspondingly raises two complementary sets of questions: What is a sign? Who are its masters, who its slaves?

Sign is a generic notion—which is to say that there are many different kinds, or species, of signs, each of which is "marked" (in the technical sense) by sets of additional properties—that Peirce (1935–1966:2.228) defined with surpassing comprehensiveness and lucidity as follows: "A sign . . . is something which stands to somebody for something in some respect or capacity." Peirce's definition embodies the core concept of *renvoi*, or transfer, Jakobson's compressed coinage (*Coup d'oeil sur le développement de la sémiotique* [1975]) for the celebrated antique formulation, *aliquid stat pro aliquo*, but it contains one very important further feature. Peirce asserts not only that x is a sign of y, but that "somebody"—or what he called "a *Quasi-interpreter*" (4.551)—takes x to be a sign of y. He then goes on to amplify this: "It is of the nature of a sign, and in particular of a sign which is rendered significant by a character which lies in the fact that it will be interpreted as a sign. Of course, nothing is a sign unless it is interpreted as a sign" (2.308). Or again: "A sign is only a sign *in actu* by virtue of its receiving an interpretation, that is, by virtue of its determining another sign of the same object" (5.569).

A sign, then, stands for its object, not, Peirce emphasized, in all respects, but in reference to a quality or some general attribute, which he sometimes (e.g., 1.551) called a "ground." The distinction between a ground and the sign that tells about it is well illustrated by a probably apocryphal but entirely plausible anecdote about Freud. This yarn hinges on three incontrovertible facts: Freud's (ultimately fatal) nicotine addiction that, after 1924, obsessively cleaved to cigars exclusively (Max Shur, *Freud: Living and Dying* [1972], Ch. 2); that cigars, in analytic symbology, can represent the idea of a male genital; and that Freud's "lectures were always enlightened by his peculiar ironic humor" (Ernest Jones, *The Life and Work of Sigmund Freud*, vol. 1: *The Formative Years and the Great Discoveries* [1853], p. 341). The story goes that, about to deliver one of his introductory lectures on psychoanalysis, Freud entered the classroom, flourishing a big cigar, whereupon the assembled medical students, fixing upon the cigar as an obvious phallic symbol, burst out in loud guffaws. "Gentlemen," Freud, not in the least discomposed, is reported to have said, "sometimes a cigar is nothing but a cigar."

The distinction implied here is both universal and fundamental, if not necessarily accurate. It corresponds to the one which St. Augustine, for instance, drew, in the *Principia Dialecticae*, with respect to *verba simplicia* ("quae unum quiddam significant"), between *res* and *signum*. By *res*, the worldly-wise and far-sighted Church father/ semiotician meant, "quidquid vel sentitur [is sensed], vel intellegitur [is understood], vel latet [is inapprehensible—as God and formless matter]"—say, like Freud's cigar when objectively apprehended as a compact roll of tobacco leaves prepared for smoking enjoyment. By *signum*, however, which Augustine defined as "quod et se ipsum sensui et praeter se aliquid animo ostendit," he might well have referred to Freud's cigar as a bipartite sign that exhibits ("ostendit") twin facets familiar since Chrysippus and his colleagues of the Stoa cleft *logos* into *semainon* ("se ipsum sensui") *vs. semainómenon* ("praeter se aliquid animo"), opposing the whole to *pragma* (Augustine's *res*), and that, in some respect—its characteristic shape, say, or agreeably penetrative function—stands for ("renvoit") the male copulatory organ for some interpreter.

The Port-Royal logicians viewed the sign in a somewhat different way, which, although interesting, was incompletely thought through. Antoine Arnauld and Pierre Nicole (*La Logique ou l'art de penser*, critical ed. by Pierre Clair and François Girbal, 1965 [1662]) held that every sign comprises two notions and that the efficacy thereof consists in exciting the second by means of the first—"à exciter dans les sens par l'idée de la chose figurante celle de la chose figurée," or the thing represented by means of the thing that represents. This relatively crude Cartesian statement, which nowhere comes to grips with the profound problem of signification, was gradually amplified and clarified in the ensuing centuries, beginning with Locke's "doctrine," but continued for a long time to cry out for a precise explication of the phrase "chose figurée." The semantic theorists of the Enlightenment simplistically identified, or, rather, labeled it—at least with respect to the area of the verbal signs that most exercised them—as a "thought" or "idea."

The ultimate solution had to be anchored in the biological make-up of organisms, as was fully anticipated by Peirce, brilliantly demonstrated by von Uexküll, and first situated in a vast, comprehensive theory by Thom. Peirce maintained that not only "is thought in the organic world, but it develops there," and that "there cannot be thought without Signs." The expansion of his argument for this position (in connection with which he adduced, for example, "the work of bees"), he felt, "would require a volume—and an uninviting one," for there will certainly exist "a danger that our system *may* not represent every variety of non-human thought" (4.551). Peirce did not survive to produce a volume such as he had clearly foreseen, but Jakob von Uexküll, who had never heard of Peirce and was therefore obliged to invent his own idiosyncratic terminology, devoted his career to the development of a body of research he had baptized "Umwelt-Forschung." This, we realize in retrospect, ultimately ripened into a highly original, elaborate, and biologically sophisticated theory of signs with an attendant methodology. His elder son, Thure von Uexküll, exhibits this in rich detail in his article "Die Zeichenlehre Jacob v. Uexküll's" (to appear in an English version in *Semiotica*, in 1979), a study which must be read as an invaluable companion piece to my tenth chapter in this book.

It is important to bear in mind two points when reflecting upon the technical writings of this great life scientist, who was born in 1864, exactly a quarter of a century after Peirce. First, that he drew a sharp boundary not between Nature and Culture, but, as his physician son underlines, "zwischen unbelebter und belebter Natur." This means, of course, that he viewed semiosis as *the* criterial attribute of life, an axiom that I also espouse throughout my own work. The second essential point to remember is that von Uexküll's conception of reality—or what he habitually called Nature—manifests itself exclusively through signs: "Diese Zeichen sind daher das einzig Reale und die Regeln und Gesetze, denen die Zeichen und Zeichenprozesse gehorchen, sind die einzig realen Naturgesetze."

The epistemological issue raised by von Uexküll is a reformulation, in biological parlance, of an ancient thesis in the history of ideas, to wit, that the mind's relationship to the world is specular. As Kant—whose metaphysic fueled von Uexküll's semiotic engine—would have it, reality itself, the *noumenon*, imposes upon the categories of the mind those forms that shape how "things" appear (*phenomena*). Recently, this seemingly perennial theme has been reopened, along several fronts, in the guise of the problem of the ontological validity of logic, which in Peirce's broad usage is, of course, entirely coextensive with "semeiotic" (e.g., as in 1.91). The solution to this problem insistently calls for a parallelism between the semiotic mechanisms of Mind and the evolutionary processes of Nature: it is with this fundamental thesis—"le monde comme image de l'homme"—that René Thom strides upon the stage to announce: "C'est à cette tâche d'analyse interne par la modélisation des phénomènes extérieurs que devrait s'attacher la Philosophie naturelle," and it is one of his greatest merits to have provided us with an arena where science and philosophy can at last be reconciled (see especially his *Morphogenèse et imaginaire, Circé* 8-9, Ch. 4 [1978]).

We now know a great deal about signs, thanks to the pilotage of Peirce, and, because of von Uexküll, about the workings of semiosic transduction in organisms linking up x, the sign, with y, the ground—or *Umwelt*—that it represents. The process of "signification," or "interpretation" of a sign—Peirce's shadowy apprehension of the "deepest and most lofty" Final Interpretant (8.184)—is, by contrast, not at all well understood, although I find Berkeley's strategy, argued in reaction to Locke's, interesting for a number of reasons (which I intend to spell out elsewhere; incidentally, Peirce [8.36], too, thought that, "In the enumeration of the signs and of their uses, Berkeley shows considerable power in that sort of investigation . . ."). Berkeley's key discovery was that what is sensed is mind-conditioned, and that the sense ideas are *like* strings of signs, or sentences in a language coded in a familiar way. The author of Nature, Berkeley maintained, communicates with us using a universal system of signs transmitted via diverse sensory channels. In short, signification takes the place of causation; the author of Nature produces ideas in Minds very much in the way in which the source of an utterance affects its interlocutor, the destination of its message. In Berkeley's own words (*Principles*, Sec. 65), "The connection of ideas does not imply the relation of cause and effect but only a mark or sign with the thing signified. The fire which I see is not the cause of the pain I suffer upon approaching it, but the mark that forewarns me of it." On this passage, Michel Foucault (*The Order of Things: An Archaeology of the Human Sciences* [1970], p. 60), justly commented: "The knowledge that divined, *at random*, signs that were absolute and older than itself has been replaced by a network of signs built up step by step in accordance with a knowledge of what is probable. Hume has become possible." What Hume had said was that the fire is, after all, the efficient cause, but, like all efficient causes, it is only a sign. Much later, it is in this very domain of signification that Thom's new contributions become so immensely valuable, elevating, however hesitantly, the problem area out of its customary metaphysical trappings into the realm of geometry: "Voir l'identité en principe formateur et la différence en principe informateur, voilà ce qu'on gagne à géometriser la signification, en première approximation" (Thom, *Morphogenèse et imaginaire*, p. 132).

W. C. Watt, another reviewer of my *Contributions* (*American Anthropologist* 80:714-716 [1978]), coins a handy label, "P-Semiotics," to set the Peirce tradition apart from Saussurean semiology. He professes to detect my "leaning" toward the former, while conceding that I do not "have any particular ax to grind." Indeed, I do not. I hope that, in Chapter 4 of this book, I made it amply plain that what "Ecumenicalism in Semiotics" is all about is getting to know the opposite sects.

Notwithstanding that Watt's exclusive dichotomy places my teacher, Charles Morris, in the uncomfortable position of the Semiotician Who Came in from the Cold, I am content to accept my provisional confinement in the pigeonhole to which Watt assigns me, although I would not be gladly counted with the echelon of those all too numerous Peirce specialists whose seemingly exclusive preoccupation lies with exegesis of the Grand Master's texts. To acknowledge Peirce's effortlessly elegant supremacy as the fountainhead of modern semiotics is not to impugn his own self-definition as a "first-comer" to the investigation of "the doctrine of the essential nature and fundamental varieties of possible semiosis"; and I trust I may presume to expand on his modest observation that "the field is too vast, the labor too great" for any pioneer "in the work of clearing and opening up . . . *semiotic*" (5.488) by deploring the widespread tendency to oversoon sanctify him.

To be sure, all of the important questions about the make-up and "essential nature" of signs were raised and reviewed by Peirce. He continued to wrestle with the answers, in solitary reflection, throughout most of his working hours until his death, in 1914. Signs, which he defined as any things which mediate between an object and an interpretant—these two, one antecedent, the other consequent, being merely correlates of signs—mostly function in communication: linking two minds, or, to apply his beautiful dramaturgic expression, "theatres of consciousness." The sign-maker, who delivers the message, Peirce called the agent that *utters* the sign, while the other, who "may be a stranger upon a different planet, an aeon later; or it may be that very same man as he will be a second after" (3.433), he called the patient mind that *interprets* the message. Before any sign is uttered, Peirce held, it already was virtually present to the consciousness of the utterer in the form of a thought; and after it was interpreted, it will, he insisted, virtually remain in the consciousness of its interpreter, where it, too, will be a sign which, in turn, should have an interpreter, and so on without surcease.

The word *masters*, as plied in these pages, is intended to work as a double agent. Of course, the contributors to semiotics mentioned in this Introduction—Chrysippus, St. Augustine, the Port-Royal Jansenists, Leibniz, Locke, Berkeley, Kant, Peirce, Saussure, Freud, von Uexküll, Morris, Jakobson, Lévi-Strauss, Thom—and the figures additionally discussed in Part Two, are all masters, whether of stellar or of satellite rank, upon whose writings mine are but marginal notices. But there is a much more pervasive sense, a far more acroamatic reading, that I had in view: a veritable master of the sign is any agent that utters and any patient that interprets one, any organism, be it man, woman, child, speechless creature, or, such as Peirce spoke of, a quasi-utterer/quasi-interpreter—in short, you or me.

But to imply that any organism holds sway over the realm of signs may be to misconstrue the real state of affairs. Samuel Butler once remarked that a hen is only an egg's way of making another egg. A nicer way of putting it might be (to borrow one of Richard Dawkins's metaphors from *The Selfish Gene* [1976], Ch. 2) that all "survival machines" —meaning people, animals, plants, bacteria, and viruses—are only a sign's way of making another sign. Signs command and constrain the behavior of us all. This conceit was implicit in Peirce's view that man himself is an external sign (5.314); that any organism in only an instrument of thought (5.315); and that—as he himself had learned from Berkeley, Kant, and others—"all thinking is performed in Signs" (6.481). The fundamental property of life belongs inalienably to signs, for "every symbol is a living thing, in a very strict sense that is no mere figure of speech" (2.222). To be a sign and to be a replicator—this is ultimately a statement of identity, for, while symbols propagate, "it is only out of symbols that a new symbol can grow" (2.302). Replicators —Dawkins's name for genes—are, in the last analysis, but signs which construct for themselves survival machines (containers, vehicles) to assure their continued existence. Thom (1974a: 194–196), referring in this connection to von Uexküll's monograph on *Signification* (1940), comes to much the same conclusion, substantially elaborating on his, as it were, axiomatic principle that "Le génome s'est constitué au cours de l'évolution par une combinatoire de segments significatifs . . . qui simulait la combinatoire des structures de régulation globale de l'organisme en voie de complexification progressive." The discipline the objective of which is to re-establish the tie between what Thom calls "dynamique globale," or what we customarily designate the signified, and what he calls "la morphologie locale," or our signifier, is familiar to the rest of us under the label of *semiotics*.

This book also touches upon several novel themes that were not even alluded to in my previous collection. Thus I would like to convince my colleagues, especially newcomers seeking research topics fraught with promise, of the merit of extending semiotic concepts and techniques to the field of social gerontology, to ask how the men and women constituting our aging and aged minority deal with their peculiar problems of intercommunication, among themselves and with the majority population that surrounds them, in their struggle to cope with, indeed, to endure, their irreversibly altered environment. For another example, I advocate the reconsideration of appalling maladies, like childhood autism, as disorders of the semiotic function, much as avant-garde physicians, such as Harley C. Shands, are already tracing schizophrenia to a developmental explanation in terms of an encoding/decoding model. Both of these vital opportunities for research, along with others, are aired in Chapter 4. Another theme that trickles insistently through this book (see especially Ch. 1) would encourage the return of clinical semiotics, in its modern simulacrum, into the ample household of its strapping descendant, general semiotics. As Leibniz reminded us (in his *Philosophische Schriften* [1875–1890], vol. 5, p. 447), "the physicians have the various signs and indications which are in use among them," meaning by signs not only what are, in medical parlance, called symptoms, but anything which may assist the physician in making a prognosis.

It remains for me to single out one more semiotic savant whose influence in radically reshaping my thinking will be palpable to readers of this book (Chs. 3–4, but especially 5). This is Oskar Pfungst, the extraordinary German psychologist (d. 1932) whose best-known book was *Das Pferd des Herrn v. Osten (Der kluge Hans)*, originally published in Leipzig, in 1907, and then in English, first in 1911, later in Robert Rosenthal's excellent re-edition in 1965. As James R. Angell precisely characterized Pfungst's work, in his Prefatory Note to both English versions, "Being in reality a record of sober fact, it verges on the miraculous." Room won't permit me to rehearse here the details of how Pfungst came to conclusively demonstrate that Hans, the stately Russian trotting horse, was never reacting to the cognitive content of the interrogative messages addressed to him but only to the involuntary movements of his inquisitors. That illusion was dispelled by patient observation and careful reasoning, Pfungst's two sterling attributes.

Although all psychologists have heard of the scandalous Clever Hans Fallacy, only a handful—such as Heini Hediger, who first drew me to this inexhaustible magic well, and Robert Rosenthal, who, as far back as fifteen years ago, grasped its basically semiotic burden—have fathomed its extremely far-reaching ramifications for human conduct, or even understood the import of these harsh words of Joseph Jastrow, who was himself introduced to the possibility of an experimental study of a psychological problem by none other than Peirce, his teacher at Johns Hopkins University: "Comparative psychology is a serious study pursued by rigid methods. Calculating and reflecting horses not only fall completely out of its range; the very belief in their possibility, let alone their reality, is a preposterous assumption that violates every basic principle of mental evolution. A flying Pegasus is as zoologically probable as a calculating horse. Carried far enough, such a belief leads to chaos" (*Wish and Wisdom: Episodes in the Vagaries of Belief* [1935], p. 209). Pfungst personally had neatly disposed of the hoax of the "'sprechende' Hunde," back in 1912, but Clever Animals just will not go away: the marketplace is still inundated with fraudulent or irrational accounts about Talking Horses, Talking Dogs, and their manifold cousinhood. The credulous public has been duped, in the 1960s, by myths about Talking Dolphins. Now the numinous whales have cast off, as Noam Chomsky once remarked in a personal communication, their wet suits and have rematerialized as "scientifically certified" preternatural chimps and gorillas—cute people in furry costumes busily engaged in attempting to acquire the rudiments of our language.

Deception, and most emphatically self-deception, is a subject too consequential to be left to the average psychologist. The workings of the Clever Hans phenomenon had, however, centuries before the advent of Pfungst, been implicitly, and sometimes even explicitly, understood by semiotically sentient stage magicians and other illusionists, the ablest of confidence men, and a host of veteran circus folk. Semiotically colored social, psychological, and physiological effects permeate and transfuse all forms of mutual contact among two or more beings, especially in conventionally structured settings where the parties, who, for biological and/or social reasons are concerned with the outcome of the interaction, share expectations about possible courses of action (cf. Russell A. Jones, *Self-fulfilling Prophecies* [1977]). If the results are influenced jointly by decisions the interactants make, this will be accomplished via modes of communication that, in general, conveniently fall under the rubric I am provisionally ticketing with the "Clever Hans" tag. The scope of the sort of semiosic control and authority, as well as acumen, implied here is so massive and involves so many facets of both human endeavor and animal behavior, that nothing short of a booklength treatment can begin to do it justice; accordingly, I expect to conclude, by the end of 1981, an extended study (already underway) on this topic, so pivotal to semiotic theory and praxis. Since this subject, for various fascinating reasons, is aquiver with emotional tension, I look forward with eager anticipation to controversy over my fragmentary remarks and the more fully developed working paper which, in the form of Chapter 5, aims to launch initially a heated debate, but in due course a thoughtful reconsideration of daily experiences of momentous implications and still incalculable consequences for us all.

Chapters 7 and 8 of this book deal with two specific issues that are classified, according to distinctions drawn by Charles Morris (1946:

219), in the subfield of descriptive semiotics. Here belong "statements as to what signs signify to certain persons" and studies of "the origin, uses, and effects" of signs. In Chapter 7, my wife and I present a reconsideration, in the light of certain semiotic principles, of the literature concerning the Plains Sign Language and the Australian Aboriginal Sign Language. This article is merely a small sample from a joint investigation of kindred phenomena, about which we have previously published about 2,500 pages of materials (Sebeok and Umiker-Sebeok 1976; Umiker-Sebeok and Sebeok 1978). The next study in this continuing series is devoted to Monastic Sign Languages; that is scheduled to appear in 1980.

Chapter 8, written collaboratively with my student Erika Brady, proffers a neoteric analysis of a much-studied episode from the *Histories* of Herodotus, in the hope that this will show that a consistent application of a semiotic point of view can bring previously unnoticed features of a text to the fore. For me, this exercise is a token of continuity with the sort of work that engaged my attention a decade or two earlier (cf. Sebeok 1960 and 1974a) but which has lain dormant in the interim.

Part One: The Sign

1. Semiosis in Nature and Culture

> ... le structuralisme réintègre l'homme dans la nature et
> ... admet volontiers que les idées qu'il formule en termes
> psychologiques puissent n'être que des approximations
> tâtonnantes de vérités organiques et même physiques. Une
> des orientations de la science contemporaine auxquelles il
> se montre le plus ouvert est celle qui, validant les intuitions
> de la pensée sauvage, réussit parfois déjà à réconcilier le
> sensible avec l'intelligible, le qualitatif avec le géométrique,
> et laisse entrevoir l'ordre naturel comme un vaste champ
> sémantique... (Lévi-Strauss 1971:614, 616.)

This chapter rests on an assumption that was formulated by Peirce, in 1905, in the following sentence: "It seems a strange thing, when one comes to ponder over it, that a sign should leave its interpreter to supply a part of its meaning; but the explanation of the phenomenon lies in the fact that the entire universe—not merely the universe of existents, but all that wider universe, embracing the universe of existents as a part, the universe which we are all accustomed to refer to as 'the truth'—that all this universe is perfused with signs, if it is not composed exclusively of signs" (Peirce 1935–1966:5.448, n. 1). By implication, I shall also contend against the position of subjective idealism ascribed to Plato's Protagoras of Abdera (cited as a character in the *Theaetetus*), embodied in that famous Sophist's arrogant adage that

Note: This paper is a substantially developed and freshly illustrated version of a short lecture delivered at the International Symposium on Semiotics and Theories of Symbolic Behavior in Eastern Europe and the West, Brown University, Providence, April 16, 1976. It is also appearing as a separate monograph published by the Peter de Ridder Press (Lisse, 1979). An Italian translation, entitled *Nature e cultura: Processi semiosici* (Università di Urbino, 1978), and a Polish translation has appeared, under the title "Dzialanie znakov w naturze i w kulturze," *Studia Semiotyczne* 8:129–147 (1978), without illustrations.

4   The Sign

"Man is the measure of all things, of things that are how they are and of things that are not how they are not."

The chronology of semiotic inquiry so far, viewed panoramically, exhibits a fluctuation between two seemingly antithetical tendencies: in the major tradition, semiosis takes its place as a normal occurrence inherent in nature, of which, to be sure, language and culture form important components; the minor tradition is disposed explicitly or at least implicitly to focus on *Homo sapiens* alone, in consequence of which his semiotic praxis is seen as closely tied to "the most diagnostic single trait of man" (Simpson 1966:476), his language. Let me adduce two sets of contemporary examples illustrating these opposite persuasions.

In the tangled branch of the field that comprehends nonverbal communication in man, a controversy has raged for some time now between two groups conveniently labeled "universalists" and "relativists," with particular attention to facial expressions but not necessarily confined to that part of the human body. Both camps claim to hark back to the classic treatment of the subject in man and animals by Darwin (1872). The universalist position maintains "that the same facial muscular movement is associated with the same emotion in all peoples through inheritance" (Ekman 1972:207), and is characteristically carried forward by ethologists, notably Eibl-Eibesfeldt (1970, Ch. 18), as well as by some prominent psychologists. The relativist position considers "facial expression as in no way innate, but akin to language and learned within each culture" (Ekman 1972:207f.), and is most commonly advocated by anthropologists, especially those who, like Birdwhistell (1975:54), have, by dint of their autobiographical circumstances, fallen under the spell of one or another brand of linguistics. The preponderance of recent evidence is compelling; it now obliges us to concur with the conclusion that "We must abandon the notion that facial expressions are a language, where arbitrary facial muscular movements have a different meaning in each culture" (Ekman 1972:278): for the data definitively prove the existence of universal expressions, which become thereby a system of signs amenable to study by standard methods of the natural sciences. The establishment of pancultural expressions does imply, however, the existence of cultural differences, and provides a number of clues as to their source as well as a framework in which their manifestations can be recorded and described by the complementary methods of the social sciences. I have discussed the distinction involved in my own idiosyncratic terminology while trying to sort out, as a first approximation, *anthroposemiotic* systems that are, by definition, species-specific, notably language and more complex constructs (such as our Soviet colleagues have styled "secondary modeling systems"—cf. Sebeok 1976:23, n. 38), requiring as material for their composition a verbal infrastructure, from *zoosemiotic* systems, that is, those component subassemblies of human communication that are found elsewhere in the animal kingdom as well (Sebeok 1972:163ff.). The two plainly continue to coexist, contrary to "a general popular belief that in the evolution of man, language replaced the cruder systems of animals," which must be, for the reasons detailed by Gregory Bateson (in Sebeok 1968, Ch. 22), totally false. On the contrary, both systems have been elaborated in human evolution into comparably intricate, independently and variously functional, yet mutually supportive, finely integrated methods of everyday interaction (and, moreover, into sophisticated forms of art). In Hediger's exactly apt juxtaposition (1976:45), "So etwa wie die vergleichende Anatomie Mensch *und* Tier umfasst, bilden Anthropo- und Zoo-Semiotik eine Einheit."

An interesting case in point is laughter and smiling, which were distinguished by some as specifically human attributes, while others were struck by the extent of the reflexive stereotypy and automation involved. Applying the comparative method, Hooff (1971, Part II) was able to show that this pair of metacommunicative signs neatly fits into the phyletic scale, since they are both traceable to primitive mammals, respectively, as the "relaxed open-mouth" and the "silent bared-teeth" displays. The existence of such homologues determines the zoosemiotic character of laughter and smiling, but their gradual ritualization, shaping, and final amalgamation around two poles in a graded series ranging from a general friendly response (smile) to play (laughter), typically enhanced by supporting morphological ornamentation in *Homo*, do not diminish our perception of their subtle social value for us in the totality of human nonverbal communication; indeed, as Hooff hints, these basic expressions radiating from the oral area may well have been influenced by the development of speech, and perhaps vice versa.

Both the most constrictive and the most comprehensive overall views of semiosis stem from contemporary France. The former, represented by Barthes, has its roots in Saussure, but I feel it is a gross distortion of his precursor's intent and program. Barthes' proclamation (1964a:80f.), that "percevoir ce qu'une substance signifie, c'est fatalement recourir au découpage de la langue: il n'y a de sens que nommé, et le monde des signifiés n'est autre que celui du langage," comes down like a butterfly net in which colorful ideas may flutter but from which they cannot escape. The latter, represented by Thom, derives directly from Peirce. I consider it a truly creative amplification of the master's doctrine: for Thom's observation (1973:106), that "seuls ceux qui savent écouter la réponse de Mère Nature arriveront plus tard à ouvrir le dialogue avec elle, et à maîtriser une nouvelle langue," liberates the spirit of the semiotic enterprise and elevates it to a level where none before him have ventured so boldly or so well equipped. Before returning to these remarks, it will be necessary to glance at certain highlights in the history of the semiotic quest as I am able to

6 The Sign

decipher them. I have done so before, on several occasions (Sebeok 1976:3-26, 150-156, 181-185; see also Jakobson 1975), but shall attempt to emphasize here those selected strands that directly pertain to the central theme of this chapter.

In a previous publication, I introduced the notion of "the semiotic tripod" to depict the triune tradition that fashioned the field. The most venerable of the three sources I mentioned is the medical, or, in Shands and Meltzer's improved coinage (1975), "clinical semiotics," the ancestral figure of which is surely Hippocrates (ca. 460–ca. 377 B.C.), often reverentially invoked as "der Vater und Meister aller Semiotik" (Kleinpaul 1972:103). Since "most Greek philosophers dealt, incidentally at any rate, with the theory of medicine" (Dampier 1966: 26), so, sliding outward in an overlapping, telescope-like fashion, emerges from the Hippocratic legacy philosophical semiotics, that then reached its highest pinnacle of achievement so far in the work of Peirce, "the heir of the whole philosophical analysis of signs" (C. Morris 1971:337) that went before. The specifically linguistic preoccupation with signs, while, of course, present from the *Kratylos* onward, is emblematized in our semiotic Pantheon by the name of Saussure, although "la linguistique comme sémiologie" began to be truly fascinating only with the injection of Thom's ideas and his application of the machinery of algebraic topology (1970:226-228, *et seq.*).

The reason why Hippocrates looms so large in the history of semiotics (to say nothing of medicine) is that, while in archaic medical practice the physician was preoccupied largely by the nature of disease, its causes and processes, he himself focused on the starting point of all medical action: "the sick man and his complaints—that is, the symptoms of disease" (Sigerist 1961:275), and that, in his interpretation of this primordial category of signs—which, as Peirce once observed, "have no utterer" (1935–1966:8.185) but "become [signs] by virtue of being really connected with their objects" (8.119; cf. 8.313), are, that is, in a more familiar parlance, species of indices[1]— theoretical consideration already began to play a very important part. In the second chapter of one of his finest books in the *Corpus*, entitled *Prognostic*, Hippocrates gave the description of the face of a moribund patient (for which the technical term *facies hippocratica* is still used today), that has become the classic example of clinical semiotic interpretation of syndromes, i.e., stable, rule-governed configurations of symptoms, and that, for this reason and to convey something of its flavor, I would like to recall in full:

> In acute diseases the physician must make his observations in the following way. He must first look at the face of the patient and see whether it is like that of people in good health, and particularly whether it is like its usual self, for this is the best of all; whereas the most opposite to it is the worst, such as the following: nose

sharp, eyes hollow, temples sunken, ears cold and contracted and their lobes turned out, the skin about the face dry, tense, and parched, the color of the face as a whole being yellow or black, livid or lead-colored. If at the beginning of the disease the face is such and if the other symptoms do not yet permit making a prognosis, one must inquire whether the patient has been sleepless, whether he had strong diarrhea, or whether he has suffered from hunger. If any of these causes be admitted, the condition may be considered less threatening. The crisis will come in the course of a day and a night if the condition of the face was due to any such cause. But if the patient does not tell of any such cause, and if the condition does not clear up within that period, you must know that this is a sign of imminent death. If the disease has lasted more than three days after the face showed these signs, ask the same questions as I recommended before and observe the other symptoms, those of the whole body and also those of the eyes. For if they shun the light or weep involuntarily, or squint, or if the one be less than the other, or if the white of them be red, livid, or have black veins in it, or if rheum appear around the eyeballs, or if they be restless, protruding or are become very sunken; if the color of the whole face be changed—all these symptoms must be considered bad, even fatal. One must also observe what can be seen of the eyes during sleep. For if some of the white of the eyes can be seen while the eyelids are closed and the patient is not suffering from diarrhea, has not taken any purgative, and is not in the habit of so sleeping, then it is a bad and very fatal symptom. If in addition to these symptoms the eyelids or lips or nose be contracted, livid, or pale, one may know for certain that death is close at hand. It is also a fatal symptom when the lips are loose, hanging, cold, and very white.

If Hippocrates was the Father of Semiotics, its Prophet—separated from him by almost six centuries—is assuredly Galen (130–ca. 200), the physician of Pergamon, author of a terse tract on the Hippocratic maxim "quod optimus medicus sit quoque philosophus" (Sarton 1954: 73, n. 95). In his voluminous writings, Galen foresaw and durably delineated the medical specialty commonly called symptomatology, but still widely known as "semeiology," or by kindred derivatives of *sēma*, throughout the West (Sebeok 1976, Ch. 2). Galen (1965:690) taught that *semeiotice* constitutes one of the six principal branches of medicine and is, in turn, divided into three parts: "in praeteritum cognitionem, in praesentium inspectionem et futurorum providentiam," meaning that the physician's threefold preoccupation must be with semiosis of the here and now, or diagnostics, and its twin temporal projections into the anamnestic past (the complete case history of the patient) and the prognostic future (extrapolation to determine the most likely course of the disease as interpreted from the foregoing).² In due time, as Majno (1975:420) remarks, "Hippocrates and Galen had stepped out of medicine and into history," but "the necessity to medicine of a Theory of Signs" (Crookshank 1938 [1923]:354; cf. Shands 1977) eventually led to a broad, if not yet global, semiotic theory of diseases which, to rephrase it in the humblest terms, asserts that the most devastating among them amount to a problem of bad communication—cells and tissues respond to misinformation, or misinterpret environmental cues to which they overreact (Thomas 1974:80).³ Therein lies the answer to the rhetorical question with which Barthes (1972:46) saw fit to conclude his survey of the relations between general semiotics and medical semiotics: "la médecine d'aujourd'hui est-elle encore véritablement sémiologique?" I would resoundingly respond, yes, more so than ever!

Medical semiotics represents only one biological thread that is inseparably woven into the warp and woof of the doctrine of signs, but it is no doubt the oldest. Coming closer to the present, I should now like to enlarge on a passing observation of mine, in 1973, where I wrote: "While generations of philosophers and some linguists were prefiguring a shadowy science of signs (of which Saussure reportedly remarked, 'Puisqu'elle n'existe pas encore, on ne peut dire ce qu'elle sera...'), seldom paying more than perfunctory heed to sign systems other than man's species-specific codes, an entirely different breed of scholars was at work developing, or, rather, redirecting *ethology*..." (Sebeok 1976:85), a field I later described as "hardly more than a special case of diachronic semiotics" (ibid.:156). Jaynes (1969) has traced this common designation for the biological study of behavior—along with that of its rivalrous sibling, comparative psychology—back to the intellectual milieu of early nineteenth-century France, notably, to the famed debates between Cuvier and Geoffroy-Saint-Hilaire. (We know, by the way, that comparative grammar arose in parallel fashion as a result of Friedrich von Schlegel's studies with the same Cuvier, the founder of comparative anatomy—see Sebeok 1976:610.) Since many students of ethology are aware of the fact that "data on animal communication have contributed a thread of continuity that, in some ways and at some times, has seemed to be the principal axis of synthesis in the entire field," as a prominent entomologist, R. D. Alexander, has most explicitly claimed (Sebeok 1972:64, 134f.), it ought to surprise no one that the essential concerns of animal behavior studies should be implicitly semiotic and its methods suitable for the attentive scrutiny of epiphenomena now distinctly understood to unfold with underlying morphological growth and differentiation. Although it might be a worthwhile historical exercise to demonstrate this intimate bond, and how it came about, some other time, I don't propose to dwell on the essential identity of ethology with diachronic semiotics of a phylogenetic bent here—that much is surely self-evident; nor to pursue the question of the extent to which Julian Huxley's zoosemiotic concept of ritualization (Blest 1961) does or does not apply in the domain of human sign behavior—a problem that was prolixly but rather inconclusively debated already over a decade ago (in J. Huxley 1966). Instead, I should like to seize this occasion to call attention to another neglected figure in the chronicles of our subject matter, the Baltic Baron Jakob von Uexküll (1864–1944), who not only helped provide the theoretical groundwork on which modern ethology rests but was also one of the greatest "cryptosemioticians" publishing in the first half of this century (see Chapter 10 of this volume). His *Bedeutungslehre* (1970:105–179), which first appeared in 1940, might even have decisively influenced contemporary semantics had its phenomenological overtones been absorbed by a single linguist of his generation (I find that I myself first mentioned this "pioneer monograph" only in 1968 [Sebeok 1972:160]). In fact, his highly original contributions to the theory of signs have gone unappreciated by, indeed, were unknown to, virtually all writers on this subject, with the conspicuous recent exceptions of the great French topologist, Thom (1968:220), who rightly characterized his writings as "souvent marquées d'une analyse subtile et profonde," and a Russian linguist, Stepanov (1971:27–32), who devoted a few responsive pages to Uexküll in his underestimated introductory textbook of semiotics.

Uexküll investigated the sensory capacities of animals, how the world is pictured in their mind, and how organisms conduct their life from within the prison of their senses, circumscribing their *Umwelt*, or subjective environment, with which their behavior stands in an overall homeostatic (feedback) relationship. He showed that an animal can respond to but a small portion of the total perceptible spectrum because its sense organs serve, as it were, in the manner of a kind of sieving or filtering mechanism for incoming sign vehicles. According to Uexküll, only those objects can become *signifiers* which are of *significance* in the life of an animal. Thus having acquired *signifieds*, the vehicles turn into bearers of sense for the receiver—the interpreter, who, in conformity with Peirce's pronouncement, is thus left "to supply a part of its meaning." Assume, for instance, that an animal has eyes similar to our own, except that it is color-blind; lacking a mechanism to detect color-chords and consequently having no means of building up an intuition about them, its *Umwelt*, other things being equal, will then perforce resemble a black-and-white representation of man's physical environment.

In Uexküll's functional cycle (Fig. 1-1), a sign vehicle (*Merkmal-Träger*), or releaser, is received from an object in the perceptual field (*Merkwelt*) by the animal's appropriate central receptor (*Merk-Organ*). The information (*Wirkzeichen*) is passed on from the inner world (*In-*

10   The Sign

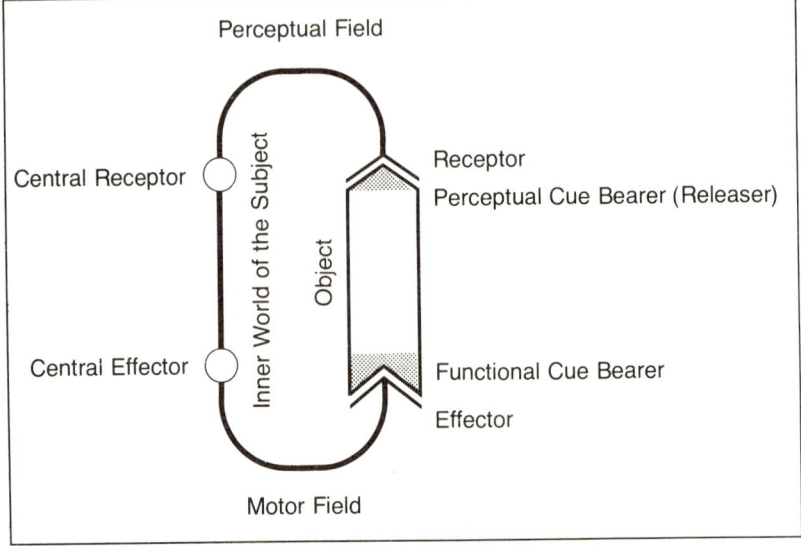

Figure 1-1. Uexküll's functional cycle. After Uexküll 1957:10, 1970:11; adapted from Eibl-Eibesfeldt 1970:6.

nenwelt) to the central effector (*Wirk-Organ*), a transformation which engenders a further sign vehicle (*Wirkmal-Träger*) that extinguishes the earlier sign (*Merkmal*), for which it functions (to switch back to the more familiar semiotic terminology of Peirce) as an appropriate interpretant. The behavior segment terminates once the sign has been interpreted.

Factors far more complex than the receptor structure can determine the *Umwelten* of different species, which may, moreover, constitute a storehouse for various categories of sign-types generated under differing contextual conditions for members of the same species. Among Uexküll's delightfully illustrated instances, an oak tree is pictured as it must be perceived by many sorts of interpreters, two of them human (1957:73–80; 1970:94–103): to the woodsman (Fig. 1-2A), the tree is an inanimate object to be accurately measured, but "in the magical world of a little girl whose forest is still inhabited by gnomes and hobgoblins" it is an object to be dreaded, for she sees a threatening demon in the gnarled bark (Fig. 1-2B). To the fox, which has built its lair among the roots, the same tree represents a home where the fox and its family find shelter from the elements. To the owl, the tree also has a protective tone, only it is not the roots but the limbs that frame it as a wall. And so on, *mutatis mutandis*, to the squirrel and the songbirds, the ant and the bark-boring beetle, and to all the other of its inmates,

Semiosis in Nature and Culture 11

Figure 1-2: *A*. Woodsman and oak tree. *B*. Little girl and oak tree. From Uexküll 1957:74f.; 1970:95.

the oak tree, an object solidly structured in itself, becomes a bundle of signs "not comprehended and never discernible to all the builders of these *Umwelten*."

Uexküll's reasoning, especially as set forth in the *Bedeutungslehre*, led him to the following generalization: every organism's blueprint (*Bauplan*) requires a link-up between its *Innenwelt* and its *Umwelt* (which includes, of course, other biologically or socially "important" organisms in its environment, such as preys and predators), and that this coupling must be semiosical (cf. C. Morris 1971:366), viz., "nach einem umfassenden *Bedeutungsplan*" (Uexküll 1970:127).[4] In his analysis, Uexküll thus not only foreshadows one of the basic tenets of cybernetics, but also makes plain and richly exemplifies what I already cited as Peirce's canonical principle of semiotics, "that all this universe is perfused with signs...": signification is demonstrably of the essence of organic existence. Uexküll's procedure, furthermore, situates signification within the still wider range of phenomena recognized by Soviet semioticians as modeling systems which, in the broad sense, refer to ideological models of the world where the surround stands in a reciprocal relationship with some other system that need not even be organic (such as a computer, or the like), and where its specular reflection—in Marxist fashion, this kind of investigation being tied to a theory of reflection—functions as a control of this system's total mode of communication (Sebeok 1976:23, n. 38). As Stepanov (1971:39) has emphasized, further adducing the idea of S. I. Vavilov's, it is a peculiarity of modeling systems that they span the entire known universe inclusive both of the stream of life and of subjacent inorganic matter. This, again, is in perfect conformity with a visionary but seldom quoted passage by Peirce, according to which "thought is not necessarily connected with a [human] brain. It appears in the work of bees, of crystals, and throughout the purely physical world... Not only is thought in the organic world, but it develops there [and] there cannot be thought without Signs" (1935–1966:4.551).

When looked at from a strictly comparative standpoint, it becomes quite obvious that the distinction of sign-types fails to coincide with the division of animates into two unequal classes, a vast speechless majority and a language-endowed minority of one. I have argued (Sebeok 1976, Ch. 8) the ubiquity of at least the signal, the symptom, the icon (in fuller detail in Ch. 6, this volume), the index, the symbol, and the proper name. Sign-types such as these are the building blocks out of which the models that teem within the *Innenwelt* are constructed and with the aid of which they are manipulated. Frankly, it is inconceivable to me that the process of signification should have emerged suddenly as an accompaniment to language development; to the contrary, the evolution of language presupposes just these prefigurements. But arguments for this position have no place here. In a more

Semiosis in Nature and Culture   13

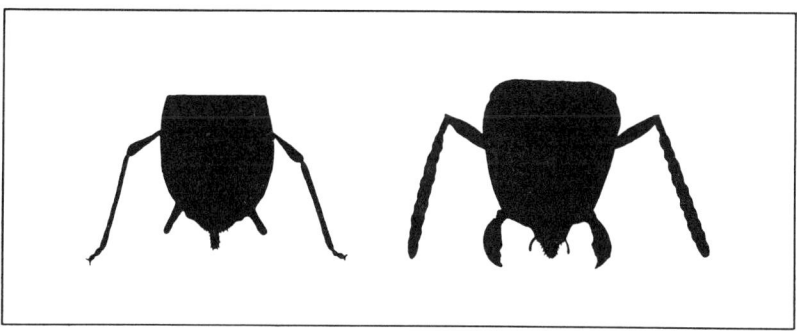

Figure 1-3: A. Icon. B. Object. Reprinted with permission from Kloft 1959: 865.

modest vein, I intend, in the next three paragraphs, merely to give one example from animal discourse for each category of Peirce's second trichotomy of signs, the one he called his "most fundamental" (2.275) division, and the one which has certainly become the most influential: (1) icon, (2) index, and (3) symbol. The illustrations I have selected for this purpose, out of a huge repertory of other possibilities, come two from the invertebrate line and one from the birds. I chose them in part for their taxonomic remoteness, in part because of the robustness of the data, and, last but not least, on account of their dramatic impact.

(1) *Icon.* This first example has to do with a certain ant-associated (myrmecophilous) aphid species, whose trophobiotic relationship was unfolded by Werner Kloft (1959). Aphids are small, soft-bodied insects, very vulnerable to predator attack, protected and tended by ants with which they communicate by an alarm pheromone that functions to stabilize their association. Their blissful liaison is further reinforced by the fact that the ants "milk" the aphids by vibrating their antennae against an aphid's back; the aphids then secrete droplets of honeydew which are consumed by the ants. Kloft insightfully realized that this congenial bond must rest on a "misunderstanding," in view of which he proposed, as a working hypothesis, that the hind end of an aphid's abdomen together with the kicking of its hind legs constitutes, for an ant worker, a compound sign vehicle, the icon, signifying, from its perspective, the head of another ant together with its antennal movement, the model: "so bemerkt man," says Kloft of the observer, "eine geradezu verblüffende Ähnlichkeit" (see Fig. 1-3). In other words, in an act of perversion of the normal trophallaxis occurring between sisters, the ant identifies the replica (the rear end of the aphid) with the model (the front end of her sister), and then proceeds to solicit on the basis of this misinformation, treating a set of vital releasers out of

context, viz., in the manner of an icon (or, to be more specific, an effigy). The multiple resemblances between this icon and the object for which it stands are so striking, subtle, and precisely modulated that they can hardly be explained away as an evolutionary coincidence. In loose adherence to Uexküll's terminology introduced above, the aphid can thus be regarded as an iconic releasing (*auslösende*) schema that sparks off the ant's chain of behavior pattern, thus bringing the ethological analysis (Lorenz 1965:268) into a common frame with the semiotic analysis.

(2) *Index.* There is a subgenus of birds, widespread in Africa south of the Sahara, that carries the scientific name of *Indicator*, the informer. Of some six species therein, one, the black-throated honey-guide, is technically known as *Indicator indicator*. The designation comes from the improbable habit of this bird of leading people to nests of wild bees (as circumstantially observed and presented in a substantial monograph by Herbert Friedmann [1955], upon whose account, as amplified by an interpretive report of Heini Hediger's [1973], I mainly rely). When the African natives reach the hive, the guiding bird waits until the comb is opened to extract the honey. Once this is accomplished, the bird picks up the scattered remains, concentrating neither on the honey nor on the bee larvae (although it will incidentally feed on insects captured in flight), but on the wax (Fig. 1-4). Such wax-eating is called "cerophagy," and the important point is that the bird does not need the wax to survive (as experiments with captive honey-guides have proved). The ethogrammatical peculiarity (one of several) of the honey-guide that I am interested in here is the manner whereby it leads men to the hives. What is involved is genuine symbiosis, or a partnership between two substantially different species: the bird is able to locate hives on remote tree-branches, but cannot force an opening; man can seldom find a hive, but has the requisite tools for access inside. So the honey-guide calls out, emitting continuous series of churring notes ("similar to the sound made by shaking a partly full, small matchbox rapidly lengthwise," according to Friedmann's vivid depiction, p. 32). Then it flies to the nearest tree, waiting motionless to be followed on a conspicuous branch. When the trip begins—and it may last from two to twenty-eight minutes, or extend from 20 up to 750 meters—the bird flies off, with an initial downward dip, its white tail feathers widely spread out. This agitated audiovisual display goes on until the vicinity of a beesnest is reached, and then the men know that when the bird stops there must be a hive at hand. The honey-guide probably detects the target by the smell of wax, and subsides when it sees or hears flying, buzzing bees. Guiding is almost always done by a single bird in any instance, implying that there is nothing in this behavior sequence, either in the auditory or optical channel, that acts as a releaser of like behavior in birds of a feather. Incidentally, I should add that the avian guides and their human followers in this communi-

Semiosis in Nature and Culture 15

Figure 1-4. The honey-guide consumes wax, but—although it is the only vertebrate capable of feeding exclusively on wax for a month—note that it by no means requires this substance for survival. Reprinted with permission of Herbert Friedmann from Hediger 1973:27.

16   The Sign

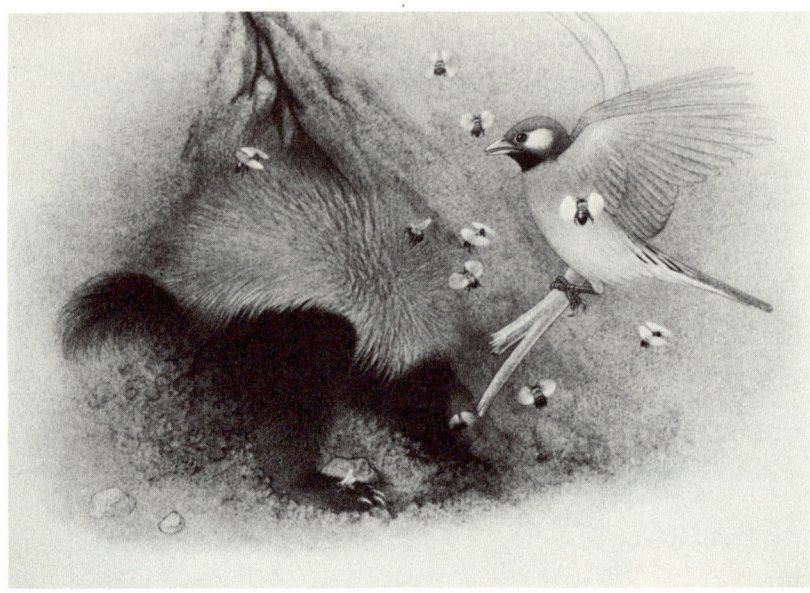

Figure 1-5. The black-throated honey-guide (*Indicator indicator*) often calls not only to people but also to the ratel, or honey badger (*Mellivora*). In this plate, the bird has led the badger to a bee's nest. Reprinted with permission from Grzimek's Animal Life Encyclopedia, by Van Nostrand Reinhold Company, New York.

Figure 1-6. The honey-guide at the wax of the combs. Reprinted with permission from Grzimek's Animal Life Encyclopedia, by Van Nostrand Reinhold Company, New York.

Figure 1-7. Artist's reconstruction of extraction of honey, watched by a honeyguide. Reprinted with permission of Sabine Schroer from Hediger 1973.

cational dyad are also capable of reversing roles: the native Africans can call forth the honey-guide by means of a specifically man-made sound, to wit, the noise of a tree being felled. The honey-guide responds to the sound produced by an ax or a machete striking against wood, a signal which can then trigger its indexical expression sequence described. It may even happen that the bird is not aware of a target when summoned; if so, it will guide in a zigzag pattern, which will, however, never eventuate in disappointment. The most remarkable aspect of this story is that, as already mentioned, the bird is by no means dependent on the wax, hence, all the less, upon the guiding sequence. It follows that, in the evolution of this behavior, factors other than merely random mutations and natural selection must have played a role; what these might have been is still opaque, and the phylogenetic conundrum is further muddied by an ontogenetic puzzle, namely, honey-guides being brood parasites, how can a nestling master the indicating habit, since it is not raised by its parents but by innocent host stepparents (the victims comprising hole-nesting birds of other species)?

(3) *Symbol*. The so-called balloon flies, of the carnivorous family Empididae, have enthralled naturalists since 1875, when the Baron C. R. Osten-Sacken, while he was visiting the Swiss Alps, made the first recorded observations of their "singular habit," as he later called it. It is the manner of their courtship that engages the attention of entomologists. In general, the males gather in swarms, carrying captured insects as "wedding presents." The male offers his gift to a female, which sits peaceably sucking it out while the male inseminates her. As soon as copulation is completed, the female drops her present, but if the empidid bride is still hungry, she may consume her amorous groom next. In the species discovered by Osten-Sacken, *Hilara sartor*, the inconspicuous, dull-colored male fly was seen carrying a white, filmlike packet of sparkling material, so light that the Baron's breath carried it away. He pursued it, at last eased it into a vial, and thus captured the first so-called fly-balloon. As more and more species of these dipterans were discovered, the full significance of their light-reflecting balloons became apparent, and Edward L. Kessel, in an elegant contribution to the literature of ritualization (1955), succeeded in unraveling the complex evolutionary sequence of patterns constituting a continuous array of homologous structures fulfilling three functions: "(1) to provide a 'come hither' invitation to the female instead of a warning; (2) to distract the female from her predaceous inclinations once they have embraced; (3) to serve as a stimulus to mating" (ibid., p. 98). His analysis comprises eight levels in all, ranging from the basic stage, the case of the species in which the male approaches the female "empty-handed," up through seven further stages in which the male attempts to defuse the cannibalistic attention of his mate with a gift. At stage 2, this consists of a juicy insect,

often as large as he is, but unwrapped. At stage 4, the prey is more or less entangled in silken threads. At stage 5, the simple, haphazard threads have been elaborated to form the complex structure, called a balloon, that encases the victim (Fig. 1-9). In succeeding stages, the prey steadily diminishes in size, hence in food value, while the balloon increases commensurately in complexity. At stage 7, the prey "is always minute and so delicate that it would seem to be useless as food" (ibid., p. 101) (Fig. 1-10). In the last stage of the evolutionary sequence—which happens to be embodied by *Hilara sartor*—"the male no longer needs to capture a prey . . . so the gift package includes no prey whatever, not even a dried-up, inedible one" (ibid., p. 102). Accordingly, I want to claim that the empty balloon—wholly devoid as it is of caloric content—has here, at stage 8, become a sign-vehicle basically signifying a reduction in probability that the male will fall prey to his female partner, that, from a strictly synchronic point of view, the link between a representamen and the object for which it stands has now become "arbitrary," and that thus (as well as in other familiar ways) this sign meets every viable definition of a symbol (Sebeok 1976:134ff.).

Each reader is invited to judge for himself the pertinence of my three biosemiotic fables to his own understanding of sign processes, especially in their developmental dimension. In doing so, one must, however, be mindful—as Peirce well recognized—that the difference between his three cardinal classes of signs (and among all the rest) scarcely ever amounts to more than a context-sensitive oscillation in relative hierarchy (Sebeok 1976:120f.), even though, in an ideal state, "the most perfect of signs are those in which the iconic, indicative, and symbolic characters are blended as equally as possible" (4.448). In considering Kloft's *verblüffende Ähnlichkeit*, remember therefore Morris's dictum (1971:273) that "Iconicity is . . . a matter of degree"; in evaluating the *Indicator*'s guiding-behavior, recall Peirce's cautionary remark that "it would be difficult if not impossible, to instance an absolutely pure index" (1935-1966:2.306); and in contemplating the realization of the American dream in the balloon fly—all packaging, no content—with the attainment of Kessel's eighth stage, don't forget that "symbolization," too, "is supposable as a matter of a continuous (qualitative) degree" (Count 1973:184).

As far back as 1963, I had occasion to point to "a vision of new and startling dimensions: the convergence of the science of genetics with the science of linguistics" (Sebeok 1972:62). In the intervening years, comparisons between the molecular code and the verbal code—the two semiotic systems thought biuniquely to share the principle linguists call "double articulation," following the medieval terminology revived in modern times—have been propounded by distinguished biologists and semioticians alike (see especially the excellent literature review by the mathematician Marcus [1974]), although a few lin-

Figure 1-8. A male dance fly inseminates a female, which meanwhile is sucking on her "wedding gift," a golden eye (*Chrysopa oculata*). This illustrates Kessel's "stage 2." Reprinted with permission from Grzimek's Animal Life Encyclopedia, by Van Nostrand Reinhold Company, New York.

Figure 1-9. Balloon at stage 5. Note size of prey relative to container; it is still edible by female. From Kessel 1955:96. Published with the permission of the Society of Systematic Zoology.

Figure 1-10. Male of a species at stage 7 carrying balloon. From Kessel 1955: 96. Published with the permission of the Society of Systematic Zoology.

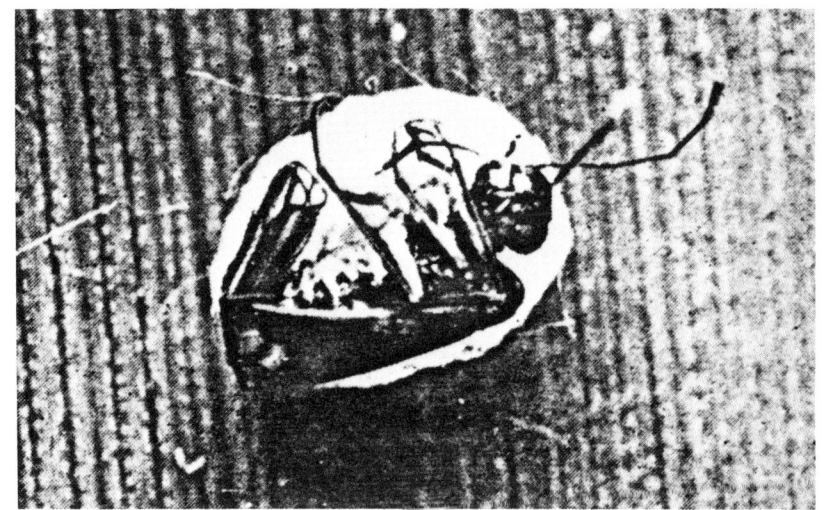

guists, like Robert B. Lees and Benny Shanon, have cast some doubts upon the validity of the analogy, let alone a possible homology. In lieu of pursuing the consequences of the indubitable fact that the genotype is indeed a set of signs prescribing alternative reaction patterns that can be profitably analyzed by semiotic methods—most productively, for the time being, within the framework of Thom's catastrophe theory (Thom 1973; cf. Ch. 6, this volume, Part III)—I should like to briefly report on the relevance of still another biosemiotic system, the overall regulatory strategy of which was formulated under the label "metabolic code" by Gordon M. Tomkins (1975) shortly before the untimely death of this imaginative biochemist and biophysicist. What is at issue here obviously falls within the sphere of what I have dubbed, rather cavalierly, *endosemiotics* (Sebeok 1976:3), without at the time paying further heed to what may be involved beyond the field of transducer physiology, which studies the conversion of "outside" signs to their initial input "inside," or considering the relative or absolute contrasts between the pathways of information outside the body and the pathways deep inside it, in brief, to what people most commonly refer as the external "physical world" vs. the internal "mental world" (cf. Uexküll's *Umwelt/Innenwelt*). I am convinced that this bifurcation is ultimately best dealt with in semiotic terms.[5]

What Tomkins attempted to do was to elaborate a model for biological regulation, or "symbolism," and the origin of hormone-mediated intercellular communication. He distinguished between two modes of regulation, both present in modern organisms, calling them, respectively, "simple" and "complex." The second evolved, most likely, later, and is the relatively more sophisticated mode. The essential feature of simple regulation is a *direct* chemical relationship between the regulatory effector molecules and their effects; translated into the terminology of Peirce, I dare say that we are dealing here with "dynamical action," which "takes place between two subjects . . . or at any rate is a resultant of such actions between pairs" (1935–1966:5.484), that is, as yet no semiosis is occurring. Complex regulation is characterized, however, by two entities not operating in simple mechanisms. Tomkins called these metabolic "symbols"—although I stick by his nomenclature, I would have preferred the less overburdened generic term "signs"—and their "domains." By "symbol," he meant to refer "to a specific intracellular effector molecule which accumulates when a cell is exposed to a particular environment"—called by others "alarmone" —and he defines as the "domain" of a symbol "all the metabolic processes controlled by the symbol." The notion of a "metabolic code," relating extra- with intracellular events, in which a specific symbol represents a unique state of the environment, arises by virtue of the fact that a particular pragmatic condition is correlated with a corresponding intracellular sign. The omnipresent substance in biological

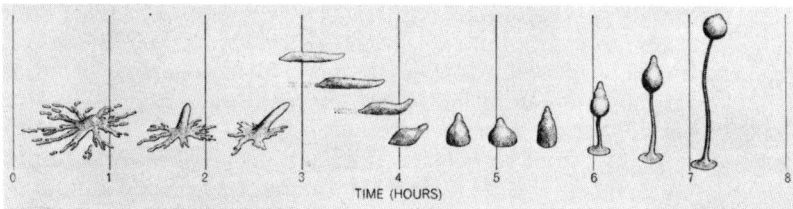

Figure 1-11. This drawing represents approximate period from aggregation (*far left*) to culmination (*far right*) in the life cycle of a typical slime mold. From "How Slime Molds Communicate" by John Tyler Bonner. Copyright © 1963 by Scientific American, Inc. All rights reserved.

regulation, adenosine monophosphate, or cyclic AMP, is a favorite example for the kind of symbol Tomkins is concerned with; in most microorganisms, it stands for a nutritional crisis, carbon-source exhaustion. A cellular slime-mold, *Dictyostelium discoidium*, serves as a dramatic pattern for the process that ensues in the absence of a sufficiency of nutrients. Thomas (1974:14), whose prime absorption centers on exploring the notion of societies viewed as organisms, writes, in his inimitable style: "Slime-mold cells [join up to form an organism] in each life cycle. At first they are single amebocytes swimming around, eating bacteria, aloof from each other, untouching, voting straight Republican. Then, a bell sounds, and acrasin is released by special cells toward which the others converge in stellate ranks, touch, fuse together, and construct the slug, solid as a trout. A splendid stalk is raised, with a fruiting body on top, and out of this comes the next generation of amebocytes, ready to swim across the same moist ground, solitary and ambitious."[6] Figure 1-11 exemplifies the life cycle of a slime mold from aggregation to the development of a mature fruiting body.

There are several important points to be noted here. First, cyclic AMP in such organisms clearly has two functions, one endocrinic, the other endosemiotic: for it is a hormone carrying metabolic information from sensor cells in direct contact with signs in the environment to more sequestered responder cells; but, at the same time, it acts as an intracellular sign signifying starvation. All semioticians will at once recognize the distinction between cyclic AMP as a biochemical *object* to be studied by physiology, and cyclic AMP taken as a *sign* significantly substituting for something else—*aliquid stat pro aliquo*. There is a genuine triadic relation here involving mediation, not reducible to a combination of dyadic relations between pairs of objects, in a word, semiosis (Peirce 1935–1966:5.484). Second, semiotic processes specifically labeled "encoding" and "decoding" can be identified in message transmission from source to target. Hormone release is often activated by neural stimulation, so in many organisms the nervous and endocrine subcodes are intimately linked. Neurotransmitters are hormones that mediate communication within the nervous system, operating over very short distances. Tomkins speculates that these substances acted in primitive cells as intracellular symbols referring to changes in environmental amino acid concentration, and that from this original concern with transducing this kind of information the primordial nerve cells might have gradually come to refer to many other aspects of the "outside" world.

Just as Uexküll's writings appear permeated by a disturbingly vitalist outlook, and just as the vocabulary used in comparing the genetic code with the verbal code is seemingly tainted by almost outrageous anthropomorphism, there are many admitted deficiencies in the scheme delineated by Tomkins, although I wholeheartedly concur with its proponent that there are also compensating "advantages in presenting a general hypothesis at this time. One is that a great deal of heretofore unrelated information is unified . . ." Any hypothesis designed to ignore local, i.e., disciplinary, variations to capture global properties should be attractive not only to life scientists but to semioticians *a fortiori*: we now have ample data at our disposal in order to gain panoptic access to genetic, metabolic, neural, intraspecific, interspecific, nonverbal and verbal, nonvocal and vocal codes, besides a host of secondary modeling systems, to keep us busy with synthesis no less than analysis for years to come. Apropos this very example of the cellular slime mold, Lévi-Strauss (1971:617), too, with his customary percipiency, opens a door to novel vistas: in a manner that is singularly dialectic, the amebocytes propel us across the threshold "de la communication comme forme de sociabilité à la sociabilité elle-même, conçue comme limite inférieure de la prédation." Communication is thus seen as the opposite of hostility, in a delicate natural balance, the lessons of which he would yield "au moraliste," but which I think would, at least initially, be safer in the hands of the semiotically inclined sociobiologist.

Is there any hope in the foreseeable future for a workable unifying scheme to yoke together these widely differing phenomena in a common explanation? In fact, a powerful theory already exists (although, to be sure, it "needs to be developed, tested, modified, and generally subjected to the full process which will turn it into a reliable scientific tool" [Stewart 1975:448]): called *catastrophe theory* by its builder, René Thom (cf. Stewart 1975), it belongs to the branch of mathematics known as topology, a field that has the satisfying property of providing a single interpretation to quite disparate data in the world in which we live. The results are expressed in geometric language, hence are qualitative rather than numerical.

The proof of this application of catastrophe theory does involve modern mathematical techniques of great rigor and sophistication; this notwithstanding, reading Thom's relevant essays (1968; 1970; 1973) is an exciting experience that reminds me of nothing so much as Bronowski's beautiful sentence (1973:453) about another giant of twentieth-century mathematical creation, John von Neumann: "What is running through the page is a clear intellectual line like a tune, and all the heavy weight of equations is simply the orchestration down in the bass."

Catastrophe theory has as its ultimate aim the classification of analogies. This means specifying a list of archetypal topological structures (catastrophes) together with rules for combining them (syntax) that could formally model all the static and dynamic morphologies of the natural world. In particular, Thom originally created his theory in the mid-1960s with the prime purpose of employing the "hard" tool of mathematics in one "soft" science, biology. Similar ideas were pursued earlier in the century by D'Arcy Thompson and later by C. H. Waddington. They both inspired Thom in his striving to model morphogenetic processes mathematically in their qualitative aspect, but, beyond his extensive discussion of the growth and differentiation of the embryo, he developed applications of far wider scope: in the theory of evolution, in reproduction, in the processes of perception and thought, in the generation, transmission, and reception of verbal signs (1970) and signs in general (1973), and the problems of signification in their broadest sweep (1968). His fundamental assumption regarding the latter is one with which I couldn't agree more: "C'est évidemment en Biologie—science plus proche de l'homme—que l'on pouvait s'attendre à voir réapparaître la notion de signification ... Or une discipline qui cherche à préciser le rapport entre une situation dynamique globale (le 'signifié') et la morphologie locale en laquelle elle se manifeste (le 'signifiant'), n'est-elle pas précisément une 'sémiologie'?" (Thom 1968:220f.). Thom's semiotic takes its point of departure (1973:85) from that of Peirce, but he materially enriches it as scarcely anyone else has since the latter's seminal 1867 "On a New List of Categories" (Peirce 1935–1966:1.545–567). I have tried to adumbrate some of the nexus between these two topologists, separated by a century, in respect to a relatively small matter, the genesis of icons in Chapter 6 of this volume. But those interested in pursuing Thom's algebraic topological notion he terms *logos* in all its immense, if as yet budding, ramifications for the study of signification in general, ultimately bearing on the question of distinguishing living organisms from inert forms, man from the other animals and animals from plants, the origin of language and syntactic structures, traced partly in terms of ritualization, more according to the principles of sociobiology (phenomenological "catastrophe"), are best advised to peruse his densely packed, terse essays (especially the one of 1968) without an intermediary.

All of the lectures that I heard or the titles of which I saw announced in the program of the stimulating international symposium for which these remarks were originally prepared seem to hew to the Sophistic line laid down by Protagoras, much later echoed in Pope's verse, "The proper study of mankind is man." It should be obvious that my presentation was more in tune with the ecumenical spirit (cf. Ch. 4, this volume) of another of Pope's stanzas from the *Essay on Man*:

Who sees with equal eye, as God of all,
A hero perish or a sparrow fall,
Atoms or systems into ruin hurl'd,
And now a bubble burst, and now a world.

My purpose was to provide informally some empirical underpinning for the prevalence of semiosis in the living universe so eloquently acknowledged by Peirce in my opening paragraph, and to buttress a previously expressed conviction of mine (1976:69) that "a full understanding of the dynamics of semiosis... may, in the last analysis, turn out to be no less than the definition of life." I trust that I have conveyed how much I would welcome a reintegration of medical semiotics into the mainstream of the general doctrine of signs; a recognition of the essential identity of aspects of this doctrine with the main thrust of ethology; a rehabilitation of neglected figures in its history, such as Galen, Uexküll, and not a few others; a full realization of the spectrum of possibilities terrestrial anthroposemiotics, zoosemiotics, endosemiotics—as well as, with ever increasing prospects, the semiotic devices used in exobiological systems—share, and in what precise ways they differ; but, above all, a fresh and unbiased examination of semiotics scrutinized under the stupendous umbrella of differential topology. These, as I see it, are the main directions in which the research undertaking semioticians are currently exploring is bound to flourish and consolidate over the years ahead.

2. Semiotics and Ethology

Gerard's terminological innovation, the org (1960:255), which he devised to designate a material system of interrelated and interacting features constituting a single whole sufficiently identifiable so that it can be distinguished from its surroundings, failed to achieve common currency in neurophysiology, but his insistent propagation of the concept has proved unexpectedly suggestive, indeed fruitful, in clarifying some basic issues of the semiotic emprise (cf. Sebeok 1976 · 26–27, 72, 98, 140). By substituting the semiotic prime "sign" for the material prime "org," we can arrive at a convenient, if preliminary, fourfold classification of the principal concerns of our discipline. Two of these are (A) synchronic, the other two (B) diachronic.

Gerard alliteratively named the twin synchronic facets of an org as its "being" and its "behaving." By "being," he meant what I prefer to call (1) structure: "Certain aspects of this recur essentially unchanged in different time-moments and constitute the enduring architecture or 'being' of the entity" (1960:255). The structural analysis of signs aims to contribute chiefly to what Prieto (1975:125–141) discussed under the label "sémiologie de la signification," and, although he associates this approach with Roland Barthes, it was by this very means that Peirce reached his three sign categories of icon, index, and symbol: "I examine the phaneron [i.e., the collective total of what is in the mind at any given time, or, roughly, idea] and I endeavor to sort out its elements according to the complexity of their structure" (1935–1966: 8.213).

By "behaving," Gerard (1960:255) meant what I would call (2), function: "The responses to any particular environment input are determined by the architecture at that particular time. Mostly, responses are adaptive (homeostatic) and transient (reversible) and constitute the 'behaving' of the system." The functional analysis of signs aims to contribute chiefly to what Prieto contrastively discussed under the label "sémiologie de la communication," an approach he ascribes to Eric Buyssens, and hence, by implication, to the Saussurean legacy, for, as Culler recently noted (1976:99ff.), "At the heart of [Saussure's] semiological enterprise are systems of conventional signs used for di-

Note: This paper was read on August 30, 1977, at the XIIth International Congress of Linguists, in Vienna. It was first published in *Spectrum: Essays Presented to Sutan Takdir Alisjahbana*, edited by S. Udin (Jakarta: Dian Rakyat, 1978), pp. 28–38.

rect communication." The point that structure, manifested through a *semiosis of ego-dependency*, and function, realized via a *semiosis of interdependency*, are complementary synchronic concepts that necessarily imply one another need not be belabored again (cf. Sebeok 1976, passim). However, in passing, one ought to be reminded of Peirce's regrettably all too true remark that the "phenomena of intercommunication have been unfortunately little studied" (6.161; see also 3.433). His observation pertains *a fortiori* to the phenomena of signification, defined in terms of the relation of signs to their interpretants, an investigation enjoying, in his view, the status of "the deepest and most lofty" (8.184) undertaking of semioticians. Yet this refers to "only *one* of the *two* chief functions of signs" (8.378), both of which still abide, each in its own way, in a pioneering, or "backwoodsman" (5.488) phase.

About diachrony, Gerard (1960:255) had this to say: ". . . secular or cumulative residue of change in the longitudinal time section constitutes the development or history or evolution of the system—its 'becoming'." Clearly, the universal problem of retaining experience has several different manifestations, despite some commonalities, and, although one is superimposed upon the other and is thus supplementary to it, it is well for us to draw a sharp distinction between these two mechanisms: (3) individual learning and (4) the ritualization (Blest 1961), by heredity in the species, of informative behavior patterns.

A most sagacious view of learning was articulated by Young (1977: 15–16), in terms that are surpassingly semiotic: "The essence of learning," this great anatomist of the brain recently told us, "is the attaching of symbolic value to signs from the outside world." What the senses can provide is "a tool by which, aided by a memory, the animal can learn the symbolic significance of events. The record of its past experiences then constitutes a program of behavior appropriate for the future." The implied phenomenological paradigm, sometimes referred to as a causal or representative model of perception, is also in good conformity with Uexküll's *Bedeutungslehre*, which postulates the interposition of a semiotic editorial screening operation between the objective world and its effects upon the perceiving mind; see Chapter 10 of this volume. As ontogeny proceeds, especially in birds and mammals, notably man, their displays "change, from an infantile to an adult repertoire, or from infantile forms to adult forms of basically the same displays," but, Smith (1977:155–156) hastens to add, many questions remain unanswered, so that "the ontogeny of communicating behavior is rich with research opportunities." The process of gradual increase in semiotic specializations and specificities of a neurophysiological character over the entire lifespan of an individual organism is known as differentiation. It encompasses the seemingly antithetical signs of growing up and growing old, as well as many of the symptoms usually associated with morbidity.[1] Underlying these three more or less traditionally specialized areas of inquiry is a shared *semiosis of alter-dependency*—whether applied to nonage, to second childhood, or to a pathogenic state of incapacity. Unfortunately, longitudinal studies of development are scarce, gerontology is itself in its infancy, and clinical semiotics has strayed far, since the times of Hippocrates and Galen, from the mainstream of the sign science.

The term *ritualization* was first used in 1914 by Julian Huxley in analyzing the display behavior of the great-crested grebe. Since then, this has become a cardinal concept of ethology (Hailman 1977:24). Huxley, in 1965, organized a large-scale symposium, sponsored by the Royal Society, on ritualization. The Society, in turn, created a study group with the more circumscribed task of exploring the nature of nonverbal communication in animals and man (J. Huxley 1966; Hinde 1972). Ethology is best defined as the biological study of behavior (Tinbergen 1963:411), but it is amply clear that, as Alexander has stated in 1964, "data on animal communication have contributed a thread of continuity that . . . has seemed to be the principal axis of synthesis in the entire field of animal behavior" (in Sebeok 1972:134–135), and as Smith (1977:2) has recently confirmed, "ethology has been most concerned with the study of communicating." The great majority of the behavior patterns of animals—usually called "displays"[2]—is assumed to have undergone a process of ritualization. "Ritualization may be defined ethologically," said Huxley (1966:250), "as the adaptive formalization or canalization of emotionally motivated behaviour, under the teleonomic pressure of natural selection so as: (*a*) to promote better and more unambiguous signal function, both intra- and inter-specifically; (*b*) to serve as more efficient stimulators or releasers of more efficient patterns of action in other individuals; (*c*) to reduce intra-specific damage; and (*d*) to serve as sexual or social bonding mechanisms." Within our present framework, ritualization may be redefined as the semiosis of *gene-dependency*, in order to emphasize the fact that here we are dealing with the progressive elaboration, in the course of evolution, of instructions stored not in the memory but in the genetic make-up of animals and man, in brief, the shaping of signs according to the requirements of natural selection. In practice, however, ritualization is very difficult to demonstrate; for one reason, virtually no paleontology of behavior exists. An additional reason is that many animals have memory systems with which to supplement their genetic systems, but the relative contribution of the hereditary and learned information stores is not always readily ascertainable. This, of course, is especially the case as regards the extended semiotic adaptations of man, whose uniqueness derives not so much from the emergence of language as from the capability for assuring his homeostasis by means of a two-track mechanism for information collection and storage, both of which are securely transmissible.

30   The Sign

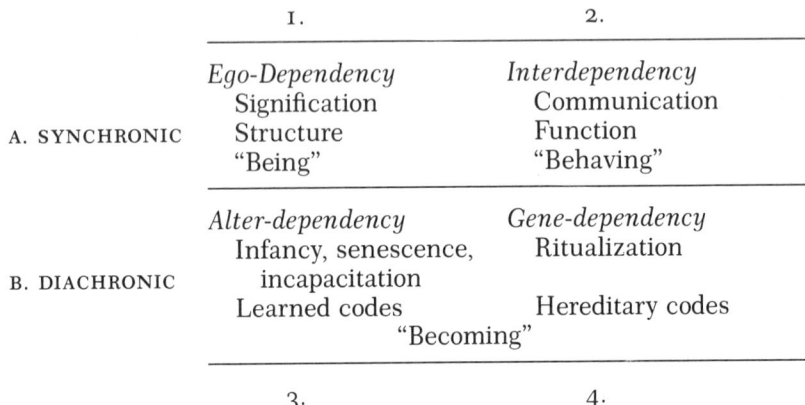

Figure 2-1. Four varieties of semiosis.

In Figure 2-1, I attempt to synopsize the distinctions introduced thus far, and to chart the principal varieties of semiosis as I see them.

The claim put forward in this chapter is that insofar as ritualization is the focal concern of ethology this branch of the life science is hardly more than a special case of the sign science. The subject matter of both subdisciplines resides in the semiotic reflections of genetic memories about the experiences of earlier brains. Abundantly supplemented by the formation of personal memories, involving transformations in the connectivity of the brain by means of a mechanism and a code the properties of which can so far only be guessed at, together they constitute our entire fund of signs transmitted from generation to generation, in part by our bodies and in part by means of such extracorporeal devices as writing and other recording tools, including, increasingly, computers.

In Chapter 1 of this volume, I described in some detail an elegant example from the literature of ritualization: Edward L. Kessel's decisive demonstration of an intricate evolutionary sequence eventuating in the emergence of symbolization in one particular species of balloon fly, *Hilara sartor*. Moynihan's outline of the ritualized behavior patterns among cephalopods (squids, cuttlefishes, octopuses) reveals the intricacies involved in studies of this sort and the sophistication required for understanding them: these *Coleoidea* have displays "designed to convey information, true or false (mimetic), from one individual to another. Others promote crypsis and might be called 'anti-displays.' Some can be cryptic in some circumstances, signals in other situations," and yet another distinction can be drawn between relatively young components and more conservative ones that can be traced back farther, into various time depths (1975:288).

Such relatively clear-cut cases are not, however, easy to come by, least of all in *Homo sapiens*, although Guthrie, for one, ingeniously sketched—"incomplete though this analysis is" (1976:8)—the comparative evolutionary history of a good many of man's so-called "social organs." Space will allow allusion to only one such behavioral complex of ours here, the category of greeting ceremonies, chosen for two principal reasons: first, because it has already been much studied from a variety of angles, and second, as an occasion for a few comments on the underlying methodology. "It might be added," moreover, "that there could hardly be a better argument for there being common ground between animal and human studies than that provided by greeting behavior" (Goffman 1971:73, n. 14). Among those who have written on the subject in recent years are the ethologist Eibl-Eibesfeldt (e.g., 1975:151–162, 465–472), two specialists in child growth and development, Blurton Jones and Leach (1972), several social anthropologists, notably Firth (1973, Ch. 9) and Callan (1970, Ch. 7), the sociologist Goffman (1971), one of the foremost students of behavior in face-to-face interaction, Kendon (1977, Ch. IV [with Andrew Ferber]), and the linguist Ferguson (1976), who postulates that *all* human societies employ *both* ritualized nonverbal signs for greetings and verbal politeness formulas conjoined with the former but linked, at the same time, "in linguistic structure to the language as a whole which is used by the community" (p. 138). As to this, he echoes Firth (1973:304), who also notes that "In greeting . . . rituals verbal and nonverbal behaviour is in close relation. Utterance and bodily action are often simultaneous or juxtaposed." Callan (1970:124) cautiously concludes that the imprecisely defined concept of greeting, "when properly worked out and documented, should be as applicable to human social life as to that of certain other animal species." Kendon, whose analysis of some of these devices employed for the management of relations between people is the most meticulous and subtle of all, is likewise prudently conservative in his windup (1977:117): "Until we know far more about the nature of human greetings and of those of the chimpanzee and other primates, little can be concluded beyond the rather general point that much in human greeting behaviour appears to be phylogenetically quite ancient."

The methodological issue, that is, how the ethologist goes about establishing that ritualization has, in fact, taken place, should be of paramount interest to semioticians (Sebeok 1976, Ch. 3), including most particularly linguists. As in so many aspects of research in this area, Darwin paved the way by "his understanding of the value of the comparative method in biology" (J. Huxley 1966:250), and especially of its extension from morphology to behavior. The kind of investigation required calls for the determination of phyletic homologies through comparison of groups of closely related species. Thus it has long been known that the silent bared-teeth display of the chimpanzee is homologous to the human smile and that the ape's relaxed open-mouth display is homologous to our laughing (van Hooff, in Hinde 1972, Ch. 8, discussed in Ch. 1, this volume), and that both sign complexes are traceable far beyond the *Hominoidea*, back to primitive mammals. Similarly, "we can find hints as to the phylogenetic development of the behavior" in the stereotyped panhuman eyebrow flash (Eibl-Eibesfeldt 1975:467–468). The methodology in ritualization studies is simply an imaginative application of the principles of comparative anatomy as expounded by Cuvier: the great anatomist took single organs and arranged animals into long graded series on the basis of both their structures and their functions, among which he considered the coupled faculties of feeling and moving primary in determining all the others. Although he was an ardent champion of the fixity of species, he also "recognized very clearly that there is a succession of forms in time, and that on the whole the most primitive forms are the earliest to appear" (Russell 1916:43). As linguists like Chomsky (1976:1) have come to "regard the language capacity virtually as . . . a physical organ of the body," ethologists have always routinely treated all behavior in this manner: "Behavior patterns," Eibl-Eibesfeldt says (1975:219), "can be compared to each other like morphological characteristics, and in this way one obtains similarity gradients that can be used to reconstruct their phylogenetic development."[3] But in order to do this, one must be able to discriminate homologies from analogies, so that a crucial part of the inquiries into ritualization boils down to a search for criteria of behavioral homology, i.e., similarity due to inheritance from a common ancestry. This search, however, is complicated by a host of special problems—for instance (Atz 1970:63–66), (1a) an extreme paucity of fossil records of behavior (cf. N. Tinbergen 1963:427), (1b) the convergence of characteristics owing to adaptations to like environmental needs, (1c) the matter of distinctive levels—identical to those which have bedeviled comparative linguistics as well from its beginnings; (2a) the lack of written records, (2b) the process of convergence that Sapir called "drift," and (2c) the problem of linguistic subgroupings, which was considered in detail by Greenberg (1957, Ch. 4). The success of the ethological procedure is borne out by the fact that classifications based on behavioral taxonomy correspond, on the whole, very closely to classifications arrived at by other means (cf. Tinbergen 1963:428); in linguistics, by contrast, we have scarcely any independent evidence for the accuracy of our genetic groupings.

The entangled roots of ethology and its sometime hostile double, "comparative psychology," were unearthed by Jaynes (1969), and ultimately traced to the famous early-nineteenth-century debates between Cuvier and Etienne Geoffroy Saint-Hilaire (see also Russell 1916:64–65, 74–78). A decisive link with our discipline was undoubtedly provided by Friedrich von Schlegel, regardless of whether he or, as Aarsleff thinks (1967:156–157), Sir William Jones deserves priority in credit for transferring the comparative method from anatomy into linguistics. It was certainly Schlegel, whose personal contacts with Cuvier are documented (e.g., ibid.: 155, n. 108), who, in 1808, referred to *die vergleichende Grammatik* and *die vergleichende Anatomie* in the same often-quoted sentence, suggesting their respective applications in the two domains *auf ähnliche Weise* (cited in ibid.: 157). It can safely be assumed that Schlegel became acquainted during his sojourn in Paris with Cuvier's methods of comparative osteology, but it matters little for our purposes whether he made the intellectual leap from organs to language (or from org to sign) on his own or, as implied by Aarsleff, through the intermediary of Alexander Hamilton. The important point is that Schlegel's *Über die Sprache und Weisheit der Indier* powerfully influenced his own contemporaries and close successors.

Despite the similarity between comparative anatomy and comparative grammar that so impressed Schlegel, and, later (1863; cf. Scharf 1975), August Schleicher's conception of the equivalence, in principle, of Darwin's evolutionary theory and the genetic model of linguistic relationship, there is, of course, one absolutely crucial difference in scope, which seems to have been underplayed by linguistics from Hermann Paul (1880; cf. Strong et al. 1891: 13–17) to our day. I refer to the evident fact that all researches across dialect or language boundaries are necessarily confined to behavior within one and the same species, *Homo sapiens*. For this reason, Huxley's offhand remark (1966: 258), that "man's capacity for true (symbolic) language... itself can properly be regarded as ritualized (adaptively formalized) behaviour," seems to me, while possibly a truism, operationally unverifiable (Sebeok 1976: 93). Ritualization cannot be ostended in the case of a singularity: since only one instance of the faculty we call language has so far been found in nature, terrestrial or extraterrestrial, there is simply nothing to compare it with as a whole. Koehler's pioneer search (1956: 85) "for roots, initia, precursors of human language in animals," an atomistic approach which has subsequently been variously pursued by at least two linguists as well as a few zoologists and anthropologists (Sebeok 1977c), has, in my opinion, not yielded fruitful results, and was therefore rightly dismissed by Lenneberg (1967: 234) as "not relevant to the reconstruction of phylogenetic history." More generally, one could add a further reservation: that while biological structures are tridimensional, the speech chain is unidimensional (in time). This contrast imposes yet another consequential limitation upon Schlegel's analogy. Too, the interpretation of the biological data involves usually quite a number of steps and thus becomes both more delicate and more sophisticated than the corresponding reconstructive procedure in linguistics.

What has been achieved in the century or so since Darwin bespoke (see Ekman 1973) that behavior has been shaped to serve communicative ends, intimating that the origin of the signifying function in man and animal alike arose out of a need for the maintenance of homeostatic equilibrium? Let me rephrase this question: what has been achieved since the realization that, in its essentials, all semiosis involves evolutionary adaptations whereby living systems come to utilize signs to constrain their time and energy ever more effectively toward reproductive success of the genotype, a process of biological regulation, or, to be more precise, goal-directedness (which is the converse of randomness)? Questions such as these were first cogently raised only in this decade in a series of already classic essays by the innovative and biologically well-schooled topologist Thom (1974a), who understood perfectly that semiosis or "la dynamique du symbolisme porte en elle (et ceci sous une forme locale et concentrée) toutes les contradictions de la vision scientifique du monde, et qu'elle est l'image même de la vie" (p. 233). Thom considers almost all biological morphogenesis a semiotic model, indeed, regards all natural phenomena as constituting imperfectly grasped systems of signs. His sketch of the appearance of language in man in response to a double need for a personal evolutive constraint and for a social constraint, or ego-preservation and group regulation (1975a:309–313), is the only scenario which, tersely expressed as it is, seems to me to be in equally good conformity with semiotics and ethology, two differently labeled disciplines that nonetheless have a common historical origin, share a set of methodological tools, and, most important, overlap in their engagement with difficult issues in the analysis of concepts having a regulation figure that Thom calls a *logos* (ibid.:327), and that is manifestly analogous to that of living beings. For Thom (1975a:329, n. 5), this Heraclitean label seems to translate into "form," that is, the structure that assures for any object its unity and its stability. Under the umbrella of his powerful theory, of great beauty, we can at last envisage, if only in outline, a biologically informed sign-science and the semiotically sensitive life-science, constituting two aspects of the general science of the *logos* of a form, what defines the boundary between living organization and inert structure, distinguishes the domain of a natural semiotics from a physics—in fine, provides us a tool with the aid of which we can set about the question of the extent to which our language provides us with a relatively correct description of the world.

3. Zoosemiotic Components of Human Communication

> Note: O. F. Kugelmass has written a brilliant paper about certain tribes in Borneo that do not have a word for "no" in their language and consequently turn down requests by nodding their heads and saying, "I'll get back to you." This corroborates his earlier theories that the urge to be liked at any cost is not socially adaptive but genetic, much the same as the ability to sit through operetta.
> —Woody Allen, "By Destiny Denied," *The New Yorker*, February 23, 1976.

1. "Zoosemiotics": Notes on Its History, Sense, and Scope

The term *zoosemiotics* was launched in 1963 and initially proposed as a name "for the discipline, within which the science of signs intersects with ethology, devoted to the scientific study of signalling behavior in and across animal species" (Sebeok 1972:61). It obviously satisfied a felt need, for—despite some initial resistance, as to any neologism, especially one with overtones of academic jargon—it rapidly diffused in two crisscrossing directions: multidisciplinary and multilingual. It has since been adopted by scholars in a variety of fields, notably biology; and it has penetrated many of the languages of Europe, East and West, and beyond, including Hebrew and Japanese. Outside of scientific writings, the word has cropped up in well-known newspapers, like *Le Monde*, and magazines, like *Il Mondo*. It was featured in at least one novel by a famous English author, as well as in a balloon emanating from the muzzle of that most distinguished of beagles, Snoopy. Discharging a professional obligation to lexicography, I endeavored until recently to keep track of these migrations, and, on

Note: This article has previously appeared as Chapter 38 of *How Animals Communicate*, edited by Thomas A. Sebeok (Bloomington: Indiana University Press, 1977).

occasion, published at least highlights from the progressive record (Sebeok 1972, Ch. 9; 1976:57, 86ff.).

What was originally intended by this term and what it seems to have come to mean to many others is quite another story, and still a bit perplexing. In most instances *zoosemiotics* has been used, roughly, as a one-word equivalent for "the study of animal communication," particularly in explicit or at least implicit contrast with "the study of human communication." This restricted usage is, however, far from what the original definition actually implied. In 1970, in a typology of semiotic systems in general, it was clearly specified that "Human semiotic systems are of two kinds: anthroposemiotic, that is, species-specific systems of man; and zoosemiotic, that is, those component sub-systems of human communication that are found elsewhere in the animal kingdom as well" (Sebeok 1972:163). Because of a colossal accretion in semiotic theory and praxis in recent years, accompanied by a well-nigh unmanageable proliferation of literature in animal communication studies, a conceptual cleansing is called for. Is *zoosemiotics* a useful term? What does it cover? How does all this fit into the vaster framework of general semiotics? Some of the difficulties of terminology and classification, which confront everyone who enters the field of study covered in the rest of Sebeok 1977a, have worried the most thoughtful of its practitioners and observers, but the only thing that is absolutely clear is that we are far from having reached consensus in this area (Hinde 1972:86–98, 395).

The subject matter of semiotics is, quite simply, messages—any messages whatsoever. Since every message is composed of signs according to some ordered selection, semiotics has been variously identified as the doctrine (Locke, Peirce), or the science (Saussure), or the theory (Charles Morris, Carnap, Eco) of signs. Correspondingly, the study designated semiotics comprises the set of general principles that underlie the structure of all signs, constituting a code, which was defined by Cherry (1966:305) as "an agreed transformation, or set of unambiguous rules, whereby messages are converted from one representation to another." Further, semiotics aims to uncover the ways in which such principles are or may be manifested in diverse messages, and to identify the specifics of particular sign systems, with comparative (including cross-taxonomic) as well as typological, synchronic (both structural and functional) as well as diachronic (both phylogenetic and ontogenetic; see section 7, below) ends in view. Semiotics is concerned, successively, with the generation and encoding of messages, their propagation in any sensorially appropriate form of physical energy, their decoding and interpretation. The methods employed by some investigators are more empirical, those by others more analytical. Some prefer to study communication, others signification (Prieto 1975, for instance, makes much of this distinction). Plainly, however, these tendencies are complementary, each implying the other. (Naturalists, as one would expect, by their inclination and training have leaned toward an empirical approach to animal communication, but solid foundations for an analytical approach to animal signification have also been laid in the classic literature of ethology, notably in von Uexküll's marvelous 1940 monograph, "Bedeutungslehre" [See Chs. 1 and 10 of this volume].)

If the subject matter of semiotics encompasses any messages whatsoever, the subject matter of linguistics is confined to verbal messages only. The fundamental competence underlying verbal messages is generally assumed to be (1) species-specific and (2) species-consistent. Species-specificity of the linguistic propensity means that the formal principles we deem sufficient to characterize natural languages (spoken or not) differ radically from those found sufficient to characterize any known system of animal communication, including especially man's so-called nonverbal communication systems. This does not necessarily imply, however, that the neural substrates and/or psychological processes involved need be substantially dissimilar—these are surely secondary and tertiary laminations that are each of a distinct order (cf. Dingwall 1975). Moreover, this conception of species-specificity does not exclude the possibility of quite sophisticated, though always only partial, code sharing, and hence communication, between man and animal (Hediger 1967; 1974 generally; Fouts and Rigby, in respect to the man-chimpanzee dyad, Sebeok 1977a, Ch. 37). Nor is species-consistency necessarily universal, for severely handicapped children may lack the capacity to master language in more than rudimentary fashion (Malson 1964; Curtiss et al. 1975).

The situation of the verbal code in a semiotic frame has been considered by almost everybody who has written on the subject since Locke (1975 [1690]:721). Late in the seventeenth century, he asserted that articulate sounds are the signs "which Men have found the most convenient, and therefore generally make use of...." Linguists —building upon Locke without attribution—generally flatter themselves by at least acquiescing in dicta like Bloomfield's that "Linguistics is the chief contributor to semiotic," or persisting in Weinreich's sentiment that verbal messages constitute "the semiotic phenomenon par excellence" (Sebeok 1976:11–12)—no doubt a conscious rephrasing of Sapir's (1931) "language is the communicative process par excellence in every known society"—just recently reechoed by Greimas (1976:9) in his remark that "la linguistique . . . est la plus élaborée des sémiotiques."

It was apparently Saussure who promoted linguistics to the status of a pilot science, or "le patron général de toute sémiologie" (Sebeok 1976:12), a programmatic statement which, when pursued blindly, can lead into many a cul-de-sac (cf. Marcus, in Sebeok 1974b:2871ff.; see also Polhemus, in Benthall and Polhemus 1975:20ff.). I have referred to the principle that is usually invoked in this connection as one of "intersemiotic transmutability," which may have been first, or was, at any rate, most insistently enunciated by Hjelmslev (1953:70): "in practice, a language is a semiotic into which all other semiotics may be translated—both all other languages, and all other conceivable semiotic structures." Elsewhere, I have questioned whether this *ex cathedra* declaration has actual support or remains, as I think, although still much cherished by linguists, hardly more than unsubstantiated dogma. In particular, I tried to show that animal sounds are often incapable of being paraphrased: "one gropes in vain for a set of linguistic signs to substitute instead of the significative unit employed by the speechless creature both to refer to his scarcely understood species-specific code and to the context of delivery, or *Umwelt*, through which the message fragment is aligned within the observed sequence of signs emitted" (Ch. 16, this volume). Even the transmutation of certain categories of human nonverbal messages into linguistic expression is, at best, likely to introduce gross falsification, or, like most music, altogether defy comprehensible verbal definition. Sapir (1931) put his finger on a "more special class of communicative symbolism," such as the use of railroad lights, bugle calls in the army, or smoke-signals, in which "one cannot make a word-to-word translation, as it were, back to speech but can only paraphrase in speech the intent of the communication."

Semiotic systems that are species-specific in man are, then, for convenience, categorized as *anthroposemiotic* (Sebeok 1972:163ff., 1976:3). Language clearly belongs here, not only in its global spoken form but also as a visible means of communication used by a small minority population among a minority of mankind with partial or total hearing impairment and by those associated with such persons (Stokoe 1972, esp. Ch. 1). Here are counted also a wide array of speech surrogates (Sebeok and Umiker-Sebeok 1976), mute communication systems preserved in certain monasteries (Barakat 1975), aboriginal sign languages used among native peoples of the Americas and Australia (Umiker-Sebeok and Sebeok 1978), complex (viz., nonisomorphic) transductions into parasitic or restricted formations, like script or other optical displays of the chain of speech signs (the Morse code, or any of the several acoustic alphabets designed to aid the blind, or sound spectrograms), optionally imposed upon chronologically prior acoustic patterns (Kavanagh and Mattingly 1972), and more or less context-free artificial constructs developed for various scientific or technical purposes (see, e.g., the respective articles by Golopenţia-Eretescu, Gross, and Freudenthal in Sebeok 1974b).

Over and above such transfers (Sapir 1931), transforms, derivatives, and substitutes, there are those macrostructures that are based, in the final analysis, on a natural language, the "primary system" on which culture is superimposed, "regarded as a hierarchy of semiotic systems correlated in pairs, realized through correlation with the system of natural language" (Sebeok 1975a:76–77, 1976:23 n. 38). Particularly, this is implied by the concept of "secondary modeling systems," propagated chiefly by the Moscow-Tartu School of semioticians (Eimermacher 1974; Sebeok 1975a:57–83; Ivanov 1976; Winner and Winner 1976). All secondary modeling systems are, therefore, anthroposemiotic by definition.

In a third category that might be reckoned anthroposemiotic are sets of signs affirmed to be uniquely used by man independently of any linguistic infrastructure (although, of course, unavoidably intertwined with verbal effects), but one must exercise great caution with respect to this division. In 1968, I blithely declared that music is "a species-specific, but not species-consistent form of behavior" (Sebeok 1972: 164–165). There is ample cause for wonder now if the first part of this allegation is true, and in what way? The relation between human and avian music was thoughtfully reviewed by Joan Hall-Craggs (Hinde 1969, Ch. 16), with special regard to the nature of the esthetic content of bird song. She concluded that "the form of music remains the privilege of birds and men" (ibid.:380), but suggested that the resemblances between the two varieties of semiosis can best be understood in terms of analogous functional requirements, such as the need to signal to distant listeners. The philosopher Hartshorne (the same, incidentally, who had served as the senior editor of C. S. Peirce's selected papers) has since reexamined the material in even more detail (1973, Ch. 3). He characterized bird song as "the best of the subhuman music of nature" (ibid.:39) and declared, "considering the enormous gap between the anatomies and lives of man and bird, it remains astonishing how much musical intelligibility the utterances of the latter have for the former" (ibid.:46).

Investigations in this area have even crystallized into a subdiscipline called "ornithomusicology" by Szöke (1963), who maintains that since birds evolved elaborate musical utterances before we appeared on the scene, it is reasonable to suppose that the development of primitive music was actually stimulated by hearing and mimicking bird vocalizations (cf. remarks by Hewes, Livingstone, and Lomax in Wescott 1974). Some species of Mysticetes, notably *Megaptera novaeangliae*, also "produce a series of beautiful and varied sounds," likewise called songs, the function of which is still a matter for much speculation but is usually assumed to serve communicative ends, possibly over great distances (Payne and McVay 1971:597); these prolonged vocalizations are frequently compared to bird songs, the chief difference being that the latter normally last only a few seconds, whereas those of the humpback whales have a cycling time of up to thirty minutes, their patterns being repeated by individuals with considerable accuracy. Whatever the ultimate merits may be of such cross-taxa comparisons and contrasts between distantly related species occupying only vaguely similar ecological niches (as considered, e.g., in terms of quite abstract geometric patterns by Nelson 1973:299–300, 324ff.), the facile grouping of music among anthroposemiotic systems appears, in retrospect, to have been premature.

The same can be said, *mutatis mutandis*, about other nonverbal art forms, for instance, abstract picture-making, a behavior that has been induced in apes (D. Morris 1962; Bourne 1971, Ch. 9), and even in capuchin monkeys, with some success. According to the ethologist Andrew Whiten, the taste exhibited by apes—their choice of color, brightness, composition—"provides a unique background against which we may try to understand the origins and fundamental nature of visual art in our species . . ." (in Brothwell 1976:40). Nicholas Humphrey's experiments show that apes prefer blues and greens over yellows and reds, leading to speculations that they favor the safety of green trees as opposed to the perils of exposure against red or yellow earth. Whiten "explains" their liking for bright light by assuming that it helps them perceive potential danger and surmises that their predilection for regular pattern might have something to do with an aptitude for handling intricate spatial relationships required to move safely through forests (ibid.:32ff.). Apes do seem to enjoy what they are doing, but forms of life that are not our direct phylogenetic ancestors, like the bowerbirds, also exhibit significant traces of a visual esthetic sense (von Frisch 1974:244ff.; Waddington, in Brothwell 1976:8; Griffin 1976:76ff.); thus male black woodpeckers chisel out nests that no less a scientist than von Frisch has depicted as architectural "works of art" (1974:189). Other birds build elaborate nests that they continue to improve upon with practice, in the sense of imparting a heavier semiotic charge: their constructions become, at least in our eyes, tidier and more elegant, but not recognizably more useful by strictly biological criteria.

Because I now consider it increasingly doubtful that any sign system that is not manifestly language-related belongs with man's repertoire of anthroposemiotic devices, I provisionally conclude, as a heuristic tactic, that all other systems used by man are to be construed as zoosemiotic until demonstrated to be otherwise. This view represents a radical shift in my position over the last ten years, one that still preserves the established dichotomy but enlarges the biological base as against the cultural superstructure, encouraging the search for true antecedents (homologies), not just the sharing of traits. It also counsels caution about a saltatory "discontinuity theory" in the terms argued for by Eric H. Lenneberg (in Sebeok 1968, Ch. 21) and supported to a degree by some notable ethologists (e.g., Klopfer, in Hahn and Simmel 1976:7–21). The strategic anthroposemiotics/zoosemiotics dichotomy will stand just as long as the riddle of the origin of language remains unsolved (Hinde 1972:75ff., 94ff.; Wescott 1974; Lieberman 1975; 1977). Recent concerted efforts at experimentation with various Great Apes notwithstanding (Fouts, forthcoming), no breakthrough is in sight; indeed, Thorpe (in Hinde 1972:174) fears that the solution is likely to elude us forever. It may well be the case, as Julian Huxley (1966:258) once remarked, and as I would very much like to believe, that language "can properly be regarded as ritualized (adaptively formalized) behaviour," but, unfortunately, he did not go on to spell out just how one could apply the essentially comparative methods of ethology to a phenomenon that stubbornly remains a singularity in our known universe. In brief, what zoosemiotics has hitherto failed to provide is a comparative perspective for language (Hinde in Benthall and Polhemus 1975:107–140), particularly with appropriately correlated operational procedures. The importance of a comparative semiotics (called for in Sebeok, 1976, Ch. 3; 1977a) cannot be overestimated, so it is encouraging to know that at least a few animal behaviorists of the first rank are not only commencing to share this long-felt conviction but have actually concluded that "the road now seems open" to realize its goals (Griffin 1976:95–106).

The relation between the mutually opposite categories in man is hierarchical, and can therefore productively be viewed in terms of a notion standard in linguistics, *markedness*. Anthroposemiotic systems are always *marked*, in contradistinction to the zoosemiotic systems that comprehend them. This means that a specific anthroposemiotic sign implies the presence of a certain property X, whereas a genetic zoosemiotic sign implies nothing about the presence of X (it may, but need not, indicate the absence of X). The marked sign is always the negative of the unmarked sign: "statement of X" vs. "no statement of X." Some major controversial issues of long standing can be clarified in this light, such as the much-debated question whether a particular facial expression signifies the same emotion for all peoples or whether its meaning depends on the culture of the expressor and the "expressee." Ekman's carefully wrought theory postulates "culture differences in facial expressions as well as universals" (1972:279). The pancultural expressions are plainly zoosemiotic—they reflect biological bias in human behavior; hence, in the technical sense of the term, they are unmarked. The consequences of social learning, which varies both from culture to culture and according to smaller groupings within a culture, include the acquisition of markedness for every possible transition state in terms of the gain or loss of whatever the feature under consideration.

"The relationships between verbal and nonverbal communication are rather tenuous," Hinde (1974:146) ruefully conceded in his latest excellent survey of human zoosemiotic techniques. Oddly, however, he has overlooked a pivotal article by Gregory Bateson (in Sebeok 1968, Ch. 22), which cogently and forcefully set forth the reasons why this must be so. There is a popular belief, Bateson said, "that in the evolution of man, language replaced the cruder systems of the other animals," but he believed this to be totally wrong, because, if "verbal language were in any sense an evolutionary replacement of communication by means of kinesics and paralanguage, we would expect the old ... systems to have undergone conspicuous decay." Such is manifestly not the case: rather, "the kinesics of men have become richer and more complex, and paralanguage has blossomed side by side with the evolution of verbal language ... [both of which] have been elaborated into complex forms of art, music, ballet, poetry, and the like, and, even in everyday life, the intricacies of human kinesic communication, facial expression and vocal intonation far exceed anything that any other animal is known to produce." In brief, the two kinds of sign systems, though they are often in performance subtly interwoven, serve ends largely different from one another, indeed, zoosemiotic devices perform functions that anthroposemiotic devices are unsuited for, and vice versa. An exquisite illustration of the "reconciliation of the human necessity of speaking with the spiritual need for silence ... within a single behavioral frame in which both components, otherwise contradictory, were indispensable" (Bauman 1974:159–160) is related from the life of Quakers, whose style of preaching, mixing a "bundle of words and heap of Non-sense," evoked astonished comment even in 1653 (ibid.:150).

2. Inner/Outer

Another coined term (Sebeok 1974b:213; 1976:3), albeit proposed no more than half seriously, was *endosemiotics*, "which studies cybernetic systems within the body." Clearly, man's semiotic systems are characterized by a definite bipolarity between the molecular code at the lower end of the scale and the verbal code at the upper. Amid these two uniquely powerful mechanisms (Marcus 1974; Sebeok 1972:62; 1977a) there exists a whole array of others, ranging from those located in the interior of organisms (von Uexküll's *Innenwelt*) to those linking them to the external "physical world" (his *Umwelt*), which of course includes biologically and/or sociologically "interesting" other organisms, like preys and predators. Semiotic networks are thus established between individuals belonging to the same as well as to different species. Jacob, who has most succinctly stated that the "genetic code is like a language," goes further: if they are to specialize, he points out, "cells must ... communicate with each other," and, at the macroscopic level, "evolution depends on setting up new systems of communication, just as much within the organism as between the organism and its surroundings" (Jacob 1974:306, 308, 312). After the new integrations have occurred, such that the coordination of elements has progressed from molecular interaction to the exchange of verbal messages, a still more novel hierarchy of integrons is set up: "From family organization to modern state, from ethnic group to coalition of nations" (ibid.: 320), a variety of elevated ("secondary") codes come into play—cultural, moral, social, political, economic, military, religious, ideological, etc. The genetic conception of integron—called "shred out" in general systems theory, in reference to evolution "from slow, inefficient, chemical transmission by diffusion at the cell level up to increasingly rapid and cost-effective symbolic linguistic transmissions over complicated networks at the higher levels of living systems" (J. Miller 1976:227)—is equivalent to the semiotic notion of "radius of communication," the progressive widening of which mirrors the history of civilization (Sapir 1931) as much as it marks stages in the maturation of every individual.

There is no absolute boundary where zoosemiotics abruptly turns into anthroposemiotics. Least of all is this a correlate of "the appearance of a new property: the ability to do without objects and interpose a kind of filter between the organism and its environment: the ability to symbolize," which Jacob (1974:319) ascribes to mammals in general. So does Washburn (1973:181), who refers to "the mammalian brain as a symbolic machine." In fact, the groundwork for the mosaic of changes that enable organisms to utilize symbols was prefigured much earlier, as Gordon M. Tomkins (1975) convincingly delineated, and was sketchily reviewed in the framework of Peirce's doctrine of signs in Chapter 1 of this volume. On the invertebrate side, insects, such as the balloon flies, have evolved a symbolizing capacity in one of their species, *Hilara sartor* (see Chapter 1; for symbolic communication in bees, see Griffin 1976:19-25). Also, John Z. Young has recently shown that the octopus deals with the world in a manner that can only be described as "symbolic." In a lecture given at the American Museum of Natural History in 1976, he said: "The essence of learning is the attaching of symbolic value to signs from the outside world. Images on the retina are not eatable or dangerous. What the eye of a higher animal provides is a tool by which, aided by a memory, the animal can learn the symbolic significance of events." Cephalopod brains may not be able to elaborate complex programs—i.e., strings of signs, or what Young calls "mnemons"—such as guide our future feelings, thoughts, and actions, but they can symbolize at least simple operations crucial for their survival, such as appropriate increase or decrease in distance between them and environmental stimulus sources ("Withdraw" or "Approach": Schneirla 1965). The use of symbols on the part of the alloprimates is, of course, a current commonplace, but it has been apparent to unbiased scientists at least since Wolfe's (1936) experiments with a group of young chimpanzees nearly a half century ago (Wolfe was an excessively timid reader of Charles Morris; ibid.: 70). As Katz (1937:237) then noted in a needless display of the double negative, "It appears that chimpanzees are not completely incapable of using non-linguistic symbols." A recent remark of Lévi-Strauss sums the matter up far more cogently: "Les animaux sont privés de langage, au sens que nous l'entendons chez l'homme, mais ils communiquent tout de même au moyen . . . d'un système symbolique" (Malson 1973: 20).

The genetic code and the metabolic code—which intimately couples the endocrine and nervous systems (Tomkins 1975:763)—are obviously at once endosemiotic and zoosemiotic, but other intracorporeal sign processes, notably the phenomenon of "inner speech" (Egger 1904; Vygotsky 1962; Vološinov 1973), may be at least partially anthroposemiotic. Thus memory experiments have convincingly shown that thinking has two richly interconnected components in man: one verbal, the other nonverbal, each with characteristic properties. The imaginal effects in this dual coding system are zoosemiotic. Neurological studies display in extreme form a functional separation between the verbal and nonverbal spatial systems (Bower 1970:509). Further, at least two scholars have independently pointed to the evolutionary intermediacy of man's dreaming, focusing their arguments chiefly on one particular kind of semiotic entity, the icon (Bateson, in Sebeok 1968:623; Thom 1975a:72–73; cf. Sebeok 1976). Moreover, tests conducted on patients with commissurectomies (in the so-called Bogen [1969] series) have also yielded rather conspicuous clues that the right half of the brain may be primarily responsible for imaging processes in dreaming. If confirmed by current sleep research experiments, these results will be highly interesting in view of the association of the right hemisphere with the normal imaging mechanisms implicated with the handling of visual-spatial tasks criterial of (nonvocal) nonverbal communication (cf. Ornstein 1972:64–65, 235 n. 17; see also section 6, below).

The field of transducer physiology studies the conversion of "outer" signs to their initial "inner" input and considers the relative or absolute contrasts between the pathways of information outside the body and the pathways deep inside it. Although one can but concur with Shands (1976:303ff.) that it is essential to grapple with "the human problem of the greatest moment . . . of so relating the outer to the inner that the minimal information derivable from inner sources comes to be a reliable index of the external situation," and that this bifurcation must eventually be dealt with in semiotic terms, this science, powerfully foreseen by Leibniz, is as yet barely developed. Its modern theoretical foundations were laid in Bentley's spellbinding paper (1941) on the human skin as philosophy's last line of defense, the argument of which rested on the semiotic of Peirce (ibid.:18). Beck, looking toward "a truly human sociobiology" (1976:157), reviewed recent work with specific regard to nonverbal communication in man.

It is, in fact, hard to ascertain where "inner" ends and "outer" begins. The human skin itself is a rich arena of momentous semiotic events throughout the life of each individual, not only within our species (Moles 1964; Kauffman 1971; Montagu 1971) but, more fascinatingly and almost wholly out of awareness, also in intricate communicative interaction with the teeming faunal and floral inhabitants of that veritable microscopic dermal ecosystem (Marples 1965). Beyond the skin toward the outside, as Hediger (e.g., 1968:83) has incontrovertibly been demonstrating since 1941, every individual, according to its species, moves in the interior of an invisible but nonetheless sharply defined insulating space circumscribed by that animal's "individual distance" (the minimum remove within which it may approach another) and its "social distance" (the maximum separation between the members of any group). These concepts are crucial in the management of animals in zoos and circuses, and in their handling in laboratory experiments, under conditions of domestication, or as pets. In a test in which the density of children was modified in a playroom, a similar process was observed in operation (Hutt and Vaizey 1966). Evidence bearing on the structuring of space and time in animals, or having to do with territoriality, overcrowding, and other sorts of distance regulation, were later extrapolated to man's perception of space and cultural modifications of this basic biological structuration. The branch of anthroposemiotics that studies such behavior is sometimes called proxemics (E. Hall 1959; Watson, in Sebeok 1974b:311–344). Its subject matter falls between bodily contact (the most intimate involvement of the *ego* with the *alter*) and patterns of physical appearance such as facial postures and bodily position, eye movements, and the nonverbal aspects of vocal acts. All of these come into play, in the main, beyond the Hediger "bubble," a variably shaped zone of personal space that admits no trespass by strangers and is defended when penetrated without permission (Fig. 3-1).

The distinction between anthroposemiotic and zoosemiotic events is thus not at all demarcated at the integumentary threshold. Both processes have important extensions past the skin, in either direction. These "boundary" communicative phenomena, to which Peirce drew our attention repeatedly (when discussing Secondness) as the shock of reaction between *ego* and *non-ego*, may prove particularly interesting for future semiotic and related researches.

3. Vocal/Nonvocal

Sound emission and sound reception are so much a part of human life that it comes as something of a surprise to realize how uncommon this prominence of the role of sound is in the wider scheme of biological existence. In point of fact, according to Huxley and Koch (1964 [1938]:26–27), "the great majority of animals are both deaf and dumb." Of the dozen or so phyla, "only two contain creatures that can

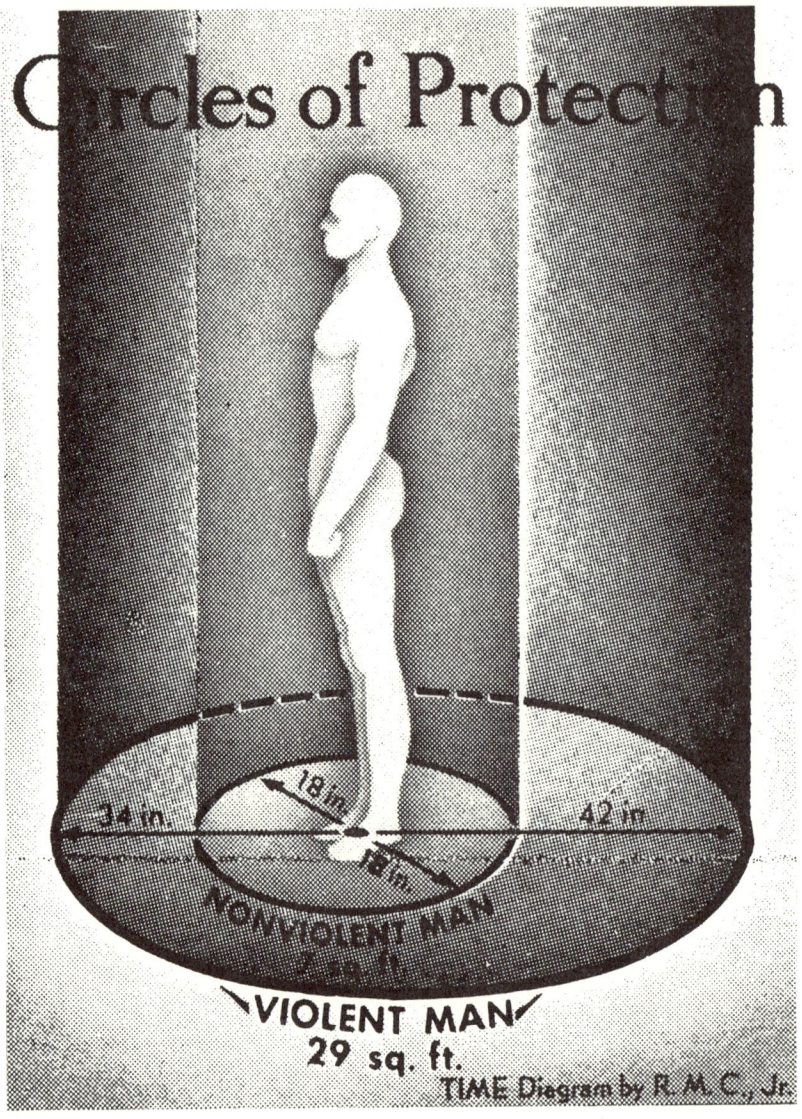

Figure 3-1. Psychiatrist Augustus F. Kinzel has differentiated violent from nonviolent human subjects in terms of their communicative radius: on the average, the former stopped him at a distance of three feet, the latter at only half that distance. The two areas of insulating space differed, as well, in shape, from nearly cylindrical in nonviolent subjects to those bulging to the rear in violent ones—an avenue of approach interpreted as particularly menacing. Reprinted by permission from TIME, The Weekly Newsmagazine; Copyright Time Inc. 1969.

hear or produce functional sound," namely, the Arthropods and the Chordates. Their respective situations are, however, quite different: while practically no members of the lower classes of Chordates are capable of sound production, the "highest three-and-a-half classes of the vertebrates are . . . unique in having all their members capable of sound-production, as well (save for the snakes) as of hearing." The methods of sound production, of course, vary enormously from group to group. Not only does our own method appear to be unusual, but Huxley and Koch (ibid.:32) confirm that it evolved only once in the stream of life. The vocal mechanism that works by means of a current of air passing over the cords and setting them into vibration seems to be confined to ourselves and, with distinctions, to our nearest relatives —the other mammals, the birds (since they possess a syrinx), the reptiles, and the amphibians (although some fish use wind instruments as well, they do so without the reed constituted by our vocal cords). So far as we know, no true vocal performances are found outside the land vertebrates or their marine descendants. Among many, notably ourselves, unarticulated vocalizations are used for status displays or to convey information about age, sex (Guthrie 1976:33), and a host of specific characteristics about the state of the emitter-in-context (Lotz 1956a:212); usually, they are employed in the manner of icons (Ch. 6, this volume).

Humans communicate via many channels, only one of which is acoustic. Acoustic communication in man may be somatic (e.g., humming) or artifactual (e.g., drumming: Sebeok and Umiker-Sebeok 1976). Acoustic somatic communication may be vocal (e.g., shouting for a waiter) or nonvocal (snapping one's fingers to summon him). Finally, acoustic somatic vocal communication may be verbal (speech) or nonverbal (Pike 1943:32–41, 149–151 remains by far the best survey of such mechanisms), with the latter being either linked to or independent of speech (Argyle 1975, Ch. 18). On the other hand, by no means all verbal systems are manifested in the acoustic medium: Classical Chinese occurs only in written form; the American Sign Language (ASL) is encoded and decoded visually; and the mode in which man communes with himself, his thinking—which, as Peirce taught, "always proceeds in the form of a dialogue . . . between different phases of the *ego* . . ." (Sebeok 1976:28 n. 45), and which constitutes one of man's unique uses of language (Bronowski, in Sebeok 1974b:2539–2540)—requires audible articulation but facultatively.

These observations, which underline obvious distinctions, are necessary because much conceptual confusion is engendered by the terminological disarray that bedevils the field of human zoosemiotics (Sebeok 1976:156–164). For example, at least two major books (Hall 1959; Critchley 1975) bear the title *Silent Language*. The attentive reader soon discovers that neither work deals with language, except in a misleadingly metaphoric sense, or even, strictly, with silence: thus

48 The Sign

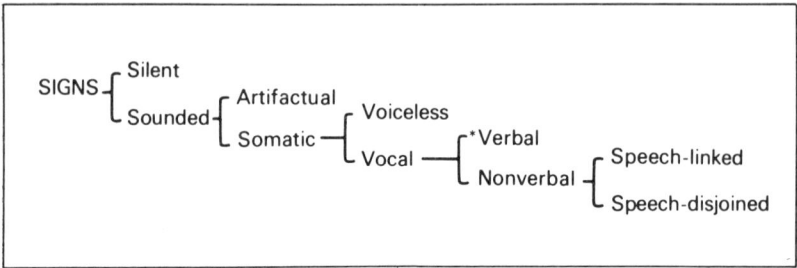

Figure 3-2. An asterisk indicates the category assumed to be purely anthroposemiotic; the status of speech-linked phenomena, such as singing (i.e., a tune plus lyrics), is best reckoned as hybrid, or transitional, if not downright fuzzy (cf. Crystal 1969:179–194). Terms to the right are progressively marked. Note that less than 1 percent of the information conveyed by speech is used for linguistic purposes as such (cf. Lotz 1956:212).

Critchley declares in his very first paragraph, "Gesture may sometimes be audible though still unvoiced."

The foregoing is summarily depicted in Figure 3-2, which substantially develops a single node from a tabular representation introduced in an earlier classification of zoosemiotic devices to illustrate the human production of signs according to the different communicative techniques involved (Sebeok 1976:30, Table 4; also in Eco 1976:175, Table 34), but which also constitutes a considerable amplification of a clarifying figure with similar intent by Argyle (1975:346, Fig. 18.1).

The superficially similar classification by Wescott (1969:152), possibly the most tireless nomenclator in this field, is both incomplete and at least partially mistaken. He distinguishes, in the acoustic channel, among three communicative systems, which he labels, respectively, *language*, *phasis*, and *strepitus*. "Language and phasis are both vocal," he continues inaccurately (cf. Dingwall 1975:32), the former being articulated, the latter consisting "solely of grunts and other vocalizations insusceptible to combination." Strepitus is then said to differ from both "in being nonvocal," e.g., hand clapping or foot stamping. Incidentally, there have been many efforts to design a system that describes all human movement in terms of the place and type of articulation of the segments of an idealized lay figure, that is, to devise a notation for muscular movement. The model, as construed in a volume of three-dimensional space so that the behavioral sequences can then be delineated as a syntagmatic concatenation of volumes, was envisaged by Bouissac (1973) and, in a measure, actually attempted by Schutz (1976; cf. Kelley 1971, which, oddly enough, is not cited).

The taxonomic fragment sketched in Figure 3-2 could be enriched in various intersecting ways. For instance, one may inquire to what degree the signs emitted by the source are "wanted," i.e., constitute its message for the destination, or have become increasingly "unwanted" (i.e., noisy) in the course of transmission. Or one may focus on whether the emission and/or the reception of a given string is conscious or out of awareness (a distinction to be pursued further in section 5, below).

4. Verbal/Nonverbal

The subject matter of linguistics, as we all "know," is communication consisting of verbal messages and the undergirding verbal code enabling them. By contrast, the concept of nonverbal communication is one of the most ill-defined in all of semiotics. No wonder the notion is often negatively formulated: as early as 1888, Kleinpaul (1972) paradoxically designated the topic of his classic manual as *Sprache ohne Worte*, or "wordless language." This concept recurs over and over in recent book titles, particularly since the appearance of the comprehensive, handsome treatise by Ruesch and Kees (1956), in the shape of "nonverbal" or "non-verbal." Sample listings, merely from this decade, include Bosmajian (1971), Davis (1971), Eisenberg and Smith (1971), Harrison (1974), Hinde (1972), Knapp (1972), Krames et al. (1974), Mehrabian (1972), Pliner et al. (1975), Poyatos (1976), Scherer (1970), and Weitz (1974). Countless monographs, special journal issues, and brief articles insist on viewing nonverbal communication as "communication minus language"; many of them are listed in Part 8 of the Eschbach-Rader bibliography of semiotics (1976:75–87), which is itself headed "Non-verbal communication" in the restricted sense. Such works tend to deepen the gulf segregating the "nonverbal" from the verbal; to paraphrase an amusing observation of Voegelin and Harris (1947:588), one might infer from some of them "that houses are built in sullen silence."

Two further interconnected problems immediately arise. On the one hand, the contents of these works so labeled encompass an astounding congeries of topics. On the other hand, the partial synonyms that have been devised to cope with this massive confusion have all proved unsatisfactory for one reason or another, as has already been adumbrated in Sebeok 1976:158–162. Such competing though only partially overlapping terms and expressions include bodily communication, body language or body talk, coenetics, gesticulation, gesture, gSigns, kinesics, kinesiology, motor signs, pantomime, proxemics, silent language, tacesics, etc., and, of course, zoosemiotics with extensions thereof. This is not the place to enter the soggy quicksand of usages appropriate to this particular trade, but what about the nature of the traffic itself? What do we know about the commodity purveyed, beyond the presumed barring of what belongs strictly to linguistics?

Mehrabian's definition of what pertains to nonverbal behavior and what its functions are is fairly typical in that it starts out with an equivocation. He distinguishes (1972, Ch. 1) between two senses, one narrow "and more accurate," the other broader but, while traditional, allegedly "a misnomer." The former embraces "facial expressions, hand and arm gestures, postures and positions, and various movements of the body or the legs and feet." The latter is equivalent to what has frequently been included under the subcategory of "paralinguistic or vocal phenomena" (also in Argyle 1975, Ch. 18). No mention is made of the obvious: that all animals communicate nonverbally, and that, in point of fact, other books, with identical titles, are devoted to just this, to the exclusion of virtually the entire human domain (e.g., Krames et al. 1974; Pliner et al. 1975; and Hinde 1972, which is evenly balanced between the behavior of man and that of the creatures devoid of language). As to the concept of "paralanguage" (Crystal in McCormack and Wurm 1976:13–27; Laver 1976:347–354)—which ought, more accurately, to be termed "paraphonation," but which the innocent inquirer may reasonably assume to bear some relation to language—it further confounds the already frustrating jigsaw puzzle. Paraphonetic features may easily be homologized with aspects of animal communication, such as the conveyance of information about sex, age, and individual identity, much as song is assumed to do in many birds. However, in preparation for a state-of-the-art paper on the topic, David Crystal wrote a number of colleagues asking them what they understood to fall under this heading; he then reported his findings: "animal vocalization (or some aspect of it), memory restrictions on language, recallability for language, utterance length, literary analysis, environmental restrictions on language use . . . glossolalia, and emotional expression in general language disturbance—in effect, a fair proportion of sociolinguistics and psycholinguistics" (in Sebeok 1974b:269).

It is indeed very difficult, in practice, always to assign unambiguously what segment of a vocal encounter (conversation, state of talk) between people concerns linguists and what segment concerns "nonverbal" interactional analysts: "please remember that the integral role of gesture in speech is quite as important for our understanding of an utterance as the one or two significant movements or indications which actually replace an uttered word," Malinowski (1965[1935]:26) warned more than forty years ago. The borderline becomes more blurred the closer the focus of analysis gets. Some of the awesome entanglements of verbal responses with other kinds of acts were first heroically wrestled with by Malinowski, but he failed to achieve the

	VOCAL	VERBAL
Language	0	+
Speech	+	+
ASL	−	+
Babbling; paralanguage	+	−
'Fig'	−	−
Song (tune with or without lyrics)	+	±
Whistle	+	0

Figure 3-3. The "fig" (thumb thrust between middle and ring fingers of fist) is an invitation to sexual intercourse in some cultures (Bäuml and Bäuml 1975: 72), a gesture randomly selected for this chart as an example of a soundless movement of the sort Efron (1972[1941]:96), one supposes, might have called an intrinsically coded kinetograph. Whistle is "Verbal 0" because it could represent merely a tune or be used as a speech surrogate (Sebeok and Umiker-Sebeok 1976).

integration he had preached because he lacked one indispensable analytic tool, an understanding of Kiriwinian verbal structure. Goffman dealt with them concretely in his masterful working paper (1975) on minimal dialogic units. They amply justify the research strategy increasingly being applied to the organization of conversations by workers like Duncan (1975), Poyatos (1976: see Fig. 4, p. 66), and others under such labels as speaker synchrony, interactional synchrony, interactional equilibrium, and conveyance of indexical information (Laver 1976:354–358).

In Figure 3-3, the two oppositions Vocal/Nonvocal and Verbal/Nonverbal, as they are realized in a few of the aforementioned phenomena, are condensed into a sample distinctive feature chart. This matrix is merely meant to be illustrative: many other oppositions, as well as many other kinds of sign systems, could be adduced at will. (The

52 The Sign

assigned values are adopted from standard linguistic usage: + means that the feature is present, − that it is not, ± that both are co-present, and o that the distinction is inapplicable.)

But the conceptual chaos does not end there, because "nonverbal" of course subsumes a considerably vaster radius than the sphere of bodily communication as such. (Incidentally, one may well ask, the so-called organs of speech also being parts of the human body, why are the several manifestations of man's linguistic endowment, notably speech itself, generally not comprehended under this or similar rubrics?) Surely, music (Nattiez 1975), the culinary arts (Barthes 1967: 27–28), a circus act (Bouissac 1976), gardening (Malinowski 1965 [1935]), a floral arrangement (Cortambert 1833), the application of perfumes (Sebeok 1972:100–101), the choice and combination of garments (Bogatyrev 1971; Guthrie 1976, Ch. 18) are only some random means among man's multiform options for communicating nonverbally. Accordingly, it would hardly be an exaggeration to claim that the range of the "nonverbal," thus conceived, becomes coincidental with the entire range of culture exclusive of language yet further encompassing much that belongs to ethology. But this way of looking at "nonverbal" seems to me about as helpful as the Kugelmass theories reported by Woody Allen in the epigraph to this chapter.

5. Witting/Unwitting

People are capable of encoding messages either deliberately or unwittingly, and to decode messages either with the knowledge that they are so engaged or without conscious awareness of what they are about. In a dyadic interaction between organisms, therefore, four possibilities exist in respect to this distinction.

The first possibility is that neither the emitter nor the receiver is able to identify the message, let alone restate it verbally. The pupil response furnishes a nice illustration of this: "While it is evident that men are attracted to women with large pupils their responses are generally at a nonverbal level. It seems that what is appealing about large pupils in a woman is that they imply a strong and sexually toned interest in the man she is with, as well as making her look younger.... The enlarged pupils, in effect, act as a 'signal' transmitted to the other person. Several observations made by others have indicated that this is what really can occur in the interpersonal relationship between a man and a woman, and apparently without conscious awareness" (Hess 1975: 95).

This state of affairs can, however, be altered either at the source or at the destination, or, of course, at both the input and the output end. For instance, a woman can deliberately dilate her pupils with one of several pharmaceuticals to enhance her appearance: such, indeed, was the custom in Central Europe in the interwar period (the drug used was a crystalline alkaloid derived from belladonna, which means "beautiful woman"). At the other end of the transmission chain, as Hediger (1976) has noted, the best circus animal trainers "haben schon längst erkannt, dass die Pupillenbewegungen z.B. ihrer Tiger wichtige Schlüsse auf deren Stimmung zulassen."

Signs that are normally unwitting, like the pupil response in man and animals, are regarded by most specialists (e.g., Peirce, Bühler, Jakobson, and American clinical semioticians generally) as constituting a subcategory of indices that, since Hippocrates, has comprehended symptoms and syndromes (Sebeok 1976:124–128, 181–182). These are of prime concern no less to semiotics than to medicine (Ch. 1, this volume). Instead of dwelling on these wide implications here, let us briefly reconsider the story of Clever Hans (Pfungst 1965[1911]). One is compelled to concur with Katz (1937:5) that at the turn of the century this case was (and is now more than ever: Hediger 1976) "a problem of first-rate importance, not merely of interest to special sciences, like zoology and psychology, but having some bearing on the deepest philosophical questions." Let us add that it is also of interest to the integrated science of communication, semiotics most particularly (cf. Rosenthal, in Pfungst 1965[1911]:xxxiii, xxxix n. 11). This eponymous horse gave its name to one of the classic errors in the history of psychology after it was finally realized "how fatally the unintentional effect on the animal of the observer can influence the results" (Katz 1937:7), and paradigmatically illustrated "the power of the self-fulfilling prophecy. Hans' questioners, even skeptical ones, expected Hans to give the correct answers to their queries. Their expectation was reflected in their unwitting signal to Hans that the time had come for him to stop his tapping. The signal cued Hans to stop, and the questioner's expectation became the reason for Hans' being, once again, correct" (Rosenthal 1966:138).

It must be emphasized that one is concerned here with what Carl Stumpf (in his original [1907] Preface to Pfungst 1965) described as *minimale unabsichtliche Bewegungen*, or unintentional minimal movements of the horse's questioner, which occasioned the colossal case of self-deception. Máday soon refocused the whole phenomenon in its properly explicit frame, designating the proposition as a *Zeichenhypothese* (1914:12) and enumerating the proofs therefor (ibid.:13–18). He also described the *unwillkürliche Zeichen*, or unwitting signs, in abundant detail (see esp. ibid., Ch. 6 and pp. 247–259), dispelling whatever lingering doubts may have existed. To be sure, Pfungst tells of other clever animals, and there have been records of many since, not just "talking" equines but learned canines, reading pigs, and at least one "goat of knowledge." The most fascinating "talking" horse was Berto, which was blind yet gave excellent results when the attendant "thought that the questions had been written on its skin or uttered aloud" (Katz 1937:17–18). All of them were assiduously coached performers intentionally cued by their trainers, who were entertainingly exposed by the prominent American illusionist and historian of conjuration, Christopher (1970, Ch. 3; see also Máday 1914, Ch. 15). In sum, the Clever Hans phenomenon lies at the very heart of zoosemiotics; the investigators were misled because they sought in the pupil, the horse—or the great spotted woodpecker (Griffin 1976:25–26), or the porpoise (Sebeok 1972:59ff.), or the chimpanzee—what they should have looked for in the teacher, man: covert and unwitting message transmissions from man to man (Rosenthal 1966, Ch. 9) as well as from man to animal (ibid., Ch. 10).

Much of the mystique that enveloped the Delphinidae in the 1960s is traceable to the Clever Hans delusion (Sebeok 1972:59–60; Wood 1973, Ch. 1; Caldwell and Caldwell, in Sebeok 1977a). In the late 1970s, a more lively issue, which has hardly been faced up to yet (but see the inconclusive discussion by D. Premack 1971:820–821; and cf. R. Brown 1973:50–51), is the pervasive, insidious penetration of Clever Hans into all the attempts so far designed to erase the seemingly ineradicable linguistic barrier between man and the Great Apes. (Eccles 1974:106, doubts "if these clever learned responses can be regarded as language even remotely resembling human language.") The possibly insoluble dilemma that experimenters in this area must confront is that man can scarcely be eliminated from any conceivable variant of the requisite training procedures, because, to put it quite starkly, every such animal is critically dependent for emotional sustenance upon its trainer—whether informed or naïve (A. Premack 1976:101ff.), even when the system used is computer-enhanced (Rumbaugh and Gill 1976a). Deprived of social contact with a human partner, the home- or laboratory-raised ape perishes, but when given the human contact, the experimenter's expectancy effects must be fully reckoned with (Timaeus 1973).

Of Clever Hans, James R. Angell noted in 1911: "No more remarkable tale of credulity founded on unconscious deceit was ever told, and were it offered as fiction, it would take high rank as a work of imagination" (Pfungst 1965). The lesson Hans tapped out as his legacy for science has not, however, been mastered even today. All efforts, without exception, that aimed to shape linguistic apes, whether the research design was quasinaturalistic or followed an essentially Skinnerian paradigm, not only offered "rich opportunities for drawing the wrong conclusions," in R. Brown's (1973:34) characteristically tactful parlance, but had their focus misplaced to begin with. The really interesting issue has to do with the nature of the communicative coupling between subject and object, hence that is precisely a semiotic problem; it was formulated by Rosenthal (in Pfungst 1965:xxxiii) in the following two sentences (and was expanded by this immensely insightful investigator in many of his other publications, where he drew on social psychological knowledge at large for fruitful hypotheses): "If we knew precisely by what means we unintentionally communicate our expectancies to our animal and human subjects, we could institute more effective controls against the effect of our expectancies. More generally, if we knew more about the modalities by which we subtly and unintentionally influence one another, we would then have learned a great deal that is new about human social behavior." The same point is made in Hediger's (1976:45–46) wide-ranging review of the Clever Hans phenomenon and its consequences, with even more explicit reference to zoosemiotics. The relevant question, he correctly emphasizes, is not how to eliminate human signs from the dyad, but how to— at long last—program a thorough investigation of all channels through which such signs actually are and might be transmitted, and thus to determine what really is happening in man-animal and man-man interaction: "Das ist eine Frage der Semiotik," Hediger insists, and, of course, this has become increasingly clear over the last decade; but the nitty-gritty of the search will also demand an exceptionally broad spectrum of cooperating disciplines.

6. Left/Right

There has been a great deal of agitation lately in the field of brain research about the question of lateralization of at least two modes of mentation in man (Dimond 1972; Ornstein 1972, Ch. 3). The yeast that fuels this ferment derives from studies termed, as long ago as the 1870s (Sebeok 1976:57–58), *asemasia*, i.e., the impairment of nonverbal communicative functions (Zangwill 1975:95–106), and, more immediately, from recent split brain experiments (Krashen 1976:157– 191). Some implications of this endeavor—essentially in its infancy— with the aim of moving toward a "true synthesis of biology and culture in the operation of human minds," were recently reviewed by Paredes and Hepburn (1976), giving rise to impassioned debate in ensuing issues of *Current Anthropology* and elsewhere. In general, however, the emerging picture seems to indicate that the left side of the brain processes verbal tasks better, while the right side deals more skillfully with visual-spatial tasks; this is underscored by a demonstration that the two hemispheres are not ontogenetically equal until the end of the first decade of life (Dennis and Whitaker 1976). Another, broader way in which scientists, such as A. R. Luria (e.g., in Sebeok 1974b:2561–2594; cf. Ornstein 1972:67), prefer to describe the division of labor is to speak of two opposed but complementary ways of thinking, such that the left brain is more likely to deal with tasks seriatim ("logically"), while the right brain manages problems as a whole, perceiving their simultaneous relationships ("holistically").

This line of research has led to the following provisional conclusion, succinctly stated (though immediately, and properly so, hedged in with all sorts of qualifications) by Bogen (1969): "the left hemisphere is better than the right for language and for what has sometimes been called 'verbal activity' or 'linguistic thought'; in contrast we could say that the right hemisphere excels in 'non-language' or 'non-verbal' function." In the current secondary literature, especially on the part of anthropologists and members of the artificial intelligentsia, one finds that this duality of information handling is labeled more starkly as "verbal to nonverbal" (Tunnell 1973:27), and one encounters such uncompromising assertions as "the appreciation of gestures . . . is the province of the right hemisphere" (Weizenbaum 1976:220). Psychological tests tend to support the view that the right hemisphere appears somewhat more skillful than the left "in nonverbal reasoning and spatial abilities" (Bower 1970:509), although both hemispheres are indubitably equipped for language representation in some ways and to some extent, the cerebral dominance seemingly involving, in Kinsbourne's dramatistic phrase, "active competition" between the two, such that "the left hemisphere is genetically destined to win" (1975: 114).

"Dominance" refers to the processing of information by one hemisphere and its ability to control responding. This variable is likely to be independent of "capacity," or the performance of some task when required by the contextual contingencies of a hemisphere. Now, according to Levy (1973:158), the left hemisphere "simply does not bother to handle information which can be handled by the right," an observation that is in good conformity with the semiotic model espoused here, especially in respect to the hierarchical notion of "markedness" mentioned above (section 1). The pithy formulation of Eccles (1974:92) expresses this best of all by asseverating that the minor hemisphere resembles a very superior animal brain, which is to say that it provides the primary locus for the coding processes we term zoosemiotic but lacks the ability to report mental functions utilizing the verbal (or anthroposemiotic) code, at any rate, vocally (i.e., it is mute). Evolutionary continuities in semiosis from animals to man as well as sudden discontinuities are thus both accounted for, but in grossly different locations in the brain. The corpus callosum serves as the principal channel of intercommunication between the two hemispheres, insuring exact synchrony (unless, of course, the commissures are surgically or otherwise severed). The messages that flow back and forth are presumably all coded neurochemically, but whether the left-to-right commerce is verbal (or digital as was suggested in 1960; see Sebeok 1972, Ch. 1; see also Bogen 1969), while the right-to-left traffic is nonverbal (or analog), remains one of many intriguing problems winking at the edge of experimental palpability. It also remains to be seen whether the two opposing schools of belief in regard to the ritualization of man's overall semiotic competence alluded to by the English zoologist Pumphrey (Sebeok 1976:67, 142) will be content with some such heuristic model; and, still further down the road, whether a proper characterization of the left hemisphere will require a judicious application of catastrophe theory (Thom 1975a; cf. Chs. 1 and 6 of this volume)—since that is the most sophisticated qualitative method designed so far to handle discontinuous phenomena—whereas the right hemisphere's smooth, continuously changing Gestalt configurations will stay amenable to traditional quantitative analysis.

7. Formation/Dissolution: Diachronic Glimpses

Diachronic considerations of two very different sorts are pertinent to zoosemiotic inquiry: one focuses on the evolution of signs and systems of signs in phylogeny (Hahn and Simmel 1976; Marler, in Sebeok 1977b); the other considers their development in ontogeny (Sebeok 1976:98-99; Burghardt, in Sebeok 1977b), as well as impairment, leading to their ultimate dissolution in the lifespan of individuals (Zangwill 1975). The former constitutes the principal axis of synthesis in the entire field of the biological study of behavior (Sebeok 1972: 135; 1976:85), or ethology, which has been insistently characterized as "hardly more than a special case of diachronic semiotics" (Sebeok 1976:156). This identification should disquiet no one who is cognizant of the common historical roots of the comparative method indispensably utilized in branches of both (Lorenz 1966:275-276): they stem from Baron Cuvier, the founder of comparative anatomy (which, in his conception, studied the static interrelationships of immutable species, created and re-created several times over), now transformed into modern phylogenetic behavioral systematics, no less than, albeit indirectly through Friedrich von Schlegel's applications, into comparative grammar (see Ch. 2 of this volume).

Any sensitive and observant caretaker is well aware that a "normal" infant is born with elaborate equipment for interacting with its human surroundings by means of a wide array of vocal and nonvocal signs. Indeed, its success in encoding and decoding vital messages is a most important measure of its very normalcy. Its semiotic growth and differentiation are undoubtedly best conceived of as a series of catastrophes (Thom 1975b). Thom's topological model, following ideas originating in biology and pursued by creative thinkers since the likes of D'Arcy Thompson and C. H. Waddington, could account for successive stages of bifurcation where, much as the development of any cell in an embryo diverges from that of its immediate neighbors, sign functions become ever more specialized and cluster to form particular constellations in a dynamic semiotic system occurring and explicable at any given time. Verbal signs suddenly emerge, superimposed upon babbling—which itself usually functions as an insufficiently explored vocal but, of course, preverbal link between the baby and its caretakers (Bullowa 1970; Bullowa et al., in McCormack and Wurm 1976:67-95). Language then continues to unfold (R. Brown 1973) until the child acquires full mastery over the language of its native speech community along with the culturally appropriate nonverbal systems of signs.

Study of the latter—which also embody the rules of when and how to use the language in accordance with personal needs and social norms—on a scale comparable with the former has barely begun, notwithstanding the pioneering instigation of this sort of research launched by Darwin in a famed segment of the diary he started in 1840 (1877). Surprisingly enough, there exists no definitive treatise of this hardly negligible area comprehending a configuration of attributes in any individual, which Chance calls "primary-group relations," a type of communication that is concerned with associations of an addresser with addressees, a process that Chance further characterizes as the wholly "nonverbal" infrastructure of social cohesion and control (1975:100). There are only a few authoritative survey articles about the state of this art, even the best of which are now getting a bit dated, such as Brannigan and Humphries (1972) or N. G. Blurton Jones (in Hinde 1972:271-296). These should be supplemented by special studies, e.g., of facial expressions in infants and children (Charlesworth and Kreutzer 1973), including tongue showing (Smith et al. 1974:222-227), and the like. The paucity of really robust achievements in this domain of nonverbal infant competences—concerning the sights, sounds, smells, and overall body management appropriate to the survival of the baby in all cultures—is the most startling fact about it. One's sense of wonderment remains far from fulfilled, although the tempo of research has become much livelier of late.

If relatively little is known about the formation of sign systems in the course of a human life, the destructive effects of injury or disease remain hardly understood at all. What Steinthal, in 1881, dubbed *Asemie*, and Jackson, following Hamilton's independent coinage of 1878, then propagated under the accurate label of *asemasia*, comprehending "the loss of gesticulating power," or of pantomime (Critchley 1975, Ch. 3; Sebeok 1976:57-58), is, alas, too frequently experienced by patients and observed by attending physicians. An example of the extent to which pantomimic movement may be unattainable by victims of severe brain damage was recorded by Luria (1972:45) from his celebrated patient Zasetsky, who was wounded in war: "I was lying in bed and needed the nurse. How was I to get her to come over? All of a sudden I remembered you can beckon to someone and so I tried to beckon to the nurse—that is move my left hand lightly back and forth. But she walked right on by and paid no attention to my gesturing. I realized then that I'd completely forgotten how to beckon to someone. It appeared I'd even forgotten how to gesture with my hands so that someone could understand what I meant." At one time, Jackson hazarded a tripartite clinical classification of the aphasias, and the third of his categories was the most global, namely, the loss of language when pantomime and gesture as well as speech are annihilated, a tragic condition so devastating as to be tantamount to social extinction.

The communicational problems that beset the aging and the aged typically fall between the two stools of social gerontology and psychosemiotics; in consequence, they have been largely misinterpreted or altogether neglected. Philip B. Stafford (personal communication), for example, has studied closely one dominant sign of senescence in our culture, "repetitiousness," and showed that, contrary to the usual assumption that this tedious habit is simply a symptom of physiological deterioration in old folks, it is rather a semiotic manifestation of an adaptive strategy useful to the elderly in capturing an audience. Nor must one take it for granted that senescence is accompanied by a mere decrease in semiotic potency: on the contrary, a restocked ambry of nonverbal skills is often required and acquired in course of the aging process to cope with the usually, often dramatically, altered social environment. Just how this is accomplished has hardly been studied so far, but I am convinced that the semiotics of old age is one of the most promising research areas for the immediate future and that it will have great import for both applied gerontology and clinical geriatrics.

Since the application of the principle of ritualization to language was not proving feasible (section 1, above), Koehler (1936:85ff.) proposed "to seek for roots, initia, precursors" to language and thought he found eleven, but then wisely concluded that "No animal has got all those initia of our language together, they are distributed among very different species, this one having one capacity, that species another. We alone possess all of them . . ." (ibid.:87). Linguists like Hockett (with Altmann, in Sebeok 1968, Ch. 5) and, to a lesser extent, Lyons (in Hinde 1972, Ch. 3) later tried similarly to disassemble the verbal code into a quasi-logical roster of components of varying numbers and to examine each function separately from a comparative standpoint, a mechanistic and desperate procedure that turned out to be a largely empty exercise, partly for the reason foreseen by Koehler, partly for others such as are given by Hewes (in Wescott 1969:4ff.). Unless and until one or more semiotic systems utilizing coding methods comparable with that of language are discovered, this sort of quest seems futile to me. Moreover, it appears increasingly unlikely that a terrestrial languagelike animal communication system will ever be located under natural conditions. The sole alternative lies, then, in the continued scanning—a long, arduous, and costly endeavor, the outcome of which is uncertain—for communicating intelligences on other planets (Arbib 1974).

Zoosemiotic systems in man, on the other hand, are eminently amenable to comparative study (Pitcairn and Eibl-Eibesfeldt, in Hahn and Simmel 1976, Ch. 5) and will, no doubt, continue to produce worthwhile findings. An example that shows just how fascinating this line of inquiry can be is Ferguson's (1976:138) suggestive research proposal that certain verbal routines, such as greetings and thanks, are "related phyletically to the bowings and touchings and well-described display phenomena of other species." The most fertile ground for the application of the methods of ritualization is surely in the domain of interpersonal rituals for which politeness formulas furnish one attractive target.

4. Ecumenicalism in Semiotics

[Catholics and Protestants] may and must talk to one another, but with a new approach; they should proceed from points on which they are united to discuss what separates them; and discuss what separates them with an eye to what unites them.—Karl Barth

... c'est la sémiologie ... qui prendrait en charge les *grandes unités signifiantes* du discours; de la sorte apparaîtrait l'unité des recherches qui se mènent actuellement en anthropologie, en sociologie, en psychanalyse et en stylistique autour du concept de signification.—Roland Barthes

... it is clear that boundaries persist despite a flow of personnel across them. ... The critical focus of investigation from this point of view becomes the ... boundary that defines the group, not the ... stuff that it encloses.—Fredrik Barth

End the Boundary Dispute!—John Barth

The Organism as a Text

In what was assuredly one of his most stupefying lectures, titled "Consciousness and language" (1935–1966:7.579–596), delivered ca. 1867, Peirce raised the question: "What is man?" His decisive answer was that man is a symbol. Peirce elaborated and deepened his argu-

Note: This article was first published as Chapter 10 of *A Perfusion of Signs*, edited by Thomas A. Sebeok (Bloomington: Indiana University Press, 1977). Some of the ideas incorporated in the last section were variously aired in lectures given at Brown University (November 15, 1976) and the University of Hamburg (January 7, 1977). They were also presented, highly condensed and with different emphasis, at the 1977 meetings of the Central States Anthropological Society, held in Cincinnati in March 1977, in the framework of a Symposium on Semiotic Perspectives in Human Relations (co-organized with the author by Dr. D. Jean Umiker-Sebeok).

ment by comparing man with some other symbol, to wit, the verbal sign *Six*, and showed that, "remote and dissimilar as the word and the man appear, it is exceedingly difficult to state any essential difference between them . . ." (7.588). Elsewhere, Peirce claimed that "my language is the sum total of myself" (5.314), a view tantamount to asserting that man is a string of signs, a process of communication (Fairbanks 1976:20), or, in short, a text. Nor is man uniquely endowed with the property of life, "For every symbol is a living thing, in a very strict sense that is no mere figure of speech" (2.222). Furthermore, "the most marvellous faculty of humanity," one which we share with all other organisms, is "that of procreation" (7.590). Yet we have even that capacity in common with signs: "Symbols grow. They come into being by development out of other signs. . . . It is only out of symbols that a new symbol can grow. *Omne symbolum de symbolo*" (2.302). Chomsky (1972:90–93)—whose way of envisioning the acquisition of knowledge of language vividly recalls (as he is well aware) some of the ideas of Peirce on the logic of abduction—reconstituted, with the linguist's fruitful reformulation of "the creative aspect of language use" (1972:6), this notion and turned it to challenging problems of modern linguistics. Incidentally, Peirce's splendid manner of argumentation was very far from an instance of the Pathetic Fallacy. Indeed, his view that signs have an inherent measure of self-responsibility was developed much further a century later by René Thom.

Thom, especially in his neoclassical essay on a theory of symbolism (1974a, Ch. 11), which adheres closely to the Peircean semiotic model (cf. Ch. 6 of this volume), has authoritatively delineated the fundamental identity of the processes of biological reproduction and semiosis, bracketed in the frame of his powerful catastrophe theory, or a kind of mathematics applicable to phenomena that are neither orderly nor linear, and hence relevant to the so-called inexact sciences, of which biology and semiotics are representative, each in its own ways. In the course of the former, a parent organism or "signified" emits a descendant, thereby engendering a "signifier" which, in an eternal and universal flux, reengenders a "signified" each time that the sign is interpreted. A signifier turns into a signified given only sufficient time, say, the lapse of a generation. By virtue of this subtle fluctuation between two morphologies, bound by the simultaneous exigencies of reversibility and irreversibility, "la dynamique du symbolisme," or, in Peircean terminology, semiosis, i.e., sign-action and sign-interpretation, "porte en elle . . . toutes les contradictions de la vision scientifique du monde, et qu'elle est l'image même de la vie" (Thom 1974a:233; cf. Sebeok 1976:69).

Two Traditions

The title for this summative essay was chosen less for its ecclesiastical connotations than to suggest that, in my view (Ch. 1, above), the scope of semiotics encompasses the whole of the *oikoumenē*, the entirety of our planetary biosphere. The chronology of semiotic inquiry so far, viewed panoramically, exhibits an oscillation between two seemingly antithetical tendencies: in the major tradition (which I am tempted to christen a catholic heritage), semiosis takes its place as a normal occurrence in nature, of which, to be sure, language—that paramount known mode of terrestrial communication which is Lamarckian in style, that is, embodies a learning process that becomes part of the evolutionary legacy of the ensuing generations—forms an important if relatively recent component. This accords with the view of the Stoics who argued, *in nuce*, "that animals have 'expressive' reason, the power of speech, by which they communicate with each other by means of signs" (Philodemus 1941:144), although they also drew a sharp distinction between the aforementioned properties, shared by animals with men, and synthetic and combining reason, ascribed by them to men alone (cf. Simone 1972:6–7). It was, however, St. Augustine (354–430), one of the greatest thinkers of all times about sign functions, who, in his brief dialogue, *De Magistro*, first wrestled with the perennial question whether it is feasible for an organism to learn through signs at all and, if so, how.

The minor trend, which is parochially glottocentric, asserts, sometimes with sophistication but at other times with embarrassing naïveté, that linguistics serves as the model for the rest of semiotics—Saussure's *le patron général*—because of the allegedly arbitrary and conventional character of the verbal sign. Much has been written within and about this tradition, which has both a conservative and a radical wing. The orthodox line was quite succinctly enunciated, in the weakest form, by Cassirer (1945:115): "Linguistics is a part of semiotics ...," but more emphatically so by Bloomfield (1939:55), who averred that "Linguistics is the chief contributor to semiotic," then Weinreich (1968:164), who declared natural language to be "the semiotic phenomenon par excellence" (cf. Sebeok 1976:11–12). The rallying cry of the ultrarevisionists was perhaps most enticingly proclaimed by Barthes (1964a:81) in an often-repeated catchphrase: "... c'est la sémiologie qui est une partie de la linguistique."

The distinction between what I have termed, although without elaboration here (but see Ch. 1 above), the major and the minor traditions has lost its force, since it is amply clear that Darwinian and Lamarckian (i.e., sociogenetic) evolution coexist in subtle interaction in the human animal (Bateson 1968) (or, as C. Morris [1976:39] marveled about him in his delightful poem, "Animal Symbolicum," "What a remarkable animal: physiological and symbolical./ Kin of every other animal, but symbol-haunted and dramatical"). Human evolution thus not only is a reconfirmation of the evolutionary processes which went on before man appeared on the scene, but continues as a dual semiotic consecution that can scarcely be uncoupled in practice: one track language-free (or zoosemiotic), the other language-sensitive (or anthroposemiotic) (Sebeok 1972:163). Semiosis must be recognized as a pervasive fact of nature as well as of culture. In such matters, then, I declare myself not only a Peircean but a (René) Thomist, yet one who stands ready to obey Karl Barth's injunction as formulated at the outset.

The Distinctive Burden of Semiotics

Ecumenicalism in semiotics means, however, far more than a plea for attempting to capture global properties of sign systems in general and for unifying local variations that are criterial for heretofore unrelated information about the genetic (Marcus 1974), metabolic (in the sense used by G. Tomkins 1975), neural (Pribram 1971, Ch. 4; Rose 1973: 100–110), intraspecific vs. interspecific (Sebeok 1972:79), nonverbal vs. verbal and nonvocal vs. vocal codes (Ch. 3, this volume) beside a host of secondary modeling systems (Winner and Winner 1976:135–137). The term, which derives from the Greek *oikos*, designating "house," seems to be appropriate because it once again calls attention to the holistic force of semiotics, which many leading contributors to the discipline have marked as its distinctive burden. This perspective was perhaps best articulated by Charles Morris, who, working initially in the overall frame of the *International Encyclopedia of Unified Science* (the program of which was unfolded at the 1935 International Congress for the Unity of Science, plans for which were laid the year before, interestingly enough for those familiar with the classical period of the Prague School, at Charles University), conceived of semiotic as an instrument of all the sciences. An acute historian of the semiotic endeavor since 1865 recently remarked about this vista that "The foundations of the theory of signs were the foundations for the unification of the sciences" as well (Fisch 1978:59). "Semiotic has a double relation to the sciences: it is both a science among the sciences and an instrument of the sciences," Morris wrote in 1938 (1971:17–18), continuing: "The significance of semiotic as a science lies in the fact that it is a step in the unification of science, since it supplies the foundations for any special science of signs, such as linguistics, logic, mathematics, rhetoric, and ... aesthetics. The concept of sign may prove to be of importance in the unification of the social, psychological, and humanistic sciences insofar as these are distinguished from the physical and biological sciences." Morris later provided for a still higher level of unification with the two last-mentioned groups of disciplines, having shown that signs are simply the objects studied by these branches of knowledge in certain complex functional processes.

A closely similar view was sanguinely expounded, in 1943, by the Danish linguist Hjelmslev, whose glossematics professed to be grounded in Saussure's *Cours*, but who was also comfortably familiar with the work of such logical empiricists as Carnap, who, in turn, acknowledged his indebtedness to Morris's semiotic. Hjelmslev (1953:69) echoed: "... it seems fruitful and necessary to establish a common point of view for a large number of disciplines, from the study of literature, art, and music, and general history, all the way to logistics and mathematics.... Each will be able to contribute in its own way to the general science of semiotics.... Thus new light might perhaps be cast on these disciplines, and they might be led to a critical self-examination. In this way, through a mutually fructifying collaboration, it should be possible to produce a general encyclopedia of sign structures." French semiotic writings of the past decade seem often to have felt obligated to take a stance, whether pro or con Hjelmslev's amplification of Saussure's outline of a prospective general science of signs; and Anglophone exegetes, like Whitfield (1969:258), who notes that glossematics views all sciences "as also being... semiotics," or like Lamb (see Lamb and Makkai 1976), are still endeavoring to reinterpret "the semiotics of culture" (Schwimmer in Sebeok 1976; Umiker-Sebeok 1977a) in various eclectic ways but seldom straying far from the broad if fragile framework erected by Hjelmslev. On the other hand, in his heroic but neglected attempt at a unification of the structure of human behavior, Pike (1967:63) has explicitly rejected both Saussure's theory of signs and Hjelmslev's version of it. Barthes, of course, as cited in the second epigraph, has persuasively and prestigiously rekindled the spark of coadunation.

The works of Morris, Hjelmslev, Barthes, and their numerous epigones on the holistic force of semiotics hardly exceed programmatic pronouncements. In truth, as Peirce came to recognize with increasing clarity after 1890, science is an ongoing quest that cannot be identified as a particular body of knowledge yet segments of which are delimitable in terms of particular social groupings of research scholars within a vaster community of investigators; as he wrote Lady Welby in 1908, "the only natural lines of demarcation between nearly related sciences are the divisions between the social groups of devotees of those sciences" (1935–1966:8.342). But Peirce also stressed that one of the first useful steps toward a science of *semeiotic*, "or the cenoscopic science of signs" (i.e., which does not depend upon new special observations), "must be the accurate definition, or logical analysis of the concepts of science" (8.343). Jakobson, in his masterful (though mistitled) essay, "Linguistics in Relation to Other Sciences" (1971a: 655–696), has sketched out a way whereby the nomothetic sciences of man, and possibly some of the natural sciences alongside them as well, might be systematized to achieve a degree of logical filiation and hierarchical ordering exactly if linguistics—alias semiotics—is used as the point of departure for their tentative serial arrangement. However, Thom's outline of a general theory seems to me to provide the first rigorously monistic model of the living being, endowed with the *facultas signatrix*, and to offer one pure topological continuum in which causality and finality are combined. Assuredly it is no accident that his dynamical topology was influenced by Peirce on the one hand (Thom 1974a:229–230), and von Uexküll on the other (Thom 1974a: xxiii, and passim).

The kinship of semiotically based programs, such as those mentioned, to the movement known as General System Theory (Bertalanffy 1968), or GST, is seldom underlined; yet their common denominator is rather obvious. As a "natural philosophy," both these variants of a single metatheory can be traced back to Leibniz (ibid.:11; Dascal 1972) and his program for a *mathesis universalis*, and it was certainly not a coincidence that the founder of GST first presented his ideas, in 1937, in Morris's semiotic seminar at the University of Chicago (Bertalanffy 1968:90). Although the two different sorts of mobilization toward synthesis continued to develop and flourish independently one from the other, their proponents have not infrequently crossed paths here and there; for example, both Morris and I were occasional participants in discussion groups of scientists assembled, from the most various traditional disciplines, in the 1950s, "for the purpose of approaching a unified theory of behavior," or, as was sometimes grandiosely claimed, human nature (e.g., Grinker 1956:v). The San Francisco psychiatrist Jurgen Ruesch was an animating spirit in this striving for integration, drawing "from theories that derive from social anthropology, sociology, philology, linguistics, and related disciplines," all of which, he explicitly acknowledged much later, "are concerned with semiotics" (1972:11–12; cf. 127). Recently, the two main preoccupations of system theorists appear to have settled on *action*, or the movement of matter-energy over space, and *communication*, or the "change of information from one state to another or its movement from one point to another over space" (J. G. Miller 1975–1976:346), but the two naturally flow together since information is always borne on a marker (ibid.:299). The distinction immediately calls to mind Peirce's alterity of dyadic or dynamical action vs. triadic or sign-action (1935–1966:5.473), which, again, brings us back to his "doctrine of the essential nature and fundamental varieties of possible semiosis" (5.488). If the writings of Peirce had been available to Uexküll, who also inspired von Bertalanffy (1968:288) (although the latter's avowed knowledge of semiotics seems to have been confined to some writings of Cassirer), GST would very likely have taken a radically different turn. The approach of von Bertalanffy consisted of treating sets of related events collectively as systems manifesting functions and properties of the specific level of the whole. This presumptively enables the recognition of isomorphies across ascending levels of organization—variously dubbed, e.g., org (Gerard 1957), holon (Koestler 1967:341), integron (Jacob 1974:299–324), or, processually, shred out (J. G. Miller 1976:226–227)—from which can be developed general principles or sometimes fundamental laws that operate commonly at all levels of organization in contrast with those which are unique to each. Semiotic ideas pervade GST, but are seldom anchored in a comprehensive doctrine of signs. For instance, Miller (1976:227) writes: ". . . the evolutionary shred out of the channel and net subsystem is from slow, inefficient, chemical transmission by diffusion at the cell level up to increasingly rapid and cost-effective symbolic linguistic transmission over complicated networks at the higher levels of living systems." However, as critics have justly pointed out—among other strictures (Phillips 1976:48–67)—GST suffers from an aura of vagueness over what is meant to be encompassed within it. The missing ingredient, the addition of which, I suggest, is most likely to dispel the fog, can only be supplied by way of a judicious linkage with a semiotic which must be firmly based upon the empirical facts of current biological thought as foreshadowed by Peirce, developed by Morris, independently furthered, in his own lambent fashion, by von Uexküll, and recently restated in the language of Thom's catastrophe theory (which, *pace* its detractors in some American mathematical circles [Kolata 1977a], has already vastly enlarged the horizons of semiotic inquiry [see Ch. 6 of this volume]). I emphasize the historical and logical associations between holism and semiotics because these are nowadays often overlooked: for instance, although Phillips devotes a section of his exploratory essay to the holistic connotations of structuralism (1976, Ch. 6), including its embodiment in Prague-style linguistics (pp. 83–84, 88), he ignores the more patently tenable and much more fundamental connections with semiotics. Precisely how semiotics can function as "an organon" (C. Morris 1971:67) of all the sciences, and the wide humanistic implications of the assumption that semiotics "provides a basis for understanding the main forms of human activity and their interrelationship" (ibid.:69), since all such activities and relations are mediated exclusively by signs, pose a host of further questions that need to be widely as well as urgently debated since, among other consequences, their satisfactory reformulation might well lead to badly needed improvement of the chaotic curricula which still inform students of the human sciences worldwide.

Communication and Manipulation

The Tampa Colloquium coincided with the heyday of an era in international relations epitomized by the fashionable slogan *détente*, which an interim President of the United States later tried to declare taboo. In the global pursuit of semiotics, we have no need for such artifices of labeling to characterize a relaxation of tensions. Wherever our workshops happen to be located—from Bloomington to Moscow, as the newest introductory manual would have it in the perhaps exaggerated heading of one of its principal chapters (Voigt 1977, Ch. 8)—the semiotic network amicably binds us together, to our immense profit, with only sporadic intrusions of that stain of darkness in the fabric that both mars the otherwise seamless web and invites ridicule upon the preposterous advocates of the intrusion of politics into our affairs (for one example, see Sebeok 1976:166). I do not mean to suggest that the practitioner of semiotics is more enlightened than the practitioner of politics, but only that the two trades are right to be uneasy with each other. Margaret Mead (1972:286) expressed the distinction between cooperative and manipulative behavior (Sebeok 1976:80) with great delicacy and her customary vatical flair when she said that in inaugurating the new science of semiotics it "is of the utmost importance that continuing work . . . should take place not in a context of power," but that "we must affirm the acquisition of this greater systematic insight as part of man's scientific knowledge *on behalf of man*. Otherwise we may expect to encounter continual blocking resistance, misunderstanding, and downright fear and hostility both from outsiders and from members of disciplines included in the new science."

Indeed, the sign expert can supply the policy maker with pointers on how to sharpen his tools designed to exploit resources in certain very important areas of human activity, such as strategic conflict, say, in the transnational arena. Game theory, in particular that subclass to which two-actor zerosum games belong, clearly articulates, in yet another kind of holistic construct (Bertalanffy 1968:90), communication with manipulation, or, if you will excuse the reiteration, sign-action with dynamical action. The book of Jervis (1970), although held to the descriptive level and without the imposition of formal game models, serves as one outstanding illustration of a creative projection of semiotic theory and techniques to the level of diplomacy in international relations. Beyond this sort of service, entailing a heightened level of awareness about games in general and about the pervasively institutionalized human con-games (Goffman 1952) in particular, an insistent exertion of the semiotic point of view may merely embarrass politician and administrator alike. It is perfectly all right for our masters to be wary of what we know, do, and might yet uncover, but is it too much to ask for their trust?

The Contribution of Adnormal, Denormal, and Abnormal Semiotics

Most of the papers delivered at our conference can be pigeonholed as multifarious examples of work touching upon the semiotics of culture (Winner and Winner 1976; Umiker-Sebeok 1977a), broadly defined, in the sense of imperative language involvement. None dealt with the necessarily language-independent semiotics of nature (Ch. 1 of this volume), a marked/unmarked opposition the many consequences of which I do not want to pursue here. Instead, I should like to allude to another set of emergent distinctions that I think must rapidly be assimilated to a unitary pansemiotic (cf. Ch. 3, section 7, of this volume). Sign processes in everyday life, or the semiotics of the *normal*, need to be closely re-examined in the light of their ontogenetic formation, or the semiotics of the *adnormal*; their dissolution in the course of a human life, or the semiotics of the *denormal*; and their modifications when caused by injury or disease, or the semiotics of the *abnormal*. In brief, two polar oppositions intersect here: one between the semiotics of ripening childhood and the semiotics of retrograde second childhood; the other, which Kleinpaul tried to make much of (1888: 103–111) in a pertinent frame, between the semiotics of the "normalen ... Formen der Gesundheit" and the semiotics of "Krankheiten."

The study of adnormal semiotics is shared with neurology and several branches of psychology; of denormal semiotics with social gerontology; and of abnormal semiotics with different medical specialties. As an example of distinguished consolidating work rooted in adnormal semiotics, let me single out McNeill's (1975) demonstration of the intimate connection between the production of speech by adults and the representation of conceptual structures on a sensory-motor level. His apt expression "semiotic extension" makes double reference to the basis of contact between "normal" adult conceptualization with the development of speech production in children and spontaneous gesticulations during speech that, "far from being mere embellishments," can also "be seen to arise directly from the operation of the speech mechanisms themselves" (ibid.:373), viewed, that is, as an external dynamic trace of the internal speech program. It is good news that McNeill is finishing a book on his fruitful notion of "semiotic extension," a kind of meaning relationship, and especially encouraging that for his underlying theory of signs he builds upon the strongest yet available—Peirce's.

The development of human communicative competence, including the unfolding of man's repertory of prelinguistic signs, "those which occur in the child's behavior before it speaks, or which later, even in the adult, are independent of language signs," according to the fruitful formulation of Morris (1964:58), involves a gradual increase in both nonverbal and verbal specializations and specificities that Eric Lenneberg has together termed "differentiation" (Lenneberg and Lenneberg 1975:1:32)—a label fittingly chosen, for it evokes, to my bent quite accurately, the proper embryological homology, or, rather, continuity. It has not yet been sufficiently realized that this amply documented process of semiotic differentiation in children not only perdures through adulthood but is also an essential feature of senescence. While the aging and the aged shed, bit by bit, semiotic competencies "normal" adults take for granted, they also tend to acquire a new-sprung stock of message-types as a part of their adaptive reaction to the impact of their changing environment with which they must all learn to cope. Since it is one of the most dramatic and significant facts of demography that the number of people characterizable as elderly—i.e., 65 years of age and older—is increasing faster than that in any other age group, and that this population trend is likely to continue in the foreseeable future, the study of caducity and communication (Oyer and Oyer 1976) is becoming an ever more urgent research concern of our decade, just as adolescence and communication was—as it still is—a pressing preoccupation throughout this quarter of a century. The heterogeneous age-related alterations in the patterns of communication—which are more likely than not complicated by a host of other variables, notably by health-related impediments—in 11 percent of our population, or about 21 million Americans alone, a figure which is predicted to rise, for this country, to about 20 percent by the turn of the century, constitutes an unprecedented opportunity for the intensive semiotic quest whose time has come. The signs of old age, seen as adaptive strategies which are reasonable in particular semiotic environments, were studied by Stafford in a pioneering thesis (1977). He showed that many such signs are routinely "misread" in the community where he did his field work as indices of physiological deterioration. He ascribes the embarrassment, alienation, and, eventually, the mental anguish of old people to the consistent misinterpretations of their messages on the part of their young interlocutors and interactants, or age mates, who don't share with them what I am here provisionally proposing to call their denormal code, resulting, according to Stafford, from a socially imposed decrease in responsibility coupled with a corresponding increase in dependence. "Old age," thus conceived, *is*, in fact, a system of signification, to which Peirce's notion of infinite semiosis is eminently applicable and which is fecundly analyzable within his trichotomous scheme of sign relations. In Stafford's favorite example, "repetitiousness" in the senescent is for them an index of old age, which, however, is regularly mistaken by others for an unwitting symptom of a physiological deficit, leading him to formulate the insightful maxim that "one man's index is another man's theme," or, as I would prefer to phrase it in the vocabulary of cryptanalytic transformations, "one generation's cleartext is another generation's encicode." Nothing short of the armamentarium of cryptanalysis must be applied to appreciate the bracketing phases of man's full life cycle from adnormal to denormal, perceived, at least within our own culture (cf. Umiker-Sebeok 1977b), as an essentially specular process.

Shands and Meltzer (1977) discuss a fascinating array of semiotic observations characteristic of certain unskilled laborers following industrial accidents. At the same time, they emphasize that the "application of semiotic principles to the field of medicine is in its infancy, although it has long been clear that the physician's stock in trade is *interpretation.*" This protracted nonage of clinical semiotics is perplexing when one considers the Hippocratic roots of the doctrine of signs as a whole (Sebeok 1976:125-126, 181-182; Ch. 1 of this volume), and particularly the explicit contributions of the immensely influential Galen (A.D. 130-201). It was Galen who classified semiotics as one of the six principal branches of medicine, and the strength of Galenism, according to Temkin's dependable account (1973:179), "reposed in no small measure in its having provided medical categories . . . for relating the individual to health and disease, [including] semeiology (the science of signs)." Galen subdivided the field into three abiding parts, inspection or diagnosis, cognition or anamnesis, and providence or prognosis. He regarded everything unnatural occurring in the body as a symptom, and a syndrome as an aggregation of symptoms (*athroisma ton symptomaton*), clearly recognizing that while both of the former directly reflect clinical observation, the formulation of a diagnosis requires causal thinking.

It is my layman's impression that the semiotic ideas have, naturally enough, penetrated most pervasively into that area of medicine which is devoted to disturbances in signing function consequent to selective ravages of brain injury—the condition Steinthal termed *Asemie* in 1881, and Hamilton (later copied by Jackson) *asemasia* in 1878, but which is, of course, more commonly known, in specific reference to a variety of abnormal language functions, by the general label *aphasia.* But since all medicine, from the Corpus Hippocraticum to the present day, is in essence hermeneutic, the pertinence of semiotics, in a deep sense, to a universal theory of disease is not surprising. Note what one leading figure in cancer research told an interviewer: "I think the most important diseases amount to a problem of bad communication. . . . Cells and tissues respond to misinformation or misinterpretation from the environment and they do so in a certain way. They overreact" (Thomas 1976:114).

Children diagnosed as suffering from infantile autism, the descriptions of which are most often negatively stated as consisting of a minimal behavioral repertoire and almost no control at all by the social environment save, perhaps, for some elementary avoidance responses, offer one kind of a challenge to semiotic analysis, because this is a form of malady which is typically characterized by disinterest in interpersonal relationships (even within the family), let alone in looser forms of association. It is often asserted that the autistic child is indifferent to faces. One such boy was pictured as mute, and what activity there was consisted almost entirely of simple, stereotyped maneuvers, "such as moving his foot back and forth, flipping a shoe lace, rubbing a spot on the floor or flipping small objects pivoted between the fingers for many hours at a time" (Ferster 1964:317). Usually, the presence or absence of a potential interactant is reported to have hardly any effect on the patient's behavior, but it has occasionally proved feasible "to achieve an increasing level of social interaction and even considerable amounts of productive speech" (ibid.:326), as in the case in point by the interposition of a machine, i.e., by means of a form of operant conditioning. It is not at all clear whether infantile autism, variable as it is, is due to some genetic defect, personality disorder, or brain damage perhaps suffered at birth, or to a combination of such and still other "psychosomatic" conditions intuitively sensed to coexist in different measure (cf. Ingram, in Lenneberg and Lenneberg 1975:2:243).

Kanner's syndrome, or infantile autism in its classical form (Creak et al., in ibid.:2:242), is recognized by an array of diagnostic features each of which represents some impoverished sign function, beginning with an underlying inability for sustained message coupling between source and destination; or, to phrase this in more positive fashion, its fundamental defining criterion limits the linkage between the child and any adult to mere symbiosis that approaches a zero-degree of normal semiosis: while the child is indifferent to his caretaker's attention, the latter's frequency of responses decreases proportionately with the amount of stimulus aversiveness and may ultimately become extinguished. The autistic child is also apparently unaware of his personal identity, and may exhibit this anomic state, among other symptoms, by a confusion of personal pronouns. He will often be echolalic in the vocal mode and correspondingly imitative in the visual mode, as well as produce significantly more stereotyped utterances and contextually inappropriate remarks than a developmentally aphasic child. Autistic children are attested to "differ even in their cries from normal children and from other subnormal children" (Cromer 1974:251). Adding to these the bizarre postures and ritualistic mannerisms, such as spinning themselves or objects, it is small wonder that the Tinbergens—as "animal ethologists who have for years specialised on social encounters in higher animals, which are of course nonverbal" (1972:11)—have focused upon autism as a prime target for their ethological approach, noting "the considerable potential" residing in this method for the investigation of nonverbal communication in man and, of course, "in general." Since, in my view, the biological study of comportment and the semiotic study of communication and signification are largely overlapping disciplines (Sebeok 1976, Ch. 5; Ch. 1 of this volume), I perceive here one common meeting ground where both methodologies could prove illuminating, although we have contributed, so far, next to nothing to either theory or rehabilitation. These brief remarks are meant to be read chiefly as a plea for the reabsorption of clinical semiotics into the comprehensive doctrine of signs, along with the signs of growing up and the signs of growing old.

Pavlov's Mice: Three Concluding Lessons

Before bringing these summary observations to an end, I would like to address the issue of overarching principles guiding semiotic inquiry. I shall do so briefly because I deal with it in substantially more detail in a separate publication (Sebeok 1978b). Also, I prefer to approach the question here obliquely introducing it by way of an anecdote from the history of physiology in the 1920s.

The episode, which is well authenticated (Gruenberg 1929:326–327; Zirkle 1958:1476; Razran 1959:916–917), centers upon Ivan Pavlov, who has justly been called "the 20th century's empiricist par excellence" (Razran 1959:916). It concerns experiments he caused to be conducted to demonstrate the transmission of conditioned reflexes in mice from one generation to the next. The experiments were actually carried out by an obscure research assistant of his, named Studentsov, whose published data showed 298, 114, 29, 11, and 6 conditioning trials for five successive generations of mice. Pavlov, who had "shared the Lamarckian predisposition, common to Russian bioscientists" (ibid.) with his country's intelligentsia, accepted these inheritance data initially or, at any rate, failed to repudiate the explanatory hypothesis even after he obtained no evidence to support it. Not until 1929, in an informal statement made during the Thirteenth International Physiological Congress, in Boston, did Pavlov offer an alternative interpretation for the amazing data: he explained that "in checking up these experiments it was found that the apparent improvement in the ability to learn, on the part of successive generations of mice, was really due to an improvement in the ability to teach, on the part of the experimenter!" (Gruenberg 1929:327, n. 1).

To me, this fascinating little story suggests three morals of particular interest to our community of semioticians, the first of which is both the most general and, at least at first blush, the most banal: that even the greatest scientist can err. What is important for us is to distinguish between certain major sources of error, and, notably, to recognize self-deception. Self-deception is akin to the extremely widespread effect known as self-fulfilling prophecy (Rosenthal and Jacobson 1968, Part 1), but will perhaps be best recognized by scientists by an emblematic

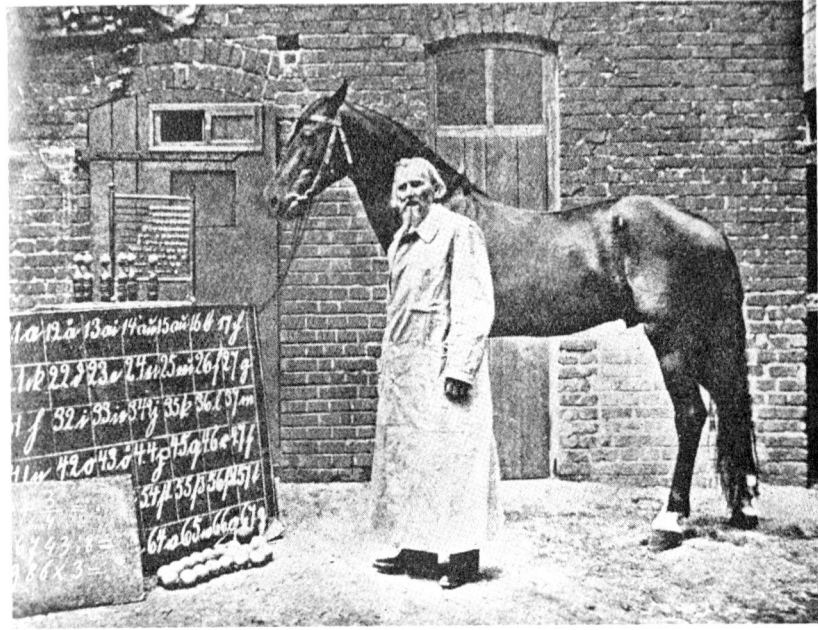

Figure 4-1. Mr. von Osten with Clever Hans. From Karl Krall, *Denkende Tiere* (Leipzig, 1912).

tag known as the "Clever Hans phenomenon." Pavlov's gullibility was due to his wish, consonant with the ambience of his times, to believe that acquired characters were inherited, just as, a few decades earlier, an unfortunate German high school mathematics teacher, Herr von Osten, very badly wanted his horse, Hans, to perform feats of arithmetic, spell and read, solve problems of musical harmony, and answer personal questions. "Pavlov, of course, was an honest scientist" (Zirkle 1958), and there is no evidence that von Osten ever had fraudulent intent; both simply fell victim to their passionate expectations.

Self-deception, then, must be sharply separated from deception of others, or deliberate fraud.[1] There are, alas, not a few cases of academic double-dealing, some British and U.S. perpetrators of which were exposed in recent issues of *Nature* and *Science*. I have followed with special attention the failed efforts of the 1960s to engage in complex communication with dolphins (Sebeok 1972:53–60), and parallel unconvincing endeavors (Limber 1977) to attribute the use of human language to chimps and gorillas in the 1970s. Without impugning in any way the good faith of most investigators of the intellectual capacities of marine mammals and primates, I see the ever-present specter of Clever Hans, except in those instances where chicanery cannot be ruled out. After all, despite the innocence of von Osten, most of Hans's performing ancestors and descendants were operated for profit in confidence games, as for instance the famous "oat-eater" Morocco, "the dancing horse" mentioned by Shakespeare (in *Love's Labour's Lost* I.ii.51), exhibited by an Elizabethan rogue named John Banks, whose methods were exposed, in 1612, by one Samuel Rid in semiotic terms that are amazingly fresh: note, Rid wrote, in *The Art of Juggling*, that the horse can do nothing "but his master must first know, and then his master knowing, the horse is ruled by him by signs" (in Kinney 1973: 290). It would surely have saved Oskar Pfungst (1965) a lot of time and effort had he known the case history of Morocco, a detailed account of which had been published (Halliwell-Phillipps 1879), but which chanced to be reckoned in the field of literary exegesis instead of experimental psychology. Various other tricks enabling animals, horses as well as dogs, cats, pigs, and many kinds of birds, to say nothing of fleas, to perform such marvels of misdirection—as by a technique widely employed by mediums but known to only those in the trade as "pencil reading"—*pour épater le bourgeois* and, of course, for a modicum of profit, are illuminatingly and amusingly bared by the fine magician Christopher (1970:39–54). (See Chapter 5 of this volume for a more detailed account of the case of Morocco.)

The second lesson is a more palpably semiotic one, the essence of which was perfectly captured by the leader of the Hans-Commission, Carl Stumpf, and his brilliant investigator Pfungst, when they spoke of "looking for, in the horse, what should have been sought in the man" (cited by Rosenthal, in Pfungst 1965:xxx). As we saw, it took Pavlov a while to shift his attention from the mice to his overly zealous assistant, back from the event being scrutinized to the experimenter, from message destination to message source. The role played by the observing subject in physics is fairly well understood and respected: since the properties of the observer, especially with regard to magnitude, are usually very different from those of the object observed, the subject is likely to remain relatively outside the system that he is studying and hence one may assume that his report will be reasonably unbiased. In the life sciences, however, and *a fortiori* in the communication sciences of man, the characteristics of the observer are likely to be similar to those of the observed and must be supposed to influence the processes under scrutiny. The subject himself will likewise be seriously affected by the stream of ongoing events (cf. Ruesch 1972:54–55). In linguistic field work, for example, hardly anybody has fully appreciated this, or, if so, conducted himself accordingly. A sophisticated exception was Leonard Bloomfield, who, according to Voegelin (1960:204), "preferred being corrected, when he made an

76   The Sign

Figure 4-2. John Banks with Morocco, the wonderful horse of 1595. In this woodcut, the steed is stomping out the numbers on a pair of rolled dice. From Robert Chambers, *Book of Days: A Miscellany of Popular Antiquities in Connection with the Calendar including Anecdote, Biography, and History Curiosities of Literature and Oddities of Human Life and Character* (London and Edinburgh: W. & R. Chambers, 1869).

error as a child-like speaker of Menomini, to asking a direct question on how do you say so-and-so to a bilingual Menomini—for fear of obtaining a false analogy. During the three summers Bloomfield and I recorded Ojibwa texts together at Linguistic Institutes, he never once asked a 'how do you say' question."

An area of special concern to us all is the art of healing, to wit, the workings of the physician-patient dyad, and the so-called placebo effect, which means the therapeutic sequel consequent to the patient's belief in the efficacy of the treatment. This is a semiotic problem in its most crystalline form: since a placebo is, by definition, a pharmacologically inert substance that the doctor administers to a patient to relieve his distress when the use of an active medication isn't called for, "its beneficial effects must lie in its symbolic power. The most likely supposition is that it gains its potency through being a tangible symbol of the physician's role as a healer" (Frank 1961:66). We learn from Shapiro's riveting sketch that, throughout the centuries from shaman to physician, this very coupling—this bond between the healer and the troubled—"comprised all that the doctor had to offer the patient" (1960:113–114); and he quotes other authorities who affirm that the history of medicine is a history of "dynamic power" of the nexus between doctor and patient (cf. once again Peirce's dynamical action and Thom's "dynamique du symbolisme"). The placebo works best with those patients who have favorable expectations from medicine and, "in general, accept and respond to symbols of healing" (Frank 1961:70), but "the fact that one of the best educated major religious groups in the United States is able to deny the rational efficacy of any treatment or medicine and to assign all treatment benefits to faith" (Shapiro 1960:114) strongly underlines the purity of the semiotic import of the phenomenon, where faith itself acquires the essence of a symbol and thus quite admirably meets Peirce's criterion of "an *imputed* quality" (1935–1966:1.558), such that the two constituent sides of the sign, the signifier and the signified, are bonded one to the other in "a relation which consists in the fact that the mind associates the sign with its object" (1.372) regardless of any factual connection. In passing, it should be noted that in medical history as well as contemporary practice one may observe a gamut of procedures in the administration of placebos from out-and-out quackery to their sensitively controlled use by responsible physicians. What all have in common is the confidence, the enthusiasm, and the ritual on the part of both interactants, and it is therefore undoubtedly true "that the ability to respond favorably to a placebo is not so much a sign of excessive gullibility, as one of easy acceptance of others in their socially defined roles" (Frank 1961:70). In other words, placebo-responsiveness assumes, so to speak, an indexical function in respect to the ability of patients to trust their fellow man as embodied by their physician or, to a lesser degree, his anointed surrogates (e.g., nurses).

The more or less synonymous sets of dyadic ties I have variously referred to in this section as source and destination of messages, observer and observed, subject and object, physician and patient, man and animal (horse or mouse, porpoise or primate), could be multiplied *ad nauseam* to encompass further particularized couplings, notably of parent and child. To my taste, the most suggestive pair of labels comes from the argot of the criminal world engagingly explicated by Maurer

(1949; see also Goffman 1952): operator and mark. This consummate metaphor works something like this, to give only one example from an area of application that ought to pique the curiosity of all who would heed Pavlov's second lesson.

From time to time, claims are made that there are dogs that actually talk. There are records in the Académie Française of one such animal that, according to no less an authority than Leibniz, "had a vocabulary of thirty words, which was put to effective use when he wanted something specific to eat or drink" (Christopher 1970:51).[2] The question is: how is such a con perpetrated, even on smart apples like Leibniz? Briefly (cynical data after Johnson 1912), a dog is conditioned, in the customary manner, to bark in response to certain verbal cues. Don, a seven-year-old German setter, who was reported by numerous observers to answer questions if food were held before him, replied to *"Was heisst du?" ("Don."), "Was hast du?" ("Hunger."),* and to other such queries, and was alleged moreover to answer categorical questions by *"Ja"* or *"Nein."* Don's behavior was thoroughly investigated by the same Oskar Pfungst who, in 1907, had unveiled the secret of Hans, and he concluded (1) that the dog does not use words with any consciousness of their meaning to the hearer, and (2) that he is not using words learned by imitation. Instead, he gave this comparatively simple explanation: the dog produced vocal sounds which induce "illusions in the hearer. . . . The uncritical do not make the effort to discriminate between what is actually given in perception and what is merely associated imagery, which otherwise gives to the perception a meaning wholly unwarranted; and they habitually ignore the important part which suggestion always plays in ordinary situations." In other words, "we may expect the majority of animal lovers to continue to read their own mental processes into the behavior of their pets. Nor need we be astonished if even scientists of a certain class continue at intervals to proclaim that they have completely demonstrated the presence in lower animals of 'intelligent imitation' and of other extremely complicated mental processes." This is also precisely what happens in the circus, as Bouissac emphasized when he referred to inferences drawn from the humanization of animals: "The most efficient training . . . evokes a behavior from the animal that, within the constructed situation, subtly creates the impression that the animal has humanlike motivations, emotions, and reasoning" (1976:118), and when he drew attention to a characteristic feature of every circus act, namely, that it "constructs its own situation, its own immediate context. . . ." "The circus act must be completed," he adds (in Sebeok 1977b:147), "by the semantic operations which are performed in the process and account for the meaningfulness that such circus acts convey to their audience."[3] The underlying principle, *that* we construct a context-based advance hypothesis about what the message will be to tune in

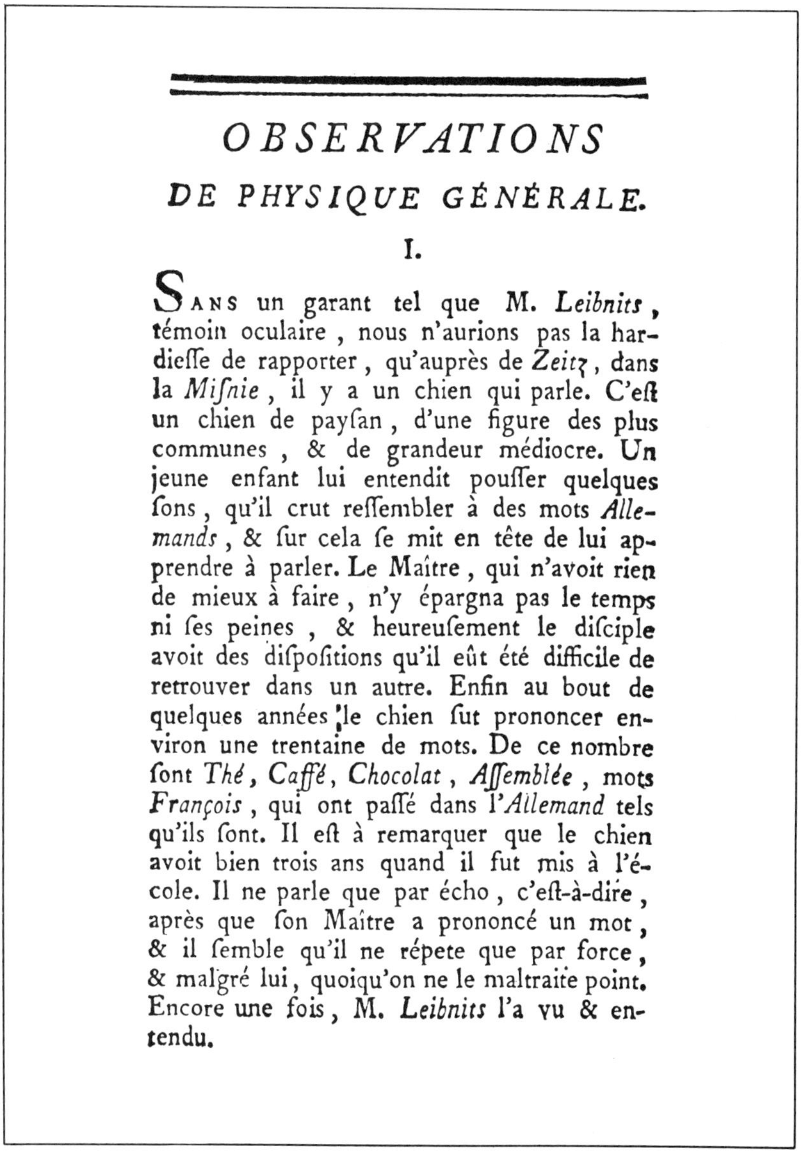

OBSERVATIONS DE PHYSIQUE GÉNÉRALE.

I.

Sans un garant tel que M. *Leibnits*, témoin oculaire, nous n'aurions pas la hardieſſe de rapporter, qu'auprès de *Zeitz*, dans la *Miſnie*, il y a un chien qui parle. C'eſt un chien de payſan, d'une figure des plus communes, & de grandeur médiocre. Un jeune enfant lui entendit pouſſer quelques ſons, qu'il crut reſſembler à des mots *Allemands*, & ſur cela ſe mit en tête de lui apprendre à parler. Le Maître, qui n'avoit rien de mieux à faire, n'y épargna pas le temps ni ſes peines, & heureuſement le diſciple avoit des diſpoſitions qu'il eût été difficile de retrouver dans un autre. Enfin au bout de quelques années le chien ſut prononcer environ une trentaine de mots. De ce nombre ſont *Thé*, *Caffé*, *Chocolat*, *Aſſemblée*, mots *François*, qui ont paſſé dans l'*Allemand* tels qu'ils ſont. Il eſt à remarquer que le chien avoit bien trois ans quand il fut mis à l'école. Il ne parle que par écho, c'eſt-à-dire, après que ſon Maître a prononcé un mot, & il ſemble qu'il ne répete que par force, & malgré lui, quoiqu'on ne le maltraite point. Encore une fois, M. *Leibnits* l'a vu & entendu.

Figure 4-3. Passage from a letter to M. de Saint Pierre reporting Leibniz's encounter with the talking dog, published in the *Histoire de l'Académie Royale des Sciences* in 1715, p. 4. I would like to acknowledge the invaluable help of P. Costabel, Directeur d'Etudes at the Ecole Pratique des Hautes Etudes, Paris, and of Claude Lévi-Strauss.

Figure 4-4. A: Don. *B*: Miss Ebers, the daughter of Don's owner, Hermann Ebers, interrogates Don: "Was ist das?" From Karl Krall, *Denkende Tiere* (Leipzig, 1912).

Figure 4-5. Blondie with Clever Daisy. © King Features Syndicate, Inc., 1977. Reprinted by permission.

our perceptual equipment to favor certain interpretations of the input and reject others, was elegantly demonstrated by Bruce over twenty years ago (1956), although *how* such contextual constraints actually work is still unknown. In sum, I read the second lesson of the Pavlov yarn as a strong injunction for us to look in the men and women (Lilly [1967] and Margaret Howe, Chauvin-Muckensturm [1974], the Gardners, the Premacks, Rumbaugh, Patterson, and their fellow trainers) for what has hitherto been assiduously sought in Peter Dolphin, the Greater Spotted Woodpecker (claimed "to represent the phenomenon of man-animal communication analogous to that found in monkeys by the Gardners and Premack"), Washoe, Sarah, Lana, Koko, and the rest.[4] This is not to deny the inherent interest of studies in animal intelligence. Quite the contrary; but I would like such studies additionally to take the crucial effects of man's participation into full account and, as in the Lana case, even the extremely subtle secondary effects of the computer used as the operator (Rumbaugh 1977, see esp. pp. 159 and 161; cf. Sebeok 1978). Incidentally, I totally concur with Hediger (1974:28-29) that the view held by some scientists that all contact between observer and observed must strictly cease in experimental (and, by extension, clinical) situations is basically untenable. There are two corollaries to this skeptical stance: first, that the source that generated the message has got to be at least as thoroughly investigated as the destination that is to interpret it; and second, that the properties of the channel(s) interconnecting the two organisms must be probed with equal diligence—which brings us to the third implication of the Pavlov story.

No one, it seems, knows how Studentsov unintentionally instructed his mice. Rosenthal, as a part of his ingenious research on the generality of the effects of the experimenters' expectancy, employed rats, but had no idea how the animals came to differentially perform as they did: "... we cannot be sure of the sense modality by which the experimenter's expectancy is communicated to the subject" (1966:165), although these rodents are known to be sensitive to visual, auditory, olfactory, and tactile cues (for recent work on the surprisingly complex social interactions of rats, and especially the functions of their ultrasonic calls, see Lore and Flannelly 1977). Rosenthal thinks, however, that the specific cues by which an experimenter communicates with his animal subjects probably vary "with the type of animal, the type of experiment, and perhaps even the type of experimenter. With Clever Hans as subject, the cues were primarily visual, but auditory cues were also helpful. This seemed also to be true when the subjects were dogs rather than one unusual horse" (1966:177).

Detailed analysis of the carryings on in a laboratory shows that there are "sighs, groans, finger tapping, guttural exclamations or muted whispers" (Pilisuk et al. 1976:515) which are seldom discerned, not to mention "illicit communication" through all the other modalities that goes, if perceived, unreported. Pilisuk and his collaborators found that such signs "did, in fact, have a significant effect upon the level of cooperative behavior," and advocated further studies of "behavior that takes place 'on the sly' since human interaction seems to be full of just such activity" (ibid.:522).

The most prescient of animal psychologists, Hediger, rightly insists that a wide-ranging, intensive program be launched to examine all known and potential channels which are or might be sign-carriers, and thus to determine what is really happening in the interaction between organisms. To this plea, he immediately adds, "Of considerable help in this endeavour is a new branch of science known as semiotics: the study of all possible signals in technical as well as biological and psychological fields" (1974:29). He then enumerates a few situations where reciprocal understanding between man and animal has been achieved via media of communication that are out of the ordinary, stressing not only that hitherto unknown channels are at work but "that familiar ones may already play a role even if outside our threshold of perception" (ibid.:34). The Hess pupil response (discussed in Ch. 3, section 5 of this volume) furnishes one nice illustration of this kind of a sign-process; the equally important eyebrow flash, "discovered" and described by Eibl-Eibesfeldt (1972:299–301), another. The pupil movement and the eyebrow flash are both extremely common if mostly out-of-awareness signs to which we respond strongly in defined contexts; they are used globally by men, except where culture overrides nature (as in Japan, where the flash is considered indecent).

A much more arcane illustration, from the underground literature of semiotics, is furnished by the case history of Eugen de Rubini, the famous Moravian "muscle reader," who came to San Francisco shortly after World War I. This young man had the uncanny ability to read the "thoughts" of others from the patterns of their muscle tensions. Had he not been carefully investigated by three of the most important contemporary psychologists, eminently including Edward C. Tolman, his feats might today be considered fictional. The very careful experiments they conducted were reported in the *Psychological Review* by Stratton, under the intriguing heading, "The Control of Another Person by Obscure Signs" (1921). Stratton and his colleagues adopted Pfungst's paradigm for Clever Hans, but they never did succeed in pinning down the precise cues employed by de Rubini, who modestly laid no claim to mind reading. He was judged to depend "to some appreciable extent, even though subconsciously, upon visual cues . . . of a highly elusive kind" (ibid.: 309–310). Tremors of the floor, faint sounds of feet, of movements of arms and clothing, together with those made by changes in breathing, were diminished signs, but not excluded under the laboratory conditions imposed. "The experimenters each and all assumed that [de Rubini's] successes depended upon sensory cues of some sort, and not upon immediate influence of mind upon mind" (ibid.: 310). This admirably cautious paper refrains from extrapolation beyond the evidence. Stratton believed that his subject "caught, in the very periphery of his visual field" (ibid.: 309), postures or motions which assisted him, but couldn't prove so. It is instructive to contrast this with the plethora of early 1960s reports of observations of sight through the face ("dermooptical phenomena"): blindfolded subjects were said to read texts without using their eyes. Observations were accumulated, although no possible mechanism ever came to mind, until fraud was discovered. The last moral of Pavlov, then, is a simultaneous call for action, along lines set forth by Hediger, but foreshadowed by Jakob von Uexküll (Ch. 10 of this volume), yet tempered by a need for unceasing vigilance in the face of imposture. Clearly, we are all prisoners of our senses, which are imperfectly understood at best, and the weaknesses of which are exploited by con-artists, academic or laic, witting or unwitting.

Figure 5-1. Ivan Pavlov in his study. From author's files.

5. Looking in the Destination for What Should Have Been Sought in the Source

---

Gibt es nicht gelehrte Hunde?
Und auch Pferde, welche rechnen
Wie Commerzienräthe? Trommeln
Nicht die Hasen ganz vorzüglich?
—Heinrich Heine,
　Atta Troll (Cap. V, Quatr. 15)

The notorious but unimpeachably corroborated case of Pavlov's mice raises, in capsule form, a variety of fascinating issues with far-reaching ramifications in several directions, but with particularly serious implications, several of which are well worth restating and pondering further (cf. Ch. 4, this volume), both for the foundations and research methodology of contemporary semiotics.

The facts, as reconstructed by Gruenberg (1929:326–327), Zirkle (1958), and Razran (1959) are straightforward enough. Pavlov, convinced that acquired characters could be inherited, thought at one

Note: The substance of this paper was delivered during a conference on Language and Psychotherapy, organized by the Institute for Philosophy of Science, Psychotherapy, and Ethics, at Wagner College, on April 17, 1977. This version appears in Horowitz, Ornstein, and Stern 1979. Several leading themes developed there were later touched upon in different lectures and seminars given, during the fall of 1977, at the University of Kansas (week of October 10), Texas Tech University (October 17), and the University of Texas at Dallas (October 18). Some were also presented, in synoptic form, under the title "Natural Semiotics," at the 76th Annual Meeting of the American Anthro-

time that this process might be demonstrated by inducing conditioned reflexes in mice and then counting the conditioning trials required through successive generations. His expectation, in conformity with the Lamarckian model of information transmission then, as later, favored in the USSR (Razran 1958), was that the numbers would significantly decrease. Accordingly, he caused an assistant of his, one Studentsov (who appears in the history of science solely as an obscure although, for present purposes, emblematic figure confined to this single episode), to conduct a series of experiments over five generations of mice, the astounding results of which the collaborator then reported to the 1923 Soviet Physiological Conference, as expressed by the following dramatically cascading figures (rounded out later by Pavlov himself): 300, 100, 30, 10, and 5.

The intellectual milieu in which Pavlov worked, and, of course, the very assumptions he brought to the investigation of the problem, accounts for his remissness in not instantly questioning the results, let alone repudiating the conclusions, obtained and announced by his "over-zealous assistant" (Razran 1959:916). "It seems reasonable to assume," Razran continues (ibid.), "that Pavlov would not have been so gullible if he had not shared the Lamarckian predisposition, common to Russian bioscientists—and to the intelligentsia in general—even before the Revolution, and if he had reviewed critically the general evidence on the topic." Only in 1929 did this uncompromisingly empirical scientist, whose honesty was never in doubt, indeed who, in a famous lecture, as far back as April 23, 1921, on the basic qualities of mind deemed indispensable to a scientist, put in a leading place exceptional facility in constructing scientific hypotheses—the capacity, that is, "to get behind the facts," as he used to say (Frolov 1938: 256)—set forth publicly an alternative hypothesis to explain the astonishing data emanating from his laboratory. As related in Gruenberg's *The Story of Evolution* (1929:327, n. 1), "in an informal statement made at the time of the Thirteenth International Physiological Congress, Boston, August 1929, Pavlov explained that in checking up these experiments it was found that the apparent improvement in the ability to learn, on the part of successive generations of mice, was really due to an improvement in the ability to teach, on the part of the experimenter! And so this 'proof' of the transmission of modifications drops out of the picture, at least for the present."

This little tale of self-deception—a variant of what Merton (1948) has dubbed the self-fulfilling prophecy, a phenomenon which was

---

pological Association, suited to the context of an all-day symposium on the "Semiotics of Culture: Toward a New Synthesis in World Anthropology" (co-organized by Drs. D. Jean Umiker-Sebeok and Irene Portis Winner, and held in Houston, December 1). The illustrations appearing in this book have all been newly added. Different versions will be published, in English and in French, in *Diogenes/Diogène*: cf. Sebeok 1978b.

later most creatively and ingeniously explored by Rosenthal (e.g., 1976:136–137) and Rosenthal and Jacobson (e.g., 1968:36), but which is perhaps best known by the tag Clever Hans Fallacy—evokes certain urgent lines of inquiry which continue to be neglected by semioticians, as well as most other students of human and animal behavior, at their peril. The issue is such an important one because the Clever Hans effect informs, in fact insidiously infects, all dyadic interactions whatsoever, whether interpersonal, or between man and animal,[1] and by no means excepting the interactions of any living organism with a computer.[2]

In what follows, I will confine my observations to the three salient features suggested by the Pavlov episode which seem to me to be especially instructive for a general theory of signs. The first of these has to do with the notion of deception, especially within or at the perimeter of the academy, and the importance of being able to recognize different kinds and degrees thereof, ranging from out-and-out fraud for financial gain (say, royalties) and preferment (in the form, for example, of a doctorate), as in a scintillating instance of fictional ethnography, cleverly unwrapped by de Mille (1976; cf. Truzzi 1977). Imposture is sometimes alleged where facts remain forever bafflingly insubstantial while nonetheless mortally damaging, as in the melodramatic Paul Kammerer scandal made famous anew by Koestler (1971): was the principal in the case deliberately trying to perpetrate a swindle, or was he an ingenuous yet suicidal victim of his own Lamarckian tendencies, or did he have a Studentsov in his lab, and, if so, was this putative staff member doctoring critical specimens of *Alytes obstetricans* either to please or to discredit (ibid.:124) his master? No possibility can be entirely excluded, just as we shall never know whether Claudius Ptolemy is the most successful fraud in the history of science, as Robert R. Newton recently argued, or the greatest astronomer of antiquity, as Owen Gingerich reaffirms. The question hinges on whether Ptolemy systematically invented or doctored earlier astronomers' data in order to support his own theories, whether he was unknowingly deceived by a dishonest assistant, or selected, for pedagogical purposes, just the data which happened to agree best with his theory (Wade 1977).

From a semiotic point of view, the deliberate exercise of fraud and deceit—the traditional confidence game or, as this is known to its practitioners, the con—is less interesting than self-deception and its far-flung consequences. For centuries, of course, one very special and continuing form of the con has been perpetrated upon marks by an operator using a tame, trained, domesticated animal, such as a horse, as his or her pivotal prop. A celebrated equine in point, popularized in a ballad published on November 14, 1595, was Morocco (see Fig. 4-2, this volume), "Maroccus Extaticus, or Bankes [John Banks', the operator's] Bay Horse in Trance," whose astonishing feats, suspected of

88 The Sign

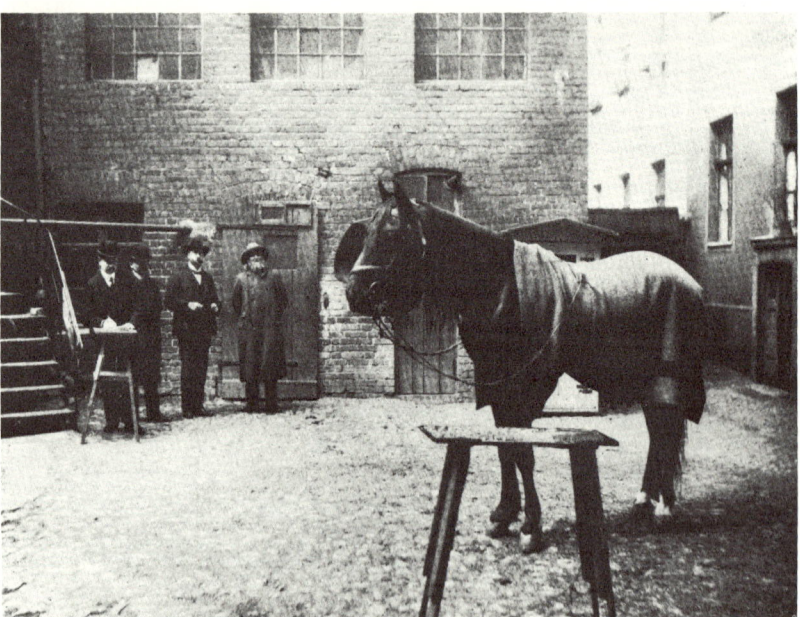

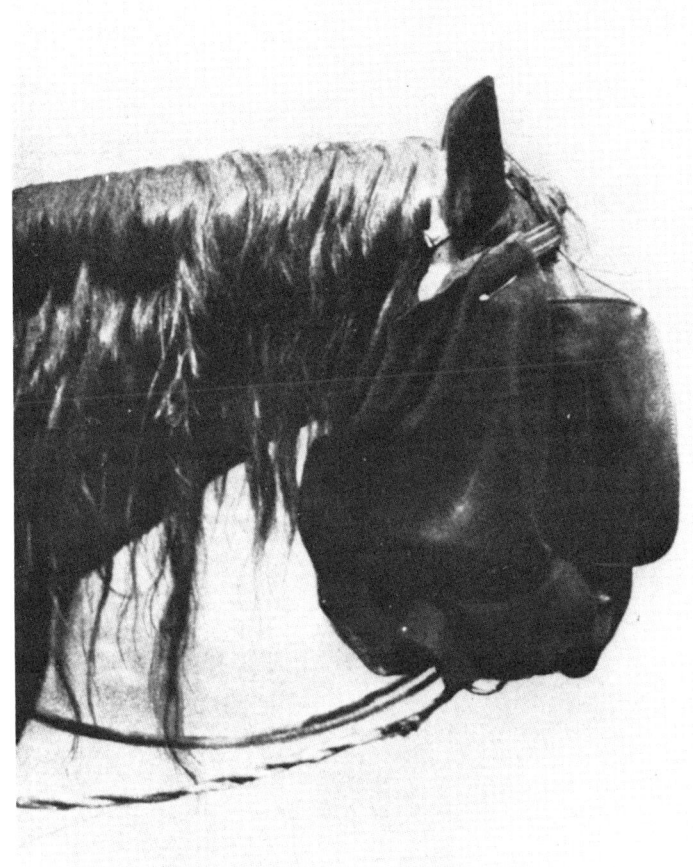

Figure 5-2: *A*. Presenting Clever Hans. *B*. Testing Clever Hans. *C*. Hans blindfolded. The place of attachment of the blindfold was tightly closed by an impenetrable flap which reached under Hans's neck. From Karl Krall, *Denkende Tiere* (Leipzig, 1912).

verging on magic, were graphically portrayed, in 1602, by Jean de Montlyard, Sieur de Melleray, in a long note (transcribed in Halliwell-Phillipps 1879:31–36) to a French translation of the *Golden Ass* of Apuleius. If contemporary accounts are to be believed, both Banks and Morocco were burned upon orders of the Pope, as alluded to by Ben Jonson in one of his *Epigrams*: "Old Bankes the juggler, our Pythagoras,/ Grave tutor to the learned horse, Both which,/ Being, beyond sea, burned for one witch . . ." (1616). Pepys witnessed just such a horse, operated for profit nearly a century later, as noted in his *Diary* for September 1, 1668: "So to the Fair, and there saw several sights; among others, the mare that tells money, and many things to admiration; and, among others, come to me, when she was bid to go to him of the company that most loved a pretty wench in a corner. And this did cost me 12 d. to the horse, which I had flung him before, and did give me the occasion to baiser a might belle fille that was in the house that was exceedingly plain, but forte belle." And Christopher (1970, Ch. 3) entertainingly relates the adventures of "the most discussed animal marvel of recent times," a mare named Lady, and her operator, Mrs. Claudia Fonda.[3] Although Dr. Joseph Banks Rhine declared Lady "the greatest thing since radio,"[4] and claimed that she possessed ESP, the skillful conjuror and historian of magical entertainment exposed the technique used by Mrs. Fonda, an obvious trick—obvious, that is, to mentalists—sometimes employed by mediums and known as pencil reading.

Christopher's key sentence reads (ibid.:45): "If Dr. Rhine was interested in testing for ESP, he should have ignored the horse and studied Mrs. Fonda." He is restating here a basic principle, explicitly recognized already in 1612 by a certain Samuel Rid, the author of a wondrously sophisticated instructional manual, or how-to-do-it book, of whom, alas, nothing further is known. This book, *The Art of Juggling*, ought to be made required reading for all would-be semioticians; here I will reproduce only a brief passage of commentary on the exploits of a performing horse, presumably Morocco:

> As, for ensample, His master will ask him how many people there are in the room? The horse will paw with his foot so many times as there are people. And mark the eye of the horse is always upon his master, and as his master moves, so goes he or stands still, as he is brought to it at the first. As, for ensample, his master will throw you three dice, and will bid his horse tell you how many you or he have thrown. Then the horse paws with his foot whiles the master stands stone still. Then when his master sees he hath pawed so many as the first dice shews itself, then he lifts up his shoulders and stirs a little. Then he bids him tell what is on the second die, and then of the third die, which the horse will do accordingly, still pawing with his foot until his master sees he hath

pawed enough, and then stirs. Which, the horse marking, will stay and leave pawing. And note, that the horse will paw an hundred times together, until he sees his master stir. And note also that nothing can be done but his master must first know, and then his master knowing, the horse is ruled by him by signs. This if you mark at any time you shall plainly perceive.

Let me underscore Rid's last sentence: "This if you mark at any time you shall plainly perceive." The point is that, until the advent of Oskar Pfungst in 1907 (1965 [1911]), no scientist that we know of had the insight to ask an animal—in this instance, Clever Hans, the horse of Herr von Osten—a question to which the inquirer himself did not know the answer. It turned out that, no matter how severely skeptical the audience, whether unschooled or expert, was, it was the observer who had involuntarily and unknowingly signed to the observed to stop tapping at the precise instant where the message destination—alive to the correct answer—expected the message source to cease emitting. "This," Polanyi (1958:169–170) says, "is how they made the answers invariably come out right" (continuing: "this is exactly also how philosophers make their descriptions of science, or their formalized procedures of scientific inference, come out right").

Actually, Lord Avebury, in the 1880s, came very close to rediscovering the correct solution in his experiments with Van, his black poodle, supplemented by his casual inspection of other dogs, some score of years before Pfungst, who himself regarded Van "as a predecessor of our Hans" (1965:178). Avebury had the right attitude to begin with, "that hitherto we have tried to teach animals, rather than to learn from them: to convey our ideas to them, rather than to devise any language or code or signals by means of which they might communicate theirs to us" (Lubbock 1886:1089). He sensitively discerned that when a dog—or a chimpanzee (see Thomson 1924:132) for that matter—is taught how to "count," the operator need not, in fact, ordinarily does not, "*consciously* give the dog any sign, yet so quick [is] the dog in seizing the slightest indication that he [is] able to give the correct answer.... Evidently, the dog seize[s] upon the slight indications unintentionally given" (Lubbock 1886:1091).

Avebury, furthermore, shrewdly connected these observations "with the so-called 'thought-reading'" (ibid.), one variant of which, commonly known as "muscle reading," came eventually to be investigated in painstaking detail by three prominent Berkeley psychologists, Edward C. Tolman among them. "Muscle reading" was shown to crucially hinge on the performer's perception of motor signs of an exceedingly delicate character, signs, moreover, "unintentionally" communicated to him "by each of the persons who acted as his guide" (Stratton 1921; discussed further in Ch. 4 of this volume).[5] It is established by now beyond serious doubt that the working ingredient of

Figure 5-3. Lord Avebury. Courtesy of N. H. Robinson, Librarian, The Royal Society.

many other mind-reading acts—much in the manner of the children's game of Hot and Cold—consists of unwitting and inadvertent nonverbal signs transmitted from audience to "psychic"; nor is this surprising, "since people constantly pass nonverbal signals to each other through such things as changes in their tones of voice and body movements. In fact, this nonverbal communication forms the basis of a well-known magic act. One performer, for example, asks to have his check in payment for a show hidden in the auditorium in full view of his audience. He then comes on stage and finds the check by reading the nonverbal cues of the audience as he wanders closer to or farther from the check" (Kolata 1977b:283, interviewing Persi Diaconis, who is both a prominent mathematician and magician; the identical illusion is discussed, in his somewhat hokey style, by Kreskin [George Kresge, Jr.] [1973:80-84], describing how "I concentrate on reading every direction, every clue, and sensitize myself to hear or see any supportive factors beyond the perceived thought. . . . It can be likened to a highly stimulating game of charades . . ."). This example is far from insignificant, since, as Diaconis emphasizes (ibid.), it suggests an enormous problem area of "how much usable information is being transmitted in this way and what the best guessing strategy is," which arises in many contexts other than parapsychology—in fact, whenever and wherever organisms interact.

As to the mental operation of guessing, it was none other than Peirce (1929:269-270) who had emphasized that "its full powers are only brought out under critical circumstances," a claim he went on to substantiate in a colorful extended narrative of a true personal incident in which the great philosopher was metamorphosed into a master sleuth (for the full story, see ibid.:267-282). As one of his editors summarizes the anecdote, it concerned "the theft of [Peirce's] coat and a valuable watch from his stateroom on a Boston to New York boat. He says that he made all the waiters stand in a row and after briefly talking with each, but without consciously getting any clue, he made a guess as to which one was guilty. The upshot of the story is that after many difficulties, and by making more successful guesses, he proved that his original guess had been correct" (Peirce 1935-1966:40 n. 15; cf. 7.45). What Peirce attempted to do by talking briefly with each man in turn was, as he put it, "to detect in my consciousness some symptoms of the thief" (Peirce 1929:281). His expectation was that the crook would emit some unwitting index, but Peirce also stressed that his own perception of telltale signs, while he held himself "in as passive and receptive a state" (ibid.) as he could, had to be unconscious, or, to use a preferred term he suggested, unself-conscious, "a discrimination below the surface of consciousness, and not recognized as a real judgment, yet in very truth a genuine discrimination . . ." (ibid.:280).[6] He mentions two conjectural principles that may furnish at least a partial explanation for his successful application of "this singu-

Figure 5-4. C. S. Peirce: an official Coast and Geodetic Survey photograph; he would not have been quite forty at the time. Photo obtained courtesy of Max H. Fisch, Peirce Edition Project, Indiana University–Purdue University, Indianapolis.

lar guessing instinct. I infer in the first place," he concluded, "that man divines something of the secret principles of the universe because his mind has developed as a part of the universe and under the influence of these same secret principles; and secondly, that we often derive from observation strong intimations of truth, without being able to specify what were the circumstances we had observed which conveyed those intimations" (ibid.: 281–282). In Peirce's incomparably insightful fashion, the first principle adduced provides the ultimate evolutionary rationale for the workings of the Clever Hans effect, while the other addresses its specifically semiotic roots.

The work on deception by illicit communication in the laboratory recently adumbrated by Pilisuk and his collaborators (1976) surely is on the right track, but merely scratches the surface of deception as a pervasive fact of life characteristic of experimental studies of human and animal behavior; Rosenthal (1976:156), for instance, admits that "deception is a necessary commonplace in psychological research," although I believe that he tends to substantially underestimate (ibid.: 388) potentially harmful consequences, particularly in the context of placebos, which may have decided toxic effects and even the power to produce gross physical change (see, e.g., Beecher 1955:1606), as well as of the dubious role of double-blind "controls."[7]

The first general lesson of the Pavlov episode thus boils down to this: be ever on the lookout against deception, but beware, above all, of self-deception. The second moral is expressly methodological, and may be best understood in a semiotic frame. It has been formulated, as we saw, in more or less the same way by Rid, Avebury, Pfungst, Christopher, and stated perhaps most comprehensively in the title of this article. Pfungst (1965:xxx) and his chief, the eminent psychologist Carl Stumpf, distilled the essence of their investigation by recognizing and admitting that the Hans Commission made the initial mistake of "looking for, in the horse, what should have been sought in the man." In physics, one speaks of couplings between the observer and the observed, and keeps asking how the former affects the latter. In psychological jargon, the experimenter becomes a proxy for "man," while "horse" can stand for any subject, whether human or animal (Rosenthal 1976). In anthropological, folkloristic (Fine and Crane 1977), and even linguistic (Ch. 4, this volume), field work, we are concerned with the distorting influence of elicitor upon native informant. In a clinical setting, we are interested in what the agentive physician's (or quack's or shaman's) personality and paraphernalia contribute towards the healing of the patient/client (Chs. 4 and 10 of this volume). In the argot of the con, the police want to know how does the operator "take" the mark? All of these dynamic/dyadic relationships between living systems have specific commonalities ultimately modeled on or, more exactly, programmed after the one universal dependence relationship which must be both basic and paradigmatic: the cybernetic cycle that prevails between mother (or other caretaker) and child. The nature of this system, "in which one partner assumes the functions of sensor and regulator for the other one and vice versa," was first outlined by Thure von Uexküll (1978), in an attempt to account for the efficaciousness of placebos. All of us are assumed to be reliving and reiterating the early months of our extrauterine existence, when gesturing, posturing, vocalizing, and eventually articulating wicca words like "mama" produced something from nothing—milk and toys, for instance—"out of the blurry, remote world of the adult gods," in Wagoner's (1976: 1598) apt and evocative conceit.

Although von Uexküll states his hypothesis in exceedingly fruitful semiotic terms, it is likewise in obvious conformity with psychoanalytic theory, which suggests consideration of this primal program as a reactivation of a pivotal early experience and one which "may be a permanent available pattern of social interchange in human life, which is not confined only to child-mother or patient-doctor relationship" (Th. von Uexküll 1978). Plausible as this formula appears, it nevertheless leaves open the question most often asked about the seemingly miraculous placebo effect and comparable forms of therapy—say, the "laying on of hands" (currently taught at the graduate level at the New York University School of Education, Health, Nursing and Arts Professions) or "mother's kiss or voodoo drums, leeches, purgatives, poultices, or snake oil" (Moertel et al. 1976:96)—or, indeed, the workings of one's belief in Christian Science (Ch. 10, this volume): namely, how are the semiotic agencies and habiliments transmuted into physiologically operational mechanisms? The answer was foreshadowed in Janet's (1925:1:43–53) discussion of the value of miraculous methods of treatment, from the shrine of Aesculapius to Lourdes. Cannon's classic article (1942) on the cause of "voodoo" death notwithstanding,[8] much fascinating research remains to be done at the borders of the sign science with the life science before this problem can be wholly resolved.

Another area of role-demand where the von Uexküll paradigm is palpably manifested is in hypnotic and posthypnotic responsiveness. As in the placebo effect—for, as Paul Sacerdote emphasizes, "hypnosis may be in many ways the most powerful of placebos" (Holden 1977: 808)—the audience, or, using a semiotic term with a broader charge, context (cf. Fisher 1965:85), serves at least four functions that combine to reinforce the realization and maintenance of so-called hypnotic behavior; these were conveniently summarized by Sarbin and Coe (1972:96–97), but may be assigned to a wider category of effects sometimes called *artifacts*, such as increased motivation and role-playing, in contrast to *essence*, which, if it really exists, refers to what is more or less vaguely known as "an altered state of consciousness," or sometimes "cortical inhibition" or "dissociation" (Orne 1959). Artifacts are systematic errors stemming from specifiable uncontrolled

Figure 5-5. Bernadette of Lourdes. From author's files.

conditions—a bouquet of subtle cues emanating from both the experimental procedure and the experimenter. Thus investigation has revealed that the paraphonetic features selected by the source—viz., forceful or lethargic tone of voice—constitute a ruling variable which must, if feasible, be carefully controlled (Barber and Calverley 1964). The hypnotized subject exhibits the behavior which he thinks the hypnotist expects of him, or, more accurately, what he thinks hypnosis is. The phrase "demand characteristics" is applied to this invigorating idea in the history of hypnosis research (Sheehan and Perry 1976), to which Jaynes' (1977:385) notion of the "collective cognitive imperative" corresponds exactly.

The intimate mutual gaze of lovers furnishes one example among many of how this fundamental paradigm is played out in young adulthood: the reason why both a boy and a girl spend so much time peering closely into each other's eyes is that "they are unconsciously checking each other's pupil dilations. The more her pupils expand with emotional excitement, the more it makes his expand, and vice versa" (D. Morris 1977:172). The pupil response is, as a rule, unknowingly emitted as well as, even more often, unknowingly perceived (Janisse 1977; Ch. 3 of this volume). "Hip dudes," metaphoric "cats," wear dark glasses, or "shades," like the Chinese jade dealers of yore, to conceal their excited pupil dilation and thus to project a cool look—one that demands heightened participation of their "transparent" interlocutors (Gump 1962:229).[9]

Semiotics, which is commonly defined as the study of any messages whatsoever, whether verbal or not, must be equally concerned with the processes of generation and encoding on the part of the most various sources, whether human or not; with the transmission of any string of signs through all possible channels; and with the successive processes of decoding and interpretation on the part of the most various destinations, whether human or not. What the Pavlov tale reminds us of is the peculiar force of the linkage joining any source with any destination. In marveling at the accomplishments of animals—especially hand-reared dolphins in the 1960s and the great apes in the 1970s—trained to engage in two-way communication with man, attention to the behavior of the human has all too often been either shunted aside by deliberate misdirection (imposture) or ignored in innocence (self-deception). Thus many people cherish the belief that police dogs are infallible as trackers, enabling them to recognize the trail of a stranger after getting the scent. However, in one historic experiment (Katz 1937:8–10), it turned out that the man in charge of the police dogs had provided unwitting cues: in other words, "it was not the dog guiding the man, but the man guiding the dog owing to his preconceived opinion about the result to be expected."[10]

Those who stage-manage the circus antics of apes have known for centuries what scientists who aim to instill manually encoded and visually decoded verbal communicative skills in such animals have still scarcely grasped. It is widely imagined, for example, that imitation of the human model in learning situations of this sort is critical. On this issue, Hachet-Souplet (1897:83–84, 91), author of the standard textbook on dressage, quotes Buffon: "'Le singe, ayant des bras et des mains, s'en sert comme nous, mais sans songer à nous; la similitude des membres et des organes produit nécessairement des mouvements qui ressemblent aux nôtres; étant conformé comme l'homme, le singe ne peut se mouvoir que comme lui; mais se mouvoir de même n'est pas agir pour imiter'. . . . Du reste," the canny author concludes, "le public se laissait prendre à cette ruse innocente." When the subject patently fails to imitate the trainer, this imperfection, too, is reinterpreted to fit with the anticipated design. Patterson (1977), for instance, instructed Koko to smile for a photograph. Her gorilla signed "frown" or "sad." The psychologist's explanation of this contrary behavior was not at all that Koko responded erroneously; Patterson's preconception of her design constrained her to assert that negative occurrences of this sort "demonstrate [the ape's] grasp of opposites." With dialectic unfolded in this vein how can you lose?[11]

What actually happens, as Hediger (1974:40) keeps patiently repeating, is that whoever poses the question about the linguistic accomplishment of apes "often already has preconceived ideas about the outcome of the experiments, indeed, he must frequently have possessed such ideas before being able to set up the experiment in the first place. Another factor is the choice of suitable experimental animals. It is up to him to choose a suitable species and individuals, treat and prepare them in a definite way. In this, the 'context'. . . , are already included many possibilities of influence by channels still largely unknown to us." The modish mirage of the Pathetic Fallacy, or the attribution of human characteristics to objects in the natural world, especially to the speechless creatures populating it, reinforced in ways that are more or less well understood (cf. Ch. 4, this volume), is so powerful that observers are not uncommonly prone to report a Barmecidal feast of signs where the more candid among them admit to having perceived none. Thus Stokoe (1977:1)—a leading expert on Ameslan—remarks about some infant chimpanzees: "These baby chimps sign as they move—very rapidly; and we often found that we had seen a sign or a sequence of two or three signs without consciously realizing that we had in fact seen it." Stokoe's encounter with baby Dar and bantling Tatu is disturbingly reminiscent of my own experience in the early 1960s with dolphins in Miami's long defunct Communication Research Institute. In that laboratory, *Tursiops* was being trained to mimic the speech of a human investigator by standard operant conditioning technique. Numerous rumors and some reports were put in circulation to the effect that the animals, especially Elvar and Chee-Chee, were indeed capable of reproducing words "appropriately." Of

Elvar, it was avouched, for instance (Lilly 1963:114): "He does not reproduce a word in 'tape-recorder' fashion or in the fashion of a talking bird. In one's presence he literally [sic] analyzed acoustic components of our words and reproduced various aspects in sequence and separately." Perhaps mistaken for a mark, I was permitted to observe one training session, and later to listen to recordings of several previous sessions. I heard only random dolphin noises, no dialogue. My puzzled demurral was countered by the assertion that these coastal porpoises articulated much too fast for their emissions to be interpreted by the human ear unaided: understanding presupposed analysis by means of the sound spectrograph and oscillographic methods. It was shown a decade or so afterward that the papers published in scientific journals by this Florida research group "provided no solid evidence in support of [such] speculations" (Wood 1973:91). The project was, accordingly, scratched, in 1968, altogether. The long shadow of Clever Hans darkened that undertaking from the start, as is perfectly patent from a sentence the principal had printed in italic type: "*And he* [i.e., Elvar] *first did it* [i.e., spoke] *when and only when we believed he could do it and somehow demonstrated our belief to him*" (Lilly 1963:114).

Stokoe (1977:1) drew another methodological conclusion from his observation in Nevada, or, more accurately, the lack of it: videotape or film "can never be an adequate substitute for trained live observation . . ." This, however, holds only if the inevitability of voluntary and involuntary influence upon the animals being experimented upon is objectively and critically recognized and assessed at every turn, and if all conceivable media of communication between men and animals are kept in constant view. Concerning the work Stokoe describes, and the like, it is not enough to exclaim in awe on what the chimps do; the real challenge is to uncover—the relationship being reciprocal—what the University of Nevada team, for one, is up to.

The use of recording devices is no panacea, of course. As F. J. J. Buytendijk's scrutiny of a film of a fight between a mongoose and a cobra established, the reaction time of their coordinate exchange of some messages is so short that it can neither be viewed by human observers nor re-viewed even in slow motion. This is explicable in terms of the concept of zero signifier (Sebeok 1976:118). "These dissimilar combatants behaved part of the time like a pair of dancers, in which each anticipated the other's next movement" (Hediger 1974: 38), that is, their reaction time was reduced to naught. Hediger believes that something similar takes place in the circus, for example, between a skilled trainer causing a panther sitting on a pedestal to strike out with a forepaw and withdrawing in exquisite accord with that movement, or a springboard acrobat adjusting his leap to the blow of the elephant's foot at the other end of the plank. In his keen observations on movement coordination, or microsynchrony, in human social interaction, Kendon (1977:75) has noted the same kind of foreknowledge: "The precision with which the listener's movements are synchronized with the speaker's speech means that the listener is in some way able to anticipate what the speaker is going to say..."

Hediger's mention of channels focuses attention on yet a third dimension of the Pavlov yarn. It is insufficient to shift one's attention back from the destination to the source. It is essential to consider, as well, the means whereby the two are conjoined. Although the visual, auditory, tactile, and chemical mechanisms of rodent communication, for instance, are understood to a degree (Eisenberg and Kleiman 1977:637–649), no one, least of all the principals, had the slightest idea how, precisely, Studentsov unwittingly disciplined Pavlov's mice; neither was Rosenthal (1976:178) able to determine to his satisfaction how his "bright" and "dull" rat subjects were differentially educated by his naïve students: "we cannot be certain of the role of handling patterns as the mediators of the experimenters' expectancies, nor of whether such other channels as the visual, olfactory, and auditory were involved." As to this, we can but reiterate Hediger's query and observation (1974:39): "How many channels exist between man and animal? We know little more today than we did half a century ago, i.e. that many other channels exist besides those of optic and acoustic question and answer. On account of the inadequacy of our sense organs and the apparatus at our disposal, such channels remain for the moment unknown. It is known, however, that many apparently quite objective laboratory experiments have given, and continue to give, false results for the very reason that many experimenters believe themselves aware of and able to control all the channels of communication existing between those conducting the experiment and the animal involved."

The following principles deserve, in consequence, attentive consideration:

(1) Any form of physical energy propagation can be exploited for communication purposes (Sebeok 1972:40, 67, 124).

(2) Channel selection is governed and constrained by the source encoder's sensorium. The source decoder will generate an acceptable reproduction of the source output if endowed (at least in part) with a correspondingly functioning sensorium.

(3) It is reasonable to assume that messages are routinely transmitted between organisms through hitherto undiscovered or as yet scarcely discerned channels. One arresting case in point is the electrical channel, "a new modality" (Hopkins 1977:286), the multifaceted communicative functions of which are in the process of being actively disclosed.

(4) The range of each of man's sense organs is significantly exceeded by those of a host of other animals. Hediger (1974:32) cites Pfungst as having demonstrated that the horse is capable of perceiving movements in the human face of "less than one fifth of a millimetre."

Pierce and David (1958:102–103) relate amusingly how a trio of electronics experts learned about the ultrasonic stridulation of crickets, drawing from this story the moral "that we hear only what we can hear, and that there may be a great many obvious differences among sounds which must forever escape our ears," wisely adding: "to some degree we hear what we expect to hear." Parallel comparisons can be adduced, *mutatis mutandis*, about the human eye, to say nothing of the olfactory field.

(5) Man has invented a variety of technical aids to enhance the ineffectualness of his channel capacity. However, such intensifying equipment "has frequently been shown to have been a [further] source of error . . ." (Hediger 1974:30).

(6) Before resorting to cheap ad hoc paranormal rationalizations, a sophisticated, if time-consuming, research program must be conducted to pin down the mechanism actually at work in each instance. Elegant and exhaustive investigations of this character are illuminatingly inventoried in Vogt's and Hyman's (1959, Ch. 6) psychophysical exegesis of the movement of the dowsing rod in water witching (cf. Gardner 1957:101–113). The contrary is illustrated by the widely publicized case of Rosa Kuleshova (Pratt 1973:63), who was reputed to be capable of "seeing," particularly reading, through her fingertips. Astute press-agentry led to a global rash of other reported "dermo-optical" manifestations (Ch. 4, this volume), in the early 1960s, all of which turned out to be phony (Gardner 1966). "X-Ray Eye Act" is the professional designation of hoaxes of this nature,[12] where the performer can easily open his or her eyes and is able to look down both sides of the nose; blindfold magic can be achieved with seemingly impenetrable coverings like bread dough, silver dollars, wads of cotton, powder puffs, folded paper, sheets of metal, adhesive tape, and, of course, a variety of cloth shields.

The small but influential segment of mankind that can afford leisure for the contemplation of such matters longs to establish communication links in two opposite directions: with the rest of animate existence (plant forms, involving phytosemiosis, as well as animal forms, involving zoosemiosis), in the matrix of which our lives lie inalienably embedded; and with supposititious extraterrestrial civilizations. Leaving unearthly aspirations and efforts aside (see, e.g., Ponnamperuma and Cameron 1974:213–215 for selected references to "interstellar communication languages"), one can confidently assert that the fundamentals of code-switching between our species and not a few others are adequately understood, not just intuitively—that kind of comprehension was the imperative semiotic prerequisite for domestication—but also scientifically, thanks, in the main, to Hediger's brilliantly creative lifelong spadework (cf., *inter alia*, Hediger 1974, and the references given in Sebeok 1976:219–220). Two-way zoosemiotic communication is thus not at issue, but such communication between man and animalkind by *verbal* means is quite another matter. The fascinating paradox of language-endowed speechless creatures has been iteratively resolved in myth and fiction, but not in reality. That search, for a resolution of the authentic kind, has lately taken a disturbingly pseudoscientific turn. An account of the socioeconomic reasons for this craze, interesting though it may be, of "humanizing" pets, quasi-feral terrestrial and marine mammals, and an occasional tame bird,[13] falls outside of the scope of this article.

Leo Szilard's satirical story "The Voice of the Dolphins" (1961) and Robert Merle's thriller *The Day of the Dolphin* (1967) are chimerical treatments of the same theme in what may well be called the Decade of the Dolphin. In the 1970s, writers have, fittingly, emerged from the brine. Peter Dickinson's "chimpocentric" tale of detection, *The Poison Oracle* (1974), where the action hinges on the linguistic capacity of an ape, and John Goulet's affecting book *Oh's Profit* (1975), the hero of which, a gifted young signing gorilla, is pitted against the merciless forces of a singularly sinister coalition of linguists, are modern transfigurations of Jules Verne's diverting (if today seldom read) parodic science fiction pastiche, *The Great Forest* (originally published with his *Le Village aérien*, in 1901). This work was inspired by the genuine, if eccentric, exploits of Richard L. Garner, who, in 1892, left America on a field trip for Gabon, where he lived in Libreville for two years. He then proceeded upcountry, where he was sheltered at a mission of the Fathers of the Holy Ghost, located on the banks of the Ogowe. In due course, he published (Garner 1892) a book on the "speech" of monkeys. His studies were themselves an odd mishmash of valuable observations, pure inventions, and colorful humbug: "Peut-être a-t-on souvenir de l'expérience à laquelle voulut se livrer l'Américain Garner dans le but d'étudier le langage des singes et de donner à ses théories une démonstration expérimentale," Verne questions tongue-in-cheek, and then goes on to invent a lunatic proto-ethologist, one Dr. Johausen (obviously Garner, but in Teutonic guise), who journeys to Central Africa to seek out "le prétendu langage des singes." Predictably, he finds just what he was expecting to find—speaking monkeys—but with a difference: "Ce qui les distingue essentiellement des hommes [est qu'ils] ne parlaient jamais sans nécessité." In passing, Verne makes some exceedingly prescient observations about language and cognition, intelligence and verbal propensity, and animal communication in general. The story ends with an ironic twist: Johausen's expectations are indeed fulfilled, and he even rises to become the ruler of the beasts, Sa Majesté Msélo-Tala-Tala, but the cost he has to pay for his achievement is enormous: that price is the loss of his most precious possession, his own language, which is to say, his humanity: "Il est devenu singe . . ." Thus, in an unending cycle, does Pop Art burlesque

104 The Sign

Figure 5-6: *A*. Georges Roux's conception of Dr. Johausen luring his "informants" to him by making music. *B*. Georges Roux's portrayal of Sa Majesté Msélo-Tala-Tala after the scientist lost his language capacity. From Jules Verne, *Le Village aerien* (Paris: Collection Hetzel, 1901).

scientific lore while Big Science apes (*le mot juste*) the presentiments of Pop Culture—no less in today's ecologically remorseful USA than in yesteryear's Lysenko-ridden USSR.

The road from Russian rodents to American apes is paved with good intentions, but for an innocent onlooker, trained in the sign science, at least three signposts pointing to a need for ventilation loom behind and ahead, each beckoning to as yet insufficiently explored byways at the dangerous intersection of two synergetic causes of error: the Clever Hans Fallacy and the Pathetic Fallacy. The trio of problems that seem, from a semiotic point of view, to cry out for immediate, impartial, intensive investigation are: the destructive pitfall of self-deception; the predominance, in dyadic encounters, of the source over the destination; and the paucity of accurate knowledge about the multiplicity and range of natural channels connecting both extremities of the communication chain.

6. Iconicity

I

A century ago, word reached President Daniel Coit Gilman of the new Johns Hopkins University that Thomas Huxley, then at the height of his fame as a leader in the life sciences and an expert in problems of medical education, as well as a renowned public speaker upon scientific subjects, was coming to this country from London. Invited to deliver the university's inaugural address, he accepted, he came, he spoke to a crowded assembly—and what ensued has been called a storm, although, in retrospect, it seems to me more like a farce. In the fashion of academic folklore, the story has survived in several variant forms; my retelling of it relies on Gilman's personal recollections (1906:20ff.).[1]

The first thing that went wrong involved what we are now accustomed to refer to, with disapprobation, as "the media." The fatigued Huxley had hardly reached Baltimore when he was discovered by the press: the reporters demanded the manuscript of his speech. "Manuscript?" he said, "I have none. I shall speak freely on a theme with which I am quite familiar." (Since I prefer to lecture the same way, I can fully appreciate Huxley's consternation!) The reporters, however, persisted: "Professor, that is all right, but our instructions are to send the speech to the papers in New York, and if you cannot give us the copy, we must take it down as well as we can and telegraph it, for the Associated Press is bound to print it the morning after it is spoken."

Huxley was caught in a familiar predicament: either he would have to write out his speech to insure accuracy of transmission and reproduction, or suffer information loss and certain distortion of his message. So he yielded, and spent next morning dictating to a stenogra-

Note: Passages of this paper that bear on the evolutionary and systematic implications of iconicity were included, in succinct form, in a talk delivered at a conference on the "Origins and Evolution of Language and Speech," on September 23, 1975, for the New York Academy of Sciences. A much fuller version was given as the opening address of the Charles Sanders Peirce Symposium on Semiotics and the Arts, on September 25, 1975; that was also the first lecture designed to mark the 100th anniversary of the founding of Johns Hopkins University. This article, prepared afterward, is reprinted, with a few corrections, from *Modern Language Notes* 91:6:1427–1456. Copyright © 1976 by The Johns Hopkins University Press. A much condensed version appeared in *The Review* 19:4:18–33, and a Polish translation, entitled 'Ikonicznosc," is in preparation for *Studia Semiotyczne* 9 (1978).

pher. Gilman noticed, the following evening, that the distinguished orator, although he kept looking at the pile of manuscripts in front of him, never turned a page. His speech lacked the anticipated glow, and the speaker his reputed charm, warmth, and persuasiveness. The President thought that perhaps the light was insufficient—but that was not it: "I have been in distress," Huxley explained afterward. "The reporters brought me, according to their promise, the copy of their notes. It was on thin translucent paper, and to make it legible, they put clean white sheets between the leaves. That made such bulk that I removed the intermediate leaves, and when I stood up at the desk I found that I could not read a sentence. So I have been in a dilemma—not daring to speak freely, and trying to recall what I dictated yesterday and allowed the reporters to send to New York."

This, however, turned out to be but the curtain raiser to the supervening alarum with comedic overtones, yet not without some sinister consequences withal. Gilman apparently did not fully reckon with the contemporary popular hostility toward biology and the widespread opinion that some naturalists were irreligious. Mindful that, for Huxley, the theory of evolution was irreconcilably antagonistic to all religion, he failed to appreciate the extent to which the odium theologicum inspired his adversaries. He had, in fact, with proper administrative caution, proposed to two of his most religious trustees that there should be an introductory prayer to precede Huxley's discourse, but, as he later reported, they said no, preferring that it be given without note or comment. This sin of omission was duly picked up by a correspondent of one of the religious weeklies in New York, who, in a sensational letter to his paper, underlined that there was no prayer. This, Gilman subsequently remarked, "was the storm-signal. Many people who thought that a university... could not succeed unless it was under some denominational control were sure that this opening discourse was but an overture to the play of irreligious and antireligious actors. Vain it was to mention the unquestioned orthodoxy of the trustees, and the ecclesiastical ties of those who had been selected to be professors. Huxley was bad enough; Huxley without prayer was intolerable."

Permit me to reproduce in full a letter that chanced to come to Gilman's hands some weeks afterward and that he eventually saw fit to publish. It was addressed by a Presbyterian minister of New York to a Presbyterian minister of Baltimore (the emphasis was supplied by Gilman himself):

New York, 3 Oct., 1876.
Thanks for your letter, my friend, and the information you give. The University advertised Huxley's lecture as the 'Opening' and so produced the impression which a Baltimore correspondent increased by taking the thing as it was announced. *It was*

bad enough to invite Huxley. It were better to have asked God to be present. It would have been absurd to ask them both.
  I am sorry Gilman began with Huxley. But it is possible yet to redeem the university from the stain of such a beginning. No one will be more ready than I to herald a better sign.

For a decade or more after this episode, one of the President's obsessive concerns became to live down the suspicions of impiety and mistrust he and his faculty had thus aroused, or, as he more vividly put it, it was that long "before the black eye gained its natural colour." His conscious efforts at rebuilding the public image of extreme conservatism in religion focusing on Presbyterianism at the Johns Hopkins were certainly a contributory, if not necessarily the decisive factor that eventually led to the professorial appointment of G. Stanley Hall as against his unconventional and undiplomatic competitor Peirce, whose contract, in Macksey's tactful phrasing, was "summarily terminated under obscure circumstances" (1970:6). This much is clearly implied by a masterful reconstruction of the 1884 ambiance in which this fateful decision was made (Fisch and Cope 1952:280–286), although the true story has yet to be teased out in full of its legendary matrix.

The harsh facts are that Peirce, who "remains the most original, versatile and comprehensive philosophic mind this country has yet produced" (Nagel 1959:185), was dismissed by the University after five years of sterling service, and he never again succeeded in holding any academic post. It is difficult to deny Nagel's inference that Peirce's "repeated failure to secure a teaching position at an institution of higher learning was a misfortune, for himself as well as for the subsequent history of philosophy," and "that had Peirce's personal fortunes been different, the state of logical and philosophical studies would today be much further advanced" (ibid.:185f.). This assessment could well be supplemented by one of Peirce's own prophetic utterances, dated 1903, where he expressed his confidence that if the doctrine of signs had been pursued "with half the *zeal* and *genius* that had been bestowed upon mathematics, the twentieth century might have opened with . . . such vitally important sciences as molecular physics, chemistry, physiology, psychology, linguistics, and ancient historical criticism . . . in a decidedly more advanced condition than there is much promise that they will have reached at the end of 1950" (Peirce 1935–1966: 5.84; cf. Sebeok 1975b). The destiny of Peirce always brings to my mind the picture of the Faustlike Professor in a 1937 film, *On the Avenue*:

> He attracted some attention
> When he found the fourth dimension.
> But he ain't got rhythm
> No one's with him.
> He's the lonesomest man in town.

2

As Wells (1971:96) has judiciously pointed out, Peirce's "notion of icon is as old as Plato's (the sign IMITATES the signified)." It was indeed Plato who bequeathed the concept of mimesis (Lausberg 1960: 554ff.) to theoreticians of literature from Aristotle to Auerbach, and then on to Wimsatt, who was responsible for consciously restoring the term *icon* into the critical vocabulary at mid-century by using it as the key word in the title of one of his important collections of essays (1954). However, the icon acquired its entirely novel perspective in consequence of Peirce's juxtaposition in the very particular context of his second trichotomy of signs—the one he called his "most fundamental" (1935–1966:2.275) division, and the one which has certainly become the most influential—first of the icon with the index, and then of both of the former pair with the symbol. The icon and the index embody sign-relations which are (to stay within the suggestive framework of the *Kratylos*, with its celebrated twin catchwords, *phúsei* vs. *thései*) in the natural mode—respectively, of likeness ("a mere community in some quality"), or of existential connection ("a correspondence in fact") —as against the symbol, which is in the conventional mode, or represents a relation that is characterized by "an imputed quality," to cite Peirce's matchless precision of expression (1.558). Peirce's trichotomy, which was but one of three in his original overall schema, has engendered a vast secondary literature. At issue are questions such as these: wherein, exactly, lie the distinctions, if they are tenable at all, between qualisigns, sinsigns, and legisigns, and between rhemes, propositions, and arguments? How are both of these groupings related to the icon/index/symbol triad? How do any of these discriminations accord with Peirce's underlying conception of a sign as something standing for an object in some particular respect (or, phrased according to the traditional formula, *aliquid stat pro aliquo*), and indispensably requiring an interpretant? The interpretant carries a particularly heavy burden; we need to be instructed in the meaning of Peirce's distraction between the immediate, the dynamical, and the final interpretant of the sign, and elucidate how far this coincides with yet a further trichotomy between the emotional, the energetic, and the logical interpretant, or habit of action. We must also be mindful that Peirce's sign categories, had his work been finished, might have advanced from ten to sixty-six classes, or even exploded into 3^{10}, that is, 59,049 fragments; and we ought, I suppose, to be thankful for his declining to consider the "difficult questions" arising from this bewildering multiplication and deciding not to "undertake to carry [his] systematical division of signs any further," but to "leave that for future explorers" (8.343).

I obviously cannot even begin to pursue the implications of such problems here, but felt that I must at least mention them, if only to establish the fact that Peirce's icon can scarcely be understood when wrenched out of the total context of his semiotic. This is exactly what is wrong with much of the international debate about the icon, which was begun by Burks (1949), but which has lately escalated into increasingly acrimonious exchanges between two groups of commentators whom I like to characterize as iconophiles vs. iconoclasts (cf. Turner 1975:155). Their polarization is exemplified, in varying opposition, by Wallis's "On Iconic Signs" (1975), which simply takes them for granted, as against Bierman's arguments in support of the contrary view, "that there are no iconic signs at all" (1962:245); and in the spectrum of contrasting Italian standpoints about iconicity variously elaborated by Bettetini, Casetti, Volli, and with especial subtlety in Maldonado vs. Eco (Ponzio 1976:355–394; cf. Eco 1976:190–217). The account of Ayer (1968) is exceptionally fair and illuminating.

Why has iconicity—and its complementary obverse, *aniconism*— meaning the prohibition, in such monotheistic religions as Judaism or Islam, of the shaping of graven images, of the use of photographs[2] among, for instance, the Amish, and, more generally, the condemnation, in many religious groups, of idolatry—become the focus of so much passionate concern on the part of so many? Wallis (1975:157), among others, has alluded to the suggestive power of iconic signs, and the implications of this puissance for the history of culture. The magic efficacy of the kind of icon called *effigy* has long been recognized in ritual experience, whether in a sermon by Donne, when he proclaimed, in 1661, that "In those that are damned before, we are damned in Effigie," or, by an appropriate relic display of puppets in front of a fraternity house on virtually any American campus in season, in a ceremony to secure victory for one's football team. The ritual system of certain cultures is constructed of iconic signs: thus, among the Rotinese, a major premise of rituals is based on the equation of man and plant, and defined by icons cast in a life-enhancing botanic idiom (Fox 1975:113f.). Such considerations notwithstanding, there has been a tendency among philosophers to treat the icon as a banal sign category of little theoretical or practical import (see Thom 1973:86), or to view the distinction between iconic and other signs as "transient and trivial" (Goodman 1968:231). Thom (ibid.), as I am, and as Peirce certainly was, is convinced that these critics "ont tort, et qu'une analyse un peu fine des processus dynamiques intervenant dans la production des images (la 'copie') pose des problèmes de nature fondamentale qui sont au coeur même de la relation Signifié⇌Signifiant qui caractérise le symbole sous sa forme achevée." Iconic signs deserve much deeper study than has been accorded them up to now, not only for compelling reasons of logic (Eco 1976; Sebeok 1976:130), but to illuminate the psychological bases of their potently, if vicariously evocative attributes. Their perturbation in human affairs of today can be poignantly illustrated by two recent affairs of far-reaching import which give evidence, to slightly paraphrase a remark of Bierman's, that iconicity can sometimes be "a life and death matter" (1962:249). I refer to the trial of Dr. Kenneth Edelin and the case of Karen Ann Quinlan, both of which I take as paradigmatic.

In the matter of Dr. Edelin, as reported by Culliton (1975:816), "In what may have been one of the most significant moves of the trial," District Attorney Flanagan persuaded Judge McGuire to allow him to introduce a photograph of the dead fetus in evidence, over the strong protests of the defense. "That picture showed a normally formed fetus with fine, black curly hair. Its face was shriveled." Culliton then depicts that Flanagan "addressed the jury vigorously, his voice filling the courtroom, his face flushed with emotion," and here is what he said:

> Is this just a subject? Is this just a specimen? Look at the picture. Show it to anybody. What would they tell you it was? Use your common sense when you go to your jury deliberation room and humanize that. Are you speaking about a blob, a big bunch of mucus, or what are we talking about here? I respectfully submit we are talking about an independent human being that the Commonwealth of Massachusetts must protect as well as anybody else in this courtroom . . .

Several jurors claimed that they were shaken by the photograph ("It looked like a baby," "The picture helped people draw their own conclusions," they reported after their verdict), and "everybody in the room" decided that the fetus was, indeed, a person.

The Quinlan case, where a pretty young girl, a prototypic Sleeping Beauty, was gradually shriveled into a rudimentary, quasi-fetal state, inevitably approaching extinction, may be read as the inverse of the Edelin case. In the former, the crucial question was, when does life begin, i.e., at what stage must the replica (homunculus) be interpreted as an iconic representation of its model (human baby)?[3] In the latter, the grave decision hinged on the question, at what point does death occur, i.e., when can an attenuating replica (regressively vegetative embryo) be deemed to have ceased to be an iconic representation of its model (typical high school senior)? Thus two of the most searing political concerns of our times—the right to abortion and the right to "pull the plug" (Heifitz and Mangel 1975)—are seen to rest on exquisite judgments by laymen about iconicity.

I should now like to say a few words about the utility of the notion of "similarity," which Peirce, on occasion, introduced into his definiens; for instance: "a sign may be *iconic*, that is, may represent its object mainly by its similarity, no matter what its being" (1935–1966:2.276). This was criticized by Eco (1976:192–200), in an interesting way, as (among others) a naïve conception, because he feels that icons are culturally coded, i.e., conventionally so in "a more flexible sense" (1976:191; cf. Knowlton's thoughtful 1966 article which, however, suffers from the author's lack of awareness of the works of Peirce). Of course, we know that Peirce had himself held exactly this view when he asserted that any material image "is largely conventional in its mode of representation," although "it may be called a *hypoicon*" (2.276), and when he singled out "icons in which the likeness is aided by conventional rules" (2.279). However this may be, the usefulness of similarity, particularly in its classical juxtaposition with a key principle in the definiens of the index, namely "contiguity," or the like (Sebeok 1976:131f.), derives from the pervasiveness of the pair in many fields of intellective endeavor throughout Western history.

Allow me to give a few illustrations of this, perhaps the most famous of which comes from anthropology. In an often quoted passage, Frazer (1951:12f.) classified the principles of magic into homoeopathic (or imitative, or mimetic) and contagious: the first is based on the principle that like produces like, or that an effect resembles its cause, and this is called "the Law of Similarity"; the second, "that things which have once been in contact with each other continue to act on each other at a distance after the physical contact has been severed," he called "the Law of Contact or Contagion," which he also says is "founded on the association of ideas by contiguity." Plainly, what we have here is magic by the management of icons (hence the construction of effigies),[4] vs. magic by the manipulation of indices.

Gestalt psychologists have examined the problem of stimulus constellations, the arrangements and divisions of wholes, and have determined two basic principles that Wertheimer has called the Factor of Similarity (the tendency of like parts to band together), vs. the Factor of Proximity (the form of grouping which involves the smallest interval). Particularly engrossing features of this study are Wertheimer's applications of these principles in both the visual and the auditory modality, and his attempts to deal not simply with similarity and dissimilarity, but with more or less dissimilarity to determine experienced arrangement; in other words, he shows that quantitative comparisons can be made regarding iconicity in regions—form, color, sound—"heretofore treated as psychologically separate and heterogeneous" (Wertheimer 1967:76). Figure 6-1 illustrates the importance of similarity in the organization of visual perception: Wertheimer shows here that identical configurations are perceptually linked, and perceived as a series of horizontal linear arrays.

In neurolinguistics, too, there appears to be substantial agreement that, as regards the typology of aphasic impairments, it is fruitful (at least as a heuristic device) to distinguish similarity disorders, "with damage to the code," from contiguity disorders, "with a deterioration of the context" (e.g., Jakobson 1971b:89f., and passim, strongly endorsed by Luria, e.g., 1973). The dichotomy of concurrence vs. sequence derives, of course, from Saussure's famous distinction between the axis of simultaneities and the axis of successivities, which he deemed a practical necessity for all of "les sciences travaillant sur des valeurs,"

114   The Sign

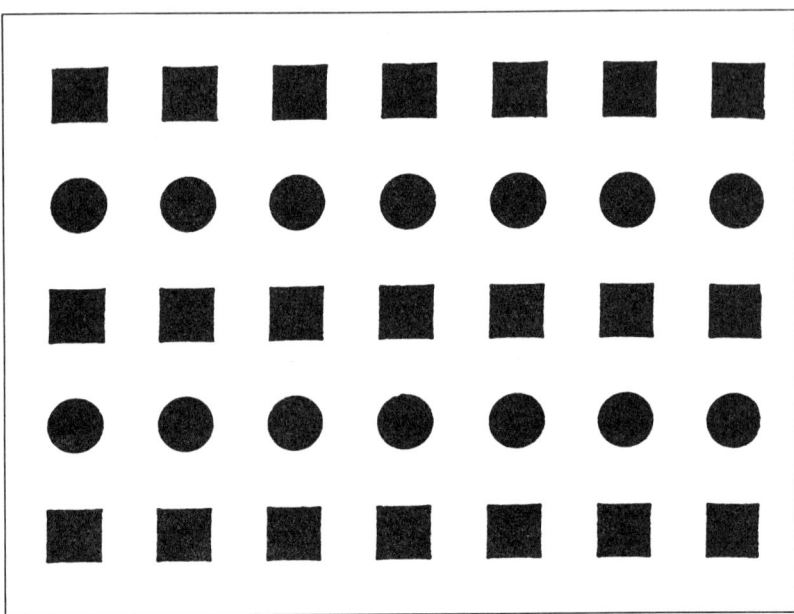

Figure 6-1. After Wertheimer 1967.

an absolute necessity in certain disciplines, and particularly so in linguistics (1967:177), where the concepts of paradigm and syntagm, and subsidiary oppositions and contrasts, have proved as seminal as they are currently commonplace notions. This might be a good place to mention that the iconic functions of language as such have been subjected to sustained observation over the past decade, and not solely on the sound level, as was the custom in earlier, superficial treatments of onomatopoeia and kindred phenomena, or on the lexical plane, where the effect of iconicity is merely virtual, but in its rich, obligatory effects throughout syntactic structures, with surprisingly revealing results (Jakobson 1965; Valesio 1969; Wescott 1971).[5] In this connection, emergence of a hypothesis by Frishberg seems to me especially worth concentrated inquiry: extrapolating from her diachronic investigation of a natural language of a deaf community signed on this continent, ASL, she conjectures that there may "exist some ideal proportion between icons and symbols that any language will approach" (1975:718); this seems quite likely, and should not be too difficult to try to falsify.

The age-old doctrine of association by similarity or contiguity has flourished, above all, in rhetoric and poetics, in the garb of tropes usually called metaphor and metonym. At the heart of the metaphor lies *similitudo* (Lausberg 1960:285), with fascinating extensions (ibid. §§ 558–564) that cannot be followed up here. Peirce explicitly identified the metaphor with one of three kinds of hypoicons, the other two being images and diagrams (1935–1966:2.277); (however, his remarks about the metaphor are meager—cf. 7.590). In passing, I should also like to point out that both sorts of tropes were recently recorded, so we are told, in the behavior of two different home-raised chimpanzees: whereas Washoe created "water-bird" for duck, a metonymic or indexical expression, being a sign in real reaction with the object noted (Fouts 1974:479), Lucy generated "candy fruit" for watermelon, a metaphoric or iconic turn, possessing the qualities signified (Temerlin 1975:120).

In sum, while I have welcomed Eco's imaginative and searching analysis of what he calls "six naïve notions" of iconism (1976:191ff.), I still favor retaining the terminology that troubles him: "similarity," and the rest, constitute, in my view, a time-honored set of primes whose usefulness in a wide range of human sciences has been amply proven, but whose pertinence to semiotic discourse becomes fully manifest only if properly applied. The notion of an "icon" is very much impoverished when viewed, as it so often is, in isolation rather than in the total context of a fully rounded doctrine of signs.

A moment ago, I alluded to the construction of what seemed like an icon by a domestic ape, Lucy. This brings me to the question of the prevalence of iconicity among the speechless creatures, and, more generally, the introduction of a biosemiotic perspective, such as I have consistently advocated for many years (Sebeok 1968; 1972; 1976; 1977a, and, with Umiker-Sebeok, forthcoming). There are, indeed, numberless instances of iconicity in zoosemiotic discourse, involving virtually all known channels—that is, forms of physical energy propagation—available for message transmission to animals. Gregory Bateson (in Sebeok 1968:614–628) has even tried to explain why genotypic controls have often evolved to determine iconic signaling, and has brilliantly argued that an understanding of human dreaming "should throw light both on how iconic communication operates among animals and on the mysterious evolutionary step from the iconic to the verbal" (ibid.:623); the same startling thought, of the evolutionary intermediacy of dreaming in man that allows for a degree of consciousness during periods of sleep and hence a certain discontinuity of the subject/object distinction inherent in iconic coding, seems later to have occurred independently to Thom (1975b:72f.).

Just a few illustrations of the use of iconic signs in the animal world will have to do for now; I have given others elsewhere (e.g., Sebeok 1976:130f.). Thus the iconic function of a chemical sign may be accurately measured by fluctuations in the intensity of insect odor trails laid by successful foragers, for example, in various species of ants. The actual quantity of the emitted pheromone depends directly on the amount and quality of the source of nourishment: "as a food supply and the odor intensity of the trail to it diminish, fewer foragers are attracted" (Butler 1970:45f.); that is, the pheromone acts as an iconic sign vehicle inasmuch as it relates in analog fashion to the waxing or waning of the guiding odor spots (although a crawling insect may use supplementary channels—redundantly or according to strict rules of code-switching—such as sight, touch, sun-compass reaction, and orientation by polarized light from a blue sky, but always, under such conditions, in an iconic fashion). Genetically programmed iconicity plays a pivotal role in deception (Sebeok 1976, Ch. 9) involving smell and taste, color and shape, sound, and, of course, behavior, as graphically described by Hinton (1973). Sometimes an animal even alters its surroundings to fit its own image by fabricating a number of dummy copies of itself to misdirect predators away from its body, the live model, to one of several replicas it constructs for that very purpose; and this is only one among a number of iconic antipredation devices contrived by different species of a highly interesting genus of spiders known as orb-weavers (Wickler 1968:56f.; Hinton 1973:125ff.). The theory of mimicry, which finds many applications throughout both plants and animals, as Wickler has shown in his beautiful book (1968), deals with a range of natural phenomena involving the origin of all species and all adaptations, which Henry Bates had emphasized already in the 1860s; however, associations consisting of models and their mimics constitute but one special set of biological events connecting signs with things signified by "a mere relation of reason," in which case the sign is an icon (Peirce 1935–1966:1.372), so that the former must be integrated, *in toto*, with the far more general and deep theory of iconicity, as we shall see.

I cannot resist recounting one particularly elegant (if sometimes disputed) final example of a complex piece of invertebrate behavior that evolved, as it were, to function as an iconic sign in the visual or tactile mode. Unraveled by Kloft (1959), it has to do with a certain ant-associated (myrmecophilous) aphid species (also discussed in Chapter 1). These small, soft-bodied insects, very vulnerable to predator attack, are protected and tended by ants with which they communicate by an alarm pheromone that functions to stabilize their association. Their relationship is further reinforced by the fact that the ants "milk" the aphids by vibrating their antennae against an aphid's back; the aphids then secrete droplets of honeydew which are consumed by the ants. Kloft realized that this congenial relationship rests on a "misunderstanding," and proposed, as a working hypothesis, that the hind end of an aphid's abdomen and the kicking of its hind legs constitute, for an ant worker, a compound sign vehicle, signifying, from its perspective, the head of another ant together with its antennal movement. In other words, the ant, in an act of perversion of the normal trophallaxis occurring between sisters, identifies the replica (the rear end of the aphid) with the model (the front end of the ant), and solicits on the basis of this misinformation, treating a set of vital biological releasers out of context, viz., in the manner of an effigy. The multiple resemblances between model and replica are so striking, subtle, and precisely effective, that they can hardly be explained away as an evolutionary coincidence (Wilson 1971:422); Figure 1-3 pictures in silhouette the hind end of an aphid (A) and the head of an ant (B).

I have already cited Peirce's rough division of icons into images, diagrams, and metaphors (1935–1966:2.277), and mentioned his seeming lack of interest in the third.[6] Icons are still too often simplistically identified with mere images, such equations giving rise to shallow and unenlightening theories, especially of art (cf. Veltruský 1976: 250ff.; G. Shapiro 1975:34, who cogently argues "that iconicity is not the central representative relation in art"; for iconicity in music, see Hospers 1967:48, and Osmond-Smith 1975). The neglect of diagrams is particularly incomprehensible in view of the fact that they loomed large in Peirce's own semiotic researches, and that they have been reviewed by at least three careful scholars, at some length, over the last dozen years (Zeman 1964; Roberts 1973; Thibaud 1975). Peirce has explicitly spelled out that "Many diagrams resemble their objects not at all in looks; it is only in respect to the relations of their parts that their likeness consists" (2.282). Elsewhere, he stressed that "a diagram has got to be either auditory or visual, the parts being separated in one case in time, in the other in space" (3.418). There follows a crucial passage, which all linguists should read through to the end: Peirce established there, among other things, that "language is but a kind of algebra," or method of forming a diagram. He then continues: "The meanings of words ordinarily depend upon our tendencies to weld together qualities and our aptitudes to see resemblances, or, to use the received phrase, upon associations by *similarity*; while experience is bound together, and only recognizable, by forces acting upon us, or, to use an even worse chosen technical term, by means of associations by *contiguity*" (3.419). He dwells upon "the living influence upon us of a *diagram*, or *icon*, with whose several parts are connected in thought an equal number of feelings or ideas. . . . But the icon is not always clearly apprehended. We may not know at all what it is; or we may have learned it by the observation of nature" (7.467). To put it tersely, I am of the opinion that no critique of iconicity that ignores Peirce's existential graphs in their multiform implications can be taken seriously or regarded as at all viable.

A surprisingly prevalent solecism assumes that icons, viz., images, are necessarily confined to the visual modality. Sometimes a semantic constriction of this sort is imposed by deliberate choice. "There is substantial agreement," according to one outstanding experimenter in search for the locus of short-term visual storage, also called iconic memory in man, "that the terms icon, visual image, and persistence of sensation may be used interchangeably" (Sakitt 1975:1319 n. 2). The only annotated bibliography on "iconic communication" that I know of takes it as consonant with expectation that all interaction thus labeled "proceeds by way of visual images" (Huggins and Entwisle 1974:5), not even pausing to contemplate alternative channels. And Watt (1975: 294) tells us that "Since 1966 the discipline which aims at constructing grammars for pictorial 'languages' has had a name, 'iconics'," dignified by others as the "science of iconics" (e.g., Huggins and Entwisle 1974: 8). A moment's reflection about the iconic components of spoken natural languages, alluded to above, should suffice to check this counterproductive terminological limitation. We ought also to be mindful, in this connection, of the many multisensory iconic representations (no doubt insufficiently studied) that pervade human and other animal existence in everyday life. One such sphere which is permeated by iconicity is, broadly speaking, that of small group ecology, illustrated, for instance, by our seating behavior (Lott and Sommer 1967) as one kind of spatial positioning: at a family gathering, we expect to find the "head" of the household at the "head" of the table, etc. As studies of various alloprimates have likewise clearly shown, "the relative position and distance of the various members of a group from one another reflect the nature of the social relations between them" (Hall and DeVore 1965:70). Moreover, Kummer has, not long ago, insightfully reviewed the essentially iconic connection of social relations and spatial arrangements in animals in general, plausibly concluding with the suggestion that "territorial tendencies... can reemerge in the handling of information" (1971:233). In other words, there exists a diagrammatic correspondence between the signans, the spatial arrangement, and the signatum, the social organization, in a fashion analogous to the isomorphic relation between a geographical area and any map that purports to represent it.

Contemplation of the icon sooner or later tends to turn from legitimately semiotic concerns, in the technical sense, to intractable, indeed, mind-boggling philosophical problems of identity, analogy, resemblance and contrast (Ayer 1968:151), similarity and dissimilarity, arbitrariness and motivation, geometry and topology, nature and culture, space and time, life and death. The experience is like entering a fun house furnished with specular reflections and distorting mirrors, doubles and replicas, emphatic stimuli and superoptimal models, and being taken for a ride in the clair-obscure on one of Gombrich's (1951) pedigreed hobby horses. Eco, with his customary stylish wit, has recently provided his readers with some guideposts through this jungle of equivocations, not ignoring the final, possibly fatal, ambiguity that "everything resembles everything else" (1976:212).[7] To his animadversions upon the icon, let me add a couple of strictures of my own, the two I have referred to previously (Sebeok 1976:126ff.) as the issue of symmetry and the issue of regression.

About the issue of symmetry, Wallis (1975:2) asserted, *ex cathedra*, in line with preponderant tradition, that "The relation of representation is nonsymmetrical: an iconic sign . . . represents its representatum but not vice versa." Simplifying considerably, we can postulate that a Polaroid snapshot was taken of a reproduction of a famous painting, *La Giaconda*. The snapshot is now interpreted as an icon (more exactly, an iconic index; see note 2) of the copy, which then becomes its denotatum, or representatum, but which is itself, at the same time, an iconic sign for the original portrait, *its* denotatum, hanging at the Louvre. But the original painting, too, stands as an iconic sign for Leonardo's model, the lady known as Mona Lisa, *its* denotatum. In this diachronic sequence, Mona Lisa came first, her portrait next, then its reproduction, finally the Polaroid photograph of that. Although Peirce's definition speaks only of "a mere community in some quality," which would seem to apply backward in chronology just as well as forward, one might accept Wallis's further specification and arbitrarily assign a progressive temporal sequence in the relation of each successive model/replica pair involved in this example.

Note, however, the following, somewhat knottier example: suppose that a renowned contemporary personage, such as the Pope, is known to me (as he is to most Catholics) only through his image—photograph, lithograph, TV picture, or some other pictorial representation—but that, one day, I get to see him in the flesh, say, waving from a balcony at the Vatican. On that occasion, the living Pope would, for me, become an iconic sign for his long-familiar image, the real chronology of events notwithstanding.[8] This kind of disorientation is quite familiar to ethologists, however, who are not at all fazed by the prevailing reciprocity in iconic relationship expressed by every species vis-à-vis its environment: I have heard ornithologists claim that, by examining the alar structures of a bird, they are able to reconstruct, with amazing accuracy, the physical configuration of the area it habitually overflies, and vice versa; or, as Konrad Lorenz colorfully put it, "The form of a horse's hoof is just as much an image of the steppe it treads as the impression it leaves is an image of the hoof" (Introduction to Wickler 1973: xi). The issue of symmetry in the bondage of icon with object, or replica with model, does not, I think, allow for a simplistic resolution, and cannot be settled by an *a priori* dictum. Time's arrow—Eddington's apt phrase (Blum 1951), used here deliberately to imply the applicability of the second law of thermodynamics (augmentation of entropy) to general semiosis—must surely be anchored among the "wired-in" feature detectors of the brain, and be accounted for by a theory of perception underlying a theory of signs.

Turning to the vertiginous problem of regression, let me illustrate this by an obvious example from kinship: An infant daughter can be said to be an iconic sign (a "spitting image" perhaps) of her mother, since there is bound to be a topological resemblance between the child, the replica, and her mother, the model. However, the little girl can likewise, though doubtless in ever attenuated fashion, stand as an icon for her father, each of her siblings, all of her other relatives, and, further, all other members of the human race, past, present, and future, but also for all primates and, further still, all mammals, all chordates, and so on and on, in unending retrogression to ever more generalized denotata. This ceaseless brachiation is a necessary by-product of a universal law of biological isomorphism whereby any viable sign vehicle, or descendant, is able to re-engender a signified, or parent, on every occasion that the sign is interpreted (cf. Thom 1973:88) (more about this particular iconic interaction in the next section). The sole feature that distinguishes living matter from nonliving (including crystals, which grow, and even reproduce) is evolution by natural selection; it is not amiss to reaffirm here something I said in 1967, that the dynamics of semiosis is *the* criterial regulatory activity which contributes to the homeostasis of every animal and to the equilibrium of such groupings as social organisms belong to. Organisms—or, at least, their individual cells—are best defined in terms of replication, which is significant precisely because it confers no obvious benefit on the replicating entity; genetic copying is the semiotic process *par excellence*, and iconicity plays a pivotal role in it.

I should like now to restate, in distilled fashion, under six points, the highlights of my argument developed in this section:

1. The notion of icon, and allied concepts, were under continuous and, at certain periods, quite intense discussion throughout the centuries linking Plato to Peirce. The tendency of ideas to consort with one another because of similarity (vs., e.g., propinquity, imputation, causal connection, or whatever) became a powerful principle for explaining many mental operations, and thus an important chapter in the history of ideas, where the story was, as it still is, retold with infinite and exquisite variations.

2. Peirce's "resemblance-association" (1935–1966:1.313, 383, 502), out of which his icon must have crystallized, derives its startling novelty from being embedded in a progressively more complex, profound, and productive semiotic matrix, which is, moreover, conceived as both a theory of communication and a theory of signification. Although Peirce's classification of signs has become the one constant lodestar in debates about iconicity since 1867, the level of discussion is substantially diminished when the icon is, as is often done, quarantined from the total context of his unique brand of the doctrine of signs, or when the intricacies of his semiotic are insufficiently grasped (having perhaps been culled from secondary sources, or worse).

3. There are no pure iconic signs; in fact, "no actual sign is an icon" (Ayer 1968:140): the transformation of deiconization is frequent, the reverse process of iconization more seldom encountered. It is plausible to assume that there may be a diachronic tendency toward an equi-

librium in mixed systems of signs (such as the gesture-languages used in some deaf communities).

4. Iconicity plays a decisive role in shaping everyday life, in all cultures. Iconic signs suffuse man's communication codes, verbal no less than nonverbal.

5. Iconic signs are found throughout the phylogenetic series, in all modalities as circumscribed by the sense organs by which members of a given species are able to inform themselves about their environment. Signal forgery, viz., the phenomenon of mimicry, in fact, all deceptive maneuvering by plants and animals, as well as humans, often crucially depends on iconicity (cf. Sebeok 1976, Ch. 9).

6. Unsolved riddles concerning this pervasive mode of producing, storing, and transmitting iconic sign tokens abound. Some of these pertain to logic,[9] some to psycho-physiology, others to ethology. Their solution awaits the advent of new analytical tools, the most promising among which by far—for it shows how the process of copying operates throughout the molecular level, governs perception, imbues the communication systems of animals as well as of man, and constitutes a fundamental principle of sociobiology, in brief, is capable of integrating globally far-reaching problems of a universal character involving mutual dynamic relations between signifier and signified (Thom 1974b:245)—are likely to come from catastrophe theory (Stewart 1975), which, someday, will render them susceptible to topological analysis.

3

In Western civilization, the entire history of semiotics germinated in Antiquity. This ramiform tradition was then passed over into medieval Europe, and so on into the Renaissance. It was substantially enriched over all these centuries. Eventually, it reached a peak of sophistication in the work of Peirce, "who was the heir of the whole historical philosophical analysis of sign and," as we have already glimpsed in respect to his classification, "has himself had a major influence upon contemporary discussion" (C. Morris 1971:337; cf. Sebeok 1976:3-26, 150-156).

Around the turn of the last century, laboring entirely outside the grand philosophical currents that culminated in Peirce's semiotic, his contemporary, Ferdinand de Saussure, contributed to the progress of the field with much more modest restraint, departing from a strictly linguistic base, as well as with constant reference back to linguistic standards but wholly with a view to the future. Although Saussure never used the term, he did provide as a passing example of an iconic sign the scales of justice (Saussure 1967:155), representing the equilibrium between sin and punishment. The actual provenance of his ideas about the typology of signs remains a tantalizing mystery (it seems inconceivable to me, for instance, that Saussure should not have read Marie-Joseph Degérando's prize-winning essay on signs, where that famed *idéologue* singled out "une seconde espèce de signes institués que j'appellerai *imitatif*...," but no really hard evidence has survived about his bibliographic resources). However that may be, he appeared to have evinced no special interest in this problem, and, although his Franco-Swiss successor, Bally (1939), did so to a limited extent, and the best among his followers, the Belgian Buyssens (see Sebeok 1976:171ff., 164), made a constructive attempt to carry out Saussure's programmatic declaration, our common fund of knowledge about the theory of signs and symbols has not been materially enhanced in the Francophone tradition as framed by the "Saussure pattern" (Sebeok 1976:53). Yet the breakthrough in the field did ultimately originate in France, to wit, in Thom's brilliant foray into this aspect of semiotics, the generation of signs culminating in symbols. As he makes very clear at the outset of his paper, however, his point of inception had its specific source in the bequeathal of Peirce, not Saussure: "Toute discussion du symbolisme ne peut que partir de la classification des signes—si simple et si profonde—que nous a léguée Charles Sanders Peirce" (1973:85). It should surprise no one that Peirce's ideas, particularly about the icon, should have found so sympathetic an echo in the work of this distinguished creator of topological models, for Peirce expected his existential graphs to also explicitly contribute toward an understanding of topological laws (1935–1966: 4.428f.), indeed, his "system is topological throughout" (Gardner 1968:56ff.; cf. Eisele, in Peirce 1976:1/xvii, where she ascribes his penetration into topology to his association with Johns Hopkins University).

A cycle of 110 years now separates Peirce's earliest semiotic stirrings —a subject in which, he confided to Lady Welby late in 1908, he then became entirely absorbed from 1863 onward (Peirce 1935–1966: 8.376), in fact, until his death in 1914—from the publication date of what I have come to regard as the single most original and important paper in this field in modern times, Thom's epochal, if excessively laconic, 1973 essay. In the nontechnical comments on his achievements with which I propose to round out these remarks, I shall confine myself chiefly to what pertains to the icon, but not, of course, implying that Thom's ideas about indices and symbols do not merit equal consideration.

In good conformity with currently held scientific opinion, Thom (1975b:72f.) assumes that the principal role of the central nervous system of animals is to map out localized regions to simulate the position of the organism in its environment, as well as to represent objects, such as prey and predator, that are biologically and/or socially necessary for its survival or well-being. That is to say, an animal is constantly informed and impelled by meaning-bearing sign-vehicles designed to release pertinent motor reflexes (IRMs), such as approach (say, toward a prey) or withdrawal (say, from a predator), or surrogate verbal responses in the human, as in a transitive SVO sentence ("the shark consumes the porpoise"), a syntactic pattern which can be viewed as a temporal transcription of a biological event in space-time, predation, as its archetypal paradigm. Among animal behaviorists, Schneirla (1965: 2) has most persuasively argued, in support of his biphasic theory, that "operations which appropriately increase or decrease distance between organisms and stimulus sources must have been crucial for the survival of all animal types" in the evolution of behavior. Thom (1975b: 73) has extended this line of reasoning to man, who, he says, by his act of naming, "a remplacé la capture (ou la fuite) par la reconnaissance de la forme et l'évocation du concept correspondant." Semiotic (logical) interactions among concepts are "des images" (iconic representations) of space-time interactions among the objects referred to.

The genesis of icons was sketched, all too briefly, by Thom (1973: 86ff.). In countless instances, images appear naturally, but copies of this sort are ordinarily devoid of semiotic value: a man's shadow cast upon the ground, his shape reflected in water, his foot imprinted in sand. Such everyday spatial images are necessarily endowed with certain physical, viz., geometric properties, but they attain semiotic status only under special circumstances. For a shadow to be cast, as in the first example, the model must be illuminated by a luminous source, the light hitting the intervening body, thus defining its shadow. In the second example, a specular image is similarly formed in the reflecting surface. In neither example is the resulting image permanent: it is bound to vanish with the disappearance of the model (or luminous source). However, the third example illustrates a new phenomenon that Thom calls "plasticity" of the receptor system. The footprint doesn't necessarily decay when the foot is withdrawn (or the sun goes under): the formative stimulus alters the equilibrium of the receptor system when impressing the shape of the model; here the image becomes a memory trace (cf. Sakitt 1975)—as in front of Grauman's Chinese Theater, in Los Angeles, where the glory of Hollywood is but a memory trace. Thom designates the dynamic state involved in such a transaction "competence," implying the possibility of irreversible temporal interaction. A modification in the first example underlines the distinction: should a man's shadow be cast upon a photographic plate instead of the unsensitized ground, his image may forever be fixed owing to the competence of that receptor system.[10] Using the concepts suggested, one can envisage formation of images equistable with their models, or more so, as termite mound constructions faithfully display in, so to speak, "frozen," or fossilized products the social behavior of these great insect architects, becoming available for a study of their behavioral evolution long after the extinction of the colony itself (Emerson 1938; Frisch 1974).

At this stage, we can claim that life has been attained. A living being L fabricates, at some temporal remove, another living being L', isomorphic with L. L' will soon supplant L. The "hot dilute soup," in which Haldane suggested that the origin of life surely occurred, must have had Thom's feature of plasticity criterial among its metabolic processes which, by means so far unknown, eventually activated the genetic code, giving rise to a self-replicating, mutable molecular system that is also environment-sensitive. The process involved is foreshadowed by the kind of inorganic local explosion that occurs in photographic emulsification. It becomes particularly plain in embryological development, which—as I intimated in citing the Edelin paradigm—may be among the most dramatic forms of iconization in bionts: it is nature's design for unfolding the growth and differentiation of a structure isomorphic with the parent by virtue of a spatial-temporal translating operation. On the molecular level, this same mechanism is realized when the DNA double helix is replicated to generate two helices, each containing one old strand and one newly made one.

At the other end of the ontogenetic ladder of life, Thom invites us to consider the phenomenon of perception: this can be regarded as a modification of dynamic competence by the sensory impact of external reality, very much as Socrates had instructed Theaetetus.[11] Any competent system, for example, the mechanical and hydrodynamic components of the cochlear partition, and the acoustic cortex, or the retina and the visual cortex, etc., rapidly recovers its percipient virginity, indispensable for total and permanent competence, while its plastic faculty guarantees that the sense impressions remain stored in the memory.

In Thom's panoramic conspectus, the formation of icons appears throughout the entire scale of nature as a manifestation of a universal dynamic of irreversible character: a model ramifies into a replica isomorphic with it.[12] Frequently, however, this process employs a reversible interaction, due to the perennial oscillation of the thermodynamics between a Hamiltonian conservative viewpoint (expressed in the First Law), and the Heraclitean viewpoint, "time's arrow" (expressed in the Second Law): "la conciliation entre les deux points de vue n'a pu se faire qu'en réintroduisant le Créateur et sa chiquenaude initiale," as Thom (1973:88) is pleased to refer to the cosmogony popularly known as the "big bang hypothesis." In all interactions between the two indispensable moieties of the sign, recognized in virtually all accounts dealing with the foundations of the doctrine, ranging from Stoic philosophy to contemporary thinking (Sebeok 1976:117f.), the relation of signified to signifier must obey this universal flux: the signified engenders the signifier in an eternal process of branching. But the signifier re-engenders the signified each time that we interpret the sign.

In biological terms, this is to say that the descendant as signifier can become the parent as signified, given the lapse of one generation. "C'est par ce subtil balancement entre deux morphologies, par son exigence simultanée de réversibilité et d'irréversibilité," concludes Thom (ibid.), "que la dynamique du symbolisme porte en elle . . . toutes les contradictions de la vision scientifique du monde, et qu'elle est l'image même de la vie."

Thom has vastly more to say, albeit in brief compass, about the image which bears on deiconization, stylization, decomposition, aging, and death (cf. our Quinlan paradigm), drawing a far-reaching distinction—with, incidentally, thought-provoking implications for the syntax of natural languages—between the physical capacity of an icon to resist the noise factor inherent in any communicative intercourse, and its biological capacity to evoke other forms biologically or sociologically important or "interesting."

Seeking common cause with Peirce, Thom probes at the heart of signification. The transcendent feature of both is a soaring imagination. Their shared scientific instrument for the invention and discovery of new truths, as well as their device for reordering old ones, is a branch of mathematics capable of dealing with discontinuous and divergent phenomena, a special part of the theory of singularities. These two figures of charismatic depth bracket a century of more or less pedestrian divagations about the sign—denoting objects of the universe, Peirce cautioned, "perceptible, or only imaginable, or even unimaginable" (1935-1966:2.230)—as well as occasionally inspired extensions and applications of semiotic notions over most parts of the verbal or nonverbal domains. The genetic code, the metabolic code (the term refers to hormone-mediated intercellular transactions), the nonverbal communicative codes used in a very high number of organisms including man, our unique verbal code and its differential participation in all manner of artistic functions, whether literary, musical, pictorial, architectural, choreographic, theatrical, filmic, of diverse hybrid formations, and, finally, comparisons among any of the aforementioned—these were all on the agenda of twentieth-century semiotic science. Peirce and Thom cast a biunique spell that enthralls us, and it would be instructive to inquire sometime into the source of this fascination. It has marked the precursor with a "name of mysterious greatness" (as William James wrote to Charles Eliot in 1895, vainly trying to secure for Peirce even a temporary appointment at Harvard—see Perry 1935:416). As for Thom, the transforming additive is that his ideas about communication and signification, about the icon, the index, and the symbol, and about the emergence of man out of his animal ancestry, don't just hang there in limbo, but are firmly encased in a successful mathematical theory of great sophistication. This is called "catastrophe theory" (Stewart 1975), the results of which are being generalized not only to systems in physics, chemistry, and en-

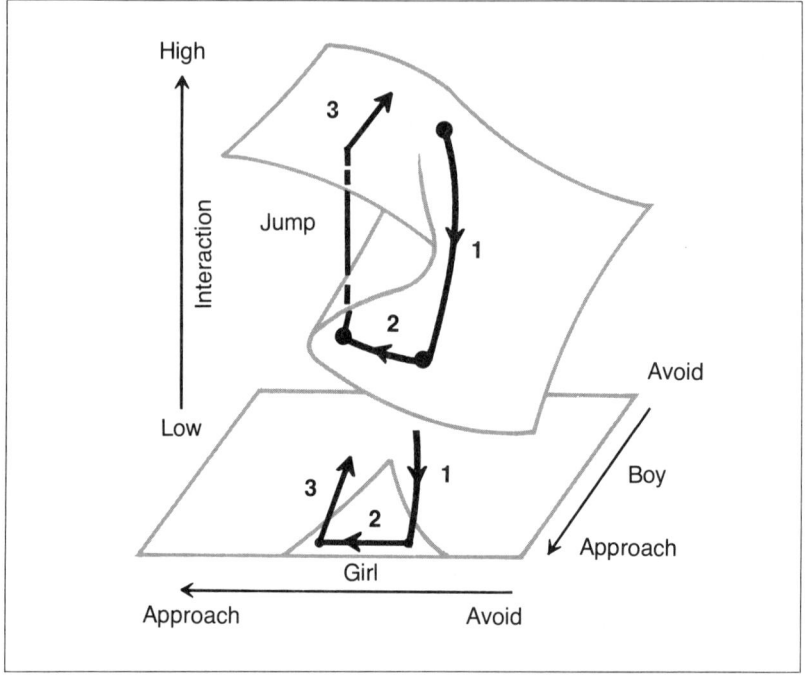

Figure 6-2. Illustration of how the meeting of a boy and girl can be a simple cusp catastrophe which can be diagrammed with accuracy. After Stewart 1975:454.

gineering, but beyond, to a wide range of problems in the biological and social sciences. In fact, Thom originally developed catastrophe theory in the mid-1960s with an eye on embryology, where his model could, in principle, account for each point of bifurcation as the development of a cell diverges from that of its immediate neighbors. Later, Thom extended his theory to evolution in general, reproduction, thinking, and, last but not least, the generation and transmission of verbal (Thom 1970; 1974b) and nonverbal signs. It so happens that images are a major feature of his theory; he has proved that, despite the almost limitless number of discontinuous phenomena that can exist, there are only a certain number of different images that actually occur. He called these "elementary catastrophes," and has shown that, in a space having no more than four dimensions (such as our "real" world), there are exactly seven such transformations. The practical uses of catastrophe theory in the much more complicated "soft" sciences, as in the study of economic growth, of social encounters (Fig. 6-2), or conversations, will be demonstrated as the presently employed crude models are gradually replaced by topological models with a small number of variables.

At any rate, Thom's work has been hailed as an "intellectual revolution" (Stewart 1975:447), the most important development since the calculus of Leibniz and Newton. I believe that his results also point in the direction which all branches of semiotics are bound to traverse in the decades ahead.

7. Aboriginal Sign "Languages" from a Semiotic Point of View

with D. Jean Umiker-Sebeok

In our culture, language, especially in its spoken manifestations, is the much vaunted hallmark of humanity, the diagnostic trait of man which has made possible the creation of a civilization unknown to any other terrestrial organism. Through our inheritance of a *faculté du langage*, culture is in a sense bred into man. And yet, language is viewed as a force which can destroy us through its potential for objectification and classification. According to popular mythology, the naming of the animals of Eden, while giving Adam and Eve a certain power over nature, also destroyed the prelinguistic harmony between them and the rest of the natural world and contributed to their eventual expulsion from paradise. Later, the post-Babel development of diverse language families isolated man from man as well as from nature (Steiner 1975). Language, in other words, as the central force animating human culture, is both our salvation and our damnation. Our constant war with words (Shands 1971) is waged on both internal and external battlegrounds.

This culturally determined ambivalence toward language is particularly apparent when we encounter humans or hominoid animals who, for one reason or another, must rely upon gestural forms of communication. Shakespeare provides a beautiful illustration of this theme in *The Tempest*, where the prospective semiotic colonization of the New World—through the transference to it of the English language—is conceived of as in effect the humanization of that world (Hawkes 1973:200). On the negative side, however, the reader is left with no doubt that such a transformation of the formally humanlike but speechless creatures which inhabit the island on which Shakespeare's characters have been shipwrecked will lead to the irreversible destruction of the harmonious relationship which exists among themselves and between them and their environment. The existing gestural com-

Note: This article, written in collaboration with Dr. D. Jean Umiker-Sebeok, is reprinted from *Ars Semeiotica: International Journal of American Semiotics* 1:69–97 (1977). All illustrations, however, are added here for the first time, from *Aboriginal Sign Languages of the Americas and Australia*, ed. Umiker-Sebeok and Sebeok (New York: Plenum Press, 1978), in which our text reappeared in abridged form (1:xiii–xxxii; 2:xv–xxxiv). A Polish translation will appear in *Studia Semiotyczne* (1979).

Figure 7-1. Conversing in the Sign Language. From Humfreville 1897:152.

munication of the islanders is viewed as an important part of their present harmony:

> *Gonzalo* For, certes, these are people of the island,—
> Who, though they are of monstrous shape, yet, note,
> Their manners are more gentle-kind than of
> Our human generation you shall find
> Many, nay, almost any.
>
> *Prospero* Honest lord,
> Thou hast said well; for some of you there present
> Are worse than devils.
>
> *Alonso* I cannot too much muse, [Aside]
> Such shapes, such gesture, and such sound, expressing,—
> Although they want the use of tongue,—a kind
> Of excellent dumb discourse.
>
> (*The Tempest*, Act III, Scene 3)

Encounters with people practiced in some form of conventional gestural system have tended, in varying degrees, to evoke conflicting emotions. On the one hand, our interlocutor, whether an Australian aborigine, an Indian of the North American Plains, or even a deaf compatriot, does not strike us as quite "human" because he does not communicate to us in a spoken language which we are able to understand. On the other hand, his use of an elaborate set of significative gestures, while not quite conferring full humanness upon him, appeals to us as a graceful and "dignified" form of communication ideally suited to service as a universal *lingua franca*, a bridge between men speaking mutually incomprehensible tongues, or, in recent years, with other, non-human primates, and thus in one way at least superior to spoken language.

Aboriginal sign languages, in particular the Plains Sign Language (hereafter PSL), have long captivated the imagination of the non-scientific world by thus holding out the promise of an escape from what Nietzsche called our prison-house of language. "Probably no other phase of Indian culture," writes Harrington (in Hofsinde 1941: 33) "has proved so interesting to the American public at large." As every American Boy Scout knows, a simplified version of PSL has long been a part of Boy Scout tradition (see, e.g., Beard 1918). Numerous volumes have been written with the general adult population in mind (e.g., Clark 1885; Cody 1952; 1970; Hadley 1890; 1893; Hofsinde 1956; Seton 1918; W. Tomkins 1929), and reprintings and new editions of these continue to appear. While PSL is presented to the public as a practical system of communication for use in certain outdoor activities where spoken language is undesirable, it is likely that what actually sells copies of such works is the almost mystical view of the

Aboriginal Sign "Languages" 131

Figure 7-2. Communication by signs: *A*. Friend or foe? "Standing off" Indians. *B*. A powwow with the Cheyennes in the Sign Language. From Humfreville 1897:156.

sign language projected by the authors, as, for example, in the following passage on the back cover of Cody 1970: "For many centuries countless warriors, traders and travelers have refined and developed this beautiful, silent language of the hands until almost any common meaning can be expressed. It is a language that is a part of nature itself, the fluttering of aspen leaves under the touch of the wind, a hawk soaring in the sky, the ponderous movement of buffalo herds, the gestures of wise old Indians of the great warrior days who were one with earth and heaven, the rhythm of waterfalls pouring over cliffs or of clouds drifting over the sacred circle of the blue above us." In recent years PSL has become a significant part of both the revival of tribal identity among Plains Indians and the correlated renewal of curiosity about the Plains Indian culture among non-Indian Americans (Kroeber 1972). Taylor (1978) reports its continued use in storytelling, where signs accompany the spoken narrative or vice versa; the sign dance, where dancers carry on a dialogue in sign language (see the description in Dodge 1882); and for formal oratory within councils or powwows (see the descriptions in West 1960). In these oratorical and ceremonial contexts, the "poetry, dramatic thought, and oratorical fire" (Scott quoted in Weil 1931:8) of PSL have become a self-conscious emblem of Plains Indian culture. Further evidence of this is supplied by West (1960), who notes that, among some tribal groups, more young people appeared to understand PSL than did older tribal members. Furthermore, PSL is now a part of the curriculum for some tribal school programs aimed at increasing ethnic awareness.

If the strong and immediate appeal of aboriginal sign language has its roots in their function as a form of mediation between the "natural" and "cultural" sides of "the talking animal," their fulfillment of this function can be attributed to the fact that they are representatives of a type of semiotic system uniquely qualified to fill a gap in our Western conception of the order or structure of the bounded universe of human and animal sign systems. As we shall see below, with the possible exception of sign languages of the deaf, the semiotic nature of aboriginal sign languages is unlike that of any other sign system by virtue of the combination of the following characteristics:

(1) Aboriginal sign languages are a complex of both natural and conventional sign relations, with, however, iconic and indexical elements outweighing symbolic ones (the reverse of the hierarchy prevailing in spoken languages).

(2) Aboriginal sign languages are semantically open both in the sense that they may be used to formulate a potentially indefinite number of messages and that the lexicon may be enlarged to suit changing demands on the system (as in spoken languages).

(3) Aboriginal sign languages are presumed to take advantage of a species-consistent (nonverbal) competence, but each sign system must be learned (a situation analogous to spoken languages).

Aboriginal Sign "Languages" 133

Figure 7-3. Tipi. Posed by Gray Wolf (Bob Hofsinde). From Harrington 1938, no. 11:29.

(4) Aboriginal sign languages make use of a visual channel of communication (and thus the roles played by the principles of successivity and simultaneity differ considerably from those found in spoken languages; cf. Sebeok, in Hailman 1977:xv–xix).

The first of the two characteristics of aboriginal sign languages noted above which set them apart from spoken language (nos. 1 and 4) is the highly "natural" relationship between their signifiers and signifieds. Kohl (1860:34), for example, describes the signs of PSL as "natural, characteristic, and easy of comprehension," Webb (1931:69) as "natural" and "universal," the "mother utterance of nature." They are "figurative" (Humfreville 1899:109) and possess "picturesque clarity" (Hofsinde 1941:32) and "picturesque novelty" (Scott 1898:219). Another early observer, Wassell, attributed the "metaphorical" character of the sign language to the poetic nature of the "savages" (1896:584), explaining that Indians are extremely sensitive to meaning in nature and therefore better qualified to develop sign language (ibid.:581). Use of the terms *picturesque, figurative,* and *metaphorical* adumbrates the iconic relationship between signifier and signified in PSL. Another favorite word used to convey the iconic character of aboriginal sign language signs is *pantomime* (see, e.g., Taylor 1978). "As one studies the sign language," Kroeber writes, "one becomes aware it is overwhelmingly pantomimic. Many signs are quite transparent, especially if one knows the culture. One begins to follow partly even on first contact, though no complete stranger would grasp much continuity. Other signs appear as 'reasonable' once one has learned their meaning by context, association, or explanation. This semantic near-intelligibility must have made the system rather readily learnable" (1972:xxiv). Kroeber suggests that a more accurate term than *pantomimic* would be *cheiromimic* (ibid.),[1] since imitation in PSL is in general restricted to the hands and arms rather than the entire body.

The signs of the Australian aboriginal sign language (hereafter AASL) also appear to be highly iconic, "imitating the most conspicuous outlines of an object or the most striking features of an action" (Berndt 1940:267–268), or, as another author writes, "characteristic of the reference" (Meggitt 1954:7). La Mont West, the only person to have done intensive field work with both AASL and PSL, implies (1963:162) that 95 percent of both systems involve "concrete symbolization of a view of the world by the selection of one or another distinctive feature to represent an object or an animal." According to the estimate of W. Miller (1978), 62 percent of the signs collected from the aborigines residing at the Warburton Mission were "iconic."

While the terms used to describe natural signs in aboriginal sign languages generally stress iconicity, natural signs, as traditionally distinguished from conventional ones, or, as they are sometimes called, symbols, are also based on the semiotic relationship of metonymy or *indexicality*, which plays a very important role in the structure of aboriginal sign languages. Harrington (1938), for example, notes that one of "the two fundamental component factors in the building up of the American Indian sign language" is "indication by gesturing at, or painting," the latter term being used by signers to designate what others might call *outlining* (ibid.: 5 : 11 : 29–31). By gesturing (or pointing), signers designate (1) cardinal directions and regions, (2) personal and demonstrative pronouns ("subjective, objective, indirective, and possessive"), (3) body parts of one's own body, and (4) colors "of almost universal occurrence in nature, such as black and white." Gesturing at the locality of occurrence of something "replaces indication of the object or abstraction," as, for example, in the sign for *to think, thought*, where the signer gestures at his own heart then brings his hand forward, thus combining "gesturing at locality of occurrence plus action mimicry." In painting, or delineating, the signer "outlines the figure of an object by tracing it with the hand or hands in mid-air" (ibid.). West, applying Harrington's categories to his own data, states that such deictic signs account for more than half of his basic units of analysis, or kinemes,[2] and nearly all of those of restricted occurrence. West further concludes that these indexical signs "comprise an open end to the kinemic system, where new kinemes of limited recurrence may be freely introduced without disruption of the more closed kinemic system participated in by nondeictic signs" (1960 : 1 : 94).

Perhaps because aboriginal sign languages first attracted amateur scientists and later, beginning in the 1950s, professional linguists caught up in an overly narrow type of formalism, aboriginal sign language studies have largely remained outside the tradition of semiotics, and nowhere in the literature does one find a consistent application of a classification of signs which incorporates a coherent and systematic distinction between the interdependent iconic and indexical sign relations prevailing in these sign languages. Harrington's analysis of PSL signs as combinations of two or more of either indexical relations or "representation by substitution or by mimicking" perhaps comes closest to a coherent semiotic classification of sign types and amply illustrates for us the complexity of describing such a visual system of communication. For example, the signs for certain colors are listed under his category of pointing or gesturing at, since, for example, the color black is indicated by pointing at one's eyebrows, hair, or some black object nearby (ibid.: 31). While this sign does involve the use of the index finger and a pointing gesture, the sign represents black by virtue of a similarity between the color of, for example, the eyebrow and the quality designated, and thus is an iconic sign rather than an indexical one (cf. Sebeok, 1976 : 129, n. 3). The pointing at an eyebrow would be an indexical sign if it referred to the eyebrow. Similarly, several of his categories of substitution, that is, where "a body part of the sign user . . . and its posture is made to represent . . . the object or abstraction" (ibid.: 31), involve mimicking actions, but

136 The Sign

1. Cardinal Directions

Up. Point Index Upward.
H H 15.

Down. Point Index Downward.

2. Personal And Demonstrative Pronouns

I, me, my. Point Index At Chest. H I 1.

Me, 2nd element in: tell me! Place hand palm up, tip of hand forward, at chin, then jerk hand backward. H T 11.

You, your. Point index at 2nd person, real or imaginary. H Y 5.

You, 2nd element in: I tell you. Place hand palm up, tip of hand forward, then jerk hand forward. H I 12.

He, him, his, visible. Point in backhanded manner toward 3rd person. H H 20, H H 22.

He, etc., invisible. Gesture in backhanded manner toward rear. H H 22.

This, here, that, there. Point index at object or locality. H P 17, H P 18.

3. Body Parts

Ear. Point at ear. H E 1. But to hear is action mimicking: hold cupped hand behind ear.

Throat. Point at throat.

4. Certain Colors

Black. Point at eyebrows, at hair, or at some black object near one.

White. Point at some white object near one (hardly at one's own teeth, for that would be misunderstood).

Figure 7-4. From Harrington 1938, no. 11:30–31.

Aboriginal Sign "Languages"   137

II. <u>Gesturing</u> <u>At</u> <u>Locality</u> <u>of</u> <u>Occurrence</u>. Gesturing at, or other indications of, the place of occurrence replaces indication of the object or abstraction. This is contained, e.g., as the first element in the sign to think, thought.

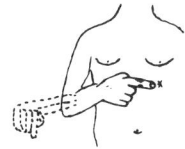

<u>To think</u>, <u>thought</u>. Gesture at heart, and then bring hand forward, to gesture thought coming forth from the heart. Gesturing at locality of occurrence plus action mimicry.

III. <u>Painting</u>. The various spoken languages of the sign talkers call this element "painting." We would call it outlining. One outlines the figure of an object by tracing it with the hand or hands in mid-air.

<u>Wheel</u>, <u>wagon</u>. Paint vertical circle with index. By modifying the tracing of circles, several wheels and the going or coming of a wheeled vehicle is indicated.

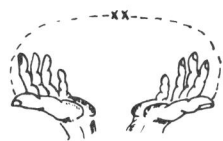

<u>Vault</u>, <u>sunrise</u>, <u>sunset</u>, <u>noon</u>. Hold spread thumb and index down toward left and paint semicircle moving toward right, first up and then down. H S 55.

<u>Corral</u>. Bring both open hands together and paint away from self horizontal outline of a corral, each hand describing semicircle. H C 26.

V. <u>Action</u> <u>Mimicry</u>. The sign user's hand or body part is made to mimic or imitate the action or motion, actual or desired, of an object or abstraction.

         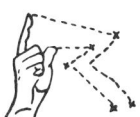

<u>To go</u>, <u>go</u> <u>away</u>! <u>To shoo</u> <u>away</u>. Gesture forward extended hand, palm turned to left.

<u>To come</u>, <u>come</u>! Beckon toward chest. H C 22.

<u>To twinkle</u>. Snap index by releasing it from end of thumb.

<u>To lighten</u>. Elevate index and with hand trace downward zigzag path of lightning.

138 The Sign

VI. <u>Instrument Action Mimicry</u>. The mimicking of the action of an instrument gets across the idea of the instrument.

<u>Awl</u>. Bore right index into left palm.

<u>Saw</u>. Mimic the action of sawing.

VII. <u>Preparation Mimicry</u>. The more strikingly mimicked action of preparation replaces the less strikingly mimicked finished product.

<u>Bread</u>. Strike first one palm and then the other into each other alternately, like patting a cake of dough. H B 47.

<u>Flour</u>. Rub back and forth across the palm side of the extended fingers of the left hand with the palm side or ball of the thumb of the right hand to mimic the action of grinding flour according to the Indian method, the fingers representing the rough understone or metate, the thumb representing the upperstone, handstone, or mano; then, if one desires, define further by pointing at something white and then making the sign for bread.

VIII. <u>Effect Mimicry</u>. The more strikingly mimicked effect or result replaces the less strikingly mimicked object which produces the effect or result.

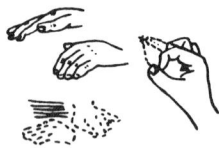

<u>Star</u>: compound of night plus to twinkle. Night. Draw hands, backs up from each side and cross them before the body. H N 6.
To twinkle. See above.

<u>Salt</u>, <u>sour</u>, <u>bitter</u>: compound of to taste plus bad. To taste: Put extended index cautiously to mouth. Bad: Mimic the action of a throwing away by closing the fist, carrying it to the right, and opening it.

Figure 7-5. From Harrington 1938, no. 11:32; no. 12:25, 28, 29.

Aboriginal Sign "Languages" 139

XIV. Characteristic Accompaniment Added. An accompaniment or outline, though actually mostly absent, is added for distinguishment, as classifiers are added to fundamentals in Chinese writing.

Horse, rider, to ride. Straddle horizontally extended index with 2 fingers of other hand to represent horse and rider. If desired, mimic galloping action.

Ridge. Hook index over upper edge of inward-turned other palm.

XV. Characteristic Outline For A Whole.

House. Place indexes to form an inverted V, tips uncrossed.

Tipi. Place indexes to form an inverted V, tips crossed to show poles projecting from top of tipi.

XVI. Characteristic Part For A Whole. A characteristic part for a whole is painted or substituted.

Mountain-sheep, bighorn. Bring hands to temples, then paint outline of curve of mountain-sheep's horns. Compare Irving, Astoria: "The bighorn is so named from its horns." (Irving, Astoria, 1855, p. 240.)

Buffalo. Hold hands on head with erect indexes curved outward and then inward at the tip to substitute for the horns of a buffalo.

XVII. Characteristic Action For A Whole. A strikingly mimicked fragment of an activity represents the entire activity, and connected object.

To snow, snow. Hang extended hand loosely, then paint sunwise circle several revolutions to show swirling, characteristic partial action denoting the whole action of to snow, and snow H S 37.

To pack up. Strike right palm on back of left hand, first on thumb side, then on little finger side. H P 1.

Match. Mimic with index on forearm the striking of a match, partial action denoting the whole action of the match, and match.

the action mimicked is not the signified of the sign but stands for the signified through an indexical relationship. For example, *bread* is used as an illustration of "preparation mimicry," where "the more strikingly mimicked action of preparation replaces the less strikingly mimicked finished product" (ibid.:5:12:25). It is indicated by imitating the kneading of a piece of dough. It is not the kneading of the dough which is the signified, nor in fact the dough, but the finished, baked bread, which stands in existential relationship to the dough. The same may be said of Harrington's categories "effect mimicry," "characteristic outline for a whole," "characteristic part for a whole," and "characteristic action for a whole."

It is the combination of iconicity and indexicality with a substantial amount of conventionalization which is seen by most authors as determining the great potential of aboriginal sign languages as a means of communication which could rival spoken language in its range of expression and semantic flexibility. Writing about PSL, Dodge (1882: 380–384), for example, notes that it is the ever increasing conventionality, or transformation of natural signs into arbitrary ones, which has enabled PSL to become expressively adaptive. Maclean (1896: 486), discussing gestural communication in general, claims that "it is properly designated a language, as among savage races it has various conventional forms, which are in a measure definite and full." Kroeber expresses this well:

> When we correctly grasp a pantomimic sign-language gesture, we have a sense of achievement, are pleased, and remember the meaning. When a gesture is puzzling, or we can conjecture several meanings for it, we feel baffled. The result is that we tend to overestimate the pantomimic transparency of the system, or at least to assume that such a transparency lies just below the surface, which is certainly not necessarily always the case. It seems reasonable to believe that the great majority of signs are representative of mimicking *in origin*, possibly all of them. But what is characteristic of the sign language as an effective system of communication is precisely that it did *not* remain on a level of naturalness, spontaneity, and full transparency, but made artificial commitments, arbitrary choices between potential expressions and meanings. (1972:xxx)

Placing the cupped hand before the mouth might be universally recognized as a sign for drinking, but its extension "to denote water in such meanings as *lake* and *island* and *drown* is a specific convention of the Plains sign language" (ibid.:xxix).

As Kroeber mentions, the important role played by iconic and indexical signs in PSL has not uncommonly given casual observers of sign language performances the impression that messages can be decoded without prior training. Voegelin (1972:xxxvi) also remarked that, in response to sign language films, "most casual observers cannot resist making a guess or two at decoding. But the same observers never attempt to decode spoken Arapaho when they hear it played back from a tape recorder." Discussing claims such as these, West (1960:2:7) reports that the comprehension tests of "naïve" subjects which he conducted as a part of his own research resulted in extremely low scores for the identification of individual lexical items and an even lower comprehension of entire sign language texts. This corroborates Humfreville's statement (1899:109) that "the sign language . . . was highly significant, though it was necessary to follow closely the thread of conversation, for the wrong interpretation of a single sign was sufficient to break the whole chain of thought."

While the conventional nature of PSL has been debated now for over a century, the following summary statement by one of the early contributors to this debate still rings true: "Some writers, as Captain H. Stansbury, consider the system purely arbitrary; others, Captain Marcy, for instance, hold it to be a natural language similar to the gestures which surd-mutes use spontaneously. Both views are true, but not wholly true. . . . The pantomimic vocabulary is neither quite conventional nor the reverse" (Burton 1862:135).

Regarding AASL, Howitt (1904:726) wrote that it "formed part of a recognized and well understood system of artificial language." The conventional nature of AASL was also noted by, among others, Roth (1897), Basedow (1925), Spencer and Gillen (1927), West (1963), and W. Miller (1978). Miller estimated that 38 percent of the signs he collected were "arbitrary." Meggitt (1954:7) remarks that, while some of the Walbiri signs appeared iconic to him, and some to the natives, others were "characteristic" to neither.

The second characteristic of aboriginal sign languages noted above —that is, semantic openness—is one which they share with spoken languages. Aboriginal sign languages are not simple semiotic systems in the sense that there is a small number of signifiers, each with one fixed conventional signified. Mallery emphasizes that PSL "is not a mere semaphoric repetition of motions to be memorized from a limited traditional list, but is a cultivated art" (1972:346), a "general system rather than . . . a uniform code," with "generic unity, not specific identity" (1880b:15). As Mounin has pointed out (1973:157), Mallery's notion of an *art* is strikingly similar to current notions of an integrated linguistic *system*. If aboriginal sign languages were simple semiotic systems, as is sometimes implied by the watered-down versions presented in popular handbooks, they could be easily learned from the appropriate use of code-books. But, as one author (Scott 1898:220) has noted in regard to PSL, those who have tried to acquire through written materials the skills necessary for signing have soon aban-

Figure 7-6. "Two and Three Are Five" and Uinta Utes conversing in the Sign Language. From Humfreville 1897:154.

doned their plans in favor of on-the-spot training with accomplished sign language users. This pedagogical situation parallels that of foreign language learning.

There is ample evidence that the Plains Indians employed sign language in a great variety of contexts, both casual and formal, and for the expression of a seemingly limitless range of abstract as well as concrete ideas. Some authors (for example, Axtell 1891:507) even maintained that the PSL was more flexible and expressive than some Indian tongues. Scott (quoted in Weil 1931:9) asserted that anything could be expressed in PSL. Maclean (1896:495) attested the fact that Indians could maintain "intelligent conversation for hours" using only PSL. Harrington (in Hofsinde 1941:33) wrote that "by a system of several hundred signs, representing all the parts of speech, the Indians of the Plains conversed together with a flow of motions which equalled the articulatory dignity of spoken speech."

Certain of the Australian aboriginal groups appear to have possessed semantically open sign systems. Stirling (1896:111), for example, tells us that "these signs constituted ... a very extensive system of gesture language, which is not only much used but is capable of indicating a very large number of objects, as well as simple ideas concerning them." The natives accompanying Stirling's party were frequently observed to carry on "a more or less continuous and ... certainly intelligible silent conversation." A year later, Roth (1897:72) reported that animals, plants, and other objects of the natural world, manufactured objects, individuals, simple and complex actions or states, number, place, interrogation, and abstract notions could all be expressed with AASL. Howitt (1904:723) also remarks that "some [tribes] have a very extensive code of signs, which admit of being so used as to almost amount to a medium of general communication," and Basedow (1925:389–390) reported that "an almost inexhaustible number of ideas can be communicated in the form of coherent 'speech'." Meggitt (1954:3) specified that the Walbiri had a very wide range of signs which could stand as substantives, verbs, adjectives, and adverbs, which could be arranged in "grammatical expressions paralleling those in spoken Walbiri" to form "whole conversations" using only AASL. West (1963:160) estimated the size of the AASL lexicon to be similar to the impressive PSL lexicon discussed in his dissertation (1960).

A second point which needs to be made regarding the conventional nature of the signs of aboriginal sign languages is that, rather than being wholly "natural" (that is, iconic or indexical) or "conventional," they are always a subtle blend of both, and the hierarchical arrangement between the natural and conventional sign relations is constantly shifting, both at the level of individual signing performances and that of the sign language as an abstract system shared by a heterogeneous group of signers.

At the level of sign language as shared by a group of signers, the linguist Sayce (1880:93) remarked that "care must be taken to distinguish between two things which are frequently confused together.

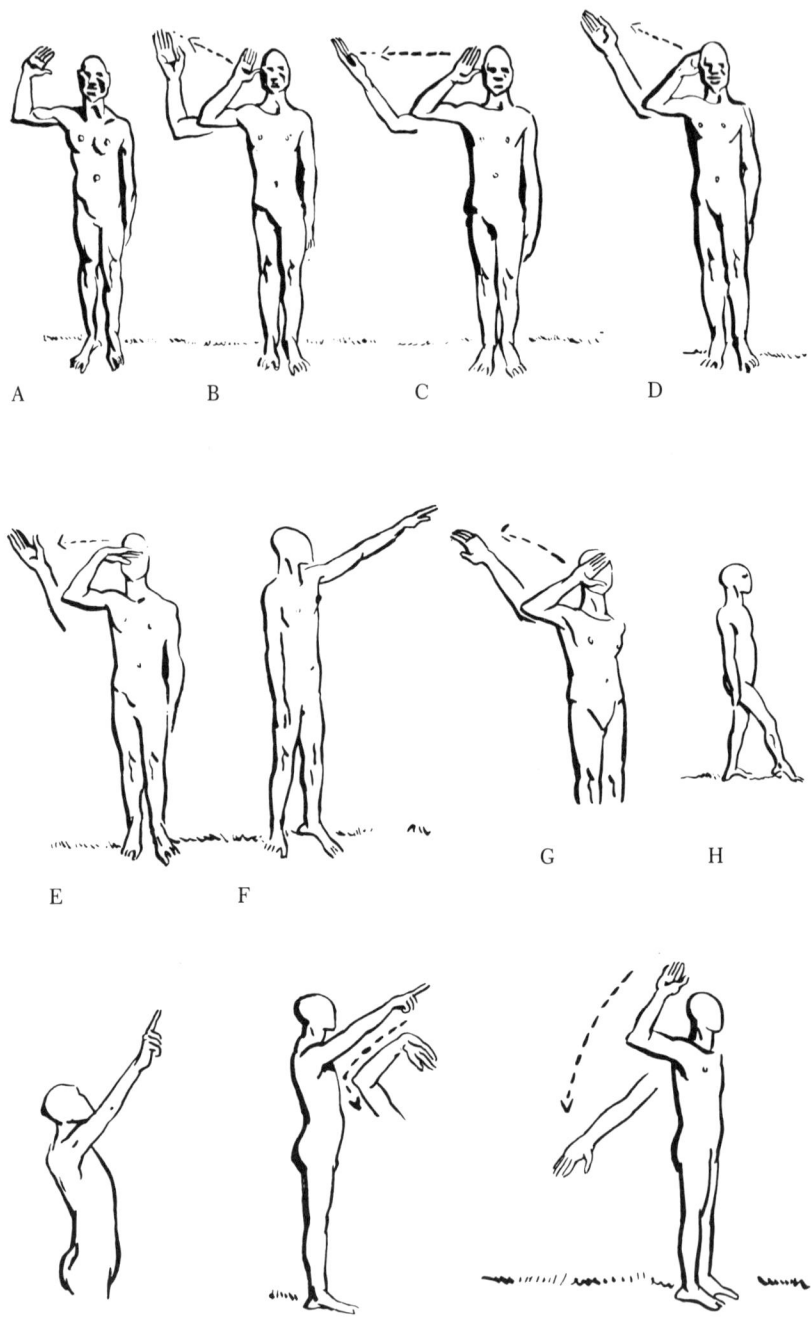

Figure 7-7. A conversation in sign language.

 A. The man stands upright, looking toward the other, who is walking away. The hand is held palm outward, and at the same time an exclamation of attraction [a] or [er] is made. The other, attracted not by sound or by having seen the sign, but because he "feels he is being wanted," turns and observes his friend.

 B. The first places his hand to his head and then extends the arm sideways, with the palm of the hand facing outward.

 C. The other answers, thereby asking what the first is wanting; he places the hand to the head and then extends the arm sideways, so that the hand is turned. At the same time he exclaims, ["'a?"] "What?"

 D. The first, thinking that he will not bother the other, responds by placing his hand behind his head and then extending the arm outward, so that the palm of the hand is open and faces outward, saying ["Ma ŋop:eilu"] "Go walk on."

 The other continues his walk. However, the first-named, on further consideration, realizes that he would like to know where the other is going. He again uses the sign as in *A*.

 E. Continuing the conversation, the first man, placing his hand, fingers close together and palm downward, in front of his face, and then extending his arm sideways with the palm of the hand facing outward, signals and says, ["'Jalwund?"] "Where you go?"

 F. The other, in replying, fully extends his left arm (in all the other movements the right arm is used) and points in the direction he intends going, saying, ["'ŋuwi"] "Over there," or "Down there."

 G. Information having been received, a different sign is used to express an ending. The first, flexing the arm, places his hand in front of his face, thumb extended; the arm is then fully extended, a little to the back, and the hand turned inward. At the same time he says, ["'Ma"] "Go on."

 H. Thereupon the departing one turns and walks away.

 After going a short distance the traveler may see something to which he wishes to draw attention. He uses the sign illustrated by *A*, transmitting at the same time the "idea" so that the first should "feel he is wanted." This man, when attracted, will respond with a sign as in *C*.

 I. The other then extends his arm upward, with the index finger pointing, the others folded back, and says, ["Na'rindjera"] "Many (people)."

 The first, not quite understanding, will then use the sign in *C*, saying, ["'a?"] "What?"

 J. Thereupon the informant again extends his arm upward, as in the position shown in *I*, and brings it downward, with the hand drawn in so that the thumb is at the back and fingers loose, saying to himself, [Na'rindjera lari"] "Many (people) coming down (the river)."

 K. The first holds his arm up, the palm of the hand facing outward, and then brings it down so that the palm now faces the ground, saying, ["Kal'lur"] "All right (or very well)."

 From R. M. Berndt, "Notes on the Sign-Language of the Jaraldi Tribe of the Lower River Murray, South Australia," *Transactions of the Royal Society of South Australia* 64(2):269, 271, copyright 1940 by the Royal Society of South Australia.

Gestures and *signs* are wholly different, gestures being natural, signs more or less conventional. A *gesticulation* is a gesture which has become a sign, and the nearer signs approach to gesticulations the more readily and instinctively they will be understood."[3] While new signs may be created using metaphoric and/or metonymic sign relations, to the extent that they are in fact a part of the sign system, that is, are used repeatedly by a community of sign language practitioners, they must be conventional at least to a certain degree. This is acknowledged by the majority of authors concerned with aboriginal sign languages. Regarding PSL, for example, both Mallery and West cite the linguist Whitney (1867) concerning the relative degrees of mimicry and the idea that there are no truly "representational" sign language gestures (see Mallery 1880a; 1880b; 1880c; 1884; 1972; West 1960).[4]

The conventional nature of the aboriginal sign language signs does not, however, prevent them from being usable as a mode of communication between individuals who come into contact with practitioners of sign languages other than their own. While, as noted above, it is doubtful whether persons unfamiliar with sign language are capable of comprehending sign language messages without a good deal of background training, the case is less clearcut concerning reports that persons practiced in some form of conventional sign language are, after minimal practice, capable of communicating effectively with one another through gesture. West proposes the following explanation for the possible validity of such reports:

> It is the combination of self-evident pantomime in the shape and motion and relationship kinemes and the general similarity of combination conventions that makes possible the ready communication between any two sign language users, whatever the provenience and degree of similarity of their respective sign systems. Another important factor in such intercommunication is the high redundancy of all sign languages. . . . We are faced with two general possibilities for communication between adepts of different languages. Each party to the communication may select the most highly pantomimic signs in his own or the other's system and use these for the duration of the conversation . . . but Scott and Bell point up the other alternative, which involves abandonment of the signs conventionally accepted in either or both sign languages and the creation of new, spontaneously pantomimic signs acceptable to the other party, by the application of generally shared principles of pantomimic construction. In such a case we have to deal not with a language at all, but pantomimic artistry. . . . In practice, of course, both the alternatives are extensively utilized. Thus the "gesture language of mankind" turns out to be not a language at all, but a combination of generally shared tech-

niques for selecting, improving, redundantly supplementing or abandoning and substituting new pantomimes for the bodies of conventionalized signs available in the respective sign languages of the conversationalists. Since these very techniques are part of the grammatical systems of each of the sign languages investigated by the writer, communication with a representative of an alien sign language is simply an extension and intensive use of the resources of the home sign language. This adequately explains the reported ability of intelligent and experienced sign language adepts to communicate with each other across language boundaries and the usual inability of poor sign talkers or individuals with no sign language experience to do so. (West 1960: 2:55–56)

One can see at work here the forces leading to the constant shifting of the balance between natural and conventional sign relations. Because, as Mallery states, "meaning does not adhere to the phonetic presentation of thought, while it does to signs" (1880b:5), the opportunity is present in every interaction involving sign language, whether between interlocutors trained in the same or different sign languages, that the pragmatics of the communication context will favor emphasis of one type of sign relation over another, thus shifting the hierarchical arrangement among sign aspects with respect to the particular context of interaction and potentially the sign system as a whole.

Despite his amateur standing as a scientist and his failure to carry out a consistent and systematic semiotic analysis of aboriginal sign languages, Mallery nevertheless approached his subject from a broad, comparative semiotic point of view. His use of the term *semiotics* (as in *native semiotics* in 1880b:4) is to our knowledge one of the earliest. In addition, he employed the expressions *semiotic code* (e.g., 1880b: 39; 1972:320), *semiotic execution* (e.g., 1972:74), and *semiotic expression* (e.g., 1972:88). We share the puzzlement of Mounin (1973: 154–156) about the source of Mallery's terminology. As he points out, Mallery gives no indication of having known of the work of Charles Sanders Peirce, and Mallery is never named by Peirce.[5] Whatever the sources of his inspiration were, the fact is that Mallery's comparison of aboriginal sign languages, especially PSL, with other auditory and visual systems in terms of a broad semiotic typology has in many respects yet to be surpassed.

First, Mallery's discussion of the hierarchical arrangement between natural and conventional sign relations anticipates Stokoe's (1974a: 127) conclusion that, while the American sign language of the deaf "can serve human language capacity as fully as can an sSign language, . . . even in as developed a language as ASL," there remains an important element of iconicity and indexicality not found in spoken language (i.e., an sSign language). It would appear that, if one were to position these three types of semiotic systems along a continuum from most natural to most conventional, sign languages of the deaf would fall somewhere between the other two.

Mallery also compares aboriginal and deaf sign languages with regard to the varying degrees to which each is influenced by spoken language. His analysis, while showing the similarities between the two visual systems in this regard, nevertheless reveals some critical ways in which aboriginal sign languages bear the imprint of spoken language where sign languages of the deaf do not. Mallery pointed out (e.g., 1880b:58) that the meanings of PSL signs are context sensitive and, furthermore, not simple representations of spoken words. "So far from the signs representing words as logographs, they do not in their presentation of ideas of actions, objects, and events, under physical forms, even suggest words" (ibid.:57–58). Stokoe's much later (1974a:118) caution that the gSigns of sign languages of the deaf cannot be relegated to simple "code representations, either as speech surrogates (1 gSign = 1 word) or of alphabetical symbols" would appear to apply as well to aboriginal sign languages. Moreover, as Buyssens notes (1967), unlike even as speech-independent a writing system as Chinese, one does not have to know the spoken language of the PSL signer in order to understand signed messages.

On the other hand, Mallery anticipated Stokoe's (1972:17) definition of PSL as a speech surrogate due to the fact that spoken language is the "primary" semiotic system of aboriginal signers, while, for the deaf, it is their sign language which is the primary semiotic system and therefore a true sign "language." Mallery writes:

> ... at the Pennsylvania Institution for the Deaf and Dumb in 1873, it was remarked that the signs of the deaf-mutes were much more readily understood by the Indians than were theirs by the deaf-mutes, and that the latter greatly excelled in pantomimic effect. This need not be surprising when it is considered that what is to the Indian a mere adjunct or accomplishment is to the deaf-mute the natural mode of utterance, and that there is still greater freedom from the trammel of translating words into actions—instead of acting the ideas themselves—when, sound of words being unknown, they remain still as they originated, but another kind of sign, even after the art of reading is acquired, and do not become entities as with us. (1880b:39–40)

While it is obvious that there is always present the possibility of intersemiotic translation between the sign language and spoken language of hearing sign language users, views on the extent to which signs represent elements of spoken language vary from one extreme, for example that of Harrington (1938:2:28—"the signs are everywhere based on spoken language and reflect it at every turn"), to its opposite, for example West's conclusion that there is "no evidence that Amerindian sign language is in any sense derivative of spoken language" (1960:I, 97). Kroeber sees PSL as being heavily indebted to spoken language when he writes that "the sign language, like writing, is a substitute for speech, not an independent or original method of communication.... The concepts which sign language communicates are basically concepts already developed in speech but translated into a non-spoken medium" (1972:xxvii). A more moderate view is taken by Taylor (1978), who, in the most recent review of discussion about this question, states that, with regard to the imitation of spoken language word-order in PSL, "a mode of expression which proceeds from the specification of the general to the particular (as in the sign language) could account for many of the sign language features which are supposed to derive from some particular language." With regard to the lexicon, however, he writes that "spoken and sign lexicons do not exhibit the same degree of independence from mutual influence" as does word-order. New signs are known to have been created in sign language as imitations of words in the spoken vocabulary, and, in turn, through back-translation from signs, new spoken words are sometimes introduced as a result of a particular sign (ibid.).

Regarding AASL, W. Miller (1978) expresses the view that the sign language system he studied was a surrogate in the sense that some signs appeared to represent spoken words and sign-order tended to adhere to word-order. It was unlike spoken language, however, in that dialect variation in words and signs did not covary. Roth (1897), on the other hand, refers to AASL signs as *idea-grams*, and Seligmann and Wilkin (1907) as *ideo-grams*, in order to stress the direct expression of ideas through signs.

It would appear that on the whole aboriginal sign languages act more as a substitute for spoken language than do sign languages of the deaf (excluding signed English and finger spelling, of course). Stern refers to the signs of PSL as *lexical ideographs*, or signs which represent a lexical unit of the spoken language without "reference to the phonemic structure of the base language" (1957:127). Such signs would fit Buyssens' definition of a speech surrogate as "un sème dont la signification est constituée par le signifiant d'une autre sémie" (1967:45), instigating a particular process of what Jakobson (1971d: 261) calls *transmutation*, or intersemiotic (as opposed intra- or interlingual) translation, which is the "interpretation of verbal signs by means of signs of non-verbal sign systems."

On the other hand, none of the aboriginal sign language dialects have been described as purely substitutive, and each is to a varying degree "independent of but translatable into natural language" (Sebeok and Umiker-Sebeok 1976:xiii). In fact, it would appear that intersemiotic translation is to a certain extent a barrier to the attainment of fluency in the use of sign language, as alluded to above with regard to communication between PSL practitioners and deaf signers. In many respects, "the sign language was, and is, regarded as an additional communications channel, in no way subordinated to the vocal-auditory" (Taylor 1978). The greater the degree of conventionalization and standardization and the less the individual signer has to rely upon translation from spoken language, the greater the fluency of sign language performances.

Mallery noted that the conventionalization of natural signs introduced by an individual is the result of an expansion of their radius of communication (cf. Stokoe 1974b), or diffusion of the signs among an even larger group of people, on the one hand, and, on the other, the increasing frequency with which they are used in different contexts, both types of situations placing demands on sign users to abbreviate the signs. PSL differs from deaf sign language and spoken language precisely because it was used by a restricted number of people—either intratribally by a subgroup within a Plains tribe, or intertribally, during sporadic contacts between representatives of different tribes—and because the variety of communicative contexts in which it was employed was small compared with these other sign systems. Mallery's way of looking at sign systems from the point of view of their meaning and function in relation to the individuals and groups which use them gives his approach a quite modern taste, as well as recalling Charles Sanders Peirce's semiotic pragmaticism (Peirce 1935–1966). With Mallery's framework, we can envision a time when aboriginal sign languages could, given favorable historical circumstances, become as conventional and almost as direct an expression of ideas as the deaf sign languages of today.

Neither AASL nor PSL has developed into a uniform system of communication, however. West's 1956 dialect survey of the Northern Plains sign language revealed that only from 20 to 40 percent of PSL signs were actually held in common by different tribes, and he concluded that the sign language could be considered universal "not in sharing of lexical items, but the application of general pantomimic principles in the formation of whatever signs are selected for conventionalization" (1960:2:54). Despite the emphasis placed by most authors on the intertribal origin and development of aboriginal sign languages, there is good reason to believe that, in fact, their primary use was for communication among members of a single tribe. Dodge (1882:384), among others, noted that the Plains Indians used sign language even in their own camps, in everyday conversation with people who spoke the same language. Webb (1931:72–74) suggested that the primary context in which the sign language developed was hunting and warfare, where spoken language was of limited use for communicating over great distances. West's survey in the 1950s supports the view that PSL was particularly important *within* Plains tribes. He found no correlation to exist between sign language use and the presence of a spoken *lingua franca*, for example Mexican Spanish in the U.S. Southwest. Furthermore, the sign language was at that time described by West as "a going concern," long after it had ceased to serve as a *lingua franca* (1960:2:63). Its ceremonial and oratorical function continued even after long-distance communication had been replaced by modern means of communication, such as radio and telegraph. Among the Crow and Cheyenne, moreover, "more young than older people knew the sign language" (ibid.), and in some areas, for example Saskatchewan, the sign language appeared at that time to be spreading. Mallery gives the following description of the tendency toward divergent patterns of conventionalization of PSL signs which result from such frequent and varied intratribal application of sign language:

> The skills of any tribe in the copiousness of its signs are proportioned to the accidental ability of the few individuals in it who act as custodians and teachers, so that the several tribes at different times vary in their degree of proficiency, and therefore both the precise mode of semiotic expression and the amount of its general use are always fluctuating. All the signs . . . were at some time invented by some one person, though by others simultaneously and independently, and many of them became forgotten and were reinvented. Their prevalence and permanence were determined by the experience of their utility. . . . Sometimes signs, doubtless once air-pictures of the most striking outline of an object, or of the most characteristic features of an action, have in time become abbreviated, and, to some extent, conventionalized among members of the same tribe and its immediate neighbors, and have not become common to them with other tribes simply because the form of abbreviation has been peculiar. In other cases, with the same conception and attempted characterization, another yet equally appropriate delineation has been selected, and when both of the differing delineations have been abbreviated the diversity is vastly increased. The original conception, being independent, has necessarily also varied, because all objects have several characteristics, and what struck one set of people as the most distinctive of these would not always so impress another. (Mallery 1880b:13–14)

Yet another factor contributing to the high degree of dialect variation of PSL is the increase in ceremonial usage noted above. It is well known that there is a tendency for the language of ritual to change at a slower rate than that used in everyday conversation. As the PSL becomes more closely tied to rituals associated with tribal identity, we would expect it to retain its "picturesque" nature and become progressively more archaic, each tribe freezing its sign dialect at a certain stage of development.

The situation becomes even more complex if one considers that both PSL and AASL were not uncommonly used simultaneously with spoken language, as a kind of "embroidery . . . to provide required emphasis" (Meggitt 1954:3; cf. Humfreville 1899; Kohl 1860; Maclean 1896; Taylor 1978; Webb 1931; West 1960, regarding PSL; and W. Miller 1978, for AASL). The high degree of iconicity and indexicality of PSL and AASL, the former frequently described as "poetry of motion" and "graceful," made them particularly suitable for use with "formal oratory" and "impassioned or emphatic conversation" (Mallery 1880b: 38). Unlike the gesticulations accompanying most speech, aboriginal sign language signs, when used with spoken language, could be compared with pictorial illustrations of written texts. Both words and signs have their own meanings in reference to their respective semiotic system, yet each influences the interpretation of the other, the visual image amplifying the verbal and vice versa. This type of intersemiotic activity must be viewed as a unique and complex process of mutual interpretation.

Turning to AASL, Stirling (1896:112) asserted that "a good deal of variation exists in different parts" of Australia, with some "blending" of signs at intertribal meeting places, such as Tempe Downs, where representatives of the Luritcha and Arunta traditionally came together. Later, Meggitt (1954:12), using Roth's collection of signs, found that the number of signs held in common between groups varied inversely with an increase in distance between them. West (1960) maintained that the amount of dialect variation was roughly similar for both AASL and PSL.

We also find that intratribal uses of AASL are as prevalent, if not more so, than intertribal ones (for mention of the latter, see, e.g., Berndt 1940; Howitt 1904; Spencer and Gillen 1927; Stirling 1896; Warner 1937). There are reports of the employment of AASL for everyday conversation (e.g., Basedow 1925; Meggitt 1954; Stirling 1896; Strehlow 1978); long-distance communication, as while stalking game (e.g., Basedow 1925; Berndt 1940; Haddon 1908; Howitt 1904; Meggitt 1954; Mountford 1938; Spencer and Gillen 1927); and communication with the deaf (e.g., Meggitt 1954; Warner 1937). AASL is also a convenient form of expression either for persons ritually defined as "dead" in the sense of being in a liminal stage between ritual statuses, as, for example, novices during initiation ceremonies or widows in mourning (e.g., Howitt 1904; Meggitt 1954; Roth 1897; Spencer and Gillen 1927; Warner 1937), or by persons of normal ritual status when conversing about taboo subjects such as sexual intercourse, dead persons, or ceremonial secrets (e.g., Meggitt 1954; Strehlow 1978). We have already noted the function of AASL as an accompaniment to speech.

A third criterion for comparison of PSL, deaf sign language, and spoken language used by Mallery was the type of communication channel utilized by each. Although he stressed the similarity in communicative potential of all three semiotic systems, Mallery warned against a glottocentric analysis of the first two which would overlook the critical differences between the requirements of an auditory versus a visual channel of communication (cf. Hailman 1977). PSL and sign languages of the deaf, as visual systems, may be able to be as expressively complex as spoken language, but they will attain such a level of complexity in quite a different way. West (1960:1:89) writes that the key to sign language grammar is to be found in Mallery's notion of "sign picture" (Mallery 1972:114). Mallery wrote (1880b:57) that "in mimic construction there are to be considered both the order in which the signs succeed one another and the relative positions in which they are made, the latter remaining longer in the memory than the former." This idea is taken up by Scott: "A conversation in the sign language has been likened to a series of moving pictures, and as the relations between object's actions in such pictures are represented by the relative positions and sequence, and are evident to the eye, so also are those expressed in the sign pictures when viewed by a person trained to see with the eye of the natural man" (1898:217). W. Miller (1978) also found that the psycholinguistic processing of AASL messages varies considerably from the way we decode spoken messages. With AASL, the internal composition, or sequence of signs, is not recalled by the addressee, while the general meaning, or "picture," of the total sequence is retained in the memory. West believed that syntactic order, or successivity, was for PSL a "redundant, non-obligatory stylistic matter" (1960:1:90). To the extent that a PSL or AASL dialect has evolved into a complex, general system of communication, we should expect it to have adopted a wide variety of semiotic strategies which are available to a visual mode but not found among spoken languages. Peng has noted three such principles of organization: (1) *simultaneity*, where two signs are produced together (see also Ljung 1965:120); (2) *reversibility*, where "a sign's movement may be reversed so as to form another sign that has the opposite meaning"; and (3) *directionality*, where "a sign may be positioned in different ways, depending upon the relative space occupied by the signer, the viewer, and the content of their conversation, so as to add a subtle connotation in one shift which would otherwise require several words in any oral language to describe" (Peng 1977:28–29). Since 1960, students of the American sign language of the deaf have developed a mode of description which combines a rigorous systemic analysis derived from linguistics proper with a fresh look at sign language on its own terms, or "from inside" (Stokoe 1974a:119). This work has begun to reveal some fascinating techniques available to users of a visual communication system such as sign language which were heretofore ignored pre-

154 The Sign

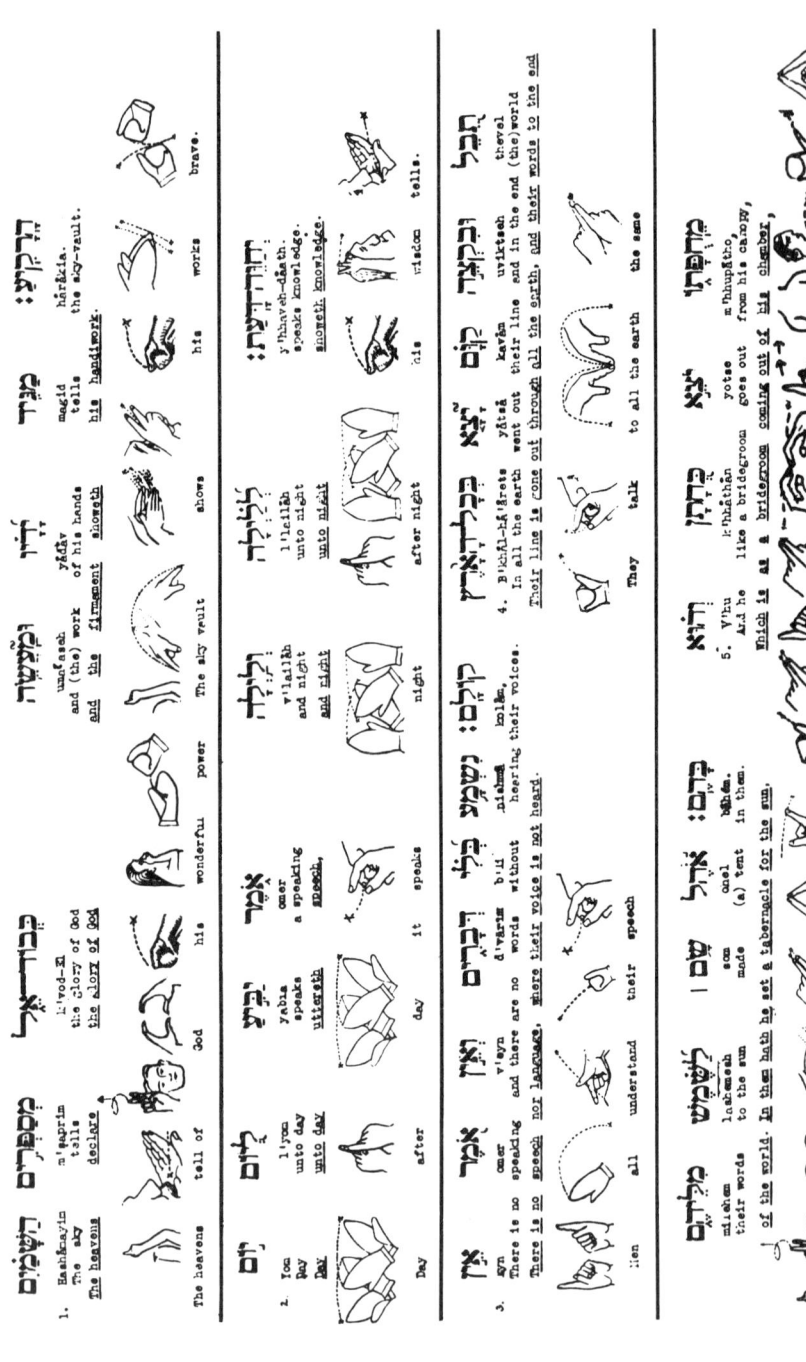

Aboriginal Sign "Languages" 155

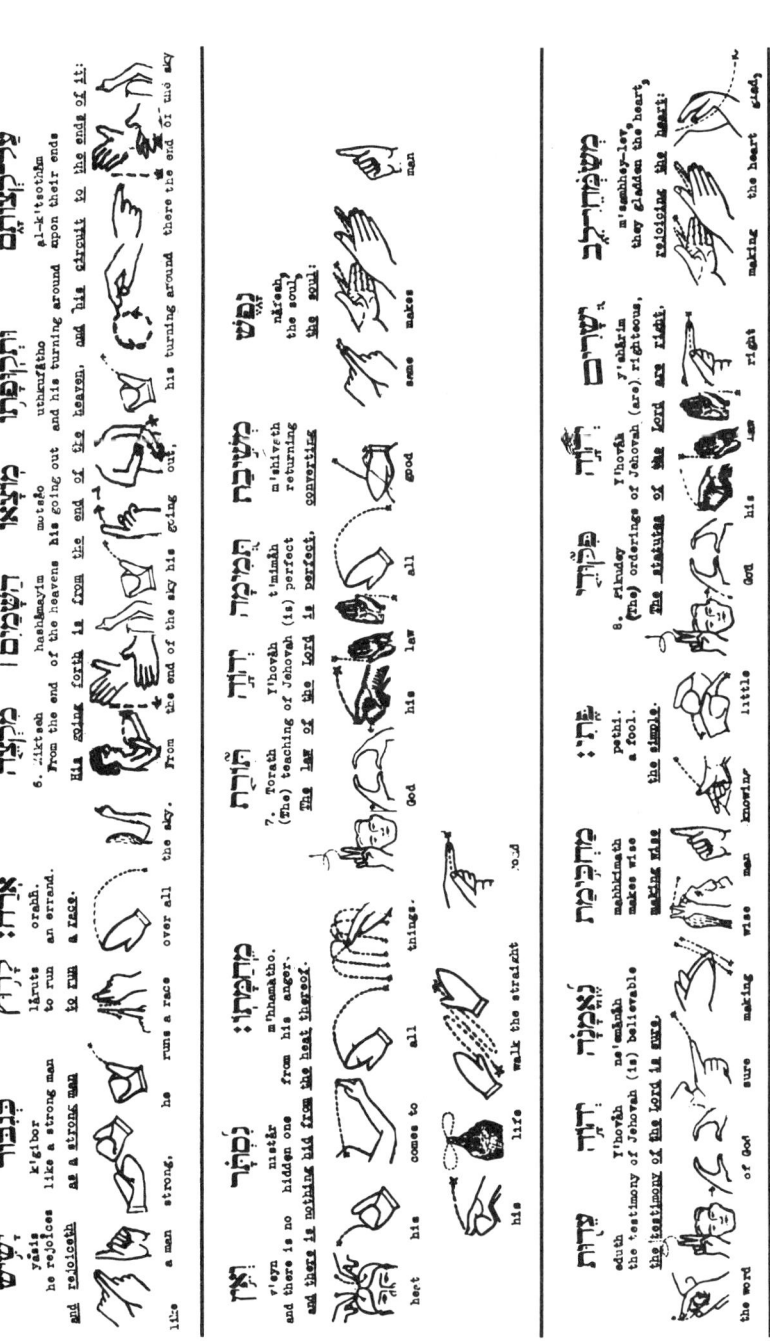

Figure 7-8. A text in the American Indian sign language: The Nineteenth Psalm. From Harrington 1938, no. 7:14–15.

156 The Sign

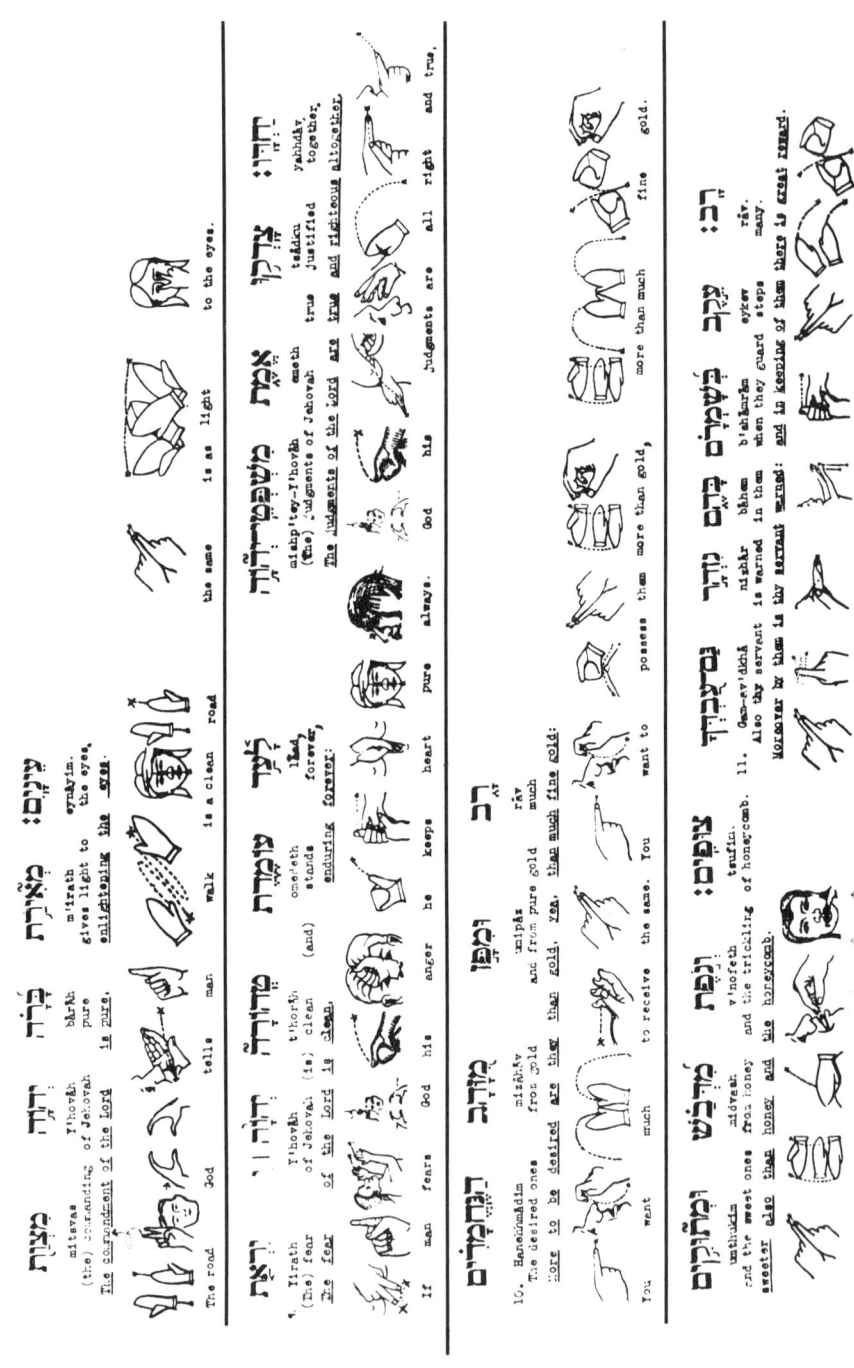

Aboriginal Sign "Languages" 157

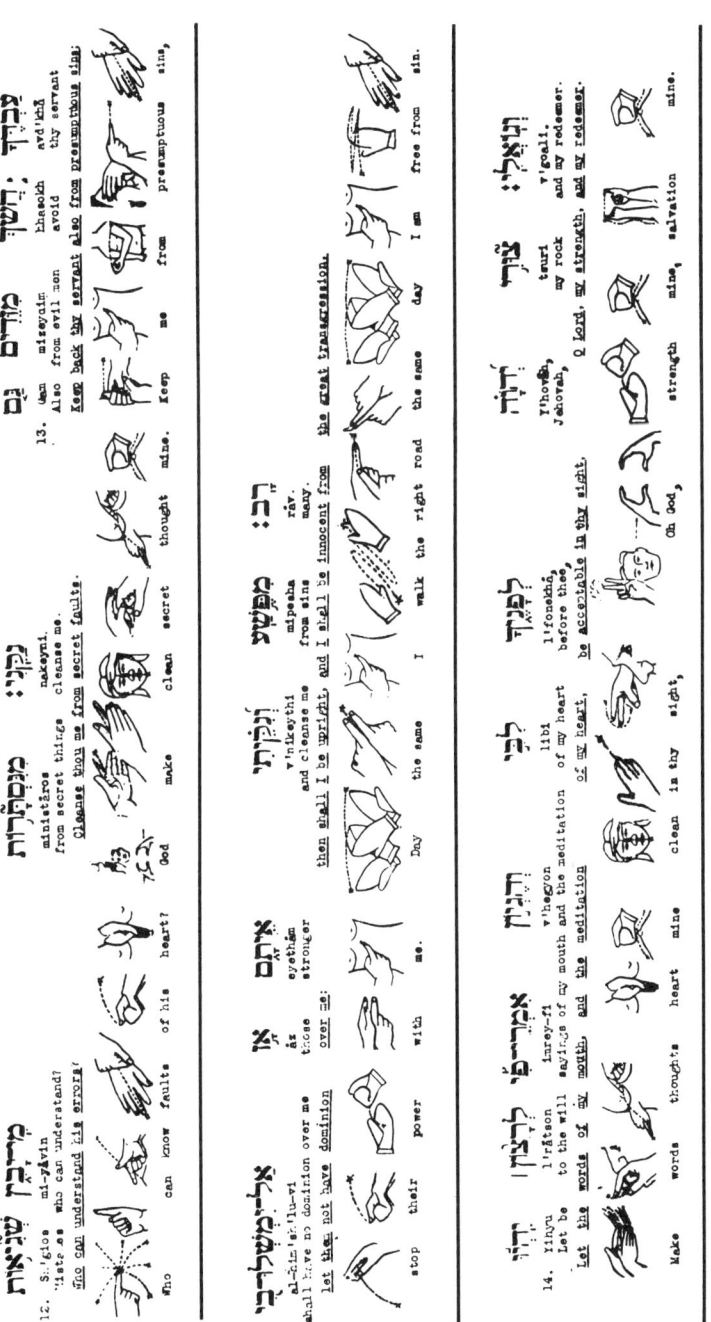

Figure 7-8 continued.

cisely because they rely on one or more of the three characteristics noted above, part of Mallery's "spatial syntax" (1972:114), where "the obligatory grammatical relationships are established not by temporal order or syntax, but by spatial relationships, both within the execution of a single sign and between positions of execution of succeeding signs" (West 1960:1:90). To date, no such revolution has taken place in aboriginal sign language studies. It would be particularly interesting to know in what way the possession of the facility of speech influences the types of communicative strategies developed in aboriginal sign languages, thus contributing to the divergent lines of development between them and deaf sign languages.

The analysis of aboriginal sign languages, like that of visual communication systems in general, has been plagued by language-dominated concepts and methods. One of the earliest of these was the analogy made between the lexicon of spoken language and that of the sign languages, where signs were treated as similar to the linguistic concept of word. As noted above, Mallery warned against basing a description of PSL on the false assumption of the identity of visual and auditory units. In addressing potential contributors to his sign language project (see, for example, 1880b; 1880c; and 1884), he admonished collectors to gather native language interpretations as well as English translations of those interpretations along with their appropriate signs. In addition to this, Mallery showed himself to be sensitive to the influence of the discursive context of the meaning of individual signs when he insisted that signs be collected within examples of connected discourse, either informal conversations or formal speeches and stories. This sort of field technique would be necessary, of course, to guard against treating signs as if they functioned like words of spoken language.

Much later, Kroeber (1972:xxxii), unaware of Harrington's earlier, sketchy attempt to analyze PSL on its own, visual terms, claimed that "what is needed is *systematic analysis of the sign language in terms of itself*." The study which Kroeber envisioned would "distinguish the characteristic pattern of motion or position from accidentals," providing a verbal description of such patterns together with outline linear sketches. The description would be made in terms of semantic categories plus executional forms, in dictionary fashion. As an illustration of what such an analysis would look like, Kroeber grouped together signs made with two hands according to whether neither hand moves, one hand moves, or both hands are in motion. Signs produced with two hands moving are grouped according to whether the hands are interacting (or crossing) or whether there is a bilaterally symmetrical simultaneous motion involved. Signs in the latter category are divided further still according to whether the motion is centrifugal or centripetal. Many of the descriptive categories mentioned by Kroeber, such as direction of motion, repetition, relation of motion to body parts, and so forth, are mentioned by Mallery (1880b: 64–65; 1884: 207ff.) in relation to his instructions to investigators concerning the notation and description of PSL. Mounin (1973: 158) has suggested that Mallery's emphasis on the importance of finding "the radical or essential part" of each sign "by which it can be distinguished from any other ... sign" (Mallery 1972: 84–85) bears a remarkable resemblance to the crucial linguistic notion of distinctive feature. Mallery, however, was unable to take advantage of the advances toward systemic analysis which were fashioned by linguists largely after he had completed his work (Jost Winteler's *Die Kerenzer Mundart des Kantons Glarus in ihrer Grundzügen dargestellt* was completed in 1875, but his dissertation remained out of Mallery's ken).

While Kroeber saw the importance of an application of linguistic technique on the level of sign morphemes, he considered it unwise to extend the use of linguistic technique beyond that level, due to the highly iconic and indexical nature of sign language signs in contrast with spoken language. His student, C. F. Voegelin, took Kroeber to task for his refusal to grant the possibility that PSL possessed a phonemic level of structure, and duality of patterning, such as found in spoken language:

> The preponderant part of all the literature on the Sign Language is concerned with its lexical resources, either on the false analogy of its dictionary and the dictionary of a spoken language or else—conversely—to show precisely the non-analogous nature of Sign Language. The genius of the Sign Language as a unique system has been approached, so far, without benefit of initial grammar, of a preliminary ordering of regularities. That the literature does, in fact, center on the compilation of the dictionary as I assert it does, is demonstrated—and justified—by A. L. Kroeber.... All publications to date, including Kroeber's and J. P. Harrington's ... have been concerned with the size and scope of this dictionary. Though not wanting to stop with a mere lexical compilation of the Sign Language, the independent views of both Kroeber and Harrington seem to suggest that one cannot go very far beyond this—farther perhaps in making classifications and subclassifications of Sign Language lexical materials ... than in sorting out arrangements of combinatorial possibilities.... Kroeber takes the lexical unit or morpheme to be the minimum component in the analysis of Sign Language: "the reason it has no equivalent to phonemes is that it began to operate only on the level of morphemes, and so far as possible semantically substantive morphemes—many relational ones would be hard to devise gestures for." There can be no question of the adequacy of Kroeber's minimum component, so far as

160   The Sign

A—Fist, palm outward, horizontal.   B—Fist, back outward, oblique upward.   C—Clinched, with thumb extended against forefinger, upright, edge outward.

D—Clinched, ball of thumb against middle of forefinger, oblique, upward, palm down.   E—Hooked, thumb against end of forefinger, upright, edge outward.   F—Hooked, thumb against side of forefinger, oblique, palm outward.

G—Fingers resting against ball of thumb, back upward.   H—Arched, thumb horizontal against end of forefinger, back upward.   I—Closed, except forefinger crooked against end of thumb, upright, palm outward.

Figure 7-9. Hand positions in gesture language. From Mallery 1880b: 70–72.

Aboriginal Sign "Languages" 161

J—Forefinger straight, upright, others closed, edge outward.

K—Forefinger obliquely extended upward, others closed, edge outward.

L—Thumb vertical, forefinger horizontal, others closed, edge outward.

M—Forefinger horizontal, fingers and thumb closed, palm outward.

N—First and second fingers straight upward and separated, remaining fingers and thumb closed, palm outward.

O—Thumb, first and second fingers separated, straight upward, remaining fingers curved edge outward.

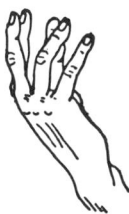

P—Fingers and thumb partially curved upward and separated, knuckles outward.

Q—Fingers and thumb separated, slightly curved, downward.

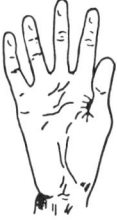

R—Fingers and thumb extended straight, separated, upward.

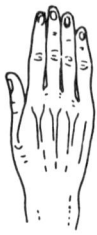  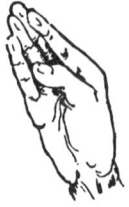

S—Hand and fingers upright, joined, back outward.

T—Hand and fingers upright, joined, palm outward.

U—Fingers collected to a point, thumb resting in middle.

 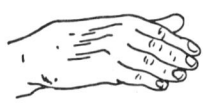

V—Arched, joined, thumb resting near end of forefinger, downward.

W—Hand horizontal, flat, palm downward.

X—Hand horizontal, flat, palm upward.

Y—Naturally relaxed, normal; used when hand simply follows arm with no intentional disposition.

N. B.—The positions are given as they appear to an observer facing the gesturer, and are designed to show the relations of the fingers to the hand rather than the positions of the hand relative to the body, which must be shown by the outlines (see sheet of "OUTLINES OF ARM POSITIONS") or description. The right and left hands are figured above without discrimination, but in description or reference the right hand will be understood when the left is not specified. The hands as figured can also with proper intimation be applied with changes either upward, downward, or inclined to either side, so long as the relative positions of the fingers are retained, and when in that respect no one of the types exactly corresponds with a sign observed, modifications will be made by pen or pencil on that one of the types found most convenient, as indicated in the sheet of "EXAMPLES," and referred to by the letter of the alphabet under the type changed, with the addition of a numeral—*e. g.*, A 1, and if that type, *i. e.* A, were changed a second time by the observer (which change would necessarily be drawn on another sheet of types), it should be referred to as A 2.

Figure 7-9 continued.

Aboriginal Sign "Languages"

EXAMPLES.

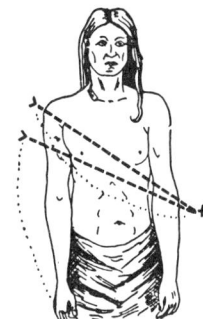

Word or idea expressed by sign: To cut, with an ax.

DESCRIPTION:

With the right hand flattened (X changed to right instead of left), palm upward, move it downward to the left side repeatedly from different elevations, ending each stroke at the same point.
Conception or origin: From the act of felling a tree.

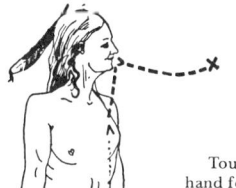

Word or idea expressed by sign: A lie.

DESCRIPTION:

Touch the left breast over the heart, and pass the hand forward from the mouth, the two first fingers only being extended and slightly separated (L, 1—with thumb resting on third finger).
Conception or origin: Double-tongued.

L, 1.

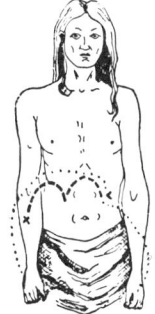

Word or idea expressed by sign: To ride.

DESCRIPTION:

Place the first two fingers of the right hand, thumb extended (N, 1) downward, astraddle the first two joined and straight fingers of the left (T, 1), sidewise, to the right, then make several short arched movements forward with hands so joined.
Conception or origin: The horse mounted and in motion.

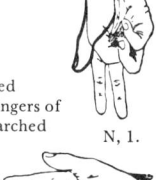

N, 1.

T, 1.

```
- - - - - - - - -    Dotted lines indicate movements to place the hand and arm in position
                     to commence the sign and not forming part of it.

      >              Indicates commencement of movement in representing sign, or part of sign.

- - - - - - - - -    Dashes indicate the course of hand employed in the sign.

      X              Represents the termination of movements.

   ⟶                 Used in connection with dashes, shows the course of the latter when not
                     otherwise clearly intelligible.
```

164 The Sign

> lexical inquiry is concerned; or even as concerns a modest grammar—*a grammar which is, strictly speaking, an appendix of the dictionary.* (1972: xxxvi–xxxvii)

Voegelin's student, La Mont West, spent the second half of the 1950s engaged in the most detailed study of PSL to date, one which resulted in his dissertation in 1960, the first volume being devoted to a formal linguistic analysis of the sign language, the second to issues such as dialect survey, sociological analysis of sign language use, and the like. West's linguistic analysis was specifically designed to set forth a kinemic as well as a morphemic level of structure and thus reveal the dual patterning of this communication system. He claimed that PSL could be described fully in terms of a total of eighty kinemes, which fell into five basic kineme classes, which he compared with units of spoken language (indicated in parentheses) in terms of number and combinatorial privileges: *hand-shapes* (consonants), *directions* (vowels), *dynamics* (stress, tone, length), *motion-patterns* (semi-vowels), and *referents* (kinemes which "specify the body parts, parts of hands or external reference in relation to which the *hand-shapes* or active hand parts are positioned or moved"—1:13). The point-by-point comparison with spoken language was a constant source of frustration to West, who makes clear that he would have greatly preferred to base his analysis of PSL on a sufficiently detailed and rigorous analysis of another gesture system, had such a study been available. He repeatedly warns the reader that the use of a language-based model of analysis could lead to the incorrect conclusion that the structure of sign language mirrors exactly that of spoken language. Since West's dissertation was the first and most comprehensive linguistic treatment of PSL and is difficult to obtain, it is worth including here at length one such admission by the author.

> It must be conceded that many decisions required in the setting up of kinemes have been made upon adherence to single criteria, often rather arbitrarily selected. Had other criteria been rated higher, a somewhat different kinemic inventory could have been set up to account for the same set of distinctions between components and subcomponents. . . . However, a second factor is also at play in giving the kinemic level less stability than the morphemic in sign language. The system is partially open-ended on the kinemic level, as well as on the morphemic. . . . On the phonemic level for spoken language the system is at least as firmly closed as the minor morphemes, except for a marginal category of onomatopoetic sounds and exclamatory sounds, which may be simply excluded from the system if they fail to pattern with it. In this sign language description, as in those for most spoken language grammars, the morphology is chiefly restricted to a treatment of major morpheme classes qua classes and of minor mor-

phemes in paradigms and individually. Since this much of sign
language morphology also forms a nearly closed system, it gives
the same, rather misleading, impression of self-contained structural integration at the morpheme level that is characteristic of
spoken language morphological statements. However, the kinemic level of sign language is far less parallel with the phonemic
level of spoken language, than is the case for the respective morphemic levels. In sign language the onomatopoetic (pantomimic)
cannot be read out of the system, since it comprises 98% of the
system at the morphemic level and a less high, but still very imposing percentage at the kinemic level, due to the high incidence
of mono-kinemic morphemes and an even higher incidence of
"fl"-like sub-morphemic form-meaning relationships. The high
onomatopoetic content of sign language makes possible and encourages the constant development of new signs. In most cases
such signs do utilize kinemic material already well established in
the system. In fact, the *motion-pattern*, *direction*, and *dynamic*
classes of kinemes participate in a nearly closed system in the
idiolect of sign language upon which this analysis is based. However, the *hand-shape* class of kinemes is slightly open-ended and
the *referent* class is markedly so. In most cases the new or rare
hand-shapes and referents can be included as allokines of kinemes already well established, since the very variety of their
occurrence insures complementarity with one or another of the
more frequent kinemes. In most cases, even, some common element of shape can be discovered between the new candidate kine
and one or another of the kinemes with which it is in complementary distribution. All too often, however, the complementarity in such cases is dependent upon rather special and unique
environments, and such uniqueness robs the statement of allokine
distribution in sign language of the authority characteristic of
statements possible for allomorphs. (1960:1:29–30)

The claims by Voegelin and West concerning the duality of PSL are, as a recent reviewer has noted, "not persuasive" (Mounin 1973:161). Mounin points out that in overlooking the visual nature of PSL, where the simultaneity of certain minimal units makes them appear to resemble the distinctive features of phonemes, there arose a confusion between phonetic transcription, based on minimal descriptive units, and a phonological transcription, based on distinctive features (ibid.: 161–162).

Despite the pressures exerted on West to remain within the then popular methodological frame for phonemic analysis and ignore questions of semantic structure, he admitted, after a summary of earlier semantically oriented descriptions of sign language, or what he called "the conceptual approach to sign language," that it "does throw considerable light upon the ease of learning and communication characteristic of the sign language" (1960:1:88–89). West would have done well to heed the advice of his chief benefactor, Kroeber, who, as noted above, stressed the importance of combining a formal grammatical analysis with a semantic one. Ljung, who applied a linguistic technique derived from Hjelmslev's and Uldall's glossematics, also known in some quarters as stratificational grammar, to PSL, also found that the meaning kept intruding upon the purely formal analysis which he was attempting. "Obviously, these gestemes are more tainted with meaning than are phonemes; compare, for example, the common circle element in *sun*, *star*, *coin*, etc., or the growth-image recurring in *grass*, *grow*, *tree*" (1965:126). Pointing to the fact that the circle element also could be found in signs for *want* and *drink*, Ljung reaffirmed Mallery's idea that the sign language, "had it been allowed to develop freely, ... would no doubt have become more arbitrary as time went by" (ibid.). The very limited success of the analysis of PSL using meaning-free descriptive techniques borrowed from linguistics points up the need for a new description of PSL or AASL, one which would take into account recent developments in the semiotics of nonverbal iconicity and indexicality as well as meaning-sensitive formal theories of conventional sign systems. Anyone attempting a new look at aboriginal sign languages should ponder the experience of Stokoe, who produced his first linguistic treatment of the American sign language of the deaf during the same period as West's dissertation, and under a comparable commitment to the structuralist framework of the day, but who soon recognized the severe limits of a structuralist analysis. In 1972, he noted, for example, that, with respect to ASL *cheremes*, "the ways in which they differ from phonemes in operation are as important as the similarities" (p. 20). Only a semiotic analysis can provide an adequate account of the whole system, with its high degree of iconic and indexical signs (1974a:127). Such a statement would be even more appropriate in a discussion of aboriginal sign languages.

Latest available reports (Taylor 1978 and W. Miller 1978) suggest that there are enough PSL and AASL practitioners active today to make fresh analyses of aboriginal sign languages feasible. In our distillation of the voluminous materials pertaining to aboriginal sign languages, our aim has been to focus attention on what makes them unique as systems of representation and communication and therefore of paramount importance for the study of other visual codes, spoken language, and, ultimately, semiotic theory. It would be regrettable were this rich and uncommon species of semiotic organization to become extinct without the benefit of another long, hard look by well-trained and appreciative eyes.

In conclusion, we would like to list some topics which are related to the principal, semiotic concern of this paper but which, because of space limitations, could not be included in the present discussion (although they will be taken up elsewhere):

(1) While we have outlined some of the points of similarity and difference between aboriginal sign languages, sign languages of the deaf, and spoken language, there are many interesting discussions in the literature (especially Mallery 1880b; 1882; 1884; 1972; West 1960) concerning the relationships between aboriginal sign languages and other gestural systems, both formal (e.g., Hindu dance gestures) and informal (e.g., monastic, Neapolitan, and Armenian signs); writing systems (particularly Chinese); and pictographs. While much of this material is slanted toward questions of the origin of aboriginal sign languages, a universal "gesture speech of mankind" (e.g., Mallery 1880b; 1882), or the gestural origin of spoken language, a careful study, which would make use as well of the modern analyses of these and other such visual systems accomplished since West's dissertation, could make a substantial contribution to the field of nonverbal communication.

(2) The same may be said for the equally significant problem of the notation of aboriginal sign languages. Many authors have tried to overcome the difficulties involved in the recording and transcription of signs, but with little success. The search for such tools is of great semiotic interest in itself and deserves separate and detailed consideration.

(3) Finally, modern poetic, discourse, and narrative analyses of aboriginal sign language texts need to be made, taking into account the framing of visual moving sign "pictures" both when used by themselves and when used in interaction with facial expression, speech, and other auditory and visual messages, such as music, especially when integrated in multimedia performances (spectacles).

8. The Two Sons of Croesus:

A Myth about Communication

in Herodotus

with Erika Brady

I

Herodotus (ca. 484–ca. 424 B.C.), widely known by the epithet the Father of History, was considered the Father of Lies by historians who followed him, such as Thucydides, Hellanicus, Xenophon, Polybius, and Sallust. These successors demanded strictly accurate accounts of close to contemporaneous events; Herodotus drew upon a wide variety of sources for his *Histories*, incorporating much anecdotal and legendary material which did not meet the more fastidious criteria of later decades and centuries. Cicero himself, who first gave Herodotus the title Father of History, was aware that the *Histories* contained fabrications of Herodotus' imagination (*De Divinatione* 2:56:116), embroidering upon narratives from oral tradition: in the very passage in which he first called Herodotus the Father of History, Cicero remarks upon his use of material not necessarily veridical historically. In the opening chapter of the *Laws*, Cicero and his brothers are discussing the relevance of accuracy in poetry, and Cicero insists that ". . . in history

Note: This article, written in collaboration with Erika Brady, is republished here from *Journal of the Folklore Institute* 15:5–22 (1978). A Greek version appeared in *Kodikas* 5 (1978). The paper was presented by E. B., in much condensed form, in the course of the 1977 meetings of the Central States Anthropological Society, held in Cincinnati, in the framework of a Symposium on Semiotic Perspectives in Human Relations, co-organized by T.A.S. with Dr. D. Jean Umiker-Sebeok, and has also been translated into Hungarian, under the title "Mítosz a kommunikációról Hérodotosznál," for a future publication. We acknowledge, with deep appreciation, illuminating comments, as well as strictures, on our prefinal draft by Claude Lévi-Strauss (cf. note 8) and by Charles W. Fornara, whose interpretative essay about Herodotus' work as "a universal history on a massive scale" (1971:1) is one of the best of its kind.

everything is meant to lead to the truth, but in poetry a great deal is intended for pleasure—although in Herodotus, the father of history, and in Theopompus, there are a countless number of legends" (*Laws* 1:5).[1] Yet there is a profound consistency even in the seemingly inconsistent characterizations of Herodotus' veracity, for it may be said that he spoke his deepest truths precisely in those legendary tales which Thucydides and his followers judged most undependable.

Early in the first book of the *Histories*,[2] the writer narrates the downfall of the last of the Lydian kings, Croesus. Many interpretations of Croesus' downfall and rescue have been formulated, focusing on historical, literary, or folkloric aspects of this text—but none has hitherto focused in specific detail upon the narrative as an account of man's attempt to communicate with ordering forces beyond himself, and the hermeneutic dilemma arising when he receives a response to his inquiry.[3] We propose to do so in what follows, although ever mindful of Lévi-Strauss's first injunction: "Un mythe ne doit jamais être interprété à un seul niveau. Il n'existe pas d'explication privilegiée, car tout mythe consiste dans une *mise en rapport* de plusieurs niveaux d'explication" (1973:82).

Croesus imagines himself the happiest of men, even when warned by the Athenian sage Solon that the ways of the gods are inscrutable. No man, says Solon, may be counted entirely blessed until his life is complete and he reposes at last in honorable death. Croesus has asked Solon whom he considers to be the happiest of men—a leading question, since Croesus merely wants confirmation of his own enviable status. But Solon's replies are evasive; twice he alludes to men who have lived good lives and who died well. Piqued, Croesus probes further whether his own good fortune does not deserve consideration, to which Solon responds as follows: "'My lord,' replied Solon, 'I know God is envious of human prosperity and likes to trouble us; and you question me about the lot of man. Listen then: as the years lengthen out, there is much both to see and to suffer which one would wish otherwise. . . . You are very rich, and you rule a numerous people; but the question you asked me I will not answer, until I know that you have died happily'" (*Histories* 1:32). Solon, Fornara (1971:79) justly observes, "spoke not just for Croesus but for all the world," yet his immediate addressee ignores the undercurrent of warning. Solon thereupon leaves Lydia, never to return.[4]

Croesus has two sons, one a fine, able young man named Atys, the other characterized as deaf and dumb, unnamed but called a "wretched cripple" by his father (*Histories* 1:39).[5] A prophetic dream warns Croesus that Atys will be killed by an iron spear. The king immediately takes all the precautions his prudence dictates: Atys is married as soon as possible, he is not allowed to engage in field maneuvers with the Lydian soldiers, and even the weapons hanging on the walls of the men's hall are removed to the women's quarters for fear that they might fall on Atys' head (*Histories* 1:34). Atys, however, feels that he cannot remain patiently at home when a monstrous boar ravages the countryside. He pleads with his father to be allowed to join the hunt, using every rhetorical device at his command:

> The young man, finding that Croesus persisted in his refusal to let him join the hunting party, said to his father: "Once honor demanded that I should win fame as a huntsman and fighter; but now, father, though you cannot accuse me of cowardice or lack of spirit, you won't let me take part in either of these admirable pursuits. Think what a figure I must cut when I walk between here and the place of assembly! What will people take me for? What must my young wife think of me? That she hasn't married much of a husband, I fear! Now, father, either let me join the hunt, or give me an intelligible reason why what you are doing is good for me."
>
> "My son," said Croesus, "of course you are not a coward or anything unpleasant of that kind. That is not the reason for what I'm doing. The fact is, I dreamt that you had not long to live—that you would be killed by an iron weapon. It was that dream that made me hasten your wedding; and the same thing makes me refuse to let you join in this enterprise. As long as I live, I am determined to protect you, and to rob death of this prize. You are my only son, for I do not count that wretched cripple, your brother."
>
> "No one can blame you, father," Atys replied, "for taking care of me after a dream like that. Nevertheless there is something which you have failed to observe, and it is only right that I should point it out to you. You dreamt that I should be killed by an iron weapon. Very well: has a boar got hands? Can a boar hold this weapon you fear so much? Had you a dream that I should be killed by a boar's tusk or anything of that sort, your precautions would be justified. But you didn't: it was a weapon which was to kill me. Let me go, then, it is only to hunt an animal, not to fight against men."
>
> "My boy," said Croesus, "I own myself beaten. You interpret the dream better than I did. I cannot but change my mind, and allow you to join in the expedition." (*Histories* 1:37–40)

Atys is killed on the hunt—not by the tusk of the boar, but by an iron spear miscast by one of his comrades.

Croesus grieves for two years, until he is forced to attend to the encroaching conquests of the Persians. Three times he sends messengers to the Delphic oracle for advice in planning a halt to the Persian invasion.

The first question is a test: Croesus orders the messengers to ask what he is doing at the moment of questioning, having chosen an activity seemingly impossible to guess: he cooks a stew of tortoise meat and lamb in a cauldron of bronze with a bronze lid. The reply of the oracle is cast in hexametric lines:

> I count the grains of sand on the beach and measure the sea;
> I understand the speech of the dumb and hear the voiceless.
> The smell has come to my senses of a hard-shelled tortoise
> Boiling and bubbling with lamb's flesh in a bronze pot:
> The cauldron underneath is of bronze, and of bronze the lid.
>
> (*Histories* 1:47)

The second line of the oracle's answer appears to be a simple statement of power, following upon the claims of the first line—but mention of the capacity of understanding the dumb and of hearing the voiceless is a veiled prefigurement of the role to be played by Croesus' unnamed son at a later stage. The message of this oracle—which has been called "das Orakel par excellence" (cf. Kirchberg's discussion of its authenticity, 1965:17f.)—is carefully written down and delivered to the king, who, however, evinces interest only in the accuracy of the last three lines of the reply that authenticate the oracle's puissance.

This portion seems straightforward enough. Delighted with the success of this demonstration of the oracle's mastery, Croesus next transmits a question in earnest: should he challenge the Persians? The oracle replies, "If Croesus attacks the Persians, he will destroy a great empire" (*Histories* 1:52).

The third and final time, Croesus sends to know if his reign will be a long one, to which the oracle replies:

> When comes the day that a mule shall sit on the Median throne,
> Then, tender-footed Lydian, by pebbly Hermus
> Run and abide not, nor think it shame to be a coward.
>
> (*Histories* 1:55)

This answer entirely satisfies the king, since he cannot believe a mule will ever sit on the throne of the Medes.

Croesus has assigned his idiosyncratic interpretation to each of these ambiguous messages (cf. Kirchberg 1965:18–23). Cyrus, the Persian king who has conquered the Medes, is the son of a noble Medean woman and a base-born Persian, a hybrid in the same sense in which a mule is the offspring of a mare and a jackass (*Histories* 1:93). Metaphorically, Cyrus is a mule. Most important of all, the oracle has not specified *which* great empire is to be destroyed if Croesus attacks the Persians.

During the campaign against the Persians, snakes swarm into the outskirts of Sardis, and the horses of the Lydians eat them. This unusual occurrence is taken as an omen by Croesus, who sends to interpreters in Telmessus for its meaning. The Telmessian interpreters warn the messenger that a foreign army will subdue the Lydians, but the message does not reach Sardis in time to convey the meaning of the omen (*Histories* 1:77). Croesus' capital is besieged, the city capitulates, and Croesus himself is captured under the following circumstances:

> What happened to Croesus remains to be told. I have already mentioned his son who was dumb, but in other ways a fine enough young man. In the time of his prosperity—now gone—Croesus had done everything he could for the boy, not even omitting to ask advice from the Delphic oracle. The Priestess had replied:
>
> > O Lydian lord of many nations, foolish Croesus,
> > Wish not to hear the longed-for voice within your palace,
> > Even your son's voice: better for you were it otherwise;
> > For his first word will he speak on a day of sorrow.
>
> When the city was stormed, a Persian soldier was about to cut Croesus down, not knowing who he was. Croesus saw him coming; but because in his misery he did not care if he lived or died, he made no effort to defend himself. But this dumb son, seeing the danger, was so terrified by the fearful thing that was about to happen that he broke into speech, and cried: "Do not kill Croesus, fellow!" Those were the first words he ever uttered—and he retained the power of speech for the rest of his life.
>
> In this way Sardis was captured by the Persians and Croesus taken prisoner, after a reign of fourteen years and a siege of fourteen days. The oracle was fulfilled; Croesus had destroyed a mighty empire—his own.   (*Histories* 1:85–86)

2

Is the episode of Croesus' downfall a historically accurate account of events, a literary fabrication, a legend or myth from oral tradition, or a mixture of different ingredients? A considerable amount of scholarly effort has been directed towards the elucidation of this problem. Herodotus' historicity in the Croesus narrative has had such unexpectedly varied defenders as Petrarch and Thomas de Quincey (Evans 1968: 11–12). Late nineteenth- and early twentieth-century researchers turned to archaeological as well as historiographic evidence to challenge the epithet Father of Lies (see, for example, Hauvette-Besnault 1894:65–180; Roussel 1927; Speigelberg 1927; Martin 1931). Attempts of this sort continue. Full-length articles still take great pains to demonstrate the possibility that the historical Croesus might indeed have met the historical Solon, and that they might have interacted in precisely the manner described by Herodotus (M. Miller 1963; see also Audiat 1940). Brief notes still interpret and reinterpret the historical significance of the Delphic oracle (Wormell 1963). Yet despite diligent and learned endeavors on the part of scholars such as these, an unadulterated historical view of the Croesus episode is unconvincing, since it either ignores or dismisses the overwhelming evidence for Herodotus' incorporation of artistic fabrication and creative assimilation of folkloric and mythic materials.

Whether or not the Croesus episode is historically plausible, there is little doubt that the story itself has absorbed and intermingles with elements of an oral tradition. The Persian Wars took place in the decade prior to the author's birth, so the historian could have had little access to first-hand accounts of the events. Herodotus himself states that he received his information on the Persian conquest of Sardis from the Lydians (*Histories* 1:86). There are no known sources or analogues to the tale as a whole (Law 1947–1948:456), although a number of scholars have remarked upon the similarity of the themes of *hybris* and *nemesis* surrounding Croesus to those features in some Greek tragedies (Levin 1960; Meunier 1968; Snell 1973). The traditional patterns and motifs apparent in the whole of the histories were noted by Aly in his work *Volksmärchen, Sage, und Novelle bei Herodot und seinen Zeitgenossen* (1921); he pounces with delight upon every indication of oral tradition at work in the Croesus episode. The threefold questioning of Croesus and the response of Solon evoke the requisite *Heimatgefühl*: "Hier ist Volkskunst" (Aly 1921:38), he proclaims with gusto.

The tragic conclusion of the portion of the episode concerning the death of Atys disqualifies the narrative as a true *Märchen*-type according to Aly (ibid.:38), yet he points out the manifest similarity between this tale and Aarne-Thompson Tale-type 410, "Dornröschen." Although the boar himself does not kill Atys in this narrative, huge and dangerous boars are commonly featured in European oral literature; Aly adduces the Greek tale of Meleager, the Grimms' tale "Das Wildschwein," and the gigantic boar of the *Odyssey* (19:11:428ff.; Aly 1921:39).

The approach to the Croesus episode as myth has declined in recent years, as critical attention has turned to the role of Herodotus as conscious craftsman and philosopher of history, rather than a passive bearer of tradition. Despite this neglect, the "old-fashioned" mythological approach cannot and should not be ignored, for this point of view has convincing supportive evidence from both philology and comparative religion. The mythological approach has so far addressed itself almost exclusively to the significance of the death of Atys. According to most interpretations, Atys is to be identified with the cult of the fertility goddess Cybele and her young lover Atthis, killed by a boar (Sayce

1883:47–52; How and Wells 1912:70–71). J. A. K. Thomson, in his work *The Art of the Logos* (1934), surmises that the cult of the Goddess and Youth might represent "a stage of religion natural at certain times in certain societies" (ibid.:83), but he feels that there is sufficient evidence to relate Atys, son of Croesus, to the cultic Atthis of the temple at the Lydian capital of Sardis. When this temple was burned, around 500 B.C., the story of Atthis was severed from its sacred roots, and finally found an attachment point in the story of Croesus, last and most famous of the kings of Lydia (ibid.). While the narrative as related by Herodotus has lost any cultic associations it may once have had, it remains to be seen whether it bears the marks of a mythological infrastructure of a deeper significance.

Most recently, some classical scholars have re-examined the works of Herodotus in general, and the Croesus episode in particular, for what these may reveal of the processes of thought which brought the *Histories* into being. This recent school does not respond defensively to the sobriquet Father of Lies. Instead of trying to prove the accuracy of Herodotus' accounts in terms of contemporary historiography, these scholars search for the uses of "untruth" in historical narrative. Seth Bernadete, in his book *Herodotean Inquiries* (1969), notes that Herodotus himself expresses unembarrassed doubt concerning the veracity of some of his accounts (ibid.:4–5). According to Bernadete, Herodotus uses his tales and legends to draw attention to the major themes of history. Coming as it does at the beginning of the *Histories*, the Croesus episode takes on a special importance, for with this story the reader's view of the succeeding events is narrowed and concentrated upon the nature of the fortunes of men (ibid.:6; compare also Immerwahr 1966:81–86; White 1969; and Schwabl 1969).

Like the other scholars mentioned above concerned with the historic and mythic aspects of the episode, Bernadete concentrates his inquiry on the portion of the story concerned with the death of Atys. Certainly this incident is pivotal, but it does not conclude the happening. The fate pursuing Croesus does not swerve until the Lydian king is about to be burned to death. The unity of this enveloping matrix has been largely ignored, with attention limited to the swift, tragic fulfillment of Solon's warning and the dream prophecy of Atys' death. The most perceptive analysis of the whole tale of Croesus is that of Segal (1971), who offers a sensitive appraisal of the events from the warning of Solon to the rescue of Croesus from execution by Cyrus. Segal remarks especially upon the dramatic and artistic effectiveness of the dumb, unnamed son of Croesus who remains with him through all the king's losses. While Segal does not point out the distinctive features that crucially oppose Croesus' sons, he is impressed by the affective force of the surviving son's silence, followed by his abrupt attainment of the ability to speak. Because the literary approach of

Segal concentrates on the entire text, structure and effect, he strikes very close to the heart of the matter.

The account of Croesus' downfall rewards many kinds of research, just as it fulfills a multileveled function in the whole of the *Histories* (cf. the second and third mandates of Lévi-Strauss 1973:83). As part of Herodotus' historical inquiry, it provides background to the rise of the Persian empire menacing the Greeks. On a didactic level, it warns of the fickleness of good fortune and the precariousness of overweening pride. There is, however, also a deep structure to this story which leads us to a broader perception of history, and a reinforcement of the fundamental lesson taught by Lévi-Strauss, that behind the world's disorder and flux there is an infrastructure of rationality and order; these qualities do not come, as Hegel mistakenly believed, at the end of history, but are omnipresent properties of the human mind, in the times of Herodotus no less than in our modern age of science.

3

The Croesus episode, in our view, represents an intricate and abstract statement about the nature and abundance of means of human, superhuman, and subhuman communication. Croesus, so sympathetically represented, becomes an embodied symbol for all human beings (Kleinpaul's universal *Vater*—see note 3), bombarded with information which all of us must decode and interpret if we are to survive. He is an all-too-successful seeker of knowledge of the future, an all-too-inadequate destination for the messages which reach him.

First, there is the counsel of Solon, a homiletic caution against the uncertain steadiness of good luck. His warning comes as an unexpected answer to a question Croesus has asked, although the king believes he knows the answer already. Croesus is merely seeking confirmation of his own belief that he is the most fortunate of men. Croesus ignores Solon's admonition: although the sense of Solon's words is straightforward enough, Croesus chooses to believe that this surface meaning is mistaken and that Solon is a fool (*Histories* 1:33).

Second, there is Croesus' dream concerning the fate of Atys (see further P. Frisch 1968:19–22). This imaging process of communion is silent, but eloquent nonetheless, and it is accurately interpreted by Croesus. The king's intended acts of preservation of his son are thwarted by the rhetorical expertness of Atys himself, whose masterful quibbling brings about his own reduction to silence by death. Croesus is warned as well by the omen of snakes, which he correctly perceives as significant, although the full interpretation does not reach Sardis before the predicted calamity has actually occurred.

Third, there is the oracular commonition concerning Croesus' second, nameless son. Croesus seeks advice about this boy's condition, only to be warned that, should this anonymous lad become speech-endowed, when that happens it will be upon a day of sorrow for Croesus. Finally, we have the oracular caveats concerning Croesus' political fate, offered in the form of cryptic messages, which, however, he again misapprehends, warranting his downfall. He is snared through the very means through which he meant to secure his success.

Note that Croesus interprets each silent communication accurately, but those communications encoded in speech both baffle and mislead him. The dream concerning the death of Atys becomes fatally deceptive only when Atys himself articulates his own interpretation, which Croesus unfortunately finds plausible. On the other hand, the messages of Solon and the oracle are mistakenly ignored in the first instance and mistakenly interpreted in the second.

In the advice of Solon, the dream of Croesus, messages from the oracle and the omen, we find an opposition between two kinds of semiotic agents. On one side, there are those agents which convey through symbolic discourse truths derived from homiletic and proverbial lore; on the other, we find information conveyed through symbolic discourse betokening supernatural knowledge of the intentions of the divine. The codes in which these three sources of information are couched require interpretation. The words of Solon and the dream warning of Atys' death, the sources of which are, in different degree, human, are thus relatively unequivocal, but the messages emanating from the oracle, having an ultimately supernatural origin, allow of several interpretations. Incapable of objectively unraveling the code of the oracular messages, Croesus is conquered by Cyrus.

In a renowned aphorism, Heraclitus (ca. 540–475 B.C.) captures the semiotic essence of oracular communication best. According to Romeo's recently emended translation, Heraclitus characterized the oracle as follows:

> The lord, who has the oracle in Delphi,
> neither discloses nor hides his thought,
> but indicates it through signs.
>
> (Romeo 1976:86)

It is the interpretation of these signifiers, with their hierarchy of possible signifieds, which Croesus fails to accomplish objectively, sensitively, and correctly.[6]

The density of symbolic communication in this narrative, almost suffocating, is most clearly embodied in and exemplified by the figure of Atys, the competent son whose putative gift for interpretation of his father's dream leads to his own death. In contradistinction to this richness of communication in oracular and prophetic discourse and interpretation, we have opposed to it its absence—silence. The silence is personified by a seemingly mute son, who not only cannot speak, but is neither spoken to nor capable of mention, for he has no name. When he miraculously breaks his silence, the result is not life destroying, as in the excessive communication of customarily verbal agents. Instead, the result is life sustaining: the Persian soldier is enabled to recognize Croesus, thus allowing him to survive. By a reversal of fortune, the silent, nameless son comes to speak and thereby to save his father's life; the competent son is, by his own eloquence, reduced to the silent anonymity of the grave. A dramatically unexpected sanction restoring the flow of communication comes to stand in antithesis to a tragically unforeseen arrest in its flow.

Lévi-Strauss, in his 1960 inaugural address, "Le champ de l'anthropologie" (1973:31-35), and more recently in a lecture delivered in London (1976:1-2), has pursued the problem of communication as explicated in myth, juxtaposing examplars of the Oedipus tale with medieval and Wagnerian redactions of the tale of Percival or Parsifal. According to Lévi-Strauss, the two worlds of the Percival myth—the castle of the Grail, and the Arthurian court—are characterized by lack of communication: in the Grail castle, a fixed waiting for a question never asked, in the Arthurian court, a nervous, alive questing for answers to questions. Lévi-Strauss contrasts the lack of communication in the myth of Percival with the myth of Oedipus, in which he perceives a world of excessive communication, "characterized by resolution of a riddle, rankness, and the explosion of natural cycles" (1976: 1)—a veritable hothouse of communication, and thus an inversion of the mythic world of the Percival tales.[7]

The story of Croesus appears to represent at least as prolific a hothouse of communication as the tale of Oedipus: we are confronted not merely with a single riddle but with a plethora of riddles, each pressing for interpretation on many levels. We are presented not only with a lone riddler, but with a multiplicity of informing sources, advisers, and counselors. In the end, Croesus himself intermittently passes from silence to discourse, turning even into a kind of Sybil, offering cryptic comment and implicit guidance to his conqueror Cyrus:

> Croesus, for all his misery, as he stood on the pyre, remembered with what divine truth Solon had declared that no man could be called happy until he was dead. Till then Croesus had not uttered a sound; but when he remembered, he sighed bitterly and three times, in anguish of spirit, pronounced Solon's name.
>
> Cyrus heard the name and told his interpreters to ask who Solon was, but for a while Croesus refused to answer the question and kept silent; at last, however, he was forced to speak. "He was a man," he said, "who ought to have talked with every king in the world. I would give a fortune to have it so." Not understanding what he meant, they renewed their questions and pressed him so

Figure 8-1. Side A of an amphora by Myson (perhaps from Vulci), now in the Louvre, depicting Croesus on a rich throne with footstool set on top of the lit pyre. The man dressed in a loin cloth, setting light to the pyre, is his own servant, Euthymos, not a Persian; this presumably indicates that the King's action is not subject to direct constraint. This famous vase appears to be the earliest record extant about the King of Lydia; the first literary reference dates from about thirty years afterward, and the account of Herodotus, discussed in this essay, half a century later. Used with permission of Hirmer Fotoarchiv München.

urgently to explain, that he could no longer refuse. He then related how Solon the Athenian once came to Sardis, and made light of the splendour which he saw there, and how everything he had said had proved true, and not only for him but for all men and especially those who imagine themselves fortunate—had all in his own case proved all too true.

While Croesus was speaking, the fire had been lit and was already burning around the edges. The interpreters told Cyrus what Croesus had said, and the story touched him. He himself was a mortal man, and was burning alive another who had once been as prosperous as he. The thought of that, and the fear of retribution, and the realization of the instability of all human things, made him change his mind and give orders that the flames should at once be put out, and Croesus and the boys brought down from the pyre. But the fire had got a hold, and the attempt to extinguish it failed. The Lydians say that when Croesus understood that Cyrus had changed his mind, and saw everyone vainly trying to master the fire, he called loudly upon Apollo with tears to come and save him from his misery, if any of his gifts had been pleasant to him. It was a clear and windless day; but suddenly in answer to Croesus' prayer clouds gathered and a storm broke out with such violent rain that the flames were put out. (*Histories*, 1:86)

In the end, Croesus is transfigured by his experiences—most particularly through the initiative of his thitherto silent son—into an effective mediator between the intentions of men and the fortunes ordained by the gods who respond to his prayers directly.

It is a masterstroke that this narrative finds its place at the beginning of the *Histories*. Chronologically, it represents a convenient, even rational starting point; didactically, it forewarns the reader to be on the lookout for the movement of an unpredictable fate through the fortunes of men and nations; indeed, this initial statement, in Fornara's (1971:77) happy phrase, "is programmatic for the entire work." Above all, the narrative contains a potent lesson concerning the nature of communication itself and the dangers of seeking to know too much and inquire too far without the gift of accurate interpretation.

Lévi-Strauss has said that ". . . all mythology comes back finally to posing and resolving a problem of communication; and the mechanisms of mythic thought, confronted by logical circuits so complex that it cannot make them all function together, consists of connecting and disconnection [of some of] the relays" (1976:2). Croesus, caught up in these intricate loops, masters the labyrinthine configurations and hookups only after, with wisdom born of bitter disappointment in the interpretation of oracular signs, he retreats into ultimate, if metaphorical, silence.[8]

Part Two: The Masters

9. The French Swiss Connection

"You know my method. It is founded upon the observation of trifles." *The Boscombe Valley Mystery* (1892)

"'Is there any point to which you would wish to draw my attention?'
  'To the curious incident of the dog in the night-time.'
  'The dog did nothing in the night-time.'
  'That was the curious incident,' remarked Sherlock Holmes." *The Adventure of the Silver Blaze* (1892)

Observers concerned with the spectacular revival and elaboration of semiotics over the last century or so have habitually wondered whether Peirce, the American philosopher, might, conceivably, have known about Ferdinand de Saussure's (1857–1913) science of *sémiologie* (exceptionally also *signologie*, but never *sémiotique*—cf. Sebeok 1976, Ch. 2), and/or whether Saussure, the Swiss linguist, might have been acquainted with at least a few of the writings of Charles S. Peirce (1839–1914) on the doctrine of signs. A possible link between these two contemporary giants could have been William Dwight Whitney (1827–1894), whose contacts with Saussure are well known; Jakobson (1971e:xxxvii) even emphasized that "In general Saussure's remarks on *sémiologie*, inspired by his meditations on Whitney, are essentially akin to the *semiotic* ideas of Peirce who, however, nowhere refers to his New England countryman."

As I remarked in a previous paper (Sebeok 1975b), there is no direct evidence whatever that Peirce met Whitney, although Peirce's father knew Whitney's brother Josiah quite well, William less well. In 1869–1870, W. D. Whitney and C. S. Peirce were fellow lecturers at Harvard, and it is not unlikely that they saw each other in Cambridge dur-

Note: This article is reprinted from *Semiotic Scene* 1:1:27–32 (1977). A Spanish translation appeared in *Lingüística, crítica literaria y literatura: Estudios ofrecidos a Emilio Alarcos Llorach*, edited by D. José A. Martínez (Universidad de Oviedo, 1978), vol. 3. Grateful acknowledgment is made for valuable information from Max H. Fisch, Robert Godel, and Kenneth Laine Ketner. Extrapolations beyond the facts are mine.

ing their sojourn there. In any case, Whitney would have known of Peirce not later than that year, and may have known of him as early as 1864, as being the coauthor of the *North American Review* article on Shakespearian pronunciation. Whitney was renowned for his editorship of the *Century Dictionary* (1889–1891), Peirce no less so for having been an editorial contributor to the same work, with responsibility for terms in astronomy, logic, mathematics, mechanics, metaphysics, and weights and measures; indeed, the editor explicitly coupled Peirce with Josiah Whitney several times in his preface to the *Dictionary*.

Another line of inquiry that, so far as I am aware, has not yet been carried out would be to comb through the Public and University Library of Geneva to ascertain whether Saussure's legacy included any publications or other papers by or mentioning Peirce. There is no telling how productive such a search may turn out to be, but the following illustrates that unexpected though seemingly trivial references can, on occasion, prove quite suggestive.

Kenneth Laine Ketner and James Edward Cook (1975) have been systematically unearthing Peirce's verified contributions to *The Nation* and making them public anew (Part One appeared in 1975, with three more tomes to follow). Ketner has recently called my attention to a review by Peirce of James Dwight Dana's biography[1] by President Daniel Coit Gilman, of the Johns Hopkins University (Ch. 6, this volume), toward the end of which the following critical sentence fragment appears: "It is difficult to believe that one of the De Saussures made a mistake in French for every three lines of print his letter fills" ([Peirce] 1899:455). Clearly, Peirce was aware of the Saussure family, if not necessarily of Ferdinand.

The Gilman book does, indeed, contain a letter "From H. de Saussure," dated in Geneva, July 3, 1857. The headnote identifies the correspondent as "the celebrated entomologist, author of *Études sur la famille des Vespides*; grandson of Horace Bénédict de Saussure, author of *Voyages dans les Alpes*; and nephew of Théodore de Saussure, author of *Recherches chimiques sur la Vegetation*" (Gilman 1899: 353). This letter then reads in full:

> C'est avec le sentiment de la plus haute satisfaction et d'une vivre reconnaissance que j'ai recu votre lettre du 29 mai par l'entremise obligeant de Mr. Fay. Chargé du departement entomologique du musée de Genève, je m'occupe d'en classer les Crustacés qui sont jusqu' à ce jour restés dans le plus beau désordre, et votre ouvrage me sera pour cela de la plus grande utilité. C'est du reste un livre indispensable à tous les musées dont le manque se fait d'autant plus sentir qu'il représente l'état actuel de la sciences, ce qu'aucun autre ouvrage ne fait.
>
> Je suis bien d'accord avec vous sur les points que vous me

signalez, mais je crois qu'il n'est pas possible de conserver les myriapodes parmi les crustacés comme le font les allemands. Je ne sais si vous l'avez fait et je me réjouis bien d'avoir votre superbe livre sous la main, afin de n'être plus arreté dans le travail qui concerne des derniers animaux, dont j'ai rapporté une très belle série du Mexique.

Je regrette que vous avez adressé votre ouvrage à la société de Physique, etc., plutôt qu'à moi personnellement, parceque les livres qui arrivent à cette destination sont remis à la bibliothèque publique, d'où il est très difficile de se les faire communiquer à domicile. J'avais cru devoir en faire la demande plutôt pour la société que pour moi, parceque j'avais pensé qu' à Washington on serait plutôt disposé d'envoyer un livre à une bibliothèque qu' à un particulier. Je dois bien vous avertir que la société de Physique n'a rien d'envoyer en échange que ses propres publications (*Mémoires de la Soc. de Physique*, etc., de Genève, 4°) qui sont mêlés d'histoire naturelle, de physique, d'astronomie, etc. Ils contiennent, entre autres, les mémoires paléontologiques de M. F. T. Pictet que vous ne possedez peut-être pas. J'ai fait, dans la dernière séance de la société, connaitre à mes collègues les démarches que j'avais faites aux fins d'obtenir votre ouvrage sur les crustacés, et la réponse favorable que j'avais obtenir de vous. Cependant si vous consentiez a me laisser posséder ces volumes à moi personnellement, vous n'auriez qu' à m'écrire une lettre *ad hoc* pour me dire que c'est à *moi personnellement* que vous envoyez vos livres, et cette attestation suffirait, d'autant mieux que de malheureuses chicanes gouvernmentales et politiques ont mis une barrière entre la société et la bibliothèque de la ville. Ma bibliothèque est du reste ouverte à tout le monde, et comme je suis pour le moment la seule personne qui s'occupe de crustacés a Genève, votre livre serait aussi bien placé chez moi qu' à la bibliothèque. (ibid.: 353–354)

The author of this letter was, of course, Henri de Saussure (1829–1905), a geologist and entomologist, who, in the mid-1850s, had conducted his researches in the Antilles and Mexico, as well as in the United States (De Mauro 1970:287). After his return to Switzerland, Henri was married, and Ferdinand was his first-born. It is not at all implausible that members of the Peirce family got acquainted with Henri while he was here, but, again, there is no evidence to prove this.

Horace-Bénédict de Saussure (1740–1799) was Ferdinand's great-grandfather, of whom it was said that, with the possible exception of Jean-Jacques Rousseau himself, he was the most outstanding of Genevese intellectuals and all-around scientists in the eighteenth century. He ascended Mont Blanc on August 3, 1784, and recorded his observations of that venture to the above-mentioned four-volume

Voyages that appeared between 1779 and 1796. The Théodore alluded to was Ferdinand's paternal uncle (1824–1903), who devoted his life mainly to civic and military tasks, having twice become a member of the federal artillery. However, he also wrote two plays, as well as *Études sur la langue française: De l'orthographe des noms propres*. Théodore was exceptional among those Saussures in that he did not become a renowned scholar in one or more of the natural sciences.

As Antoine Meillet wrote in his obituary notice of Ferdinand, the great linguist was born into a milieu "où la plus haute culture intellectuelle est depuis longtemps une tradition" (in Sebeok 1966a:2:92). In this respect, as in so many others, Saussure's biography reminds one of Peirce's, son of the famed Benjamin Peirce, the mathematician and natural philosopher, to whom the son was so indebted for an intellectual outlook steeped in scientific analysis.

Another prominent mathematician, Heyting (1962:195), spoke much later of "grades of evidence" in a most enlightening way. In an encouraging passage, he said: "It has proved not to be intuitively clear what is intuitively clear in mathematics. It is even possible to construct a descending scale of grades of evidence. The highest grade is that of such assertions as $2 + 2 = 4$. $1002 + 2 = 1004$ belongs to a lower grade; we show this not by actual counting but by a reasoning. . . . Such general statements . . . belong to a next grade. They have already the character of an implication." The edifice of conjectures erected in this article is obviously built upon bits of very low-grade circumstantial evidence. The objective of the exercise was certainly not to argue for a preconceived thesis, but to gather in one place the strands pointing to Peirce's Swiss connection, and to suggest one or two research possibilities that appear to merit further exploration for the sake of the historiography of modern semiotics.[2]

10. Neglected Figures in the History of Semiotic Inquiry: Jakob von Uexküll

The multiple decussations of the sign science—which Saussure (1967:36, 188N21) suggestively dubbed, in a strictly medical context, *signologie*—with the life science (Medawar and Medawar 1977) are hardly ever mentioned in historical accounts of either semiotics or biology, perhaps because such points of intersection seldom fall in the center of anyone's field of vision. Yet these penumbral zones merit careful cultivation if only for historical reasons. Thus we must be mindful of the common origins of Hippocratic medical biology, especially as transformed by Galen's anatomical knowledge and exactitude of mind into six categories for relating the individual to health and disease (*merē iatrikēs ta men prōta esti, to te phusiologikon kai to aitiologikon ē pathologikon kai to hugieinon to sēmeiōtikon kai to therapeutikon*; see Galen 1821–1833:xiv:689)—one of these branches being an explicitly spelled out tripartite *sēmeiotike*—and the more general philosophical notions of the *sēmeion*, particularly as conceived by such philosophers as Chrysippus, the third leader of the Stoa at Athens. The Stoics defined logic as the science about the signifying expression (*sēmaínōn*) and about signified things, i.e., what Sextus later recalled as the "incorporeal" (*asómatos*) matter of discourse conveyed by the sign, named the *lektón* (or *sēmainómenon*, emphatically not to be identified with "concept," and also to be sharply distinguished from the object in view). The ultimately and essentially biological nexus between the Stoics and the physicians in regard to what is signified, the *topos peri sēmainómenon*, was perspicaciously captured by an extraordinary polymath, the neurophysi-

Note: This paper was read August 27, 1977, at the III Wiener Symposium über Semiotik and published in Borbé 1978. It is the first of a series of studies intended to review contributions to the doctrine of signs on the part of scholars previously overlooked in this context. A parallel appraisal of Karl Bühler is in preparation at the invitation of the II Congress of the International Association for Semiotic Studies, scheduled for delivery in Vienna, July 1979.

Figure 10-1. Jacob von Uexküll. With grateful appreciation to Th. and G. von Uexküll.

Figure 10-2. Jacob von Uexküll in the laboratory. Courtesy of Th. and G. von Uexküll.

Figure 10-3. Jacob von Uexküll in the laboratory. Courtesy of Th. and G. von Uexküll.

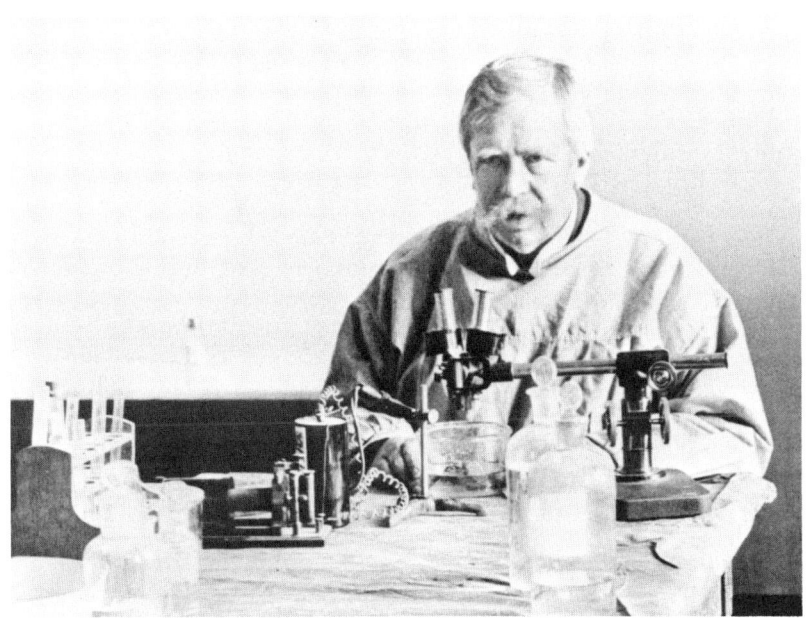

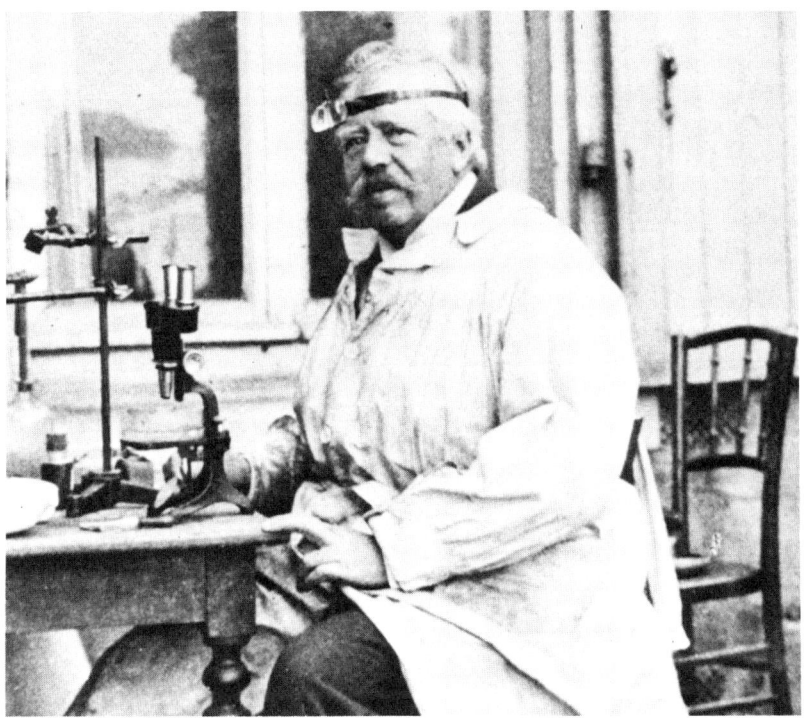

ologist McCulloch (1965:390), in his very vivid simile, ". . . something in the head like a fist in the hand [is] called the *Lekton*," or, couched more succinctly, "What's in the brain is the Stoic *Lekton*." Whatever else the Stoic semioticians may have meant by it, *lektón* surely designated the effable (cf. Bréhier 1962, Ch. 2), a motor schema representing a bodily state of the organism against which any event—verbal or nonverbal—is measured.[1]

Visionary physicians—like a handful of utopian semioticians—have independently called, in increasing numbers, for a reconvergence of their respective arts since Crookshank's provocative essay "The Importance of a Theory of Signs and a Critique of Language in the Study of Medicine," first appeared in the early 1920s (cf. Sebeok 1976:182). Also from the medical side, Thure von Uexküll (in press) has recently sketched out three categories of communication systems, discepting crucial problems of intersemiotic transmutation among them, with the aim of yielding a first approach to the "Aufgabenkatalog einer medizinischen Semiotik." Meanwhile, on the other side of the Atlantic community, Shands keeps pursuing the same goal in his multifarious approaches to clinical semiotics, probing some of its unexpected implications for medical inquiry (e.g., in Sebeok 1977b, Ch. 5).

It is not my purpose here either to dwell upon the antique roots of Western medical and semiotic execution, or to review the current conjoint efforts of even a few of the most creative practitioners of each. Before turning to other aspects of my principal subject, I should, however, like to display one arresting topic plainly of mutual interest to both but scarcely fathomable by either in isolation. This has to do with the so-called Placebo Effect (cf. Sebeok 1977b, Ch. 10, Section 6), that was proclaimed already by Galen in his apothegm "he cures most in whom most are confident" (cf. A. Shapiro 1960:117). The appellation designates the relief of symptoms supervening upon a patient's belief in the efficacy of his treatment, independent of or but tangentially related to the pharmacological component of the administered medication. In other words, the outcome of the treatment hinges not on a pharmacodynamically induced mechanism but a semiotic one: the therapeutic benefit of the "drug" (or other treatment) chosen by the agent—a shaman, a physician, or a sanctified surrogate, such as a nurse—is of little or no consequence to the patient and may, on occasion, even be deleterious. Until modern times, the history of medical practice was virtually tantamount to the inculcation of a trustful relationship between doctor and patient, since almost all medications the actor had to offer the one who was being acted upon were placebos (A. Shapiro 1960:113). The substance of the treatment itself didn't really matter. One example of (literally) antipodal deflection in remedial procedure must suffice: "A Dr. Raymond at the Salpêtrière in Paris found 70 per cent of patients suffering from a variety of diseases, including tabes, were treated successfully by suspending them by their feet, causing the blood to flow into their heads. A collaborator of Bernheim at Nancy, a Dr. Haushalter, reversed the procedure and suspended the patient's head upwards and obtained a similar per cent success in a variety of organic and nervous diseases" (ibid.).

The Placebo Effect is a semiotic transaction of the most fascinating, pellucid character. Its mitigating force derives from "the action, ritual, faith and enthusiasm" (ibid.) on the part of both interactants, or, in the words of Frank (1961:66), the chemically inert substance "gains its potency through being a tangible symbol of the physician's role as a healer." In a conventional clinical setting, the placebo seems to work best with those patients who expect medicines to help them and therefore accept and respond to symbols of healing. Going a long step further, Mary Baker Eddy, the remarkably astute founder of Christian Science, enshrined the "I shall please" phenomenon and promoted its semiotic distillate to pure, puissant dogma: "Mortal belief is all that enables a drug to cure material ailments" (Eddy 1934:174), she instructed her votaries, since "the so-called laws of health are simply laws of mortal belief" (ibid.:184). "A patient's belief is more or less moulded and formed by his doctor's belief in the case," she taught, "even though the doctor says nothing to support his theory. His thoughts and his patient's commingle, and the stronger thoughts rule the weaker" (ibid.:198).

In sum, placebo responsiveness works universally—in our society no less than in medically perhaps less sophisticated tribes—because the medicine man validates and iteratively revalidates his power through whatever ritual is culturally appropriate, assuming that the requisite structural conditions prevail. These involve three complementary factors: the message source or healer, the message destination, or patient, and the context of message delivery, including the group, each with its ceremonially pertinent paraphernalia. Lévi-Strauss, in his essay "The Sorcerer and His Magic" (1963, Ch. 9), enumerates the three human aspects of the operative belief thus: "first, the sorcerer's belief in the effectiveness of his technique; second, the patient's . . . belief in the sorcerer's power; and, finally, the faith and expectations of the group, which constantly act as a sort of gravitational field within which the relationship . . . is located and defined" (ibid.:168). Whether issuing spittle or ink for a prescription, faith in the act requires the attributes of a symbol, the species of sign whose relation to its object "is an imputed character" (Peirce 1935–1966:1.558), although, as Lévi-Strauss also cautioned (1963:184), "the mystical communion" between the interactants "does not have the same meaning for both parties and . . . ends by reducing the treatment to a fabulation."

Technically, a placebo is, however, something less than a symbol: it is that constituent of it which Peirce named an index (1935–1966: 2.293), or it is that peculiar kind of sign which has "a Symbol for its indirect Interpretant" (2.294). The semiotic categorization of a placebo as a more or less attenuated indexical symbol, or a metonym (Sebeok 1976:132), is no mere pedantic exercise. Beyond a certain conceptual clarification and the logical consequences thereof, its pigeonholing has practical import especially in a paper concerned with the ideas of J. von Uexküll, who counted among his closest disciples the neurologist and psychotherapist Bilz (G. von Uexküll 1964:156), author of a little known but most arresting disquisition, aptly titled *Pars pro toto* (1940), about indexicality in the realm of human and animal behavior. In this rare contribution explicitly at the interface of the life science and the sign science, Bilz—strongly influenced by the pioneer investigator he admired so greatly—argued that the *pars* "*bedeutet* nicht nur das, wovon er stammt und was er damit repräsentiert, sondern er *ist* schliesslich dasselbe!" (1940:71). Bilz dealt with "die Bindung des Kranken an seinen Arzt," characterizing the physician by a curiously evocative epithet as a *Lückenbüsser* (ibid.:93), roughly rendered as stopgap. He proposed a model for defining the nexus between subject and object that was in good conformity with both von Uexküll's theoretical biology and a then prevalent conception of universal sign function, Cassirer's (1953:86) "*symbolics* and *semiotics*" (see also Bilz's commentary on C. G. Jung's notion of *Übertragung*, Bilz 1940:95).

Before leaving this omnipresent and, as I think, primal theme of the Placebo Effect—to which I intend to return elsewhere, in the wider setting of the Clever Hans Fallacy (Sebeok 1978b)—I should like to call attention, in passing, to misguided efforts to reduce the indexical variables to zero, spurred no doubt by an authentic increase in the number of therapeutically effective drugs and the consequent menace to some physicians "by a real or imagined loss of self esteem and prestige among colleagues and in the community and by the threat of uncertainty or loss of magical powers" (A. Shapiro 1960:122). Undertakings like this, while they may sometimes have given rise to positive results —one such incidental by-product was the invention of the "double blind" design in psychopharmacology (Goldstein 1966:43), now generalized to behavioral research, e.g., to formally test the vocabulary of signs taught to a chimpanzee (Linden 1976:26–27)—are foredoomed. Not wishing to belabor this again, let me just repeat the thrust of an earlier observation, that, while the elimination of the index from the equation is, in the end, unfeasible, this is not even the really interesting issue, which, rather, "has to do with the nature of the communicative coupling between subject and object, hence [is] precisely a semiotic problem" (Ch. 3, this volume).

A most important area of convergence between biology and semiotics focuses upon a science now everywhere called ethology, which is very largely concerned with phylogenetic ritualization (cf., e.g., Lorenz 1977:207–214), and which could, therefore, with equal justification, be regarded as that diachronic branch of the sign science that has to

Jakob von Uexküll 193

do with the evolution of the—phyletic as well as cultural—behavior of communicating. As Smith (1977:2) recently emphasized, "Of the various biological disciplines that are involved with behavior, ethology has been most concerned with the study of communicating." The immediate interest of this equation (Sebeok 1976:85, 156), for which there are perfectly good historical reasons (outlined in Ch. 2, this volume), derives from the special position von Uexküll occupies in the early twentieth-century development of ethology, and his recognition, in spite of their fundamental philosophical dissidence, as one of the "most important teachers" of Lorenz (Lorenz 1971:274; cf. G. von Uexküll 1964:161; R. Evans 1975:96).

It has been said that von Uexküll's work "has had relatively little effect on animal behavior studies compared with the great originality of its content" (Klopfer and Hailman 1967:126). There are various more or less persuasive explanations for this, but none of these need trouble us here. My immediate concern is with the remarkable, if altogether implicit, semiotic orientation of many of his publications. This has previously been observed by scarcely a handful of readers. I find that I first mentioned his name in this connection as far back as 1963 (Sebeok 1972:61), and thereafter with increasing frequency; e.g., in 1968, I referred to his *Bedeutungslehre* as a "pioneer monograph" (ibid.:160; cf. Ch. 1, this volume). The earliest relatively extended appreciation I know of was accorded to specifically this aspect of his writings in, of all places, a Russian textbook of semiotics (Stepanov 1971:27–32). In Germany, Gipper (1969, Ch. 6; cf. 1972) meticulously examined the relevance of some of his leading ideas for the subsidiary field of *Sprachinhaltforschung*, and Krampen (1978) mentioned the implications of the *Werkzeug/Merkzeug* dichotomy for pragmatic systems. Gipper (1969:369–370) also recognized one ineluctable fact, namely, that the biologist's theory of cognition derives from the philosophy of Kant, "deren a-priori-Kategorien J. von Uexküll zur theoretischen Grundlegung seiner Anschauung heranzog." Not only are the consequences of this historical link taken into account "nicht immer mit der nötigen Sorgfalt" (ibid.:370), but its indirect reverberations through Cassirer's writings need ultimately to be considered, since his notions of symbolic function, and most particularly his biological bias, are elaborations of Kantian conceptions. For Cassirer, the problem of form, i.e., elevated to the central problem of epistemology, became the genuinely constitutive principle in respect to which, he claimed for his master, "Kant stood nearer to modern biology than he did to that of his own day" (cited in 1953:28). One must be mindful that, for Kant [1790], "Symbol ist eine Anschauung, die man Begriffen a priori unterlegt, und die eine 'indirekte Darstellung des Begriffs... vermittelst einer Analogie' enthält" (Haller 1959:135). In 1962, Lorenz (in R. Evans 1975:181–217) published an interesting extended commentary on "Kant's Doctrine of the A Priori in the Light of Contemporary

Biology." The recollection of von Uexküll was manifestly present there, with his celebrated maxim about freedom and restraint: "The amoeba is less of a machine than the horse" (ibid.: 186).

Sooner or later, von Uexküll's *Umweltlehre*—which constitutes the kernel of his semantics, or *Bedeutungslehre* (1970 [originally, 1940]) —must be inspected, both against its philosophical background and within the matrix of modern sensory physiology, to explore its semiotic explanatory power. The term *Umwelt*—which, of course, implies the tenet that any organization necessarily perceives the world in its own image rather than mirrors the universe "as it is"—with its many quasi-synonyms, including the excessively comprehensive and thus misleading abridgment *Welt*, is notoriously hard to translate. Nevertheless, its sense is quite clear. It is captured, in varying degree, by such overlapping English terms as *ecological niche, experienced world, psychological* or *subjective* or *significant environment, behavioral life space, ambient extension, ipsefact*, or, expressions that I prefer, *cognitive map* or *scheme*, or even *mind set*. This is perhaps best explained in the opening paragraph of von Uexküll's *Theoretical Biology* (1926:1): "Kant writes, 'Space is merely the form of all appearances of the outward senses, i.e., the subjective conditioning of sensibility, by which alone intuition of the outside world is possible for us.' The biologist would express this in the following way,—'The existence of space is dependent on the inner organisation of the subject's personality, which clothes the sense-qualities in spatial form.'" The startling implication of Kant's view of space, and of time as well, is that an organism cannot, through sense perception, be immediately aware of things—external objects or, by proprioception, internal ones either—as they really are, because spatial and temporal objects are altered in the very act of being apprehended: objects, having only the primary qualities, are but the causes of our experiences. The world known through the senses, i.e., von Uexküll's *Umwelt*, can only be a phenomenal world. The world of real objects is knowable only through reason (*Vernunft*), and solely by this act of symbolic cognition can some true propositions —thoughts about words, thoughts about thoughts, in brief, signs about signs (cf. Peirce 1935–1966:5.295)—be apprehended.

What is so interesting about Kant's ideas and von Uexküll's biological anchoring of them is that sensory processes and the ultimate homeostatic regulatory mechanisms of information-processing, comprehending the universal twin life-principles of "feedback" and "feedforward," are now understood to be programmed "in a way that gives modern sensory physiology a curiously Kantian colour" (Medawar and Medawar 1977:147). An appropriate alteration in the environment activates the sensory system through a receptor that is specific for a very limited number of modalities, say, certain wave lengths of light, and thereafter the initial receptor sign proceeds through a sign-processing system which ultimately generates the behavioral response. As von

Uexküll (1926:118) taught: "What we learn with regard to all our actions comes from the sense-signs alone, which serve to control our movement." In the retina, for example, the cones and rods collect light energy; this initiates a chain of chemical reactions which in turn leads to permeability changes in the adjoining nerve membranes. This idealized scheme applies to the human brain no less than the bacterium. In other words, sense organs "respond to changes in the environment and translate them," in the manner of transducer mechanisms (details of which are scarcely known; cf. Sebeok 1976:3; Ch. 3, this volume), "into the currency of nerve impulses" (Medawar and Medawar 1977: 145), or map one energy form into another. Thus the spatial and temporal pattern of the stimulus is transformed into impulses of varying patterns and frequencies. The *modality* of the sense is "not a property of the sense organ but is determined centrally" (ibid.). So also are the nature and quality of what is sensed: in our visual cortex, for instance, all axes of orientation are represented for each receptive field position, which leads the Medawars to conclude that (ibid.:147) "Kant's ideas no longer sound as extravagant as they once did." To this I may add that they in no wise conflict with the pragmaticism of Peirce either, for he also insisted on "a crystal-clear discrimination between the Object and the Interpretant of knowledge" (1935–1966:4.539)—that is what we have to finally reckon with here. Speaking not of psychology "but the logic of mental operations," Peirce spelled out his meaning: "A complex of percepts yields a picture of a perceptual universe" (ibid.). Organisms thus perceive not the *Ding an sich*, i.e., "things as they are," but signs, and from these signs, each according to its pre-existing *Bauplan*, or blueprint, build up mental models of the world that are equivalent to Peirce's interpretant, the function of which, according to him, is performed by another sign or a set of signs that occur together with the given sign (sign-alignment; cf., on the syntagmatic function, Bilz 1940), or might occur instead of it (in what linguists would call, in paradigmatic fashion, sign-alternation). What an animal communicates, in other words, is an edited selection from what, to it, is space/time. In passing, it may be worth mentioning here that one conspicuous facet of the logician Montague's posthumously highly fashionable semiotic program, applied to natural languages, is intended to deal with rules that govern the denotations of expressions in all possible worlds, not just in a particular world, designated "the actual world," and has hence become known as "possible-world semantics" (a current adaptation of Leibniz's "true in all possible worlds" approach to analyticity; by the way, the distinction between the analytic and the synthetic was introduced by Kant independent of the distinction between the *a priori* and the *a posteriori*, with which it is often confused). This is claimed by its practitioners, despite certain grave difficulties, to have "succeeded in producing solutions to semantic puzzles of long standing, in the form of generalizations of widely accepted mathematical theories" (Thomason, in Montague 1974:56), and raises certain large and unexplored issues about psychological reality, including the general limits imposed by our cognitive capacity on the kinds of alternative worlds we can consider, as touched upon in Partee's provocative discussion (forthcoming).

The fundamental semiotic problem von Uexküll attempted to deal with was to connect the real world with the phenomenal world in a biologically satisfying way, and to give a detailed accounting of what he referred to as a contrapuntal relationship between an organism and its environment. In retrospect, the solution seems simple enough, as phrased, for example, by Lorenz (1977:9–10) after Kant: "the system of sense organs and nerves that enables living things to survive and orientate themselves in the outer world has evolved phylogenetically through confrontation with an adaptation to that form of reality which we experience as phenomenal space. This system thus exists *a priori* to the extent that it is presented before the individual experiences anything, and must be present if experience is to be possible. But its function is also historically evolved and in this respect not *a priori*. The paramecium, for example, makes do, so to speak, with a one-dimensional 'ideation of space' but we cannot know how many dimensions there are to space *an sich*." The task of von Uexküll (1926:xv), clearly inspired by Kant, was twofold: a reconsideration, in then current biological terms, of the body's steering mechanisms, especially its sensory apparatus and central nervous system, and the study of the biological mooring of the epistemological relationship between the perceiving subjects (animals) and their objects of perception (*Merkwelt*, or perceptual world). His view of spatial and of temporal qualities, which Kant had called "the material," was cast in a semiotic frame. It begins with a sophisticated, elaborate, and original classification of signs, the complexities of which can only be hinted at here, but which should be understood as a steady striving for a kind of information ecology.

Von Uexküll referred to space forming qualities as local signs and to their connections as direction signs, distinguishing between two types, transverse signs and longitudinal signs, and discussing the properties of each in much detail. For example, he contrasted local signs and direction signs by the distinctive feature of reversibility, which he judged unique. He elucidated the transformation of the two kinds of outer direction signs into corresponding inner signs, a very important identification, "for they enable us to bring to a common measure our own movements in the outside world" (1926:10). To the key question, "What does the space look like that surrounds animals?" he suggested, procedurally, that we first determine what the visual space of a human being is like, then modify this according to the faculties of the animal under investigation. This is achieved by decisions about the animal's repertoire of signs, although the result can only yield us "intuited space" (ibid.:42).

His exposition about time was parallel: apperception is a life-process carried out in phases, he argued, each of which manifests itself through a sense-sign, which he named the moment sign, invariant as to its magnitude and intensity, variable only in its content. Notions of number, calculation and estimation, and of threshold phenomena, ensue, and here he introduces the concept of order sign. A fascinating aside about the unity of the *ego*, "always furnished with a moment-sign" (ibid.:53), curiously evokes and complements a famous passage in Peirce (1935–1966:4.6) about the way in which thinking always proceeds in the form of a dialogue, itself necessarily composed of signs, between different phases of the *ego*.

Next, von Uexküll arrives at the concept of the mark sign, the *Merkzeichen*, also called perceptual or receptor sign, or stimulus (contrasted elsewhere with *Wirkzeichen*, which gives internal information, and differentiated from *Merkmal*, a bundle of perceptual cues [cf. 1957: 9]). Mark signs are again of two types: those for qualitative differences and those for different grades of intensity. Mark sign, illustrated by the human discrimination of color percepts, refers to an alteration in content that is just perceptible to the attention; thus the number of mark signs for color "increases with the skill of the individual observer in distinguishing colours" (1926:76), thus giving us a measure of the amount of color in his *Umwelt*. Klopfer and Hailman (1967:126) commented on this: "If an animal is color blind but otherwise has eyes similar to our own, the animal's *Umwelt* can be approximated by a black-and-white photograph of its physical environment."

Corresponding to the internal mark signs, von Uexküll speaks of external "indications." Note the kinship of this idea to Peirce's reactional sign of dual character, to wit, his index, "which is such by virtue of a real connection with its object" (1935–1966:5.74). "When indications make their appearance in the world, they are already in the grip of these laws, and this without any reference to the objects with which they are associated," von Uexküll remarked (1926:78). Compare the foregoing with Peirce's "The premises of Nature's own process are all the independent uncaused elements of facts that go to make up the variety of nature which the necessitarian supposes to have been all in existence from the foundation of the world. . . . These premises of nature, however, though they are not the *perceptual facts* that are premisses to us, nevertheless must resemble them in being premisses" (5.119). The sum of indications were called by von Uexküll "world-as-sensed." In this connection, it is further worth noting that von Uexküll anticipated certain basic cybernetic concepts: indications, he noted, "enable the animal to guide its movements, much as the signs at sea enable the sailor to steer his ship," and the animal, "by the very fact of exercising such direction, creates a world for itself" (1926:126). This he called the inner world (*Innenwelt*).

In the course of the development of his "theory of indices" (1926:

137–140), von Uexküll makes the following highly interesting observation: "Now suddenly we see why it is that we cannot omit from biology the study of the theory of knowledge. For this alone teaches us to reduce our human indications to the simplest factors, and then to combine them once more" (ibid.: 139). In my opinion, this section comes to grips with the rationale for combining the life science with the sign science, for, to paraphrase von Uexküll somewhat, a semiotic that is biologically uninformed "is sheer amateurishness."

Animals are composed of two halves: a receptor half and an effector half. The former corresponds to the world-as-sensed, the latter to the world of action, and together they make a comprehensive whole, the "surrounding world." How is the system of mark organs linked up with the system of action organs? To depict this bond, von Uexküll posited a functional cycle (*Funktionskreis*), which he regarded as the elementary unit of behavior. His oft-reproduced information flow diagram of it (Fig. 1-1 in this volume, adapted from von Uexküll 1926:155, 157; 1957:10; 1970:11; see also Lorenz 1971:274) may, at first glance, appear simplistic, but it amounts to a reasoned conspectus for a vast program of research, of semiotic no less than biological import.

The ethological investigation of any species traditionally begins with an inventory of all ascertainable patterns of behavior, nowadays commonly called the animal's ethogram, but recognized already by Jennings (1906:300) as the organism's "action system," the discovery of which the American scientist considered the first requisite to understanding its behavior: "It is usually possible to determine with some approach to completeness the various movements which a given organism has at command," for, as a rule, these form a coordinated system.[2] A like determination of the number and properties of each of the organism's functional cycles became, accordingly, von Uexküll's primary goal. One such cycle (or "circle," as one of his translators would have it) has to do with "the enemy" (1926:155), or, more broadly, with living beings that are biologically significative, such as prey and predators: their forms and behaviors, attractive or repellent, act as releasers for long-range motor processes, such as pursuit or flight. The initial task is to catalog the receptor and effector cues that compose the arcs of each cycle, "and to analyse their causal interaction with the structure of the organism, on one side, and that of environment on the other" (Lorenz 1971:275). The rest of this paragraph continues the quotation from Lorenz, but his statements are themselves a very close paraphrase, interlaced with many literal citations, from a 1921 book of von Uexküll's:

> The organism's 'inner world' (*Innenwelt*), comprising the whole of its bodily structures and/or functions, is causally influenced from the side of the 'perceptual field' (*Merkwelt*), that is to say, those parts of environment which affect its receptor organs, in

other words those which are selected, out of innumerable others, by the specific organization of the receptors. The conception of the latter does not by any means include the sense organs only, but also the whole organization which, within the central nervous system conveys specifically releasing stimulation in the direction towards effector organizations. The function of receptors is not only to receive releasing stimuli, but also to exclude all others from becoming effective. All the stimulus data originating from receptor cues converge centreward into a network of interactions (*Merknetz*) which constitute the central representation and the unity of the receptor cue. On the effector side, a corresponding network (*Wirknetz*) serves to integrate and co-ordinate the single muscle contractions into an activity which represents an adaptive response to the cues received. The task of investigating the biology of any species of animals can be regarded as fulfilled only when all functional cycles are fully analyzed and when we have gained full knowledge of what "strings" keep the organism suspended, in a steady state, within its environment. These strings of course, are, as we all know, causal chains interlocking by hook and eye. It is mechanical problems that are confronting us on every side.

Lorenz observed that the research program mapped out by von Uexküll was "pretty nearly identical with that of ethology" (ibid.), but it can just as well be viewed, especially if read in the light of an extended polemic essay von Uexküll published in 1940 under the title *Bedeutungslehre* (1970:105–179), as a program for a semiotic investigation of the most elemental kind. Von Uexküll reasoned that every organism's blueprint, the *Bauplan*, implies a pre-established and pre-stabilized harmony of two structures: outer, or environmental, with inner, or organic, and that the nexus between the two structures is a strictly semantic link-up: "Die Lebensaufgabe von Tier und Pflanze besteht darin, die Bedeutungsträger bzw. Bedeutungsfaktoren gemäss ihrem subjektiven Bauplan zu verwerten" (ibid.:118). Stepanov (1971:28) drew attention in this connection to what I noted above, von Uexküll's prevision of certain fundamentals of the art of the helmsman, precisely those, I think, that eventually came to provide teleology with a proper mechanistic base in biology.[3]

The functional cycle of von Uexküll sites human signification within the range of a particular set of semiotic systems that the so-called Moscow-Tartu school has dubbed secondary modeling systems (Ch. 3, this volume), by means of which (roughly speaking) models of the world or its fragments are reconstructed. The Soviet scholars had in mind systems which are secondary in relation to the primary system of natural language, the infrastructure, as it were, over which such superstructures as literature are built. But this notion is part of a still wider range of phenomena, tied to a theory of reflection (cf. the classic Marxist principle that consciousness is a true reflection of the objective world) over the entire domain of every species, comprehending both the inorganic and organic distinctive features of each surround (cf. Ch. 1, this volume) (of which, by the way, there must, by definition, be at least as many as there are animals). Reflection is a necessary function of every mind, if mind is taken in Peirce's sense (1935–1966:4.550 n.), as "a propositional function of the widest possible universe, such that its values are the meanings of all signs whose actual effects are an effective interconnection." It was one of von Uexküll's greatest merits that he squarely faced, as Peirce did before him, the inevasible fact that signification is not a peculiarity of language, or even of human cognition, but occurs, in various manifestations, throughout organic existence. Only a semantic theory cast "in some form of idealistic nominalism akin to Fichte's" can afford to ignore the facts that "there cannot be thought without Signs," and that thought is and develops in the organic world (Peirce 4.551).

A fascinating by-product of von Uexküll's semantic model has to do with a problem being debated with increasing vigor today because of a recent accumulation of reports which tend to be widely interpreted as evidence for homology in cognitive schemata across primates, especially between apes and man. Thus Rumbaugh and Gill (1976b:565) have conjectured that, "to the degree an organism has hominian intelligence, it has the private, covert, processes of symbolism and attendant concept formation; and that whatever the nature of these processes are, they *are* linguistic." With many others, they further "hold that language is inherent in the covert cognitive operations that provide for the comprehension of relationships, the formulation of strategies for problem solving, and other expressions of creativity." In the previous decade, disturbingly similar claims were being promulgated, *mutatis mutandis*, about the more remote mind of the dolphin: for example, Bateson's (1966:571) first expectation in studying their communication was that it would likewise prove to be "primarily about relationships," and he concluded (p. 575) that, in certain important respects, "the vocalizations of the dolphin resemble human' language rather than the kinesics or paralinguistics of terrestrial mammals." The ambitions connoted by statements of this kind are a far cry indeed from Wittgenstein's (1929) pessimistic epigram: "Wenn ein Löwe sprechen könnte, wir könnten ihn nicht verstehen" (1953:223:32). The reverse assumption fuels many research programs in animal communication today, including Griffin's boldly imaginative proposal (1976:89–95) for what he has termed "participatory investigation" to provide a window to the animal's mind. Griffin adds: "If we consider the recent history of this field [i.e., animal communication studies], it is clear that far more complex communication behavior has been found than any scientist would have ventured to predict 30 years ago" (ibid.:94). In fact, however, this was exactly the forecast made, as far back as 1920, by von Uexküll (1926:177) in two truly arresting sentences: "... modern psychology affirms that all animals, or at least the higher animals, have a human intelligence, which is not expressed simply because the bodily organisation sets limits to it. If we succeed in getting an animal to produce a suitable sign-language by means of its organs, we can converse with it as with human beings." I hardly need to underline that this uncannily modern—although by no means necessarily correct—view constitutes the most fundamental canon of all current projects of two-way communication with apes, namely, that language is not contingent upon speech, or airway, but upon features of the brain, or the supposedly high-order cognitive mechanisms (or "intelligence") common to the species[4] (although powerful opinions to the contrary are also often voiced—cf. Limber 1977:290–292, and the question is still very far from being settled; for my own views on this subject, see Sebeok 1977b, Ch. 3 this volume, and esp. 1978b).

A principal reason why von Uexküll's contributions are generally ignored by natural scientists, including most ethologists, today, is his rejection of the fact of evolution, which he characterized as "absurd" (1926:263). His preformationistic convictions not only vitiated his biology in their eyes but also deprive his model of a viable diachronic dimension for us (which must not, however, be taken to mean that his conception of life was static; like Goethe's, his interest was not in *Gestalt*, or fixed form, but in *Bildung*, or form change, in which the static *Gestalt* is but a momentary phase in a dynamic process). Nevertheless, it should be noted that his view of embryonic shaping was far from naïve: "there is no framework in the germ, but ... there is a *rule*" (ibid.:182), he argued, which could be characterized, borrowing from modern linguistics, as a *generative* rule, and which, he emphasizes, "is not a mere formula; it is a natural factor" (ibid.:230). Its analysis was made possible by Mendel's revelation of the workings of heredity. What Mendel's discovery of the genes provided for von Uexküll was congruity, that is, the presence of "all the pegs and sockets of the counterproperties" (ibid.:317) between the features of the external world, which exercises no direction-giving influence, and the living genome, which possesses no organs that could give it knowledge of these features, and a certain rule to complete the congruity required by the functional cycle. In two words, von Uexküll's theory provides *signs* and *rules*; it thus aspires to become the kind of life science as well as the kind of sign science that Peirce called nomological (1935–1966: 7.83–84), and that Piaget calls nomothetic (1970:3; Piaget's usage goes back at least to Windelband, in 1894, echoed by A. Huxley, in 1963—cf. Sebeok 1976:150). However, it was only when Thom's catastrophe theory came along (Thom 1974a; 1975a; cf. Sebeok 1976; Ch. 1, this volume) that this high aspiration for "law-seeking" ripeness began to loom as a palpable possibility, and Thom (1975a:xxiii) duly credits von Uexküll among his best-known forerunners, particularly for his description of the essential difference between the dynamic of life and the anthropomorphic constructions with which it is often compared (1975a:200). He is referring here to Uexküll's (1970:123-124) opposition between the mechanism of such a machine as a watch and the growth of an animal, for example a *Triton*. In both of these cases, there is an underlying construction plan. However, for the watch, the plan controls a centripetal process, in the mollusk a diametrically opposed centrifugal process. What all this means is that the artifact must always be built up by completion of its several parts—cogs, springs, etc.—which are then mounted on a common support, whereas the animal's parts are assembled temporally in the order in which they appeared, as biologists would nowadays insist, in the course of evolution, and spatially from inside toward outside. The animal's components are each endowed with what von Uexküll called their *Ichton*. The unitary *Bedeutungton* is then integrated, as it were, out of a hierarchy of specialized *Ichtöne* "die sich nun in verschiedene aufeinander abgestimmte Töne sondern und die Formbildung entsprechend einer von vornherein feststehenden Melodie ablaufen lassen" (ibid.:124). As in the sea urchin, the independently working "reflex persons," when acting in unison, come to constitute a "reflex republic" (ibid.: 39-40), in von Uexküll's provocative and much controverted pair of metaphors. Thom's point, as he has repeated on various occasions, is that "C'est évidemment en Biologie—science plus proche de l'homme —que l'on pouvait s'attendre a voir réapparaître la notion de signification." This emerged under two entirely different historical circumstances, the first associated with the theory of perception: he credits von Uexküll for having made the first approximation under the specific constraints of his time and discipline. A subsequent occasion for the reintroduction of signification into the life science is suggested by more recent progress in genetics and molecular biology. Of this succession of efforts, Thom questions rhetorically whether "une discipline qui cherche à préciser le rapport entre une situation dynamique globale (le 'signifié'), et la morphologie locale en laquelle elle se manifeste (le 'signifiant'), n'est-elle pas précisément une 'sémiologie'?" (1974a:194-196). For von Uexküll, certainly, all of nature was an expertly knit web of *Umwelten*, intertwined according to a fantastic master plan. In terms of a doublet perpetuated by Frege in 1892, he avowed: "Alles in ihm hat Sinn und Bedeutung" (von Uexküll 1935: 378).

The theses of von Uexküll, taken as a whole, raise a host of philosophical issues, some of which are of particular concern to inquirers into problems of communication and signification. For instance, his functional cycle implies a clear distinction between an "outer" *Umwelt* of objects and the *Innenwelt* of the subject, traversed by signs converted at some limen. An area that has interested me for some time

(Ch. 3, this volume), and which is studied most intensely by transducer physiologists, is just the boundary phenomena between the polarities of *ego* and *alter*, viz., the communicative radius or the topological configuration of space/time that Hediger uncovered and analyzed in many animals. In mentioning this, it is worth noting that von Uexküll (1935:379) himself alluded to this "bubble" concept in man when he remarked: "Jeder von uns Menschen trägt sein Himmelsgewölbe mit sich herum wie eine riesige undurchsichtige Seifenblase." Animal psychology, wrote its foremost contemporary practitioner, Hediger (1972:566), "glaubt, sich verstehend, in gewissem Sinne mitempfindend in die Situation eines Individuums einfühlen zu können, nicht zuletzt aufgrund ethologischer Daten und aufgrund genauer Kenntnisse der betreffenden Umwelt, zu welcher Uexküll . . . den Schlüssel geliefert hat." It was, of course, Hediger himself who eventually came to formulate, in quite precise scientific terms, the conception of the "bubble," which, in turn, underlies all researches in the so-called proxemic behavior of man (Hall 1968), so far remaining a surprisingly underdeveloped branch of anthroposemiotics.

The *Umweltlehre* of von Uexküll requires no more than that the categories of experience and knowledge be isomorphic to the real universe—not that the two halves of the cycle fully correspond with one another, let alone that the *Innenwelt* completely represent the world. A rather circumscribed repertoire of guiding signs sufficiently serves the purpose of the organism, which is the sustenance of its survival. He explained (1936:14) that to trace a map "muss man die sinnlichen Anschauungen ausschalten und sie durch Symbole ersetzen, die sich einer gedanklichen Konstruktion einführen lassen." A map is not a picture, "sondern eine Zusammenstellung symbolischer Zeichen," or "eine abgekürzte Beschreibung in einer konventionellen Zeichensprache," as we know from Peirce (1935–1966:3.419), who likewise taught that a map cannot be read unless the law of the projection is understood, "nor even then unless at least two points on the map are somehow previously identified with points in nature." Another simile was suggested by von Bertalanffy (1955:257), whom I paraphrase, underlining the obvious: that the indexical sign "red" is not identical with the various hazards it stands for; it suffices for this signifier to indicate them, that is, to be isomorphic to "stop" as "green" is isomorphic to "go," allowing orientation and therefore the preservation of the informed interpreter. The *Umweltlehre* encompasses an immense range of problems of relativism of categories from the perspectives of language and culture that evoke especially the ideas of W. von Humboldt and Benjamin Lee Whorf (not to be pursued here, for these have already been dealt with exhaustively by Gipper 1969; 1972).

Upon reflection, von Uexküll's semiotic epistemology brings to mind some salient aspects of Popper's interactionist views of objective knowledge, and particularly his pluralist thesis of multiple worlds.

Popper (1972:74) introduced the terms "world 1," to denote the physical world, "world 2," the world of our conscious experiences and subjective knowledge of all kinds, and "world 3," especially the world of language, spoken or manifested in whatever other substance (cf. von Humboldt's *Sprachwelt*), and also including the logical content of entire libraries, computer memories, myths and scientific theories, mistakes and arguments, as well as the world of artistic products and social institutions, which, according to taste, could also be singled out as "world 4" and "world 5" (the latter, of course, roughly correspond to what I have referred to above as secondary modeling systems). World 2 can be taken to refer to each individual's private state of mind, which J. C. Eccles subdivides into three levels: outer sense, comprehending the ordinary perceptions provided by all our sense organs; inner sense, i.e., the world of our emotions, and both memory and foresight; and self, or pure *ego*, our perduring consciousness throughout our entire lifetime. Whereas world 2 is our primary reality, world 1 is a derivative construct, a realm of secondary reality. World 3 is, so to speak, a region in the public domain, and relates uniquely to man: all other animals are blind to all of it. Popper intends by this partition to emphasize the limited autonomy of each world: world 1 is often asserted to be the only one that "really" exists; world 2 is sometimes called behavior, and world 3 is verbal behavior. Killing belongs to world 1 (Peirce's "action by brute force," or dynamical action, as in 1935-1966:5.484), intimidation belongs to world 2, and "impersonal arguments" (Popper 1972:84) belong to world 3 (both of the latter exemplifying different kinds of *semiosis*, in Peirce's sense). Translating into my own terminology, (nonverbal) zoosemiotics would enfold world 2, (verbal) anthroposemiotics world 3 (Sebeok 1972, Ch. 8).

Popper further propounds several theses on epistemology and his third world (which, in philosophical tradition, resembles most closely the universe of Frege's objective content of thought). His critical position vis-à-vis Kant, whom he classes with "belief philosophers," is particularly interesting to us in this context, but on the issue of our intuitive grasp of time he sides decidedly with Whorf and thus, by extension, with von Uexküll: he finds Whorf "utterly convincing" and concludes that "our intuition of time may change with our changing theories" (Popper 1972:135). The crux of his argument hinges on biological, viz., evolutionary considerations. Popper (ibid.:112-115) sharply distinguishes production problems from the produced structures themselves. The approach from the side of the products is what he calls the "objective" or world 3 approach, and the behaviorist, psychological, and sociological approach the "subjective" or world 2 approach. This discrimination goes to the heart of the relationship between the observer and the observed, the *Ding an sich* and its appearances, manifestly calling for a phylogenetic answer to the question how our cognitive structures and functions, which Popper calls the perceiving apparatus, got the way that they did. This relationship is, of course, an essentially semiotic one, for it involves a process, learned while we are young, of decoding extremely complicated messages reaching us from our *Umwelt*, according to "innate dispositions" keyed to "reality." In brief, says Popper (ibid.:63) "our subjective knowledge of reality consists of maturing innate dispositions."

The worlds 1, 2, and 3, since they belong to the same universe, surely interact, continuously and intensely, but, adds Popper, "it can easily be shown that knowledge of the universe, if this knowledge itself forms part of the universe, as it does, must be incompletable" (in Ayala and Dobzhansky 1974:280). This indeterminacy can be illustrated by returning to von Uexküll's exemplar of a map: "Take a man who draws a detailed map of the room in which he is working. Let him try to include in his drawing the map which he is drawing. It is clear that he cannot complete the task, which includes an infinity of smaller and smaller maps within each map: every time he adds a new line to the map, he creates a new object to be drawn, but not yet drawn. The map which is supposed to contain a map of itself is incompletable" (ibid.). This is a statement, in picturesque form, of Gödel's incompleteness theorem.

The modes of interaction between world 1, world 2, and world 3 are depicted by Eccles (1974:93) in a diagrammatic flow chart which delineates the principal lines of communication to and from the brain and within the brain, that is, from peripheral receptors to the sensory cortices, and so to the cerebral hemispheres, and vice versa, displaying the output from the cerebral hemispheres via the motor cortex, and so to the muscles. Eccles's diagram can be read as a fleshed-out version of von Uexküll's functional cycle, but specific to mankind and hence less generalized—circumscribing, say, the ambit compassed in von Uexküll's book of memoirs (1936), as delightful as it is insightful. In this graph (Fig. 10-4), the minor hemisphere has "the status of a very superior animal brain," according to Eccles (1974:92), because evidence is lacking that this brain has some residual consciousness of its own, and the mind that it is postulated to house is prevented from communicating to us since it is naturally speechless (cf. Ch. 3, this volume). (The two hemispheres do communicate one with the other as indicated, through the untransected corpus callosum.)

The entry of consciousness into semiotic inquiry was independently foreseen and emphasized by Peirce and by von Uexküll. Whether consciousness is regarded as a phenomenon accessible to science, or as a logically untenable epiphenomenon—the Ghost in the Machine— the *expressions* of it, in all animals by means of their species-specific nonverbal competencies, in man by his superimposed verbal competence as well, constitute a proper domain for semiotic researches. Peirce devoted a dazzling lecture to "Consciousness and Language" (1935–1966:7.579–596), and was especially preoccupied with the relation of the sign he called the interpretant to intelligent consciousness

206 The Masters

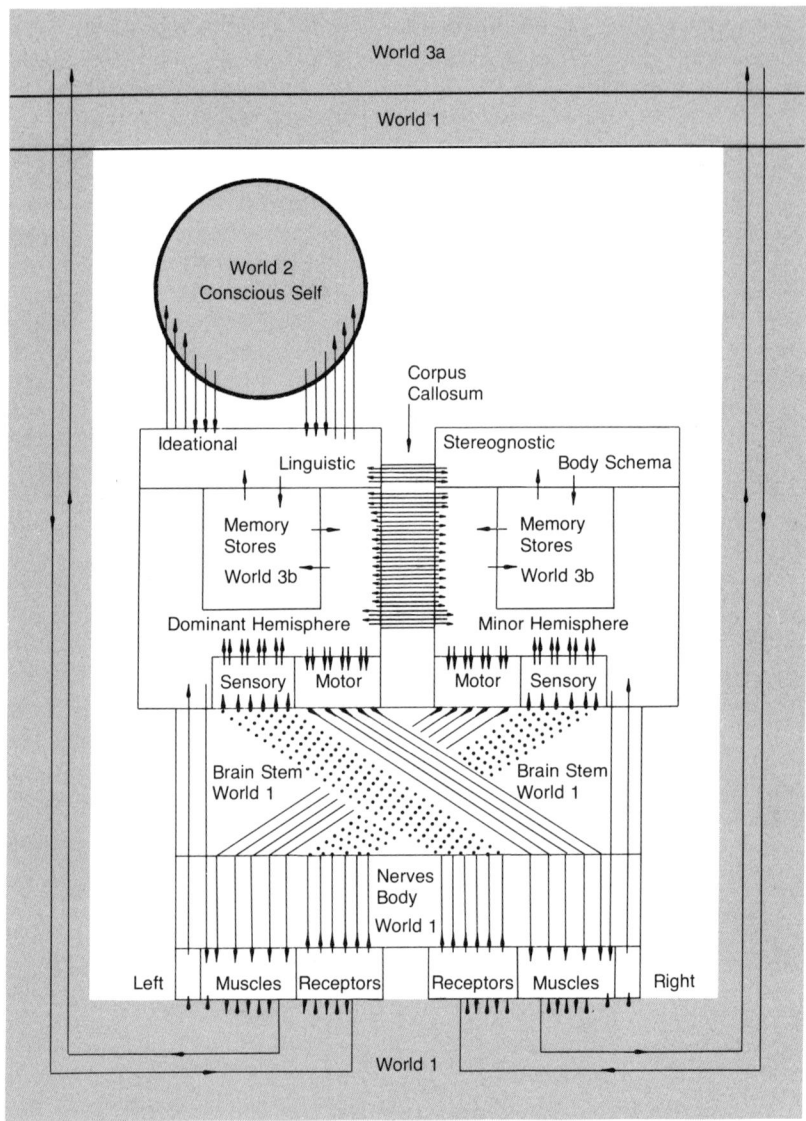

Figure 10-4. Modes of interaction between world 1, world 2, and world 3, as pictured by Eccles after Popper. See text for sources and explanation of this graph. From *The Understanding of the Brain*, by John C. Eccles. Copyright 1973 by the author. Used with permission of McGraw-Hill Book Company.

(e.g., 2.303). Von Uexküll was concerned with the discontinuity—for the animal's perceptual world is constantly changing—of subjectivity and the impermanence of the subject-object distinction in animals. This breach in continuity persists in man's alternating patterns of wakefulness and sleep. During the paradoxical (REM) phase initiated in the pontine reticular formation to which many sensory nerve fibers carry the signs that are implicated in the maintenance of consciousness, that is, during states of vivid dreaming, the ninety-minute stage of sleep when the right hemisphere is almost completely unshackled from its otherwise dominant counterpart (Ch. 3, this volume), this discontinuity of subject-object is still preserved in the course of man's imaging processes, which are therefore regarded by some as an evolutionary transition in several different ways (cf. Ch. 3, this volume). Von Uexküll particularly considered the problem of self-observation, and was convinced that "What we are conscious of are only those [indications] that appear in the mark-organ of our brain, when we perform plastic actions" (1926: 357). At the conclusion of this, his most consequential, book, he touched on the questions why the organization of the subject remains so incomplete, why the impulses that build up our bodies elude our knowledge, why certain realities remain inaccessible to investigation, and why, in the end, biology must proceed from elements of intuition. A way—and the only way so far—in which solutions to these and allied puzzles might be found through a sophisticated synthesis of the life science and the sign science has now been shown in Thom's already classic essay of a theory of signs (1974a; Ch. 11), constructing high upon foundations laid by two of his giant, if vastly different, precursors, Peirce and von Uexküll.

Figure 11-1. Gyula Laziczius. With thanks to Academician Péter Hajdú.

11. Gyula Laziczius

In the course of a report on some highlights of the Eighth International Congress of Linguists, a distinguished Hungarian specialist in Finno-Ugric languages makes a bitter charge. "It is common knowledge," he laments, "that no Hungarian contributions to the theory of structuralism exist" (Lakó 1958:197). This sweeping indictment—belied a dozen pages later by the obituary of Gyula Laziczius,[1] an internationally appreciated contributor to the structuralist movement, but a prophet with hardly a follower in his own land[2]—may well stand as an epitaph in memory of this dedicated linguist, whose career was shaped by a series of harsh ironies.

Laziczius was born on August 18, 1896, in Újpest, a district of the capital where he died on August 4, 1957. During his life of threescore years, he was able to function barely a decade and a half as a productive scholar, so many and so oppressive were the reverses visited upon him. Having completed his elementary and secondary schooling in Újpest, he enrolled at the University of Budapest, in 1914; but his studies were interrupted by World War I, which he spent partly in a Russian military prison. Upon his return, in 1918, he continued his higher education and, after graduating in 1920, earned his living as a teacher, for some years, in a variety of secondary schools. In 1922, however, he was dismissed from his post, for political reasons, and ten years were to pass before he was able to free himself from stultifying clerical jobs and, in 1932, resume teaching. The following year, he completed a thesis for his "habilitation": "General Phonology, with Particular Reference to Hungarian and the Slavic Languages." In 1935, he became a corresponding member of the Academy; the next year, an adjunct professor of Hungarian linguistics; then, in 1938, he was called to occupy, as an extraordinary professor, the newly established chair of General Linguistics and Phonetics (which was, incidentally, the first comparable academic position to be established anywhere), and became an ordinary professor of these subjects in 1940. During World War II, he suffered a series of tragic personal misfortunes, including the loss of a son, under particularly grim circumstances. In 1949, he was forcibly retired from his chair, once again for political reasons. He spent the eight remaining years of his life with hardly any

Note: This article is reprinted, with minor alterations, from *Selected Writings of Gyula Laziczius*, ed. Thomas A. Sebeok (The Hague: Mouton, 1966), pp. 11–21.

opportunity for conducting scientific work, and in penury, scarcely managing to make a living as a hack translator. His heart condition of old deteriorated steadily after his discharge, but he survived for a few more years thanks to the medicines supplied to him by a famous American colleague.

In the 1920s, while Laziczius did office work by day, he gave his free time to the area of scholarship which first engaged his attention: Russian literature and philosophy. His doctoral dissertation, presented in 1929, dealt with "Bĕlinskij and Hegel" (see 1966:27–37); and he also published a series of articles on Tolstoy, Dostoevski, and other topics drawn from nineteenth century Russian thought. His maturation as a linguist coincided with the formative period of structuralism, the mid-twenties, when members of the Prague School as well as some of their American colleagues began to emerge from their chrysalis stage.

His first important article, "On Phonology," appeared in 1930, followed shortly by "The Phonology of a Hungarian Consonant Change."[3] These papers showed the direct influence, in the first place, of Saussure; of the "Prague" linguists, notably Trubetzkoy and Jakobson; and, not least, of Sapir, whose "Sound Patterns in Language" made a considerable impression on Laziczius ("I believe that Edward Sapir was the first to introduce phonemic considerations in the study of sound changes" was the opening sentence of the second of his articles cited). Phonemics, as Laziczius conceived of it at the time, constituted an independent branch of descriptive linguistics, devoted to the study of the function of speech sounds—this formulation allied him most closely with the Prague point of view, which Mathesius had designated "functional linguistics"—and he undertook to state its three principal goals: to identify the sounds which possess either a lexical or a grammatical function in a given language; to decide how such elements are distributed in this or that language; and, most important, to examine and compare phonemic systems, i.e., to study typology. Unless phonemics leads to the formulation of comprehensive generalizations, it will have failed, he insists, since individual events, no matter how interesting by themselves, have nothing to do with science. It is characteristic of Laziczius's procedure that he promptly attempted to apply the theory he displayed to a concrete corpus, and he showed how the phonemic point of view contributed to the solution of a well-known problem, that of the disappearance of word-final short vowels in old Hungarian.

Laziczius was deeply aware of his predecessors and contemporaries in the structuralist movement (Bühler and Twaddell were among those from whom he profited in later years). Yet he was by no means content to remain merely a disciple: "bien que j'aie toujours approuvé l'idée fondamentale de la phonologie, je considérais avec un certain scepticisme les enseignements qui se cristallisaient peu à peu autour de ce fonds commun" (1948:294).[4] Though he eventually became an innovator in phoneme theory, the first of his major works, *Introduction to*

Phonology (1932), gives less evidence of this than of his remarkable erudition, his grasp of essentials, the lucidity of his formulation, and his versatility in applying a new technique in a field excessively burdened with tradition. Like his other two books, which came out in 1942 and 1944, this, too, was published only in Hungarian, a fact which, of course, prevented the instant international recognition it would surely have been accorded had it been written in a more accessible language. It is, indeed, one of the classic expositions of the field, which, even today, repays careful reading.

The book is divided into three sections, roughly equal in length: (1) general phonemics, (2) Hungarian phonemics, and (3) historical phomemics. Among the most valuable chapters in the first part—which is otherwise vintage "Prague"—is a sketch of the history of phoneme theory, from the days of the Kazan' school of Baudouin de Courtenay and Kruševskij through the First International Congress of Linguists (1928); it is plain that the author had complete and critical mastery of the entire literature of his subject.

The second part not only contains the earliest—and in many respects still the best—description of the phonemes of Hungarian, but it also constitutes an original and brilliant exposition of structural dialectology, far ahead of its time. Laziczius succeeded in reducing to a simple and clear structure the apparently chaotic phonetic diversity which separates Hungary's eight dialect regions, and in relating this to the system of the literary and spoken standards; whether or not a structural dialectology is, *a priori*, possible did not concern him, for he was perhaps the first linguist to resolve the question to his own satisfaction and to that of the few who possessed the equipment to grasp his argument.

It is in the third part of the monograph, however, that Laziczius breaks most decisively with the atomism of the Neogrammarians and boldly outlines the principles of historical phonemic analysis.[5] "Sound changes in language always and without exception occur as mutations," he declares emphatically, and goes on to elucidate, with the aid of this novel instrument, several key problems of Hungarian linguistics. His final chapter, on the "Interdependence of Sound Changes," is a plea for intertwining the threads of isolated diachronic events, for searching out those "developmental tendencies" which characterize the particular state of a language, and for recognizing those internal pressures which condition linguistic changes.

Laziczius's later departures from phoneme theory as developed by Trubetzkoy centered around three problem areas: the definition of the phoneme in terms of psychological notions; the nature of phonetics; and the relationship of phoneme to allophone.

In regard to the first point, he in effect joined with most American linguists in sharply rejecting Trubetzkoy's use of "undefined psychological terms,"[6] but expressed himself as favoring the sociological approach of certain other Russian linguists, notably Vinokur and Šor. He also repudiated Trubetzkoy's conception of phonetics as a natural science. This view, he argued, is not borne out by either the history of or current practice in the field: "Sans considérer certains buts pratiques (enseignement des sourds-muets, etc.), on l'a toujours mise au service de la linguistique" (1948:298). The gap between the two subjects—phonetics and phonemics—is not one of principle; it is, rather, an artificially induced breach motivated by academic politics, one which must be bridged, he argues, by a return to the tradition of Sweet, namely, the reintroduction into phonetics of the functional techniques of phonemic analysis: "les phonéticiens eux-mêmes se sont rendu compte à plusieurs reprises des différences fonctionelles qu'il y a entre les sons d'une langue donnée. Même s'ils n'avaient pas fait cette découverte, on ne devait pas leur refuser le droit d'en tirer profit. Pourquoi réserver cette distinction à la phonologie? Dans la science," he winds up on a characteristic note, "il n'y pas de monopoles" (1948:302).

It was Laziczius's view of the nature of the phoneme, however, and the ensuing amiable controversy between him and Trubetzkoy, for which he became most famous internationally.[7] Bühler's well-known model, dividing the act of speech into three aspects, furnished the philosophical peg upon which Laziczius hung his linguistic garment. These aspects were, it will be recalled, those features of sound which refer to the designation (*Darstellung*), those which are characteristic of the source (*Kundgabe*), and those which constitute the appeal to the destination (*Appell*). Laziczius's first point was that phonemes function in all three aspects and not just referentially; his second point was that, among linguistic signs, one encounters, beside phonemes and allophones, also another category, which embraces those elements which he dubbed *emphatics*—we would call them expressive features—which function only in reference to the speaker and the hearer but not the content; and, third, that the allophones function only in reference to the speaker but not either the hearer or the content. All three—phoneme, emphatic, and variant—were, moreover, Laziczius insisted, to be regarded as equally conventionalized. He was the first one, followed by van Wijk and Malmberg, to point out that the claimed proportional relationship, *phonology* to *langue* equals *phonetics* to *parole*, is incorrect, since the allophones are also socially determined.

While Trubetzkoy admitted the unilateral nature of phonemic investigations, he was of the opinion that data concerning expressive elements were so meager and unreliable that one could but speculate about their role in language, and he ended by relegating them, together with the features functioning in reference to the speaker, to a special discipline, namely, *phonologische Stilistik*. Laziczius, in his several replies, defended and elaborated upon his position, incidentally furnishing many novel data in its support; and he continued to accuse Trubetzkoy and his followers of a number of "errors," chief among them being their confusion of expressive elements and allophones.

Whatever one may think of this exchange, or of the merits of Laziczius's theory, the fact remains that he was the first to describe in functional terms (however gropingly perhaps) the relationship of what some would now prefer to think of as distinctive, redundant, and expressive features. Realizing their importance only lately, linguists and psychologists alike, in collaboration and individually, have begun attempts to disentangle afresh, and with the aid of the newest tools of our trade, these interwoven threads that make up the total ribbon of communication.[8]

The appearance of his *Introduction to Phonology* (1932) ushered in Laziczius's most productive period: over the next twelve years, he published many papers dealing with all sorts of problems in Hungarian, Finno-Ugric, and general linguistics. Some appeared in leading periodicals abroad, commanded esteem, and brought him invitations to lend his name to the masthead of a number of journals, notably, *Acta Linguistica*, *Archiv für vergleichende Phonetik*, and *Zeitschrift für Phonetik und allgemeine Sprachwissenschaft*. He also came to play an increasingly authoritative role in international congresses of both phoneticians and linguists. At home, he was elected Secretary of the Linguistic Society of Hungary, and to full membership in the Academy.

Laziczius's researches were by no means restricted to language in its phonic aspect, for his articles touched as well on many different topics in morphology and lexicology, synchronic and diachronic. Writing "On the Question of the Formation of Finno-Ugric Tenses" (1933), for example, he introduces and discusses the notion of morphological zero (which must be treated exactly as we handle "material data, but naturally only within the system, when a corresponding opposition is available"); and proceeds to a fascinating and learned psycholinguistic excursus against the so-called "axiom of parallelism," that fuzzy, pseudo-Whorfian concept, which still has a remarkable number of adherents—the one about the color-blind Chinese (can they distinguish blue from green?). In "The Size of the Hungarian Lexicon" (1942c), he makes the point that a quantitative approach to linguistic materials serves no useful purpose if the units counted were not established according to sound principles. "La définition du mot" (1945), the last new paper he published abroad, was composed during the painful war years; therein, he evaluates several definitions of the word and adds yet another: words are linguistic signs composed of specific phonic elements capable of functioning in a linguistic context (*Zeichenfeld*) as well as in a nonlinguistic environment (*Zeigfeld*), and constituting, at a particular moment and in a particular speech community, a system.

I have mentioned Laziczius's friendly debate with Trubetzkoy; but I must add that the art of dialectic was the method he favored most for the exposition of his views—and he excelled at it. He participated in many disputes, reasoning always with awesome cogency but often with perhaps needlessly offensive acrimony, earning himself a host of enemies. Typically, his papers open with a reaction to someone else's thesis, which he proceeds to demolish by argument supported with both data and a prodigious knowledge of the relevant literature; his antithesis is then stated and applied to some concrete linguistic problem which he elucidates in a higher synthesis. Once, when he was charged by a colleague with malice aforethought, he replied: "In my opinion, in science there is no such thing as an attack; there are only theories and hypotheses, data and proof, and he whose trump is the higher is right. . . . Attack is not my meat, but criticism is my right, indeed my duty" (1935c). And his attitude is further indicated by an observation he made "On the Margins of an Article": "Every piece of scientific writing, save when it touches on virgin territory, is more or less contentious in character" (1940).[9] In his passionate search for the truth, he was prepared to tilt with anyone, from distinguished foreign colleagues like Trubetzkoy or Bühler (e.g., Laziczius 1939; reprinted, 1966:64–70), to Hungarian notables like Zoltán Kodály (e.g., Laziczius 1938).

The seeming multiplicity of Laziczius's linguistic activities was at last reduced and incorporated into a single, overarching theory of language, which he presented in the second of his major works: *General Linguistics—Questions of Principle and Technique* (1942a). The twelve chapter headings may impart some of the flavor of the book: (1) The Autonomy of Linguistics; (2) The Subject Matter of Linguistics; (3) Bühler's Third Axiom—The Place of Linguistics; (4) Language as Sign Event; (5) Language as System; (6) Subsystems in Language; (7) The Unity of Language; (8) The Distinction between Language and Speech as a Methodological Principle; (9) Sign Event as a Methodological Principle; (10) Expression of Meaning and Expression of Emotion; (11) The Distinction Between Synchrony and Diachrony; and (12) Other Errors of Method.

Laziczius thought of this monograph as only a prolegomenon to his grand design: by clearing away the underbrush of methodological misconception, he wished to prepare the ground for a four-volume work, to be devoted, respectively, to phonetics, phonemics, lexicology, and syntax. Unfortunately, he was able to complete only the first of these, *Phonetics*,[10] although a version of the book on the morpheme and fragments of the one on syntax also survive. (He died, in fact, while he was completing a chapter on "The Central Problem of Syntax.")

Phonetics has already been reviewed in the United States in some detail.[11] It is a fine, mature, and, in some respects, unique book, one which pays equal attention to the genetic and the acoustic stages of the speech event; accords special treatment to each of the prosodic phenomena of duration, stress, and tone; and includes meticulous and critical accounts of the historic controversies around the diphthong and the syllable. In discussing the chapter on acoustics, the reviewer in *Language* had noted that, in consequence of wartime isolation, "the author had no access to the latest research in this field, which . . . has progressed enormously during the last few years in the United States especially." By the summer of 1948, when I had met and been entertained by Laziczius, he appeared to have read and thoroughly absorbed all that had been published on "visible speech," and he volunteered that this new literature had given him no cause to modify his theories in any fundamental way.

In Laziczius, we see the confluence of the best in Russian and American, Swiss, Czech, and Danish linguistic thought, which he enriched from his own nation's resources. It is not likely that, in our age, another general linguist of his stature will appear in Hungary. Laziczius wrote his major works in Hungarian, but he was a scientist in the main stream of modern linguistics, a river which, like language itself, overflows the boundaries of nations, and will not stay confined to continents.

12. "Dialect" from a Zoosemiotic Perspective

... minél több részletvonalból rajzoljuk meg egy-egy nyelvjárás képét, annál hívebb lesz a rajzunk. Minél több kritériumot vonunk be vizsgálódásunk körébe, annál pontosabb eredményt várhatunk tőle. E tekintetben kétség nem is merülhet fel.[1] (Laziczius 1932:54)

Hungarian scholars (e.g., Horányi and Szépe 1975:6) occasionally allude to the explicitly semiotic preoccupations of Laziczius. Thus it is well known that several sections of his introduction to general linguistics develop consequences from the twin Saussurean notions that verbal phenomena are semiotic in character and that signs are organized into systems (Laziczius 1942b:26ff., 69ff.). The semiotic of Laziczius hardly goes beyond that of Saussure, but it does transcend his master's conception in one important specific respect: while Saussure appears never to have envisioned the possibility of sign processes, within the broad framework of social psychology (or, in Naville's account, sociology) (Sebeok 1974b:219f.), occurring outside of human existence. Laziczius—in a remarkable digression—contrasts verbal signs with sign processes uncovered by Karl von Frisch in the honeybee (Laziczius 1942b:31; cf. Sebeok 1972:11 n.). Laziczius's chief inference, namely, that the bee can be the source of a message and its destination, but that this message can never denote, i.e., that it can have no cognitive function ("A méhek nyelve... az ábrázolásra már képtelen"), turned out to be erroneous: in part, because it was based on a 1923 report which, in the investigator's own words, "had missed the most interesting aspects" (Frisch 1967:vi); and, in part, because Laziczius was unduly constrained, I think, by an excessively simplistic model of the communicative act propagated by Karl Bühler (e.g., Laziczius 1966:16, 46, 61, 64), from whose work, one can confidently assume, he learned indirectly of the eminent Munich zoologist's ex-

Note: This article, commemorating the eightieth anniversary of Gyula Laziczius, was first published in Hungarian, under the title "A 'dialektus' állatszemiotikai szempontból," in *Nyelvtudományi Közlemények* 78:435–440 (1976); this English translation is meant as a companion piece to the preceding.

periments (cf. Bühler 1934:vif.; Sebeok 1972:35f.). However, what matters to us is not that subsequent developments in zoosemiotics (Sebeok 1974c:192) have seemingly invalidated a passing observation that Laziczius embedded in a linguistic context, but that he foreshadowed with great sensitivity what has since become a very live issue indeed: "Is a comparative semiotics possible?" (Sebeok 1970).

In this necessarily brief commemorative tribute, I wish to call attention to a problem area that would certainly have excited the scientific imagination of Laziczius had the relevant data been uncovered in his lifetime: given the indubitable fact that many animals, including, *inter alia*, species of insects, frogs, birds, and mammals, have developed dialects—some inherited, others learned, but environment always interacting with heredity in a highly complex fashion (J. Brown 1975:433; Wilson 1975:168)—how does this broaden our thinking about linguistic evolution, or, to pose two somewhat different questions, what conceivable evolutionary function can we ascribe to the diversity of human dialect patterns, and what corollaries of interest to the linguist does a consistently comparative, i.e., cross-specific, semiotic approach suggest?

Let me begin by concisely reviewing a few salient cases of dialect variation reported in the vast literature of animal communication (Sebeok 1968; 1977a), starting with an example from the social insects (one that would especially have delighted Laziczius, and to which this great cosmopolitan scholar would have instinctively tuned in), stemming from the Carniolan race of the honeybee, *Apis mellifera carnica*, upon which most of the enviably precise research by von Frisch and his students has been concentrated (Frisch 1962; 1967:293-320). Comparative investigations in six races, i.e., genetic strains, of *A. mellifera* have revealed that the area indicated by a round and by a tail-wagging dance, respectively, and the dancing rhythm, differ for each, such variations having been appropriately referred to as dialects. As I have related before (Sebeok 1972:46f.), this dialect phenomenon was then exploited in an ingenious way, as a result of which it was found, in conformity with the von Frisch communicative hypothesis, that, for instance, the Italian (*ligustica*) race of workers underestimated from (viz., "misunderstood") the tempo of the Austrian (*carnica*) dances, whereas, conversely, the Austrians overestimated from (viz., "misunderstood") that of the Italian dances in a mixed colony composed of the two strains.

The second mammal, next to man, in which the phenomenon was reported, less than a decade ago, was the elephant seal, *Mirounga angustirostris*, where consistent differences in the threat vocalizations of males were observed and described. The geographical variations in their vocal behavior were explicitly said to resemble local dialects in humans; the mode of transmission, it was felt, "would account for the rapid development of dialects in separated geographical areas and their apparent perpetuation from one generation to the next," leading the investigators to suggest the conclusion "that man is not the only mammal in which normal vocalizations are learned from other species members" (Le Boeuf and Peterson 1969:1656). There is further evidence—ultimately, subject to interpretation that depends on the resolution of taxonomic disputes—that the pika, *Ochotona princeps*, pothead whales (several *Globicephala* species), and the squirrel monkey, *Saimiri sciureus*, show geographical variation in their calls that may most accurately be characterized as dialects.

In passing, it should be emphasized that it would be wrong, in this mammalian context, to limit the concept of "dialect," despite the etymology or the preponderance of pertinent research, which has focused upon the acoustic modality, to regional variations in just the sound pattern. One has but to recall that in man even sign languages may clearly be divided by dialect area boundaries, a lack of uniformity which has been adumbrated for Ameslan in respect to at least two Southern and three New England states (Croneberg 1965:313ff.), but which obviously needs much more extensive documentation than can be accorded here.

Geographic variation in bird vocalizations—especially songs of courtship and of territorial advertisement—have been most meticulously studied, and this literature was thoroughly reviewed by Armstrong (1963:88–111), and later by Thielcke (1969). Several inquiries have shown that the patterns may be distributed as a kind of mosaic, where each local population is characterized by a song type which distinguishes it from neighboring populations, but which may also recur elsewhere. The rain-call of the chaffinch, *Fringilla coelebs*, is a classic example of mosaic variation on the European continent. (In linguistic geography, configurations of this nature are sometimes referred to as "lateral areas" [cf. Bonfante and Sebeok 1944:383f.].) Thielcke proposed to reserve the term *dialect* only for vocalization variants with a mosaic distribution, but, as of seven years ago, the descriptive data failed to provide any explanation of "how mutually independent dialects arise within the same species or even within the same song." Although, he surmised, the "function of dialects is perhaps to reduce variability in order to increase the effectiveness of the signal," he concluded that we "know nothing about the function of dialects" (Thielcke 1969:322).

The occurrence of dialects, then, is widespread in birds, but their developmental basis has hitherto been analyzed in only a few species. It is important to be mindful that *dialect* refers here to differences between demes within a species that contrast in their vocalizations from other demes: what is implied is that there are variations in phenotype, but not, of course, that these are due to learning alone (J. Brown 1975:663f.). In species where the nature and extent of the variation have been most thoroughly described—notably, the white-crowned sparrow, *Zonotrichia leucophrys*, inhabiting the San Francisco Bay area—learning and cultural transmission of the dialect features from generation to generation have been proved to be important, not genotypic (in a simple sense) but phenotypic (Marler and Tamura 1962:375). Extrapolating from these data, as well as from another sparrow, the chaffinch, and a parrot species, *Amazona amazonica*, Nottebohm (1970), in the course of an important overview of the study of avian vocalizations, re-examined the possible evolutionary significance inherent in the formation of vocal dialects. This far-reaching contribution immediately stimulated the thinking of several linguists concerned with the search for possible mechanisms at work in human dialect formation (e.g., Grace 1970, esp. n. 2; Labov 1973:246f.).

Nottebohm's argument proceeds from the observation that vocal learning is strongly correlated with the occurrence of dialects and complex song repertoires. In most instances, then, the evolution of plastic ontogenies—which means that some of the features of the song are acquired by learning from other members of the deme—can be assumed as subserving two fundamental purposes: "(1) mating like with like, and (2) wooing, stimulating, and retaining a partner" (Nottebohm 1975:79). Thus males must learn to utter the dialect of their birth area, because females develop a preference for the song dialect of the region where they are born, and will eventually express this preference in the choice of their mate. Were this not so, gene flow would occur between adjacent populations, tending to eliminate vocal differences, attenuating or doing away altogether with the effectiveness of dialect barriers. In the contrary case, "dialects acquired as vocal traditions would persist even in the presence of genetic variability" (Nottebohm 1975:80). It is, therefore, not true, as earlier investigators used to claim (e.g., Armstrong 1963:89), that bird dialects crucially differ from dialects of human speech in that the former are wholly controlled by heredity whereas the latter are culturally developed population markers, without an obvious evolutionary function.

As Labov has pointed out, "The value of Nottebohm's contribution is not in setting forth a theory or an hypothesis that we can test immediately, but rather suggesting an alternative view to broaden our thinking about linguistic evolution" (1973:247). The question at issue is the value of language diversity for humans, providing, more generally, for relative cultural isolation and the maintenance of cultural pluralism. It is interesting to note that, in the present climate of linguistic inquiry, with its pounding re-emphasis on universal grammar, both a new impetus and a model for the search for an underlying mechanism that could account for the "fantastic diversity of human tongues, often geographically proximate," in brief, for what Humboldt has called, a century and a half ago, *die Verschiedenheit des menschlichen Sprachbaues*, seem to have been pressed home to us from outside the field of linguistics. "How can such exceeding variety have arisen," Steiner wonders, "if, as transformational grammar postulates and biology hints, the underlying grid, the neuro-physiological grooves, are common to all men and, indeed, occasion their humanity? Why, as carriers of the same essential molecular information, do we not speak the same language or a small number of languages corresponding, say, to the small number of genuinely identifiable ethnic types? No one has come up with a satisfactory hypothesis" (Steiner 1971:69).

Nottebohm's suggestion is that dialects in birds may provide a relative degree of genetic isolation by the role they play in the mating behavior, but without any "necessary irrevocable commitment to actual speciation," adding that, whereas "genetic isolation of small populations may lead to high rates of extinction and even possibly to excessive inbreeding, differences in vocalizations are probably rarely insuperable barriers to breeding, and thus the microevolutionary process is kept more flexible and open." Further, he himself raises the intriguing possibility that dialects "have played an active role in human evolution," and that these "might have influenced the emergence of local physiological adaptations" (1970:955). Some anthropologists concerned with extant tribal societies that, at least until recently, lived in ecological balance with their environment, are beginning to examine the question of the extent to which language area patterns facilitate intergroup contact among hunters and gatherers and simple horticulturalists, allowing a flexible response to local environmental stress (Hill, forthcoming). This trend represents a truly creative synthesis of dialect geography and areal linguistics on the one hand, with ecological and evolutionary biology on the other. A further corollary of this research intimates a solution for the perennial puzzle why we all pass through the divide of linguistic puberty, that is, a stage of maturation beyond which the human individual's language-learning ability is dramatically reduced: this deficit, too, must be the product of evolutionary selection, functioning, as in birds, to encourage diversity in dialect patterns. No doubt, Laziczius would have approved of this kind of multidisciplinary endeavor, utilizing zoosemiotic theories and data to illuminate anthroposemiotic conundrums, for it is in good conformity with his over-all scientific program: "A kutató munka egyre újabb matériákat igyekszik feltárni, egyre mélyebb aknákból igyekszik gyarapítani a meglévő anyagot, hogy minél teljesebb, minél többrétű legyen."[2] It is not inconceivable that, were he writing today, a remark he once made about Schleicher could, *a fortiori*, be applied to himself: ". . . ha valaki élete végén megkérdezte volna, hogy mit tart nagyarányú és sok tekintetben értékes munkásságából a legfontosabbnak, bizonyára azt válaszolta volna: a természettudományi módszer átültetését a nyelvtudományba"[3] (Laziczius 1942b; 107, 109f.).

13. Roman Jakobson's Teaching in America

"Socrates is an evildoer, and a curious person, who searches into things under the earth and heaven, and he makes the worse appear the better cause; and he teaches the aforesaid doctrines to others.". . . Socrates . . . corrupts the youth . . . does not believe in the gods of the State, but has other new divinities of his own. (Plato's *Apology*, trans. Jowett)

In a Foreword to a recent collection of some of my essays in verbal art, I briefly recounted my first meeting with Jakobson, on the sultry 27th day of August, 1942, when we spent a long afternoon absorbed in animated conversation in the garden of Franz Boas's house in Grantwood. I recorded that, among other topics, "he spoke to me at generous length about the highly ingenious accomplishments of the Russian Formalist school and its productive reformulations by the Prague Circle, stressing the close ties of both with structural linguistics." I noted that our friendship dates from that occasion, "as does my abiding absorption with the study of the verbal arts" (Sebeok 1974a: vii ff.).

Now I have been honored with an invitation to comment on Jakobson's "teaching" during his American period, that is, following his arrival and settlement in this country after his dramatic Hegira from Czechoslovakia, and then, successively, from Denmark, Norway, and Sweden. Since teaching is a far more intimate expression of scholarship than any formal publication can possibly be, this narrative must necessarily be laced with autobiographical observations; and since Jakobson's instructional activities are so vast in scope, I can generalize with confidence only from such glimpses of it as good fortune has bestowed upon me. These date, in the main, from the war years and immediately thereafter, while Jakobson was Professor of General Lin-

Note: This article is reprinted from *Roman Jakobson: Echoes of His Scholarship*, edited by C. H. van Schooneveld and Daniel Armstrong (Lisse: Peter de Ridder Press, 1977), pp. 411–420.

Figure 13-1. Roman Jakobson. Courtesy of Professor Jakobson.

guistics and of Czechoslovak Studies at the Ecole Libre des Hautes Etudes (1942-1946), then Visiting Professor of General Linguistics (1943-1949) at Columbia University. I never attended his courses at Harvard University, where he served, from 1949 until his retirement in 1967, as Professor of Slavic Languages and Literatures and General Linguistics, nor at M.I.T., where he became Institute Professor in 1957. However, throughout this entire period, I heard him lecture on various other campuses on occasions too numerous to recall in detail. We have attended a good many conferences together, both in the United States and abroad. In particular, he has frequently been our guest at Indiana University. I recollect four of his sojourns with especial pleasure: his first visit to Bloomington during the war; his concluding report at the fortnight's Conference of Anthropologists and Linguists, in July 1952 (Jakobson 1971a: 554-567); his enthusiastic participation in the Conference on Style, in April 1958, in the course of which he delivered what may be his most often cited paper, "Linguistics and Poetics" (published in Sebeok 1960: 350-377); and a sequence of lectures delivered here during the 1964 Linguistic Institute.

When Jakobson and I first met, I was a graduate student in transition on several levels: literally, from the University of Chicago (and utter penury) to Princeton (and the promise of relative affluence afforded by a splendid fellowship). At the same time, I was also intellectually at sea, thrashing about somewhere in the middle of the common Atlantic pool that J. R. Firth so eloquently delineated a few years later (1949). My early linguistic attitudes had essentially been molded by two men, neither of whom was at Chicago any longer: Manuel Andrade, who died prematurely, and Leonard Bloomfield, who reluctantly accepted a call to Yale in 1940. After their departure deprived me of their comfort and steady linguistic counsel, I read voraciously according to my own appetites, and thus came to discovery of the Linguistic School of Prague and a glimmer of understanding of the distinctively Russian flavor the late Trubetzkoy and the very lively Jakobson had imparted to it, transforming its classical doctrines as these had sprung from native soil (cf. Vachek 1966). When Andrade suddenly died, he had already "gone a long way toward developing a semiotically grounded linguistics, much farther than any studies yet made in this field," and his ambitious program "involved the building of the whole of linguistics upon semiotical foundations; he believed that in this way linguistics would obtain a metalanguage appropriate to the description and comparison of all languages" (C. Morris 1946: 223). I was strongly influenced by Andrade's highly original views and their applications, but far from sufficiently equipped at the time to carry his project further, especially since his remaining notes and manuscript fragments were scarcely utilizable. In any event, no one else was much interested: he was ahead of his time in our prevailing linguistic milieu, and this pupil of Boas is remembered today, if at all, only for his technical work on Quileute and several Middle American Indian languages. As for Bloomfield, who became my next advisor, he had just published a masterful essay proclaiming that "Linguistics is the chief contributor to semiotic. Among the special branches of science, it intervenes between biology, on the one hand, and ethnology, sociology, and psychology, on the other: it stands between physical and cultural anthropology" (1939:55). In his classes and private sessions, however, Bloomfield refrained from discussing broad issues; his concern, no doubt rightly, was with imparting the formal skills required of any practicing linguist. It was at his pounding insistence that I was set on the path of specialization in Finno-Ugric languages and linguistics, despite the very nearly total absence of instruction in them within the Western Hemisphere, a circumstance which forced me into an autodidactic stance, yet one which ultimately led to the institutionalization of this field in America. Bloomfield's procedures, essential for training though they may have been, left me unsatisfied and restless, for they gave a disjointed, choppy, incomplete picture of linguistics. I could, therefore, understand, in some measure, why, some twenty years later, a new generation of linguists deemed it fit to set up a straw man in his name, selecting him as an emblem for a brand of inadequate behaviorism; Jakobson was, of course, perfectly correct in maintaining that "sur bien des points Bloomfield reste supérieur au mouvement qui se réclame de lui . . ." (Faye, Paris, and Roubaud 1972:47).

Such, then, in capsule form, was the initial state of my affairs when, at the age of twenty-one, I journeyed across the Hudson, from New York City, to seek out the cosmopolitan linguist, already acclaimed throughout Europe, but not yet acclaimed in America. I was sufficiently well acquainted with some of his writings to have aroused my curiosity to enlarge my knowledge in a face-to-face meeting. The afternoon turned into an intense tutorial, extending late into that summer evening, in the course of which two subjects were discussed in the manner of a Greek symposium, as it were, liberally interspersed, that is, with drink and food: Jakobson's apperception of phonological theory, and his notions about poetic language. Although the phonemic principle was well known in America, and accepted even then by all modern schools of linguistics, Jakobson convinced me then and there that any further development of linguistic sound analysis must proceed by dissolving the phoneme into distinctive features, and that binary opposition can consistently be applied as a patterning device for the entire phonemic material. And while Bloomfield had instilled in me his conviction that "the artistic use of language by specially gifted individuals" enjoyed general favor as a substitute for the observation of language (1939:5ff.), Jakobson opened my eyes and ears to the true, exciting potential of a poetics when practised by a master of linguistics. This was, indeed, a propaedeutic experience leading toward the kind of holistic vista of the language sciences that I had been vainly groping for at Chicago. I therefore resolved to stay in close touch to learn more.

The first formal opportunity for doing so developed within the framework of the Ecole Libre des Hautes Etudes, assembled under the auspices and on the premises of the New School for Social Research. Jakobson described it as "a university founded by French scholars who were refugees from the Nazi occupation," where we "were teachers and students of one another" (Mehta 1971:232), and where "dès le début les différences entre étudiants et professeurs se trouvaient abolies par le fait que les professeurs eux-mêmes allaient écouter les conférences de leurs collègues" (Faye, Paris, and Roubaud 1972:34). Thus Claude Lévi-Strauss came to introduce Jakobson (and the rest of us) to structural anthropology, while Jakobson opened the door for Lévi-Strauss (as he did for many others) to linguistics. I remember that both had the courtesy to come to my raw course on the history of the Hungarian language—my very first teaching assignment—whereas I attended as many of their lectures as my commitments to Princeton would allow. I tried never to miss Jakobson's packed seminars, after which we usually went to a nearby bistro to continue animated conversations about the topic of the evening.

It was at the Ecole Libre that I heard Jakobson lecture for the first time, and I would like to refine here my impression of his platform style, which seldom varies whether he speaks in French (and he did in those times, in New York) or in any other language. I had once written of "the many-valued, unmistakably Jakobsonian, rhetorical strategems that are sprinkled among the expository statements . . . there by tactical intent, at once to persuade and to seduce" (Sebeok 1965b:86). With conspicuous exceptions—his very carefully worded summation of the results of the Ninth International Congress of Linguists, which he read verbatim on August 31, 1962 (in Jakobson 1971a:593-602), was one—the lectures of Jakobson give off an air of uncontrived happenings (in the semiotic sense of Nöth [1972:130ff.]). He appears to rely on miniature cue cards, consulting them mostly for melodramatic effect rather than content.[1] The feeling he conveys is that he creates, shapes, and edits his topic of the moment to express it in a rhythm best suited to his auditors' pulse; after Jakobson's Madrid lectures in 1974, a Spanish newspaper report characterized them as harmonious musical performances directed by the lecturer and played by the audience. The over-all effect is that his students—all of his audiences become his students—are moved unusually close to him, to the extent of even becoming protective. One cannot help recollecting that Jakobson once professed in the Moscow School for Drama; he had kept in touch with a former actor of the Moscow Art Theater, and later made effective use of him (Sebeok 1960:354). I am strongly reminded of a passage in which Stanislavsky comments on his own methods: "To achieve a harmony . . . one needs more than outer, physical tempo and rhythm; one needs inner, spiritual tempo and rhythm. One must feel them in the sound, in the speech, in the action, in the gesture, in the movement, in fact, in the entire production" (1959:443). Sometimes a genuine improvisation replaced a "happening": when, shortly before Christmas of 1942, he received a cable from Copenhagen announcing the death of Viggo Brøndal, he substituted for his lecture an unforgettable, yet impromptu eulogy of his friend which deeply affected all of us present, although no one in the audience had ever met this important but remote personage of the Cercle Linguistique de Copenhague.

The ambience pervading and surrounding our group was international indeed: "Il y avait des gens qui passaient par là, qui venaient nous écouter ou qui venaient parler eux-mêmes. Toutes les langues possibles s'y mêlaient," Jakobson related in an interview (Faye et al. 1972:34). Americans—both established scholars from Columbia and neighboring institutions and much younger ones, partially drawn from the Language Section of the War Department (then located at a New York address, 165 Broadway, which became the eponym for a heroic era in American linguistics)—were gradually attracted into Jakobson's orbit. (Somewhat disconcertingly, he was followed around, as well, by an indeterminate cloud made up of East European and Russian groupies, to whom he was unfailingly gracious and kind, although they did erode his time.)

Many of our crowd moved on with him to Columbia, where, in 1943, he offered an evening seminar on the topic of case systems, stemming from a trail-blazing monograph he wrote in 1935.[2] Each student in this seminar was assigned to analyze exhaustively the case system of a language of his choice, present his findings orally, then revise the presentation in the light of the ensuing discussion. I selected Finnish. The resulting paper became a chapter of my eventual dissertation, dealing with the form and function of several Finno-Ugric case systems. Although my Ph.D. degree was awarded by Princeton (in 1945), Jakobson served, to all intents and purposes—and with the enthusiastic concurrence of my chairman, Harold H. Bender—as my thesis supervisor; it was thus, and in this sense, that I chanced to become his "first American student." Incidentally, at Jakobson's behest, this same monograph came to forge an initial link between John Lotz and me and, in due course, the lives of the two Hungarian linguists continued variously to commingle with his, as mentioned elsewhere (Ch. 14, this volume).

Jakobson's strictures on the work-in-progress of his students could be very telling: about one of my early papers, he gently hinted that he thought I had written it with my left hand; of another, he remarked that it seemed to him especially interesting for what I had left out. On the other hand, when a finished piece of work gained his coveted approval, he would stand behind it with his full authority. While he generally tends to be reasonably equable and tolerant of criticisms leveled directly at himself—responding usually, in due course, to a coherent set of them, without invidious identification (the "Postscriptum" to *Questions de poétique* [1973] being a good example)—he would not countenance indirect attacks disguised as censure of his students. His loyalty to them—and, by his own count, "about a hundred of [his] former students are professors in this country" (Mehta 1971:232)—remains abiding and fierce; in cases such as Soffietti's Columbia thesis on Turinese phonology, his defense can result in deplorably acrimonious clashes with colleagues like R. A. Hall, who, of course, perceived the polemic in quite different terms (1975:141ff.). When, as sometimes happens, two of his former students collide, he will not, however, hesitate to take sides strictly on the merits of the case at issue (Jakobson 1971c:209), painful as that may be. Little wonder, then, that generations of his disciples, down to the youngest, many of whom declared that they went to Cambridge for the opportunity of working under him, are steadfast in their allegiance, proclaiming "his ability to illuminate a question from various points of view" (Gribble 1968:7).

It would be seriously misleading to pretend that Jakobson's teachings were an instantaneous and resounding success in America. Far from it: these were roundly condemned by an influential cabal of autochthonous and lately-naturalized linguists—mostly a generation or two older than mine—clustering around "165 Broadway." In a lecture delivered on December 27, 1974, as part of the Linguistic Society's Golden Anniversary Symposium on "The European Background of American Linguistics," he characterized his foes of this era by an abusively intended Aesopian epithet, *administrators*, which, however, was so veiled that it was widely misinterpreted. In truth, these men were mostly misguided chauvinists, afflicted with a hubris doubtless induced by the pressures and fears of an uncertain military conflict in the backdrop. Regrettably, the behavior of this small but powerful clique—which caused Jakobson and his friends untold anguish, to say nothing of economic loss—left a sinister stain on the otherwise magnificent tapestry of achievements of American linguistics of the 1940s. Fortunately, this dark episode was transpierced by brilliant shafts of light emanating from giants like Boas and Bloomfield; their instant appreciation for Jakobson's decisive presence must be allowed to compensate for all the rest, which had better stay buried along with other, similarly motivated, wartime debris.

The affidavit against the teachings of Jakobson was much the same as the charges preferred by Meletus, summed up in the epigraph at the outset of this record. "This inquisition," Jakobson might have continued in the words of Socrates, "has led to my having many enemies of the worst and most dangerous kind, and had given occasion to many calumnies.... There is another thing:—young men ... come about me of their own accord; they like to hear the pretenders examined, and they often imitate me, and proceed to examine others; there are plenty of persons, as they quickly discover, who think that they know something, but they really know little or nothing; and then those who are examined by them instead of being angry with themselves are angry with me. . . ."

In the fall of 1943, I took up permanent residence at Indiana University, where Velten, Voegelin, and I soon invited Jakobson to come for some lectures. Voegelin asked him to send some feasible topics, and was startled to receive a list of nearly one hundred titles. Jakobson arrived in Bloomington by bus, greeting me with the question, "Where are the Indians?" He spoke on the cultural and social history of Slavic languages (1968), several of which were then taught here intensively to Army personnel, and was then also asked to give an *ad hoc* talk in J. R. Kantor's seminar. Kantor was an extreme behavioristic psycholinguist, who relished controverting with linguists (1936). For some reason, Jakobson chose as this seminar theme "The Theory of Signs," which, as far as I know, was his first presentation of semiotics in this country. He had hardly finished when Kantor bounded forward, shouting, "Why, that was nothing but medieval philosophy!" "Not at all," I remember Jakobson retorting, "it goes back at least to Plato!"

So Jakobson continued to flourish, as he related to Philip Rahv, "now and then in hostile, and often in amicable contexts" (Jakobson 1972:18). For the summer of 1946, the late Stith Thompson organized the first Folklore Institute, assembling at Indiana University a highly interesting mélange of scholars of various ages. Among the welcome participants were Roman and Svatava Pírková Jakobson, who, as I recall, were driven out to Bloomington by Alan Lomax, who came to join his father, John A. During approximately the same weeks, the much more venerable Linguistic Institute was in session at Ann Arbor, under the inspired direction of Charles C. Fries. I happened to be among the members of the visiting faculty of the University of Michigan that summer, and so was a well-known American specialist in Slavic languages, who, in 1944, had been the unfortunate recipient of a particularly savage review by Jakobson of his *Introduction to Russian*. Although the facts were beyond dispute, the tone of this piece generated much resentment. It was the custom then to conduct during the Institute weekly luncheon conferences, led chiefly by distinguished visitors. When Fries canvassed the faculty for nominations, I proposed Jakobson, but was first hooted down. However, I kept nagging away, and, with Voegelin's sympathetic support, finally prevailed upon Fries. I then fetched Jakobson from Indiana by car, and, on July 24, he addressed the assembled faculty and student body on "Comparative Metrics as a Problem of Modern Linguistics." His once and always antagonist[3] sat not far away in the audience. Jakobson kept disarmingly referring—and, seemingly, deferring—to him as "my great and good friend," this unexpected warmth causing the victim (at least momentarily) to melt, and me irrepressibly to giggle. At any rate, and in spite of the novelty of the topic in linguistic circles of those times, his debut at the Institute was, by all accounts, a *succès fou*. Fries thereafter turned into one of his ardent admirers, and Jakobson has, since then, become one of the most sought-after guests at Linguistic Institutes.

His stellar role in the 1952 session, along with a sensational performance by Lévi-Strauss (1963:67–80) was an especially memorable *tour de force*. Among a particularly distinguished group, leavened by such famous scientists from abroad as the late Bar-Hillel, Hjelmslev, and Sommerfelt, we listened to his pivotal presentation that introduced fundamental semiotic concepts to an essentially native audience, most of whom heard the name of their turn-of-the-century compatriot, Charles Sanders Peirce, for the first time; many were, I think, incredulous to have the Russian colleague characterize this American as "one of the greatest pioneers of structural linguistic analysis," as well as "a genuine and bold forerunner of structural linguistics" (1971a:555–565), but as usual, time was to bear out amply his farsighted assessment (Sebeok 1975b).

The hallmark that stamps all but the most solemn of his public utterances is Jakobson's wit. He sprinkles his lectures with humorous asides, often calculated to point up the discrepancies between reality, with its shortcomings, and a state considered desirable by the speaker in temporary collusion with his listeners. Anecdotes about him could fill a modest-sized monograph; although I have always suspected that he secretly engendered most of them himself, such stories tend to take on a life of their own, becoming collective property much in the manner of his and Bogatyrev's "Die Folklore als eine besondere Form des Schaffens" (in Jakobson 1966:1–15). Possibly the best known has to do with Jakobson's arresting accent. While his mastery of the grammatical and lexical resources of spoken English is elegant, and of its rhetorical effects superb, his pronunciation has remained shockingly alien, giving rise to a remark most often ascribed to Kuryłowicz (Mehta 1971:229), but, in fact, circulating in numerous variants: "Jakobson can lecture perfectly in six languages—unfortunately, all of them Russian." His proficiency in handling discussion is histrionic and, partly as a consequence, a lot of fun to watch. I was once chairing a lecture where he spoke for a scheduled hour or so to a large assembly of students. When the time came for questions, his mostly young auditors were shy, and too overawed to speak up. After a few moments of awkward silence, Jakobson turned to me, holding his hand high: could he address a query to himself, he wondered? I nodded, he put his question, then went on to answer himself, thus expanding his lecture for another rapt hour. Some years ago, in the early 1960s, the Director of the Newberry Library convened a meeting of a dozen or so linguists in Chicago, culminating in a convivial banquet, where we were called upon to relate "Jakobson stories" in turn, most of which I have now forgotten. What does linger in my memory is the spontaneous outpouring of affection with which the many hilarious incidents—true or alleged—were suffused. Not a trace of malice disfigured that glow. I remember remarking on that pleasant atmosphere to friends who walked me back to my hotel: I felt that, after nearly twenty years of searching, Jakobson, who was born on October 11 and hence jocosely fancies his affinity with Columbus, had found the symbolic Indians he vainly looked for upon first alighting in Indiana, and they had finally made him their honored chief. After this mutual discovery, the benefice of his teaching continued to radiate serenely out of Cambridge, prompting even his callowest followers to proclaim that he had, indeed, "played a key role in the development of linguistics in America," and acknowledge that "he has a lasting, and often decisive, influence on our scholarly development" (Gribble 1968:7). The youth of America thus turned out to be luckier than the youth of Athens, whose elders succeeded in killing the man of whom Crito said "that of all men of his time whom [he has] known, he was the wisest and justest and best" (Plato's *Phaedo*, trans. Jowett).

14. John Lotz:
A Personal Memoir

Far from being a cynic, if that word describes one who sensibly resigns himself to the second-rate, John Lotz was also the least sentimental of men. The mawkishness of the Spartan saw, Latinized as *De mortuis nil nisi bene*, was surely inconsonant with his skeptical intelligence, his powerful sense of irony, and especially his passionate dedication to the truth. While he was, privately, a man of deep, even self-lacerating, feelings, he was, in his public persona—as manifested in his daily conduct, his administrative dealings, and, above all, throughout his writings—logically consequent and cerebral to a degree of intellectual refinement rare even among the best of academics. He did not suffer fools gladly. His controlled impatience with his colleagues and subordinates who failed to measure up, with regard to their mental keenness, to his high expectations of them rendered his contacts with such associates uneasy in the best of times and much worse after 1967, the year he became President and Director of the Center for Applied Linguistics (CAL), with an attendant substantial increase in his managerial chores.

Lotz was quintessentially a Hungarian,[1] despite the fortuitous site of his birth (of Hungarian parentage, on March 23, 1913) in Milwaukee, Wisconsin—a quirk of fate of which he was nevertheless inordinately proud, and that endowed him with a citizenship that served him well after 1947, when he reclaimed it, in Stockholm, prior to joining the faculty of Columbia University. I well remember attending a meeting, in 1972, of a committee charged with responsibility for planning a strictly U. S. Colloquium on Semiotics—the group consisted of the two of us, the logician Henry Hiż, the linguist Roman Jakobson, and the art historian Meyer Schapiro—where Lotz remarked wryly that he was "the only genuine American present," the other four members having been born in Europe. Withal, Lotz—whom his intimates uniformly addressed as János—was very much a Hungarian, not merely in respect to his surface predilections, as for superior cuisine and wines, or

Note: This essay is the first of a two-part appreciation of John Lotz and his contributions. It originally appeared in the *Ural-Altaische Jahrbücher* 46:1–26 (1976); the appended list of Lotz's publications has, however, been omitted here.

Figure 14-1. John Lotz. From author's personal collection.

the like, but to the very core of his being, as only a native speaker of the language that forms an intensive, systematic object of his contemplation over a lifetime can be. In 1947, Lotz told me that he was then in the habit of rereading, each and every year, the entire range of published materials pertinent to the Hungarian language, including complete journal runs, besides, of course, keeping abreast of the current linguistic literature on and in Hungarian. I do not know, but doubt, whether he was able to continue with this rigorous discipline after his titular changes from Visiting Associate Professor of Hungarian Studies (1947–1949) to Associate Professor of General and Comparative Linguistics (1949–1956) and, finally, to Professor of Linguistics (1956–1967), at Columbia University, corresponding to a redefinition of his teaching responsibilities. He was likewise steeped in Hungarian literature, notably lyric poetry, which he could, and often would, spontaneously recite at great length; indeed, he was an outstanding expert on Hungarian metrics, and, in 1966, was awarded the PEN Medal for Hungarian literature by the PEN Club in Budapest. That same year, he spent eight months in Hungary (with his wife, Ann, and two sons, John Martin, then aged eight, and C. Peter, three), as a Fulbright-Hays Research Fellow, guest of the Hungarian Academy of Sciences, and Guest Professor of Linguistics and Hungarian at the University of Budapest. In 1972, he returned to that university as Guest Professor in Hungarian, and, a few months before his death (August 25, 1973), he was elected an Honorary Member of the Hungarian Academy. It has been rumored that he had planned to retire in that country, but the indigenous press reports that claimed so do not accord with what he confided in me the last time we spoke with one another, in a frank and wide-ranging conversation, in the fall of 1972.

Whatever his cultural commitments may have been, the facts are that Lotz was a continuous resident of Hungary for only sixteen years of his life (1919–1935), in contrast to double that number of years that he spent in the United States (1913–1919, 1947–1973); and for twelve intervening years he lived in Sweden (1935–1947). After a brief spell of elementary schooling in Detroit, his parents—Martin and Catherine (May) Lotz—settled in Somogyvámos, where he finished his primary education in 1923. (I understand that Lotz's parents were motivated to move back to Hungary because they were unable to find a Protestant elementary school for their son where the instruction was in Hungarian; no Catholic school would do.) He graduated from the Lutheran Gymnasium in Bonyhád in 1931, and was thereupon admitted to the University of Budapest and its elite Eötvös-Collegium, where, under the influence of Zoltán Gombocz—to whom he owed much, and to whose memory (and Béla Leffler's) he dedicated his first major work—he received a first-rate humanistic education, concentrating upon philosophy, Hungarian language and literature, and several Germanic languages; his dissertation—for which he won the

Eötvös-Prize—dealt with "The Concept of Time in History." Upon completion of his examinations, in September 1935, in Pécs, he obtained a fellowship in Germanic studies and philosophy at the University of Stockholm (1935–1937), was then awarded his doctorate in Hungary (1937), and settled down in Sweden, for the next decade, to a succession of academic posts at the University of Stockholm: Lecturer in Hungarian (1935–1939), Director of the Hungarian Institute (1936–1957), Docent (1939–1947) and Associate Professor (1942–1947) in Hungarian. In 1936, he also became Editor of the Publications of the Hungarian Institute,[2] which, until its expiration in 1963, included twenty items, among them Lotz's own early masterpiece, *Das ungarische Sprachsystem* (1939), and, incidentally, an abbreviated version of my dissertation (1946), which turned out to be instrumental in bringing us together in person during the following summer. The series also featured several other important early writings by Lotz himself, for example, his monograph on verbal forms in the *Jókai Codex* (1938); his first collaborative study with Roman Jakobson (delivered as a lecture on April 8, 1941, expanded English version published in 1952); and Wolfgang Steinitz's classic *Geschichte des finnisch-ugrischen Vokalismus* (1944) as well as his sketchy *Geschichte des finnisch-ugrischen Konsonantismus* (1952).

The psychologist David Katz introduced Jakobson—newly arrived from Norway—at the end of the summer of 1940, to the brilliant young Hungarian resident, whose circle included Steinitz as well. Lotz "became strongly interested in a structural search in linguistics, of which first elements were already in his Hungarian Grammar," Jakobson recently wrote me, reminiscing about their early period of acquaintanceship in Sweden. "He was eager to learn from me all that we of the Prague Circle had to say. We had long conversations and discussions and we organized a kind of mini-circle, we two and Steinitz. Every week we met in Lotz's flat and read improvised communications and discussed various problems of general linguistics, always on some concrete language, mostly Finno-Ugric or Slavic. J.L.'s and my joint study on Mordvinian verse resulted from one of such meetings. I gave a few lectures in scientific societies of Upsala and Stockholm and J.L. took part in them." As an incidental result of these exchanges, Steinitz came to dedicate his *Vokalismus* to Jakobson while the seminal "Axioms of a versification system," by the latter with Lotz, opened an era of intellectual cooperation between two outstanding linguists of wholly differing backgrounds and formation, whose interests chanced to initially converge especially on metrical topics. (Much later, in 1957, Lotz contributed the brief entry on Jakobson to the *Encyclopaedia Britannica*.)

When Jakobson emigrated to America, he carried tales about the scintillating Hungarian, and, during a hot August afternoon we spent together in 1942, at Franz Boas's house, in Grantwood, he unfolded a plan to create for Lotz an academic opportunity where the two of them could pursue their work together in a common framework. It took five years to realize this scheme, which eventually envisaged the expansion of the famous Columbia Slavic Department, created by Ernest J. Simmons in 1946, and chaired by him until 1959, into a department of Slavic and adjacent languages.

Jakobson also urged me to establish direct contact with Lotz, and I wrote him immediately. He responded promptly, sent me a copy of his *Sprachsystem*, which I then reviewed for *Language* (Sebeok 1943), calling it, over thirty years ago, "a remarkably good work, . . . excellent and original . . ." Considerable correspondence and intensive exchange of ideas between us ensued, in spite of wartime delays and interruptions. Lotz asked to see a copy of my dissertation, then offered to publish a portion of it, edited by himself. I accepted his assistance with gratitude, but asked to see the proofs. However, these never reached me for, as we learned afterward, the ship bringing them was torpedoed. The monograph was therefore published in the raw, and I received my first copies only some two years after the war.

In 1947, I applied for a fellowship to the American-Scandinavian Foundation, and, with its generous support, was enabled to spend over two months of that year in Stockholm. During this sojourn, I saw Lotz practically every day, from mid-morning often late into the night. For some weeks, Tamás Tarnóczy, the leading Hungarian acoustician, was a third companion; his "Vibration of the Vocal Cords and Their Opening Quotient" was later likewise published by Lotz. A social highlight of that summer was a sumptuous dinner party, given by Louis Hjelmslev's publisher, for Lotz, Malmberg, myself, and, of course, the senior Danish linguist of those times; the occasion eventuated in ever closer contacts with the Scandinavian colleagues, which again had reverberations at Linguistic Institutes from 1952, when both Lotz and Hjelmslev became first-time Visiting Professors, to 1964, when Malmberg joined us, in turn, at Indiana University.

Lotz and I read Vogul and Ostyak texts together, and formulated plans for a comprehensive investigation of the language and culture of the Cheremis people, a research project that, in 1948, I developed further with the assistance of Ödön Beke, and that kept me busy throughout the next decade. Lotz wished to hear from me all I could relate about the wartime work of American linguists and postwar trends in descriptive linguistics, a quest that intensified significantly when, as a result of Jakobson's persuasive efforts, a letter arrived from Simmons with a call to Columbia. Two remarks of Lotz's, from those days, stick in my memory: half jokingly, he would characterize his theoretical stance as "post-structuralist," and his comment, very often repeated in reference to contemporary descriptivist studies, *annál a valóság bonyolultabb* ("reality is more complicated than that")—both tags, as it turned out, prophetic.

During his Swedish period, Lotz wrote a tremendous amount, but published relatively little. I saw and critically read, at his request, a large pile of his manuscripts, maybe a dozen or more that he considered "nearly ready," but most of which have not even yet been released for printing.[3] Four principles informed all of his publications, as he explicitly recognized and stated in the *Sprachsystem*:

(1) "Im Ausdruck ist die größte *Exaktheit* erstrebt" (p. 8);

(2) "In der Anordnung war die größt mögliche *Klarheit* das Ziel" (ibid.);

(3) "Das Material ist nach der strengsten *Konsequenz* bearbeitet" (p. 9); and

(4) "Der Gegenstand wird *objektiv* behandelt . . ." (p. 10).

Writings which he deemed deficient in respect to one or more of these criteria of scrupulous construction he refused to make public. Incidentally, he had an extraordinary gift for the graphic representation of linguistic data: his structural diagrams have never been equaled as to their lucidity in conveying very complex topological relationships; the most baroque display accompanied his paper on "The Structure of the *Sonetti a Corona* of Attila József" (1965), where the four-colored design, isomorphic with the poem analyzed, was so striking that Lotz received a commercial offer to have it mass-produced on a tablecloth. He was also a passionate and outstanding chess player, who especially enjoyed the company of mathematicians. In 1950, he became the principal investigator of a Russian grammar project for mathematicians, supported by the American Mathematical Society. During his New York period, his most frequent chess opponent was to be the prominent topologist, Samuel Eilenberg. If, on the other hand, Lotz had any degree of sensibility for either the visual arts or music—other than schmaltzy Hungarian folksongs, fragments of which he would often pour forth in his distinctively lusty baritone—he kept the fact well concealed. On Sundays in Stockholm, Lotz used to drag me to soccer games, his fondness for which was later transferred to rugger (I think he had played association football himself in his youth). In 1969, at a Conference on Sign Language, I heard him read a paper analyzing the hand signals used by referees—a semiotic cameo that, stubbornly, he would not let anyone read, let alone publish.

After Lotz received Simmons's portentous invitation, he questioned me closely about academic life in America, but hesitated for many weeks before accepting. One practical problem involved the disposition of his tremendous quadripartite private library of general linguistics, Uralic studies, logic, and Hungarian studies; eventually, of course, this was moved to Manhattan, where it continued to grow. Even though, ultimately, much of the Hungariological section became the property of Columbia, many of his books had to be relocated in a separate flat in the building, several floors beneath the apartment occupied by the Lotz family, on 50 Morningside Drive. At the end of the summer, he received a U.S. passport, and returned to America. As he told several friends later on, he found the intellectual atmosphere of the New World much more stimulating than the one he left behind, and, so far as I know, never regretted his decision to reimmigrate to his native land. He retained, however, a thread of connection with Sweden until 1966, reflected by the title of Inspector of the Hungarian Institute at the University of Stockholm, and frequently went back for visits.

Upon his arrival in New York, Lotz resumed his contacts with Jakobson, who writes: "Until my move from Columbia to Harvard (late 1949), our co-operation continued to develop, particularly in discussions on distinctive features and on relations between phonology and morphology. One of the results of this work was our common study on French consonantal pattern in *Word* [actually, "Notes on the French Phonemic Pattern," in vol. 5, no. 2, of that journal, in 1949] and Lotz's presentation and defense of my paper on the relation between phonology and morphology in the Paris Congress of Linguists, in 1948 [the Sixth; see pp. 451–453 and 464–470 of the *Proceedings*, 1949, for Lotz's contributions], which I could not attend. We first planned to write a primer of phonology devoted to the analysis of distinctive features, J.L. and I, but after my move to Harvard, our preliminary discussions were unfortunately discontinued and they yielded to my work on *Preliminaries to Speech Analysis*, done in collaboration with Fant and Halle" (the latter a former student of Lotz's, as well as Jakobson's). At about this time, Lotz began what was to become a lifelong preoccupation with acoustic phonetics, and coproduced a number of films in that field. The most widely viewed among these films were *Some Aspects of the Speech Event* (1953), and *Hungarian X-ray Film* (1961), both slow-motion pictures with sound. His work in cinematography had two peripheral but important long-range effects, both connected with the facts of sponsorship: the support of the Wenner-Gren Foundation brought Lotz closer in touch with its Director of Research, Paul Fejos; and the collaboration of the Haskins Laboratories cemented his friendship with the physicist Franklin S. Cooper.

Fejos, the remarkable force who infused anthropological researches the world over with his special brand of dynamic imagination, was also a Hungarian, who had been an internationally recognized director of both art and ethnographic films prior to coming to head the foundation. He was, moreover, always interested in technological innovations, so he enthusiastically backed Lotz's initial ventures with the camera from 1952 to 1954 (his subsequent undertakings in this area were financed by several agencies of the U.S. federal government). Fejos, who had, even earlier, supported Lotz's Sayan Samoyed project (1951–1953), continued to assist Lotz. Although their relationship always remained ritually formal, each was quite exceptionally fond of the other. Lotz took part in several symposia at Burg Wartenstein (the foundation's European conference headquarters), and notably organized one on the topic "Toward the Description of Languages of the World." The two of us also designed a conference together, on "Language and Medicine," held at Wenner-Gren's New York offices. Both of these took place in 1970, after the leadership of the foundation—which Lotz, along with many of us, continued to regard as the best-managed of all comparable granting agencies—had passed to Fejos's widow, Lita Osmundsen. Nor did the confidence of this foundation in his competence and capacities ever falter, for it generously contributed, up to Lotz's death, to his final, most ambitious project, encompassing the totality of the world's languages.

The Haskins Laboratories is a private research organization that has become a mecca for phoneticians the world over. Founded by Caryl P. Haskins, a myrmecologist and polymath, in 1935, the work of its phonetics component has long been guided by Cooper, who, in due course, succeeded the founder to the presidency of the whole. Lotz conducted a variety of acoustic investigations under the aegis of the laboratory, as reflected by his films (some of which were, however, shot at the University of Rochester, and others at the Columbia-Presbyterian Medical Center), and Cooper figures as a collaborator in them all; Lotz also coauthored a number of papers growing out of his experiments there. Cooper joined Lotz as an Adjunct Professor at Columbia at the latter's initiative, and, in the late 1960s, came to serve on the CAL Board of Trustees, also at his behest. It is worth noting, in passing, that these products of Lotz's, mainly from the 1950s, utilized not merely Hungarian materials, but also Arabic, Chinese, Russian, Spanish, and Thai.

An episode of Lotz's life at Columbia, which should by no means be glossed over, for it bedeviled his existence over a number of years, was the rift, eventually permanent, with his colleague, André Martinet, the distinguished French linguist who then headed the Department of General and Comparative Linguistics in which Lotz was his junior. A fair assessment of this regrettable story, which ended with Martinet's resignation from Columbia and departure for the Sorbonne, must be left to those who were privy to both sides of the record, as I was not. The Linguistic Circle of New York, which Lotz served as its secretary during the period leading up to the incidents in question, certainly figured in the events that are now a part of its history, and so did, particularly, its journal *Word*, then edited by Martinet with Lotz as a principal staff reviewer. Indeed, from 1950 onward, he contributed to *Word*—besides his joint article with Jakobson, already mentioned, and his important study on "Vowel Frequency in Hungarian"—over a dozen book notes and longer reviews, but these ceased abruptly in 1952, after which he never again wrote for this periodical or continued to have any truck with the Circle.

During his early years at Columbia, one of Lotz's principal intellectual interests came into focus, perhaps catalyzed by his acquaintanceship with a vigorous, enhancing young officer of the Rockefeller Foundation, Chadbourne Gilpatric. This was his concern with systems of communication other than speech, already patently manifest in his *Sprachsystem*, which paid more than perfunctory attention to Hungarian orthography—a rather uncommon feature of contemporary grammatical treatises. He returned to his preoccupation with script several times, notably in a series of papers produced during his last years: "The Conversion of Script to Speech as Exemplified by Hungarian" (1969), "The Role of Script in Describing the Languages of the World" (1971), "How Language is Conveyed by Script" (1972); and he even compiled a working bibliography of what he considered "the most significant contributions in Western scholarship dealing with the problem of script" (1972). In 1951, he wrote an acute, if excessively laconic, paper on the relation between natural language and constructed scientific languages, or calculi, dubbing the latter "parasitic," i.e., always dependent on the former. His curiosity about animal communication crystallized about 1950, in a preliminary analysis of the signaling behavior of the honeybee, "in order to get a perspective on the specific characteristics of human languages," a theme to which he returned over and over again. His work in poetic language encompassed not only Hungarian but several other Uralic languages (as already mentioned, Mordvinian, and also Kamassian), as well as, later on, Germanic (1956b), Greek (to appear), and, of course, metrics in general, a subject on which he wrote some of his most memorable and influential articles. During his first sabbatical leave of absence, in the early 1950s, he was to have produced, with the aid of a Rockefeller grant, a major synthesis of his ideas on semiotic, but he never brought this off. Many years afterward, when he was the Director of the Center for Applied Linguistics, he commissioned me to prepare a state-of-the-art report for the center on semiotic in the late 1960s, which I did. As a direct consequence, I received a formal appointment as CAL's "consultant" on semiotic, and, as an outgrowth of this assignment, the center assumed formal sponsorship of the U.S. Colloquium on Semiotics (alluded to above), at which Lotz himself was to have presented a major position paper on the relation of language to other systems of signs. However, he died before this could be accomplished, and the center reverted—in the words of its own Deputy Director—to a condition of "selective ignorance" about this area. At any rate, since the theory of signs is now a major international touchstone of intellective endeavor—although some might call it a fad—there is no doubt that Lotz foresaw its development as a tool of analysis, if not a formal discipline, more than a decade before its seemingly spontaneous worldwide explosive onrush.

In the summer of 1952, we brought Lotz to Indiana University to participate in a Conference of Anthropologists and Linguists, held for a fortnight in the framework of the Linguistic Institute. In Bloomington, he was reunited with Hjelmslev, Jakobson, and, from Finland, Valentin Kiparsky; he became acquainted there with Lévi-Strauss; he mingled with many of the most prominent linguists of the United States. In 1953, he returned to Bloomington as a member of the faculty of our second Linguistic Institute, cosponsored with the Linguistic Society of America (of which he had become a life member in 1949). He now inched his way deeper into the American way of life by enrolling as a student in the university's driver education program, and, upon passing his test, preened himself ebulliently in a college sweatshirt that proclaimed him an alumnus of that institution. (Unfortunately, he turned out to be a spectacularly careless, indeed dangerous, driver, who later occasioned one major road accident and was involved in innumerable minor scrapes.) Asked for his impressions, by a well-meaning dean, about the great State Universities of the Midwest, he baffled him with the aphorism, "Better late Gothic than never," which became quasi-proverbial among his friends.

At the end of that summer, he decided to drive out with me and my family, in easy stages, to Albuquerque (where I held a visiting appointment at the University of New Mexico, for the following semester). Although Lotz was, by then, a forty-year-old bachelor, he turned out to be not only a boon companion to me, but an altogether considerate and generous house guest, who showered us with presents, including a (really unwanted) kitten—perhaps out of nostalgia for his own, metonymically named Ice Cream, awaiting his return to Manhattan. He was unfailingly kind to my infant daughter who, some eighteen years later, spent a summer as his research assistant in Washington. In Albuquerque, we both saw a great deal of Stanley Newman, and another visiting linguist, from Cornell, Gordon Fairbanks. The four of us soon founded the Linguistic Society of New Mexico, which never boasted of more than four members, but which was divided into two sections, A. Hungarian, and B. Foreign, with Lotz alone holding membership in both.

While we were still westward bound, Lotz began to complain of feeling unwell; in Albuquerque he experienced disturbing symptoms which, looking back, turned out to be the earliest intimations of a rare, debilitating disease of the blood that was properly diagnosed and finally treated only in the 1960s.[4] He took the train back to New York in a somber mood, worried about his health, but nonetheless ready to assume his new duties at Columbia as Chairman of the country's first Department of Uralic and Altaic Languages.

In addition, Lotz became Director of Columbia's Language and Communication Research Center, a nebulous administrative device created to handle grants and contracts within its purview between Columbia and agencies of the government and private foundations. One major product of this unit was a publication containing basic data on the peoples and languages of the Caucasus (preliminary edition, 1955), the main sections of which were compiled by four other scholars, with three of whom (one a student of his) Lotz later—at various times, in varying degree, and for different reasons—came to be on distinctly bad terms.[5] His Preface—which did not appear in the final edition—is noteworthy for its reference to "a continuing research program on language communities of the world," for it shows that the outlines of the world's languages project, formally inaugurated only in 1971, had already assumed a firm shape in Lotz's mind.

In the spring of 1956, Lotz negotiated a grant from the Ford Foundation enabling him to convene a conference of all scholars then affiliated with American institutions working in Uralic and/or Altaic fields. A "Report on Uralic and Altaic Studies" resulted, and, either by uncanny foresight or a most fortunate coincidence, was submitted to the foundation early in the fall of 1958, just a few weeks, that is, after the enactment of the National Defense Education Act. A copy of this report was also sent to the American Council of Learned Societies, which then promptly acted to sponsor a Uralic and Altaic Committee, chaired by Lotz, to provide a forum for continuing discussions about the development of the field.[6] The far-sighted President of the ACLS, Frederick Burkhardt—Lotz's ardent supporter then, as later, when he became a member of CAL's Board of Trustees—appointed him Director of Research of the Uralic and Altaic Program of the ACLS, in which capacity he served (on a part-time basis), with the highest distinction, between 1959 and 1965. Owing to his tireless efforts, the ACLS was awarded two sizable successive contracts by the U.S. Office of Education, under Title VI of the NDEA, to develop research and studies in Uralic and Altaic languages and areas (June 16, 1959–January 31, 1965). Details of the program appear in Lotz's report, published in Bloomington, in 1966. The administrator of Title VI, that is, the individual who pushed both unlikely contracts through the Office of Education, was my late Indiana University friend and colleague, William Riley Parker, who later commented on the realization of Lotz's dreamlike Grand Design: "I know of no other venture under NDEA, then or since, in which the taxpayer's money was more wisely spent, either in the national interest or in the interest of American scholarship and education." He also paid tribute to his "vision and practicality and erudition . . ." (Parker 1966:vii–ix). Lotz prized the esteem of both Burkhardt and Parker, was gratified by his connection with the ACLS, and, above all, regarded the program, which, in Parker's words, mobilized "every available human resource in the United States," as his greatest organizational achievement, which, indeed, it was. It lent him an aura of entrepreneurial success, which was later cited as a capital reason for his candidacy for the Directorship of CAL.

Early in the fall of 1956, Lotz attended the Vth International Congress of Anthropological and Ethnological Sciences, held in Philadelphia, where he met an archeology student from the University of

California, Ann M. Norsworthy. He followed her out to Berkeley and, after a brief courtship, married her on July 6, of the following year. In 1958, his first son, doubly named after his father and his grandfather, was born.

In 1960, Lotz and I both received invitations to attend an international congress scheduled to be held in Budapest. Each of us reponded promptly, affirmatively, and gratefully, delighted at the prospect of visiting Hungary for the first time after the war. Together, we presented our respective passports to the proper authorities in Vienna, but, owing to some petty bureaucratic chicanery, both of our visa applications were denied. He went on to Sweden, eventually to spend 1962–1963 as a Visiting Professor of Linguistics at the University of Stockholm, then rejoined me in Vienna one year later, and, a few days afterwards, his documents now in order, I saw him off at a railroad station for his journey back to Budapest—so short a distance away in kilometers, such an immense distance when measured in terms of the many eventful years that had elapsed since his last visit. In 1964, he was appointed to a Selection Committee by the Ford Foundation to establish cultural exchanges with Hungary, an effort that he devoted much of his time to, then and later on.

Beginning in the late 1950s, the linguists of America were grouped in three interlocking, mutually supportive national organizations which, as it were, through multiple channels, spoke in unison for our profession in the United States: the Linguistic Society of America (1924–), the ACLS Committee on Language Programs (1941–), and the Center for Applied Linguistics (1959–). The third of these, CAL, was founded by Charles A. Ferguson, who, in 1966, retired as its first President and Director (although he remains, to this day, its *éminence grise*). A search committee for his successor was established with J Milton Cowan, the LSA's second Secretary-Treasurer, at its helm. If the position were to be filled by a figure with stature and qualifications comparable to Ferguson's, he or she must be a scholar of international reputation, a canny administrator, a fund raiser of demonstrated ability, and someone with at least a reasonable interest in that kind of linguistics which, in some sense of that vague adjective, is referred to as "applied." This was a tall order, and the search was correspondingly protracted. At last, Lotz was called to fill this important professional post, which he then held during the next four exacting, increasingly turbulent years (1967–1971). In several important respects, his appointment did seem ideal: Lotz's academic credentials were, of course, impeccable; his recently completed work on behalf of our Uralic and Altaic community demonstrated his capacity to undertake fiscal chores from inception to final accounting; and his interests appeared broad enough to encompass "applied linguistics," which was then often simply equated with language teaching (see his several contributions, back in 1942, to M. Allwood's *Living Language Teaching*, or his even earlier *Hungarian Reader for Foreigners* [1938, 1962]). However, I questioned at the time whether he was wise to leave his, on the surface, sheltered and reasonably tranquil academic existence for the hurly-burly of Washington, the stresses and strains of which were to tax his already precarious health, assuredly contributing to a major heart attack requiring his prolonged hospitalization; his decision to move, as it turned out, came to expose him to well-nigh intolerable indignities that, in the end, embittered his declining years. When he called up, one evening, to inform me of his job offer, I expressed mixed feelings about it, and asked what his chief reasons could be (aside from considerations of the obvious emoluments) for accepting it. He replied that he thought that the next few years might be stormy ones on campuses such as Columbia's (a prediction which turned out to be quite correct, although the upheaval there was as curt as it was violent, and, in the end, essentially ineffectual); and that, for the sake of his family (now augmented by a second son, born in 1963), he would prefer to reside in a Washington suburb rather than in the heart of Manhattan. These were two splendid personal reasons for changing location, I concurred, but noted that he had said nothing positive about the Center, nor expressed any sudden urge to adapt himself to the peculiar, in fact, unique, requirements of this semipublic clearinghouse between our profession on the one hand and representatives of a host of other disciplines, a maze of U.S. federal agencies, and the arcane world of private foundations on the other.

At any rate, the Lotz family did relocate in Chevy Chase, Maryland. He assumed the directorate of the Center at a time when it had just about peaked in respect to the scope of its activities, with a commensurately swollen staff, financed with soft money. The initial task he set for himself was to gain quick control over the budget, which was leaking quite alarmingly, a goal that he accomplished all right, but not without severely treading on many entrenched toes and thereby incurring the implacable enmity of several veteran staffers who were claiming CAL as *their* turf, by dint of seniority. His opinion of many—but by no means all—of his inherited subordinates verged on contempt which he scarcely bothered to disguise, and thus he was, in short order, irreversibly alienated from his "rear guard," a hardly dispensable power base. Unfortunately, the few new men and women that he himself hired for the Center appeared, to outside observers such as me, hardly to ameliorate the overall average of professional acuity.

Lotz's notorious secretiveness, bordering on the conspiratorial, did not help matters either. He shared with members of his staff no more information than he felt they needed to know, and sometimes even less. This deprivation was, I sensed, more deeply resented than the loss of some more palpable perquisites that marked his advent, and it was not uncommon, nor perhaps surprising, for ambitious—or maybe merely curious—CAL employees to bypass him in their dealings with complaisant members of the Board of Trustees, or with certain granting agencies whose officers should have known better; but he was either unconcerned or helpless to impose more than fitful discipline. Only in 1969, when, in my capacity as the newly elected Secretary-Treasurer of the LSA, I came to open up a suite of offices within the Center, adjacent to his own headquarters, did I grow fully aware of an atmosphere of tension on the premises, and come to realize, feeling like a guilty bystander, that CAL, although on an even keel as far as its businesslike management was concerned, was far from a happy ship, and that the now often melancholy Lotz himself might well have been its most disgruntled inmate (I also had occasion then to call to mind another familiar Lotz adage: "Happiness is a bourgeois prejudice"). Lotz was clearly bored by many aspects—some would insist the key aspects—of his job; often, I thought tactlessly, he would scorn seemingly sincere persons concerned with pedagogical and other applications of linguistics, and deride earnest organizations with outlandish acronyms that he deemed as pretentious as he judged their efforts self-seeking humbuggery. Meanwhile, he incessantly complained about his deteriorating health, so that some accused him of hypochondria; but those who knew him well were not deceived and knew that his ailments, no less than his ennui, were only too real. It was at this juncture that scabrous and, I dare say, slanderous, rumors about this thoroughly virtuous but positively ill man began to circulate. He was aware of them and their source, but made no attempt that I know of to refute them.

One of Lotz's principal duties involved the constant care and feeding of the Ford Foundation, his associations with which (initially in the person of the late Cleon O. Swayzee) went back to the mid-1950s. The foundation served as midwife to the Center, and has been a constant source of its basic support throughout these past fifteen years. Quite understandably, the officers of the Ford Foundation who cared most about CAL and the program it stood for developed something like a proprietary interest in its achievements, demanding to know Lotz's own long-range program plans, while showering him, or so he complained, with naïve pronouncements about technical issues that he felt they were not professionally competent to cope with. In my own dealings with much the same cadre of officers on the Linguistic Society's behalf, around the same period, I did not find this to be so—but vested interests were not, of course, involved in our case. At any rate, Lotz would not reconcile himself to the simple fact that who pays the piper calls the tune, and his aversion to Ford grew apace. His unwillingness to articulate and forecast his policies, let alone adapt them to the tastes of the times, cost him the loss of his second source of power, vested in several amiable and essentially well-disposed, though possibly overly tenacious, men and women upon whose recommendations the survival of CAL depended. By contrast, it should be stressed, his relations with several major government agencies—notably, the U.S. Office of Education—remained excellent, and CAL's overall level of support from federal sources was substantially higher during the years of his leadership than it is, for instance, right now.

Lotz's generous hospitality and that of his gracious and delightful wife were a byword about Washington. During these last short years, it was at their suburban residence that I enjoyed seeing him best. It was in this house, or garden, that he was at his most reflective, gently witty, and least intolerant of the frailty of others. My business brought me to the area, and thereby into close contact with him, quite often, and it is my remembrance of our evenings together, our many long talks—lately conducted half in English, half in Hungarian—concerning the affairs and problems of our respective, in some measure overlapping, organizations, on politics and corruption (which, for Lotz, were virtually synonymous), or about numberless other topics, that gives me the greatest pleasure. It was Lotz's wont to address me with the gruffness of an elder brother. I sought his advice—as often as not discarding it—as if he had been my sibling. His life style was radically different from mine, and so were his definitions of modern linguistics[7] and of its contemporary giants. I had a more detached perspective of his associates than he did, and could afford to be more charitable toward at least some of them. We disagreed about many things, but I cannot overemphasize the intellectual stimulation that I derived from one quarter of a century's communion.

One evening, Lotz was entertaining a minor dignitary of the Washington scene, in the presence of a dozen or so "establishment" linguists, including members of his Board of Trustees. Some remark of this hapless, bewildered official set Lotz off on an ill-tempered tirade, which had all the makings of an ugly incident. I never learned either its cause or its substance. It was obvious, however, that the customarily urbanely entertaining Lotz had, for once, lost control of himself. Before the harangue could escalate, the party broke up, to cover a momentary breach in the fabric of the conventional world; but the occurrence left a residue of lingering embarrassment, as well as of a displeasure that was never to dissipate. This episode, I believe, set off the crumbling of Lotz's third and last pillar of authority, which was, *de jure*, vested in the board. Within a few months, he retired from the headship of the Center.

This much is fact. Lotz, I was told, tried to reach me afterward, but, during the spring, I happened to be lying in the isolation ward of a hospital, unable to handle even phone calls. We didn't see each other until many months later, while we both chanced to be in Hungary. His version of "what really happened," as he related it to me in Szeged, in August 1972, and the subjective testimony of the other parties concerned (viz., various trustees, staff members, people from Ford) are all different. They have all been contested, producing a distinctly cubist view of the event, *Rashomon*-like in its manifold perspectives and arguing for the ultimate unknowability of truth. No useful purpose would be served by rehearsing the statements of the other witnesses to this tragedy here, but Lotz's perception of it must be recorded. He summed it all up in one trenchant, if startling, phrase: "The Anglo-Saxons did me in," naming two members of the CAL board in particular. I interpreted this to be a figurative way of expressing his conviction that his resignation was forced because his own moral standards clashed with the ethic of his most influential masters. In this, I am sure that he was right, for their cultural differences were pervasive, profound, and perhaps unbridgeable; but I also am bound to repeat in this context one of his favorite maxims, *annál a valóság bonyolultabb*!

As already alluded to several times in this memoir, Lotz had conceived the idea, at least by the mid-1950s, of a large-scale, long-term scheme for describing the languages of the world according to a uniform plan, but he began to hammer out his vision into concrete terms only in the late 1960s. He once told me that he had hoped to devote his full time to this project after his retirement (which, in the normal course of events, would have commenced in 1978). He approached the project in several successive steps, well thought out and expertly realized. In 1971, he convened an all-American conference of linguists, in Washington, for a discussion of format problems; this was shortly followed by an international symposium, held at Burg Wartenstein, on roughly the same topic. (An unprecedented feat was that Lotz was able to secure the participation at the Austrian conference of two prominent colleagues from the Soviet Union.) An international standing committee was then set up, with Lotz as its secretary, and with ample initial financing that he was able to secure from the ACLS, Wenner-Gren, and the U.S. Office of Education. The next step in the design called for the opening up of an office—presumably a branch of CAL, to be managed by Lotz, with a small staff—in Vienna, but this was not realized. The last public news of the project was contained in Lotz's progress report, delivered in Bologna, to a large audience at the Xth International Congress of Linguists. With a change of administration at CAL, Lotz's efforts were then abruptly arrested, and, to all intents and purposes, the project vanished from view. Who can say when it will be resurrected?[8]

In Szeged, where I spent a depressing week with Lotz, he gave the impression of an utterly weary man, beset by his failing health, compounded by perplexities of an uncertain future. Indeed, he underwent minor but painful surgery there, yet insisted on proceeding to Bologna, where his scar got infected, so that he had to go back to Szeged to have this attended to. He eventually returned home, only to be hospitalized with pneumonia. Upon his release, he appeared to rally, or so it was reported, and finally was able to put his affairs in order with a representative of the CAL board, reaching an equitable settlement. On August 25, he felt well enough to want to take his family out to dinner at the Piccadilly, one of his favorite Washington restaurants, where he had a fatal heart attack at dinner—an ironic oxymoron that he would have appreciated.

I lack the literary gift for conveying my emotions about Lotz, but a poem by e. e. cummings, which leapt into my mind when I heard of his passing, poses the anguishing question I would myself raise:

> Buffalo Bill 's
> defunct
>   who used to
>   ride a watersmooth-silver
>   stallion
> and break onetwothreefourfive pigeonsjustlikethat
>   Jesus
>
> he was a handsome man
>   and what i want to know is
> how do you like your blueeyed boy
> Mister Death

15. Parasitic Formations and Kindred Semiotic Sets: Notes on the Legacy of John Lotz

Lotz's scientific activities encompassed a wide range of semiotic topics, including notably the following:

(1) Natural languages in their several manifestations, including especially (a) speech and (b) script.

(2) Natural languages in approximation to polar opposite states, namely, (a) tending toward context freedom, as in calculi, and (b) tending toward context sensitivity, as in verse.

(3) Other sign systems—(a) in man, for example, the professional hand-signals used by referees during football games,[1] and (b), in animals, the communicating behavior of the honeybee.

(4) In 1955, he also made a singularly ingenious (although hardly known) foray probing the uncertain frontiers of verbal formulations and their averbal setting.

His ambition, to complete a major synthesis of his semiotic ideas, "in order to get a perspective on the specific characteristics of human language," was thwarted (Ch. 14, this volume), but the problem area preoccupied him throughout his productive career. He succeeded in working out only scattered fragments of the whole; from these, however, one can glean some of the themes and arguments which, in all likelihood, would have informed the book he had envisioned.

From the welter of his legacy, this recollection proposes to capsule but a few essential aspects of his overall scheme, particularly to recapture his position on the conjoint topics 3b, 2a, and 1b.[2]

Note: This article is a companion piece to the preceding; effectively, it constitutes Part II of that Memoir, as prevised in the note on the first page of Chapter 14. It is being simultaneously published in the *Ural-Altaische Jahrbücher* 50:138–143 (1978).

The Structure of Bee Communication (3b)

In all the years of our acquaintanceship, I heard Lotz speak about only two kinds of animals: domestic cats and honeybees. During his bachelor years in Manhattan, he had a cat named Ice Cream, who, inscrutably, either jumped or accidentally fell to her death while chasing pigeons from his library's window ledge overlooking Morningside Drive. His care for cats was personal, affectionate, and engaged in their welfare. His attitude toward honeybees was detached, scientific, and concerned solely with their semiotic competence.

Aristotle, or an informant of his, accurately observed and described the so-called "dancing" of hive bees in the *Hist. Animal.* IX, 624b, as Haldane (1955) has noted, so the phenomenon must be at least 2,300 years old and presumably very much older. Von Frisch's first incomplete account, in the early decades of the century, of the communicatory function of the honeybees' "dance," particularly the direction of food found and its distance, both of which are indicated with great accuracy (Sebeok 1972:34–53), and the many amazing discoveries of additional features (as well as the sharp controversies and puzzling gaps in knowledge [Wenner 1971]) that have unfolded since have involved the more or less systematic professional attention of an ever increasing number of language scientists, including especially psychologists (such as Bühler) and linguists of various persuasions. Lotz was among the first linguists anywhere—and, after Laziczius (Sebeok 1972:11 n. 6, 36; 1976, Ch. 7), the second of three Hungarian linguists—to point out the importance "for linguistics, and for semiotics in general" (1951), of these remarkable discoveries.[3] He published a succinct analysis of the structure of bee communication in 1950, compressed into a multifaceted diagram, which I reproduced in *Language* in 1963 with an extended commentary of my own. As far as I can determine, however, Lotz was totally uninterested in animal communication per se; his only concern was to display the data available at that time in a form that he deemed comparable with his conception of linguistic structure. He subsequently (1951) spelled his views out under six headings, which I now recall, supplemented by my bracketed remarks as these appear pertinent nearly three decades afterward.

(1) "In bee communication, the field of reference is rigidly limited to the finding place of pollen and nectar and to the quality of these, whereas the field of semantic reference in human language is unlimited (universal)." [The bee dance can, in fact, be regarded as a miniaturized re-enactment of the journey that the signing bee has returned from and its projection upon which some informed bees may be about to embark. The field of reference symbolized is probably always novel, since the worker generally reports about a site never before experienced either by her or her sisters. The location of a new nesting place as well as a food find is communicated by the waggle dance.]

(2) "In bee communication, the somatic gesture, the dance, cannot be decomposed into component units: at the most the two phases of simple turn and wiggling constitute a semisyntactic structure, whereas human language operates on the principle of the selective combinability of minimal signs, morphemes." [At least the following additional dance forms, all of which have communicative functions, have been detected in the intervening years: jostling run (*Rumpeltanz*); spasmodic dance (*Rucktanz*); buzzing run (*Schwirrlauf*); grooming or shaking dance; jerking dance; and trembling dance. The relationships of these stereotyped locomotory forms to one another are far from fully understood.]

(3) "The bee dance cannot be decomposed into 'empty' constituents which are recombinable . . ." [True; the bee code lacks the feature of duality and all that its presence would imply.]

(4) "The bee dance 'maps out' the environment around the hive; it is an *icon* of the referential reality, which is only rarely the case with human speech symbols. . . . The syntactic structure, of course, might bear iconic reference to the internal processes (thinking, emotion, volition, etc.)." [I don't agree with either assertion in the first sentence: in the bee dance, the indexical or the symbolic aspect is often predominant (Sebeok 1976:133–134), and language is replete with iconicity (Ch. 6, this volume). These subjects deserve closer study.]

(5) "In bee language no conversation is possible; in the sending of a message there is an inconvertible relationship between a foraging bee and the recipients." [Contrast Lindauer's (1961, Ch. 2) vivid description of "debate" in a swarm, exceptionally lasting even up to a fortnight, over the quality of competing nesting places; cf. Sebeok 1972: 45.]

(6) "The pragmatic aspect of human language has its correspondence in the vigorousness of the dance and the length of time it is executed." [Quite so.]

In general, bee communication—not only by means of the "dance," but also via the chemical and acoustic channels—is turning out to be a great deal more complicated than it could be imagined in mid-century, and the total semiotic repertoire of man, comprising his verbal and averbal codes together, stands revealed as far more labyrinthine than was thought possible in the innocent 1950s.

Constructed Scientific Languages (2a)

Lotz's manner of writing was plain, deliberate, brusquely to the point, but, even by his standards of composition, his 1951 essay, contrasting natural languages and constructed scientific languages, or calculi, was excessively terse.

The point of his consequential note was to call attention to a category of semiotic sets that he dubbed *parasitic* formations, by which he meant superstructures optionally imposed upon spoken language. He underlined the fact that a natural language "has no limitations for any semantic or pragmatic function," which is tantamount to calling it a *universal* language. However, "just because of these broad social and semiotic implications, the semantic references of a natural language are vague." To counteract this inherent indeterminacy, certain special conventions come into play when the need to introduce a calculus arises.

A calculus doesn't just happen to be parasitic, but this must always be so, a necessity which also implies later acquisition. This conclusion leads Lotz to reject the contention that a child could learn the *Principia Mathematica* instead of English, asking, rhetorically, "How would P. M. nursery rhymes or the emotional outbursts of a child sound?"

Lotz felt that concentration solely upon the analysis of the formalized symbolism is insufficient. It is necessary to mind the manner in which this symbolism has been derived from a natural language. This, then, emerges as a central problem in metasemiotics, requiring a reinvestigation of the relation between natural language and the calculi.

Script (1b)

Lotz's lifelong preoccupation with script was firmly grounded in a semiotic outlook, clearly expressed already in his early masterpiece, his 1939 Hungarian grammar. The key sentences are these: "Das Grundprinzip, das dann den Aufbau des ganzen Buches bestimmt, ist *die Zweiseitigkeit, die Zwillingsnatur der Symbole*, zu denen auch die Sprache gehört, d. h. sie sind die Verbindungen eines *Zeichens* (*Form-physikalisch-physiologisch*) und eines *Inhaltes* (*Bedeutung-psychisch*). Nur diese Verbindung kann man Symbol nennen, eine Seite allein nicht. . . . Die *Formlehre* erörtert die *Schrift*, die *Rede* (*Laut*) und ihr Verhältnis zueinander." These, then, were his overall goals, a program he proclaimed and carried out in the book (see Sebeok 1943), and kept on elaborating, up to his death, in a variety of articles.

In general, three sets of principles underlie Lotz's writings about script:

(1) Script must be treated in its own terms, i.e., it cannot be derived altogether from speech. Internal analysis of both media is required before the isomorphism between the two systems of verbal signs can be understood. Script contains elements not contained in speech, and vice versa.

(2) The role of script within the total framework of the structure of language—which Lotz represented diagrammatically in Kavanagh

and Mattingly 1972:123, Figure 1—requires its establishment in three relationships: script to the semantic coverage; script to the morphemic units; and script to speech.

(3) There are certain features in the relationship between the two semiotic systems which are not simply juxtapositional. Among the media in language communication, speech is the unmarked category in contrast (among others) to script. Lotz believed that the process of a writing was, however, intimately tied to linguistic processing as a whole.

The most important of his many-sided contributions to this still relatively neglected area consisted of this, that he raised, in rather concrete and precise terms, a host of empirical questions which are bound to be investigated further in the immediate future.[4] His treatment of Hungarian script must, however, be regarded as definitive.

Many years ago, I casually inquired how Lotz happened to formulate his conception of the sign in the manner that this appeared in the Introduction to his 1939 book, and he told me that he had thought at the time that his youthful phraseology was entirely fresh. Only afterward did it dawn on him that his statements were an echo of Saussure, particularly as they reverberated through commentaries of Lotz's revered teacher, Zoltán Gombocz. I remember his rueful added observation that this sort of resonance suffusing one's writings of long-forgotten readings must be a commonplace in humanistic discourse.

16. Marginalia to Greenberg's Conception of Semiotics and Zoosemiotics

> The special position of linguistics arises from its two-fold nature: as a part of the science of culture by virtue of its inclusion in the mass of socially transmitted tradition of human groups, and as a part of the nascent subject of semiotics, the science of sign behavior in general. . . . Since linguistics faces in these two directions, it should be aware of the implications for itself both of the semiotician's discussions of language and of the general science of culture. (Greenberg 1971:1)

"That linguistics is a part of semiotic is commonly admitted," Charles Morris noted, but adduced the works of only two European linguists, Saussure and Hjelmslev, and two American ones, Bloomfield and Greenberg, to document his claim (1964:62). Of this latter pair, the senior scholar never attempted to come to grips with any consequences of his own explicit recognition of this hierarchical relationship, although he had succinctly formulated it when asserting that "Linguistics is the chief contributor to semiotic" (Bloomfield 1939:55), echoing a view that can be traced back at least to Locke, in 1690, and that is repeated ever more insistently by contemporary linguists laboring in the wake of the Saussurean heritage. Greenberg, however, is one of the few early contributors to the field to have seriously faced up to at least some of the implications of looking at both natural languages and systems of animal communication from a semiotic point of view (Chomsky [1959:218] by no means exaggerated when character-

Note: This article is reprinted from *Linguistic Studies Offered to Joseph Greenberg on the Occasion of His 60th Birthday*, ed. Alphonse Juilland (Saratoga, Calif.: Anma Libri, 1976), 1:183–192.

Figure 16-1. Joseph Greenberg. Courtesy News and Publications Service, Stanford University.

izing "Greenberg's proposals [as] the most carefully worked out of their kind . . ."). Nevertheless, it should be noted that Greenberg's semiotic evidently derives directly from that of Morris (with overtones of Carnap), and has, accordingly, remained predominantly behaviorist in motivation and orientation. In paying this tribute to my old friend and erstwhile collaborator (Osgood and Sebeok 1965), I would like to provide a few remarks—hardly more than annotations, really—specifically concerned with some of the issues raised, or, at any rate, implied, by the multifaceted inquirer's ventures into the realm of signification.

As long as fifteen years ago, I clearly recall being struck by two incidental paragraphs of Greenberg's (1961 : 1144f.) about communication in bees. In particular, he introduced in this context the notion of a universal metalanguage—metasemiotic would be a more accurate term—observing that "Anything the bees can say we can translate into human language, but there are an enormous number of things . . . which bees cannot translate from our language." The underlying principle of intersemiotic transmutability was most lucidly—perhaps initially—enunciated by Hjelmslev (1953:70): "In practice, a language is a semiotic into which all other semiotics may be translated—both all other languages, and all other conceivable semiotic structures." This, having been variously restated by prominent linguists, has since been elevated to dogma. Recently, for instance, it was most starkly spelled out by Shaumjan (1977; to be expanded into a full-length monograph) as follows: cognitive flexibility—owing to the productivity of natural language, reinforced by its attributes of richness and variability—is the feature which "makes it possible always to translate a message expressed in some sign system into a message expressed in a natural language, whereas the reverse is not true: not every message expressed in a natural language may be translated into a message expressed in some other sign system." (Cf. also Greenberg's own formulation [1957:64]: "Even when, as is possible in the case of gestures, we may learn them before language and independently of language, we may later explain them in terms of language, but never vice versa.") I would like to question whether the first half of this *ex cathedra* declaration has empirical support. Before doing so, however, I wish to return briefly to the problem of metacommunication in the animal kingdom that I have already alluded to in several previous articles (Sebeok 1963:458 ff.; 1965:6f.).

I assume that a metacommunicative operation is said to have taken place whenever meanings were elicited, and acted upon, by messages referring to a code. This is a type of semiosis found even in insects. Thus it is well known that honeybees often exclude intraspecific foreign workers—the guard bees may even kill them when food is scarce—while admitting to their nest colony certified members. The crucial decision as to membership appears to be made by recognition of odors acquired from the environment (although the possibility of a genetic component in the highly eusocial bees has not been ruled out). I have previously compared the display of the open scent gland of a returning worker to a pass badge with a duplex function: it is used both as its own designation and, autonomously, as a message referring to the *Apis* code, i.e., a metacommunicative message (Sebeok 1963; cf. Michener 1974:223).

The *locus classicus* of metacommunicative signing is, of course, to be found in mammalian play invitation, first described in dogs by Darwin (1872:63) with characteristic charm: "There seems... some degree of instinctive knowledge in puppies... that they must not use their sharp little teeth... too freely in their play.... When my terrier bites my hand in play, often snarling at the same time, if he bites too hard and I say *gently, gently*, he goes on biting, but answers me by a few wags of the tail, which seems to say 'Never mind, it is all fun.'" The theoretical foundations were then worked out by Bateson (1972: 177–193) some eighty years afterward, and a wide variety of metasigns employed to switch the signification of representation belonging to the object semiotic of different vertebrates (man included) have since been more or less catalogued (Aldis 1975, Ch. 9). Metacommunication may, moreover, occur in broadcasting status information, as in macaques and baboons. In sum, the phenomenon is so widespread that it can no longer be maintained that "only human language has this property" (Greenberg 1961:1144).

What about the proclamation of asymmetrical convertibility of codes attributed to Hjelmslev, and statements, like Shaumjan's and Greenberg's, to the same effect? Consider, as one counterexample, the failure of all efforts hitherto to standardize bioacoustic terminology: the animal literature is full of a hodgepodge of incomprehensible terms drawn from physics, phonetics, poetry, music, and "the authors' own experience and imagination" (Broughton 1963:5), with a host of *ad hoc* onomatopoeisms, like the chirp of *Cercopithecus nictitans*, allegedly "sounding like 'tshe(a)k,'" or the chimpanzee's "loud WAA BARK" and its "WRAAAA CALL," which is to Jane van Lawick-Goodall "one of the most savage sounds of the African jungle" (1971: 276), but evoking in each of her readers unverifiable phantasmagorias. Animal sounds are incapable of being paraphrased, and, even if replicated, e.g., on the highest fidelity of recordings, come across out of context so attenuated as to be immediately uninterpretable. What is missing in cases such as these is the clear and practical applicability of Peirce's concept of the interpretant: one gropes in vain for a set of linguistic signs to substitute instead of the significative unit employed by the speechless creature both to refer to his scarcely understood species-specific code and to the context of delivery, or *Umwelt*, through which the message fragment is aligned within the observed sequence of signs emitted.

The hallmark of man's humanity surely stems less from his language endowment as such than from the much more remarkable fact that he has two different, complementary communicative repertoires at his disposal, one verbal, the other not. The former is, clearly, in no sense an evolutionary replacement for the latter, which, far from having undergone conspicuous decay, continues to flourish in mankind with a complexity and intricacy surpassing those of comparable systems found elsewhere in the animal kingdom (cf. Greenberg 1957:62 —"Prelanguage signs continue to function even in human societies as gesture and otherwise"). The two codes serve overlapping yet largely distinct functions: "The nonverbal act can repeat, augment, illustrate, accent, or contradict the words; it can anticipate, coincide with, substitute for or follow the verbal behavior; and it can be unrelated to the verbal behavior" (Ekman and Friesen 1969:53); but, in many cases, the transmutation of nonverbal messages into verbal "is likely to introduce gross falsification," for a variety of reasons enumerated by Bateson (1972:419). Whereas the category of gestures Ekman and Friesen (1969:63) call "emblems," following a usage propagated by Efron (1972), is comprised of signs with a manifestly verbal interpretant, "a direct verbal translation, or dictionary definition, usually consisting of a word or two, or perhaps a phrase," other categories defy comprehensible verbal definition: these must be illustrated in handbooks by line drawings, photographs, or some other kind of iconic interpretant. This common predicament is faced, for instance, by Oléron (1974:12), who attempts typically to resolve it "par un commentaire des signes gestuels présentés parallèlement sous forme photographique," although he adds at once that his verbal description is unavoidably "schématique et allusif donc à l'insuffisance ... d'une telle description."

While the force of Peirce's affirmation that "the meaning of a representation can be nothing but a representation" (1935–1966:1.339), which he called the interpretant, certainly stands, there is no compelling evidence for the view that every nonverbal sign must invariably address somebody verbally, create, that is, "an equivalent sign, or perhaps a more developed sign" (2.228) out of the language code. Indeed, a consideration of recent advances in split-brain studies, particularly of the effects of partial commissurotomy on interhemispheric integration tasks in human subjects (Gazzaniga 1975:568f.), tends to make the contrary assumption suspect *a priori*. Neurological findings of the past decade suggest, extrapolating crudely from the modest data available so far, that the left hemisphere of our brain, in particular, the temporal-parietal lobe, specializes in verbal coding, or, more generally, sequential, temporal, and digital operations, while the opposite, possibly smaller half mutely manages spatial and stereognostic relationships. In normal people, the lateralized specialities of the various left and right brain areas can—and ordinarily do—make their contribution to the cerebral activities of their twin shell through the corpus callosum, but, as Bogen (1969) has recounted, certain dichotomies in behavior, having been assigned through the years to either the one or the other hemisphere, persist (cf. Dumas and Morgan 1975). The model of the brain function that seems to emerge from the new data is a dynamic one, producing an ultimately integrated behavioral response, but nonetheless admitting spheres of influence with only partially overlapping tasks. This picture of a dual processing system appears in good conformity with what we generally know about the interaction of the nonverbal with the verbal code, as well as with Bateson's specific views (1972:416-431) about redundancy and coding, but it fails to support the claims of Hjelmslev and his successors. It also compels one to ponder the full implications of Peirce's extraordinarily acute insight that "signs require at least two Quasi-minds ... and although these two are at one (i.e., *are* one mind) in the sign itself, they must nevertheless be distinct. In the Sign they are, so to say, *welded*" (1935-1966:4.551).[1]

Let me turn next to the prescient essay, first presented in 1947, epitomized in the epigraph cited at the outset of this paper (Greenberg 1971:1-10). In his article, the author meditates upon some consequences of the Janus-like position of linguistics among the sciences. He tells us, quite correctly, that linguists—he must surely have had American linguists in mind—have, on the whole, "been more aware of their affiliations with cultural anthropology than with semiotics," a state of affairs that he attributes to "the recency of the semiotician's interest in the general features of language." Earlier in the same paragraph, he refers to semiotics as a "nascent subject," and the aspect of it he chooses to elaborate upon, in particular, is the trichotomy, "first advanced by Morris, and now widely adopted," of syntactics/semantics/pragmatics (1971:1ff.). All of which raises a congeries of fascinating historical questions.

First, note Greenberg's insistent use of the lexical shape *semiotics*, which—his citations notwithstanding—can never be found in the works of either Morris or Carnap. They both used *semiotic*. Greenberg's 1947 usage curiously anticipated, by fifteen years, Margaret Mead's reintroduction and forceful advocacy of the former label in 1962, after which it spread rapidly and decisively the world over. I have discussed this entangled story in some detail (Sebeok 1976:47-58), but now regret having overlooked Greenberg's earlier idiosyncratic presentation, and cannot help wondering how the *-ics* form came to him, why he abandoned it a decade later (Greenberg 1957:1), and whether, as seems eminently plausible in retrospect, his article was familiar to Mead.

As to the tripartition of semiotics, this actually derives from Peirce, as Rulon Wells had pointed out (Sebeok 1976:14). Nor has every linguist been equally enchanted with it; for one, Greenberg's late Columbia colleague, Uriel Weinreich, thought that it "turned out to be of little use in connection with natural sign phenomena" (ibid.: n. 25).

Nevertheless, many of us, myself included, found these distinctions serviceable in a variety of applications, at least as a provisional classificatory grid for sorting out, e.g., sign-processes in animals. A careful reading of Greenberg's elaboration of these three aspects of semiotics reveals that, in the course of it, he has creatively anticipated developments that have reached their peak in anthropology of the last decade under names such as "ethnosemantics," "ethnoscience," "folk taxonomy," "formal analysis," "componential analysis," as well as more enduring and now semi-independent disciplines, such as sociolinguistics, for which he used the warier expression "social linguistics" (1971:7). It is interesting to discover that, when speaking in a pragmatic frame of stylistic features, he is concerned "whether it is part of the standardized behavior of a people to speak at meals or keep silent," whether "a Sunday sermon will follow a certain organization beginning with a scriptural text and will employ a certain definable style," and with standardized greetings (1971:4). Topics such as these are now routinely considered in semiotic inquiry by workers ranging from Barthes to Kendon, but bring to my mind, above all, a neglected contemporary American classic of "cryptosemiotics" (Sebeok 1976:ii), the monumental book by Pike (1967), because Greenberg's influence is so pervasive there throughout (see Pike's index, 1967:739).

It is, at first blush, puzzling that Greenberg should have placed so strong an emphasis upon the novelty of semiotics, especially in its filiation with linguistics. He had evidently read, for he cites it (1971: 10, n. 2), Charles Morris's most famous book, published only the year before he delivered his paper, and must have known the chapter on "The History of Semiotics," where Morris delineated, if superficially, the "long and interesting history" of the subject. And Greenberg's familiarity with Saussure, who had professed in the first decade of the century that language is "rien de plus qu'un *cas particulier* de la Théorie des Signes," goes back to his graduate student days (1971: 340). True, the historiography of semiotics is, even today, far from having been worked out, with numerous important gaps remaining to be filled in the future (Sebeok 1976:3–26, 150–156; see also Jakobson 1975). On the other hand, a discipline that has been traced back at least as far as to Hippocrates (ca. 460–ca. 377 B.C.)—who was designated "der Vater und Meister aller Semiotik" by Kleinpaul (Sebeok 1976:181)—can hardly be considered impenetrable either: a Genevese provincial *faux pas* claiming that "Le premier à concevoir cette science semble avoir été F. de Saussure..." (Sebeok 1976:153) can no more be condoned than the equally parochial transatlantic multiple solecism that allots the doctrine of signs to "Originally a branch of pragmatist philosophy (à la William James and Charles Sanders Peirce)" (Lamb and Makkai 1976:352). Greenberg is, of course, too sophisticated a scholar to commit such blunders, so one has to assume that his argument was shaped with long-range strategic intent, and in preparation for his more famous essay, written in 1947, "Language as a Sign System" (supplemented by three appendices [1957:1–17, 95–99]), where he attempted to demonstrate how to deal, in a technical way, with general formal properties of sign systems and, as a special case, of language which was then—indeed, still is—"a very important and insufficiently studied topic" (Chomsky 1959:203).

In a highly suggestive passage, Greenberg introduces "the dimension of time," thereby adding nine more combinations to the "total field of language, as here defined" (1971:7), his remaining nine permutations being synchronous. In semiotics, diachrony has two quite different applications. The first has to do with the evolutionary process by which a behavior pattern gradually alters to become increasingly effective as a sign (in biology, usually referred to by the less precise label "display"). A preponderance of cases involve "ritualization"—a term originated, in 1914, by Julian Huxley—which has become a focus of biosemiotic research activities and coterminous with the entire field of ethology. Ethology, loosely referred to as the biological study of behavior, is thus more accurately defined as diachronic semiotics on a phylogenetic scale. There are very few durable anthropological studies of ritualization so far. Permit me to call attention to one of the best (almost unknown to Anglophone scholarship), because it should be grist for Greenberg's semiotic mill: this is Koenig's fascinating exploration of the ethogram of military uniforms in the perspective of their culture-historical development. He demonstrates that the practical functions that originally existed have long since been obliterated in order to maximize efficiency in communication (Koenig 1970:15–182). (Greenberg considered "the over-all degree of efficiency" of communication in a separate essay later on [1957:Ch. 5], containing a number of observations of interest to the semiotician, but space does not permit a review of these here.)

The second application of diachrony pertains to the development of semiotic competence and performance during the life span of an organism, and comprises a field I dubbed, in 1974, psychosemiotics (Sebeok 1976:141; see also Ullman 1975:781), or, as Greenberg particularized, "the syntactic, semantic, and pragmatic aspects, treated from the ... individual ... point of view ... diachronically" (1971:7). (At the core of psychosemiotics lies, of course, psycholinguistics, to which he was likewise one of the first major American contributors with his perdurable interest in the connection between language universals and psychology [Osgood and Sebeok 1965].)

In rereading this 1947 essay, I was startled by Greenberg's remarks about chess, which, almost a quarter of a century afterward, he expanded into a full-length address, "Is Language Like a Chess Game?" (Greenberg 1971:9, 330–352). He called chess a quasi-language because, "as the individual moves of the game seem to have no reference to anything outside themselves, the semantic dimension is lacking..."

The rules of the game are syntactic; the behavior of the players he assigned to the pragmatic aspect. Modern semiotic theory, however, endeavors to take into account the fact that even those sign systems that seem to be purely syntactic—notably including musical and non-representational visual artistic products, glossolalic texts, etc.—allow for a semantic interpretation of their combinatorial possibilities. This was recently underlined by Jakobson—who has been keenly aware of the traditional comparison of natural languages with chess since at least 1927—in pointing to the possibility of an introversive semiosis where the referential component may, to be sure, either be absent or minimal, but the emotive connotation is retained even so,[2] and where, therefore, "un renvoi d'un signe à un autre [est] présent dans le même contexte ou sous-entendu . . ." (1975:16).

Summing up, we see that Greenberg's writings at mid-century have prefigured two main trends in current semiotic practice. He was a direct catalyzing influence in furthering the advent of symbolic studies in anthropology; and he was a pioneer working toward the integration, in a rigorous way, of the study of sign systems into a viable mathematical theory.

The "rewarding field" that he envisioned at the interface of anthropology and semiotics, and which he wisely said that "a mature science of culture is unlikely to emerge without" (1971:10), has now arrived with a vengeance (Turner 1975; Schwimmer 1977). The ongoing debate numbers among its contributors such modern masters as Douglas, Firth, Geertz, Leach, Lévi-Strauss, Singer, Victor Turner—to say nothing of the Tartu school and its epigones outside of the Soviet Union—who toil, under a variety of labels, old or new, and with assumptions that differ considerably in the extent of their veridical foundation, to clarify the universal problem of semiosis departing from what is known of cultural particulars: for, "simply stated," Turner tells us (1975:159), oversimplifying, "we master the world through signs, ourselves by symbols."

Greenberg has shown the relevance of mathematics to semiotics, particularly to linguistics, but results that Chomsky called nontrivial (1959:203) were hard to attain. They became a distinct possibility for the "soft" sciences only with the devisal by René Thom of his "catastrophe theory," and with its eventual applications to all sorts of discontinuous and divergent phenomena that notably include the generation of signs. The first approach in this new vein, published only three years ago, was Thom's marvelous sketch of a theory of symbolism .(1974a:229–251). It provides a relatively crude model for very complicated processes, but it does furnish a topological tool with which to grasp what may be involved in semiosis as a fundamental domain of biological regulation.

Appendix I

The Semiotic Self

Freud (1933:119) viewed anxiety in plainly semiotic terms when he defined it "as a signal indicating the presence of a danger-situation." His concept of anxiety as a sign, or string of signs, focused on a mechanism of defense which triggers the only kind of escape from an internal danger available to the organism, a flight from awareness. (Two of the most "significant" characteristics of signal anxiety may thus well be silence and invisibility.) Grinker (1966:131–132) developed some consequences of this way of analyzing the properties of anxiety states in declaring his belief "that anxiety is a signal to the self and others which indicates that organismic adjustments to present or expected situations are being made in dynamically related somatic, psychological and behavioral processes," and that, in mild form, "anxiety is of great significance as a signal of threat for it precedes or accompanies active preparation for adjustment." Paradoxically, anxiety may, in intense form, also produce serious kinds of self-inflicted (mental) illness (the heightened response being due to positive feedback).

What both Freud and Grinker loosely designated as a "signal," Peirce would have called an index—the kind which tends to be unwitting as opposed to the indices of fear—and, which, according to one of his approximations, "forces the attention to the particular object intended without describing it" (1935–1966:1.369); the relation between an index and the object signified may be a direct physical connection (1.372) or a correspondence in fact (1.558). Now, for Peirce, an emotion "is essentially the same thing as an hypothetic inference, and every hypothetic inference involves the formation of . . . an emotion" (2.643). He held, moreover, that "an emotion is always a simple predicate substituted by an operation of the mind for a highly complicated predicate," and gave this specific explanation for the arousal of anxiety: "The emotions . . . arise when our attention is strongly

Note: This draft was prepared for presentation in a Conference on the Semiotics of Anxiety, sponsored by the Werner-Reimers-Stiftung, in Bad-Homburg, Germany, December 8–11, 1977. It has not previously been published, but I plan to develop it into a much longer paper, to be presented at a follow-up conference on the "Genealogie der Angst," scheduled to convene in Copenhagen in November 1979.

drawn to complex and inconceivable circumstances. Fear arises when we cannot predict our fate; joy, in the case of certain indescribable and peculiarly complex sensations. If there are some indications that something greatly for my interest, and which I have anticipated would happen, may not happen; and if, after weighing probabilities, and inventing safeguards, and straining for further information, I find myself unable to come to any fixed conclusion in reference to the future, in the place of that intellectual hypothetic inference which I seek, the feeling of *anxiety* arises" (5.293; italics in original).

The foregoing citations are intended to set the stage for a necessarily succinct consideration of some aspects of anxiety by the ancillary use of the tool kit of the sign science, and to serve as a convenient point of departure for the discussions to ensue. The model which immediately comes to mind is the one being developed to account for the vertebrate immunologic system in Darwinian terms (i.e., based on random variation and selection), which may, moreover, be best posed in this context as a problem involving information flow.

The immune reaction has two fundamental components: recognition and response, or how an antigen—defined as any object that provides an antibody response—is recognized and how a structure exactly complementary to it is synthesized. Recognition is required for all positive responses and (very likely) for various refractory states, which is to say that tolerance is not simply tantamount to lack of recognition. The molecular basis of recognition is, of course, a set of immunoglobulins, or proteins in the blood that have antibody activity.

The immune system responds in two ways: there is a proliferation of recognition units; and there is a stimulation of reactions which can be broadly characterized as directed to antigen elimination. The diacritic trait of antibodies in general is their specificity, a matter of shape: "the business end of the antigen fits, in lock-and-key fashion, a receptor on the surface of the cell" (Schmeck 1974:44). The qualifying property of an antigen is its foreignness—its property of being non-Self. "The teleological rubric 'foreign = bad' has been pretty dependable, for immunological activity is now known to be essential for life" (Medawar and Medawar 1977:99). It is assumed that, in evolution, the earliest living entities "invented" the immunologic system in order to segregate themselves from the rest of the soup of surrounding organic material, in order to keep their Self distinct from the Other. The dilemma in assaying the native from the alien derives from the fact that all things are constituted of much the same chemistry. In solving this problem, the immunologic process became "our license to live in the sea of micro-organisms and as individuals everywhere" (Robert A. Good, in Schmeck 1974:37). In brief, the immunologic system functions as a prime defense against infection and thus is pivotal in the maintenance of body integrity "by distinguishing between 'self' and 'nonself'" (ibid.:36); the triple pillars of the so-called "new immunology," according to the Medawars (1977:98), are "a study of the biology of self-recognition, the molecular basis of specificity and the process of information transfer in biological systems."

Miscarriages of this immunologic process, like the aberrations of signal anxiety alluded to, are the consequences of faulty communication; allergies, hypersensitivity, autoimmune phenomena are responses of cells and tissues to misinformation or misinterpretations of signs emanating from the environment; this is "the price we must pay for possessing a response system attuned with the exquisite sensitivity necessary to discern and react upon non-Self components" (ibid.: 111).

It is the thesis of this working paper that this superb, although not flawless, gift of discrimination is, in fact, doubly expressed in man, by two parallel recognition systems and associated defense mechanisms. the immunologic memory, which consists of an array of cells whose surface receptors allow them to respond to particular types of molecules, supplemented by another, commonly called anxiety, which protexts the Self in the sense that this is a continuous activity, or way of life, in a word, behavior. What is maintained by anxiety, another sort of memory, is not biological substance but the pattern of behavior that it operates. Both repair mechanisms are homeostatic, both ensure the continuity of the individual for a finite time, but the former is essentially provided by inherited instructions while the latter also has a large learned component. I am, by the way, in complete agreement with Professor Hediger's twin conclusions (1959:30) that the syndrome we label anxiety in man has its roots (1) in our animal ancestry, "besonders der Säugetiere," as well as (2) "in der Normalpsychologie."

One consequence of Hediger's first conclusion—which he amply documents in his remarkable paper just cited—is that it suggests locating the sign processes together named anxiety on the borderline of the realm of endosemiotics with the continuum of zoosemiotics, i.e., what Thure von Uexküll (1978) proposes to call, respectively, the "level of vegetative life" and the field of "averbal or preverbal communication" (the second of which, he, by the way, explicitly notes, involves the notion of body image).

It may be necessary, at this point, to step for a moment beyond ancient anatomical schematism to the modern field of transducer physiology, and to recall "the human problem of the greatest moment," as Shands (1976:303) quite correctly designated it, "of so relating the outer to the inner that the minimal information derivable from inner sources comes to be a reliable index of the external situation." This bifurcation, which was so powerfully foreseen by Leibniz and fascinatingly discussed by Bentley (1941), must finally be dealt with in a semiotic frame, as I recently had occasion to argue elsewhere (Ch. 3, this volume). If they are to specialize, cells must communicate with each other, but, as Jacob (1974:308) has underlined, "evolution depends on setting up new systems of communication, just as much within the organism as between the organism and its surroundings." Immunity must have arisen early in evolution; as exchanges multiplied, anxiety eventually emerged, a supplementary form of semiosis —an early warning system, so to speak—selected to favor reproduction, especially in the higher vertebrates, and notably the mammals (cf. Hediger 1959). As the capacity to integrate becomes more sophisticated, the rigidity of the program of heredity attenuates, the brain grows more complex, the ability to learn ever more refined. Learning consists of selectively attaching, in the *Innenwelt*, semiotic values to objects in the *Umwelt*. In the felicitous phrasing of Young (1977:15f.), "Images on the retina are not eatable or dangerous." What the senses can provide is "a tool by which, aided by a memory, the animal can learn the symbolic significance of events. The record of its past experiences then constitutes a program of behavior appropriate for the future." Anxiety, in this framework, constitutes a kind of induction device the special purpose of which is to increase the probability of continuance of the Self; this formulation accords equally well, I think, with Freud's as well as Peirce's view of the state of anxiety.

Anxiety, then, is activated when the Self is menaced by an event (a catastrophe, in Thom's parlance—see e.g., 1974a:239) deemed of sufficient importance by the endangered organism. The triggering index may take a quasi-biological shape, such as the olfactory trace of a leopard predator for a baboon prey, or be of a semantic character, such as some verbal assault whereby a stranger presses in upon the territories of the Self (e.g., Goffman 1971:46). Note that the spatio-temporal nature of the tie between the sign and the interpretant (viz., anxiety) in animals tends to be superseded by a linkage perceived by man as causal.

In other words, these are the outlines of a teleonomic conception of anxiety, in its beginnings as a regulatory mechanism based on indexical associations of a Pavlovian sort, gradually acquiring the symbolic attributes of causality of the kind intimated by Peirce. In animals (except, perhaps, in domestication) anxiety involves the great biological verities of alimentation, sexuality, and the like. In man, however, this transitivity of the indexical relation is generalized to objects and concepts which may be biologically altogether indifferent.

In these brief notes, I could not dwell on the question where the "inner" Self begins and the "outer" Other begins, but the boundary is, clearly, beyond the skin. This basic problem was essentially solved, beginning in 1941, by Hediger's invaluable insights and demonstrations, and thereafter applied with varying degrees of success to humans by a host of followers (cf. the field of proxemics). Hediger's (1959:25) standpoint, with which I can but enthusiastically concur, is expressed in the following paragraph: "Fluchttendenz, Furcht vor Feinden, Angst vor allgemeiner Bedrohung oder wie immer wir dieses

Phänomen nennen wollen, welches die gesamte körperliche Organisation und das gesamte Verhalten dominiert, ist also derjenige Affekt, dem im Tierreich die absolut überragende Bedeutung zukommt. Er bietet den wirksamsten Schutz, ist der stärkste Motor in der Ontogenese und Phylogenese. Sein Fehlen hat den Tod des Individuums und der Art zur Folge."

In conclusion, permit me to summarize the main propositions advanced in this paper—

(1) There are at least two apprehensions of the Self:

    (a) *immunologic*, or biochemical, with semiotic overtones; and

    (b) *semiotic*, or social, with biological anchoring.

(2) The arena of the immune reaction is contained within the skin; the arena for signal anxiety is normally between the perimeter of the Hediger "bubble" and the skin of the organism, the former containing the latter.

(3) Invasion of (a) is initially signified by the immune response, of (b) by anxiety, with the latter serving as an early warning system for the former.

(4) In evolution, (a) is very old, whereas (b) is relatively recent. There is a corresponding advance from a purely metonymic nexus to one perceived as causal efficacy.

(5) Communicational errors occur in both processes, and may have devastating effects upon the Self.

Appendix II

Displaying the Symptoms

Review of W. John Smith, *The Behavior of Communicating: An Ethological Approach* (Harvard University Press)

Two of the obsessive preoccupations of our time intersect in and constitute the expertly interlaced semiotic theme of this book: the nature of communication and the communication of nature. Fascination with the manner in which animals commune with one another and their two-way commerce with man is persistently attested to by our allegories and myths. Animal communication is a perennial and doubtless universal literary motif variously exemplified by Plato's philosophical dog and Walt Disney's Pluto, Aesop's fabled menagerie and Robert Merle's science-fiction apes and dolphins. The curious 1892 book of Richard L. Garner, on *The Speech of Monkeys*, belongs in a twilight genre between science and outright hokum; it is an archetype of sorts for a currently very popular form of mass entertainment that featured mainly porpoises in the innocent 1960s and stars widely touted American chimpanzees or gorillas in this pseudo-sophisticated decade.

In his scarcely read lampoon, included with his *Le Village aérien* (1901) and much enhanced by Georges Roux's beguiling illustrations, Jules Verne introduces his maniacal German proto-ethologist, Dr. Johausen (obviously modeled on Garner), to drive home the point about monkeys that "ce qui les distingue essentiellement des hommes" is that they "ne parlaient jamais sans nécessité." Johausen was convinced that cognition preceded expression, that nothing prevented beasts from speaking save their lack of intelligence, and, above all, that the so-called language of the apes "n'était que la série des sons que les mammifères émettent pour communiquer avec leur semblables, comme tous les animaux." Verne's venturesome character did much better science than his living exemplar, although, in a dramatic climax, the explorer pays for his only partially successful field trip though the loss of his own faculty of language: "Il est devenu singe."

The science of animal behavior—and, as Julian Jaynes has traced them in their complex and sometimes confusing ramifications, the

Note: This review article originally appeared in the *Times Literary Supplement*, no. 3939 (September 9, 1977).

associated terms *ethology* and *comparative psychology*—began germinating in the era following the Baron Cuvier's exasperating debates with his former collaborator, Etienne Geoffroy-Saint-Hilaire, around the 1830s.

This branch of the life science, which, as the Medawars recently noted, perhaps a trifle optimistically, is "now everywhere called *ethology*," hinges on a crucial insight: that behavior patterns are just as amenable to study, especially compared to each other in respect to their similarity gradients, as are organs and physiology. This was certainly taken for granted by Darwin, and no contemporary biologist ever doubts the applicability, tricky though it may be in the execution, of the idea of homology to behavior.

In semiotics, the sign science, however, this biological truism is still considered a startling bit of chicancry. Thus Chomsky, I think, is rather exceptional in his recent advocacy of the point of view that we may, indeed ought to, "regard the language capacity virtually as we would a physical organ of the body," and that we "can investigate the principles of its organization, functioning, and development in the individual and the species" by methods according with this viewpoint, which is, of course, in perfect conformity with what we know about the process Lenneberg and others called differentiation—a gradual increase, from conception unto extinction, in morphological/behavioral specializations and specificities. This concept is productively fitting to the semiotic maturation of all living beings, be they speechless or uniquely language-endowed.

The philosophical prefigurements and early scientific accomplishments relating to animal communication were quite adequately assessed in Friedrich Kainz's *Die "Sprache" der Tiere*, published as a separate book in 1961. This somewhat eccentric essay has, however, been totally ignored in the ensuing Anglo-American literature. Even W. John Smith never mentions it, but then his forty-four-page listing of references, which is, despite his modest disclaimer to the contrary, exceptionally comprehensive, includes only a small portion of the vast "foreign" literature. During the thirty-four years that separate Kainz's original survey (1943) from Smith's present compendium, which he himself characterizes as still only "a prologue to the study of communication," the number of scientific publications on the subject has at least quadrupled. Two detailed technical reviews have appeared in the interval, with contributions by diverse authors, dealing with many aspects of animal communication: the first (Sebeok 1968), consisting of twenty-four chapters, and a new one (Sebeok 1977a), more than twice as long, of thirty-eight chapters (both collections with superb articles by Smith).

Side by side with the accelerating torrent of technical contributions there runs a rivulet of summative books, often in a popular vein, perhaps the most proficient among them the functional classification by

Hubert and Mabel Frings (1964), reissued in 1977 with a new chapter on "Recent Advances and Future Prospects."

In the meantime, ethology—and such cognate fields as sociobiology or behavioral ecology—have, in general, continued to prosper, having been at last anointed, in 1973, by the awarding of a triple Nobel Prize under the mantle of physiology and medicine. Beginning with Darwin, in 1872, "ethology" has extended uneasy pseudopods, ever more aggressively in recent years, in the direction of anthropology; "human ethology" is now a recognized subdiscipline with the customary academic accouterments, the claims and limits of which are subjects of an international debate which took place in Germany in the fall of 1977.

The hallmark of ethology, since its earliest days (Saint-Hilaire), has been naturalistic observation, in contradistinction to laboratory analysis (Cuvier). Smith, as his book's subtitle signals, firmly aligns himself with the ethological tradition, which has certainly yielded dramatic discoveries. These notwithstanding, one must not take the opposition too seriously. For example, the integration of signing into the behavioral repertoire of a chimpanzee to effect eventually spontaneous interaction between her and both humans and other animals was accomplished in the controlled microsphere of a quasi-laboratory. And some of the profoundest and most consequential revelations in the entire field, having to do with, among other topics, communication about space/time, have come from a lifetime of exceptionally distinguished work (surprisingly passed over in total silence by Smith) by Heini Hediger, conducted in the macro-region of the circus and the zoo, which fall, with respect to "coarseness," somewhere between the ethologist's natural environment and the psychologist's laboratory.

Smith's main title poses an initial dilemma of which he seems not altogether aware: while no one is likely to gainsay that all communicating is behavior, it is difficult to single out any behavior that is not communicating. MacKay, in 1972 (Hinde 1972:3–25), and Glasersfeld, in 1974, have, for instance, tried to elucidate what counts as communication in the context of animal behavior, but very few have paid heed. The trouble is that the moment you commit yourself, as Smith does, to a consistently semiotic stance, you must fully reckon with the implications of Charles S. Peirce's dictum that the entire universe "is perfused with signs, if it is not composed exclusively of signs." It turns out, however, that Smith considers only, or mainly, one class of behaviors, those acts called "displays," a term which he says originated in Julian Huxley's 1914 work on the signaling movements of great crested grebes (actually, both the noun and the verb *display* were used by Darwin, in much the modern sense, already in 1871). The corresponding expression in semiotics is a category of signs designated "unwitting index," or in some restricted contexts, "symptom."

Smith tells us that the displays of animals should not "appear foreign to us," because our own nonverbal means of communicating "are fundamentally similar in form and origin." That they nevertheless do seem so is due to the fact that the design of each speechless organism is suited for life in a singularly delimited environment. This stipulation conforms to the biological theory of Jakob von Uexküll—one of the most important framers of modern ethology, whose Kantian meditations first conjoined in an interesting way the life science with the sign science—according to which animals are capable of perceiving only a particular set of features from their environment; thus frogs, in their optical channel, can detect about six classes of relevant events, or types of change, occurring in their surroundings. This indigenous editorial process is said to fabricate what he called their *Umwelten*, from which they derive their circumscribed choice of a small range of possible communicative actions governed by an arbitrary semiotic code, preset by past history and capable of being mutually grasped by both the message source and its destination. Uexküll's exposition is so lucid and convincing, his synthesis so creative, that it is small wonder that it came to serve as a principal inspiration for René Thom's revolutionary topological ("catastrophe") theory.

What is surprising is that very few linguists have ever heard of Uexküll's polemic *Bedeutungslehre* (1940), although it provides the only cogent biological anchor for all current adaptations of Leibniz's "possible-world semantics." It is more puzzling yet that Smith, whose series of contributions to the study of vertebrate semantics, in the 1960s, are the best of their kind, since Uexküll's, should have consistently ignored his most outstanding and intellectually consanguineous predecessor.

Leaving these general strictures aside, and mindful of its self-imposed limitations, it can be confidently stated that this book of Smith's is the choicest work on the subject ever written, one which is bound to remain the definitive treatment of it for years to come. Its technical proficiency is authoritative (Smith being, by trade, a noted ornithologist), and its interactional perspective consonant with the most vital trend in the contemporary behavioral sciences, including especially Goffmanesque sociology. In addition to its assured place in the literature of biology, it will furnish an invaluable resource for the fundamental and seminal branch of today's sign science which has lately come to be known as natural semiotics.

Appendix III

Teaching Semiotics: Report on a Pilot Program

Background

The Pilot Program in Semiotics in the Humanities at Indiana University was undertaken under a generous grant from the National Endowment for the Humanities between August 1975 and July 1976. The program was focused on *semiotics*, which can be informally defined as a science that studies all possible varieties of signs, and the rules governing their generation and production, transmission and exchange, and reception and interpretation. Concisely put, semiotics has two complementary and interdependent aspects: communication and signification. As I have delineated in a number of recent publications, semiotics is an ancient discipline, stemming from a pre-Socratic clinical tradition, which then led to the development of three fundamental semiotic traditions—the medical, the philosophical, and the linguistic—that have thoroughly intermingled at various periods in Western intellectual history, although there were times when they strove for autonomy. Beginning in the mid-1960s, semiotics underwent a spontaneous and rapid international development that led to the emergence of semiotic workshops in Eastern and Western Europe, North and South America, and Australia, Israel, and Japan. The influence of the semiotic method has variously encompassed or influenced all subjects commonly called "the humanities," most of the social sciences, some of the behavioral sciences, and even such natural sciences as, notably, ethology, as well as genetics and physiology. Although most often involving the "sciences of man" (especially the nomothetic sciences), semiotics has also become a powerful tool in animal communication studies. Further, one may speak of the semiotic behavior of machines, such as computers.

Note: This report, edited for publication by Daniel Laferrière, represents a much-condensed version of a privately distributed narrative. The abridged version previously appeared in the *Semiotic Scene* 2:23–30 (1977). For further information, see my Preface to Sebeok 1978a.

This explosive development no doubt partially derives from the pressure and technological improvement of the mass media, in consequence of which the problem of communication has proved to be one of the most pivotal ones of our civilization. It is readily understandable, therefore, why so many disciplines were reoriented and have converged upon the study of the general laws of cultural and natural signification. Another pertinent factor here has, of course, been the emergence of a few charismatic figures at the turn of the century (e.g., Ferdinand de Saussure in linguistics, C. S. Peirce in philosophy), and such creative contemporary synthesizers of their major traditions as Roman Jakobson.

The intent of the project was to inaugurate and facilitate the integration of semiotics in the Humanities curriculum at Indiana University. Scheduled for the 1975–1976 academic year, it consisted of: (1) a lecture course, Signaling Behavior in Man and Animals, conducted by the project director under the sponsorship of the Honors Division, and open to qualified undergraduates and interested graduate students; (2) a series of lectures and seminars in connection with the course offered by outstanding visiting semioticians, who also advised on the shaping of a program in semiotics; (3) a survey of Indiana University Library holdings in semiotics, with recommendations for relevant acquisitions.

It is my feeling that the pilot program has indeed increased the Arts and Sciences faculty's awareness of the usefulness and importance of semiotics as a general method of analysis, and has opened the way to the integration of semiotic studies into the existing curricula in various departments.

Project Activities

The activities undertaken during the grant period were in close conformity with the original project description. The core was a lecture course conducted by the project director, with the participation of numerous visiting speakers.

The *lecture course*—Signaling Behavior in Man and Animals—which ran consecutively throughout both semesters of the academic year, was offered under the sponsorship of the Honors Division; it was therefore open to a highly select and qualified group of undergraduate students drawn from a number of departments. Through an *ad hoc* arrangement with the Department of Linguistics, the enrollment was opened up to interested graduate students as well. The number of students enrolled was 39: first semester, 12 undergraduates and 5 graduates; second semester, 16 undergraduates and 6 graduates (the second semester increase is noteworthy in light of the more common experience that, during the second semester of a one-year course, the enrollment tends to decrease). An indication of the breadth of interests among the students is a listing of their majors: anthropology, biology, computer science, education, English, folklore, history and philosophy of science, linguistics, mass communication, and political science. In addition, some visitors, including faculty members, attended the class as auditors.

Two texts were assigned for course work: "The Semiotic Web," by Thomas A. Sebeok (1975-1976) and *A Theory of Semiotics*, by Umberto Eco (1976).

The course syllabus follows:
1. Introduction: the scope of semiotics; terminological problems
2. Historical outline of the field
3. The classification of signs
    a. Functional (in communication)
    b. Structural (in signification)
    c. Historical
        i. phylogenetic ("ritualization" in ethology)
        ii. ontogenetic (e.g., acquisition of communicative competence in individuals)
4. Semiotic systems of man (anthroposemiotics)
5. Semiotic systems of animals (zoosemiotics)
6. Semiotics in relation to
    a. The "sciences of man" (humanities, social sciences, and behavioral sciences)
    b. Selected natural sciences (ethology, genetics)

The course began with an introduction to semiotics, given by the project director, followed by a general outline of the field. Theresa Calvet, Research Associate of the Program, lectured on French structuralism on three separate occasions during the first semester. On September 24, Özséb Horányi, of the Hungarian Academy of Sciences, spoke on "A Semiotic Approach to Photography." A lecture on "Peirce's Theory of Signs" was given by Max Fisch, Peirce Edition Project, Indiana University–Purdue University at Indianapolis, on October 22. John N. Deely's lecture, on November 5, "Towards the Origins of Semiotics," dealt with the semiotic theory of Jean Poinsot. (Professor Deely was from the Philosophy Department of Saint Mary's College.) A special session of the class was held on November 13 to enable students to hear Erving Goffman's presentation "On Pictures." During the second semester, Bogusław Lawendowski, of the University of Warsaw, then a Research Associate at the Research Center for Language and Semiotic studies, spoke on "Semiotic Aspects of Translation" at the February 18 class meeting. Throughout both semesters the *guest speakers* supplemented their public lectures with visits to the class, where some made formal presentations followed by discussions and others invited questions on the subject of their public lectures. The discussions were often continued by several of the students at a nearby coffee shop. Often the visiting speaker would join the students and Ms. Calvet in these talks. In April, the project director gave three lectures to sum up the field of semiotics, and Ms. Calvet gave a lecture on the philosophical background of C. S. Peirce's work.

In addition, Milton Singer, one of the evaluators of the program, was persuaded to present a public lecture, "Culture Theory Tilts to Semiotics," during his early March visit as a member of the Evaluating Committee. His lecture was cosponsored by the Department of Anthropology.

Each lecturer supplied a list of recommended readings that were printed in the newsletter, *Semiotics at Indiana University*, and distributed to the students and other interested persons in advance.

Attendance at the public lectures ranged from about 30 to over 500; the number steadily increased as the year progressed, climaxing with Roman Jakobson's address.

Six of our guests, Umberto Eco, Paul Ekman, Peter Marler, Sebastian Šaumjan, Harley Shands, and William Stokoe, were interviewed on the Educational Network's continuing television program, *It's About Time*, conducted by Paula Gordon. The programs were very successful and drew additional attention to our efforts in the community and throughout Indiana.

News releases were provided to the *Indiana Daily Student* and the *Bloomington Herald-Telephone*. Announcements of our activities were placed in the University Calendar. *Semiotics at Indiana University*, a newsletter designed specifically to keep the local students and faculty aware of the progress of the program, to carry announcements concerning the public lectures and bibliographies of relevant materials, was initiated under the editorship of Ms. Calvet. Six issues were produced during the academic year and present a chronological account of the project's activities. This newsletter was mailed out not only to locally interested faculty and students but also to persons at other universities and to the funding agency.

The Indiana University, Bloomington, Office of Research and Development (to which the Research Center for Language and Semiotic Studies reported) appointed a faculty Steering Committee. This Steering Committee not only provided the project director with overall guidance, but made a point of meeting with every visitor, to ascertain his point of view and to get other information about current trends in semiotics.

In addition, the Office of Research and Development also appointed a Curriculum Planning Committee.

At the beginning of the year, the Dean of the Indiana University Libraries, W. Carl Jackson, appointed a special committee (consisting of Polly Grimshaw, Librarian for Anthropology, Folklore, Sociology;

Betty Jo Irvine, Librarian for Fine Arts [later replaced by Jill Cladwell, who also covers Cinema]; Barbara Halpron, Librarian for Philosophy, Psychology, chairperson; and Hugo Kunoff, Librarian for English). Almost all of the visitors were scheduled to meet with this group for consultations. They were shown the library holdings most pertinent to their particular segment of concern in semiotics, and, having evaluated them, they offered further recommendations. At the request of the Library Committee they provided bibliographies of semiotic works particularly relevant to their fields. A report from the Library Committee, with its recommendations as to an acquisitions program for semiotics and the expenditures for such a program, was made.

Results

The purpose of the Pilot Program was to increase awareness of the usefulness and importance of semiotics to the students and faculty at Indiana University. In order to measure the impact of the program, evaluations were made by an outside Evaluating Committee, the RCLSS Visiting Committee, the previously mentioned Steering Committee, students, and visitors.

Evaluating Committee. Milton Singer, Professor of Anthropology of the University of Chicago, and Rulon Wells, Professor of Philosophy and Linguistics at Yale University, then also President of the Linguistic Society of America (as well as past President of the Charles Sanders Peirce Society), both outstanding contributors to semiotics, were the two committee members. Before coming to Bloomington, they visited with Drs. Max Fisch and Edward C. Moore of the Peirce Edition project located at the Indiana University–Purdue University at Indianapolis campus. During their four-day stay with us, they spent the first three days meeting with students, faculty (including Steering Committee members), administrators, and the Library Committee, and writing a brief report for presentation at the March 4 dinner meeting of the RCLSS Visiting Committee. On the fourth day, they also sat in during the morning meeting of the Visiting Committee responding to questions raised about the program and related matters.

The *Visiting Committee* for the RCLSS consists of six distinguished individuals who convene once a year to assess the overall activities of the center.

Steering Committee. Associate Dean Turner distributed a questionnaire to the members of this committee late in the program. The five questions dealt with attitudes in the departments toward a semiotic approach, the likelihood of redistributing presently available funds and personnel, and comments and observations concerning the Pilot Program. The responses were anonymous. Of the five who replied directly to the questions, all indicated an interest in the semiotic approach.

On the judgment of the semiotic approach to the discipline, one indicated it was of great value and three that it was of moderate value. One respondent felt that his/her department would be willing to devote a half-time academic position. The fact that four of the respondents considered that a semiotics program should be created if no extra demand is made on departmental resources probably reflects the difficult budget situation.

Visitor Comments. Dean Turner wrote letters to all of the visiting lecturers requesting their opinions on the advisability of semiotics in the university's curriculum. Replies were received from Paul Bouissac, John N. Deely, Paul Ekman, Max Fisch, Alain Rey, Harley C. Shands, and William C. Stokoe. Their letters provide detailed and helpful information for the development of a curriculum in semiotics.

Student Comments. Specially designed questionnaires were distributed to the students in the class at the end of the second semester. Eight responses were received. Of the eight respondents, one had attended six public lectures, one had attended seven, and six had attended eight or more of the public lectures. Of the eight, all but one had attended the class both semesters. All said that the course had helped them to integrate their concept of the social sciences and had given them a perspective of the field of semiotics and its application. Comments on the overall program ranged from favorable to enthusiastic, and five of the eight indicated that they would recommend a similar course to other students.

In general, my impression as director of the program is that it has had a positive impact on the university community in that administrators, faculty, students, and even laymen have become aware of a hitherto unfamiliar discipline that can be of importance in their understanding of the Humanities.

It should be mentioned that the public lectures that were delivered in connection with this program are being collected and will be published under the editorship of the project director by the Indiana University Press in its Advances in Semiotics series (Sebeok 1978a).

Additional Information

1. Research associates. During this past year, there were five research associates in the RCLSS, with terms of appointment ranging from twelve months to four weeks. Foremost among them is Theresa Calvet, who served as my assistant on the program. Ms. Calvet is a doctoral candidate in philosophy at the University of Louvain, with a special competence in Peirce, especially his doctrine of signs.

The other four research associates were Özséb Horányi (Hungarian Academy of Sciences), who was with us throughout September 1975;

Zofia Jancewicz (University of Warsaw), who spent last September and October at the Center under an IREX grant; Bogusław Lawendowski (University of Warsaw), who is here for a year under the auspices of the ACLS' American Studies program; and Boris Ogibenin (Ecole Pratique des Hautes Etudes, Paris), who was with us throughout March.

2. Administrative assistant for the program was Margot D. Lenhart, a member of our RCLSS staff, who in addition to her regular duties was responsible for all of the travel and local arrangements for our visitors.

3. As a direct by-product of the program, the university has recently created an Ethology Committee, and has designated me as its chairman *pro tem*. This committee has been assigned the task of working toward the academic development of ethology at Indiana University, an endeavor paralleling the development in semiotics.

4. The program cooperated with the conference, "Comparing the Arts," which was held under the NEH Program Grant to the Indiana University Comparative Literature Program. At our initiative, on the eve of the conference, March 11, Roman Jakobson delivered his lecture, "Science of Sounds as Signs." Two of the visiting scholars were active participants in the conference: Paul Bouissac served as a workshop leader on "The Semiotic Approach," and Décio Pignatari addressed the conference on the "Metalanguage of Art."

5. The program maintained very close contacts with the Film Studies Program, with which we collaborated by inviting Raymond Bellour. Several students who participated in the Semiotics Program are interested in film, and one has started a new film journal, *Media Montage*.

6. Roman Jakobson's visit created such interest that I have been asked to teach an all-campus Jakobson seminar during the Fall Semester, 1977, for the Department of Linguistics. I have also been invited to conduct a course, "Semiotics and Human Ethology," for the Department of Anthropology.

7. Of broader interest, perhaps, is that in part at least because of our leadership here, several other U.S. universities are now shaping or contemplating semiotics programs of their own (esp. Brown and Colorado).

In mentioning our leadership, I am not referring merely to the Pilot Program, but to a number of enterprises which make Indiana University the pre-eminent U.S. institution at the frontiers of semiotics in our hemisphere:

(a) Semiotic Society of America—This new organization, which was incorporated only early in 1976, has its Secretariat located on our Bloomington campus; its publication, *Semiotic Scene*, is now produced at Tufts University.

(b) Publications—The official monthly journal of the International

Association for Semiotic Studies, *Semiotica*, is edited in my office, as it has been since its inception in 1969; since then 25 volumes have appeared (and many more are in press). In addition, three series of books have also been edited, or are now being edited, in our Research Center for Language and Semiotic Studies: Approaches to Semiotics (some 60 volumes so far); Advances in Semiotics (4 volumes published so far, with 4 others in press); and Studies in Semiotics (12 volumes published so far, with many others in press).

(c) The Peirce Edition Project–Funding has been approved by the NEH and NSF for the Center for American Studies at Indiana University–Purdue University at Indianapolis to produce a new edition of the writings of the American philosopher Charles Sanders Peirce. The edition is expected to run to a total of fifteen volumes over a seven-year publication period and to provide the first complete chronological set of Peirce's writings, and the first new edition since the 1930s. The project will be under the general editorship of Max Fisch and will be directed by an Advisory Board of Scholars with interest and competencies in the diverse intellectual fields with which Peirce was involved. I am on the Advisory Board and have agreed to provide general direction for the preparation of Peirce's writings dealing with semiotics.

Notes

1. Semiosis in Nature and Culture

1. Although Bühler (1965:28), too, defined the symptom as "Anzeichen, Indicium," he tied it up in his organon model closely to the message source: the symptom is such, in his view, precisely "kraft seiner Abhängigkeit vom Sender, dessen Innerlichkeit es ausdrückt..." The reason I feel uncomfortable with definitions that qualify symptoms as "unwitting" or "unintended" indices are explained in Sebeok 1976:127.

2. In Neuburger's judgment (1906:385), "die galenische Semiotik verwertet die meisten Beobachtungs- und Untersuchungsmethoden, die das Altertum ausgebildet hat." On Galen as a neglected forerunner of general semiotics, see Chapter 10 of this volume.

3. A paper bearing on this topic, "Krankheitssymptome als Übersetzungsfehlerverbalisierung nonverbaler Kommunikation als Problem einer Semiotik der Heilkunde," was given by Thure von Uexküll, on June 5, 1976, at the II. Wiener Symposium über Semiotik, and will appear in the proceedings of that conference. The author is a son of Jakob von Uexküll, whose fundamental contributions to semiotics are discussed below.

4. Uexküll's scheme could, I think, productively be accommodated within Zeeman's developing model of the brain (1965), thus making it amenable to mathematical exploration and generalization to cover any information with tolerance properties; in particular, this would allow for the combination of language structure with tolerance structure along lines later worked out in some detail by Thom (1968; 1970).

5. Cf. the semiotic analysis in Shands 1976:303ff., grappling with "the human problem of greatest moment... of so relating the outer to the inner that the minimal information derivable from inner sources comes to be a reliable index of the external situation."

6. Acrasin is the same as cyclic AMP, which the amebas release in pulses, signaling back and forth to one another during the process of aggregation induced when local conditions turn bad; (for details, see Bonner 1963; for an up-to-date analysis of intracellular communication in this remarkable organism in the wider context of this feature in developing embryos, see Anthony Robertson's chapter on "Cellular Communication" in Sebeok 1977a). Needless to add, Thomas's "bell" is an acoustic metaphor for Tomkins's chemical symbol.

2. Semiotics and Ethology

1. In Chapter 4, Section 4, of this volume, I introduce and discuss two intersecting polar oppositions corresponding to the categories distinguished here:

the semiotics of the *adnormal* vs. that of the *denormal*, and the semiotics of the *normal* vs. that of the *abnormal*.

2. A display is a kind of sign that is called, in common semiotic parlance, an unwitting index (or a symptom). Darwin used both the verb and the noun *display* in this sense, anticipating modern ethological usage; for instance: "... as all the males of the same species display themselves in exactly the same manner, it appears that actions, at first perhaps intentional, have become instinctive" (1871:2:92).

3. Marx (1961:1:3:372), for reasons of his own, stressed the extension from morphology to behavior when he wrote, for example: "Darwin has interested us in the history of Nature's Technology, *i.e.*, in the formation of the organs of plants and animals, which organs serve as instruments of production for sustaining life. Does not the history of the productive organs of man, of organs that are the material basis of all social organization, deserve equal attention?"

4. Ecumenicalism in Semiotics

1. Koestler's (1971) sparkling chronicle of the tangled Kammerer affair, which he dramatized as "the case of the midwife toad," shows how painfully elusive the truth can be, and how difficult it is to decide among these two basic forms of deception, their intermixture, and still other alternatives. In the matter of Kammerer, the question will perhaps forever stand unresolved.

2. I have prepared an article, "Close Encounters with Canid Communication of the Third Kind," which will discuss this matter in detail. It is in press, to appear in *Wechselbeziehungen Diachroner und Synchroner Sprachwissenschaft: Festschrift für Oswald Szeinerenyi zum 65. Geburtstag* (Amsterdam: John Benjamins, 1979).

3. By the way, Hachet-Souplet (1897:85) has pointed out that "Il n'y a, au point de vue théorique, aucune différence entre le dressage du singe et celui du chien." In practice, however, circus trainers differentiate between the quadrupedal and the "privileged" quadrumanous species (viz., dogs vs. monkeys). Surprisingly enough, the excellent literature of dressage seems only very exceptionally to be utilized by psychologists who aim to impart language training to primates. It is a pity that the two traditions so seldom intersect.

4. A "shill" is an accomplice who plays a confidence game so that the mark sees him win (Maurer 1949:306). In reporting the unmasking of Don, Johnson (1912:749) makes a strong point of the fact that "Extensive comment has been made in the German and even in the American daily press on [the dog's] reported conversational ability." In the circus, posters (Bouissac 1976, Ch. 10) provide "the semiotic key" to the act, reinforced by carefully planted advance publicity. It would be easy to document the metaphorically shill-like role that popular magazines and other mass media, especially TV, as well as naïve colleagues, unknowing shillabers, have played in the promotion of the dolphin mythology of the 1960s (Sebeok 1972:60) and the chimp mythology of the 1970s. As in any con, it is very difficult to "knock a mark," i.e., to convince him that he is being duped. Such diehard marks are called addicts. My experience has been that attempts to ameliorate academic addicts are met with

resentment, even downright hostility; the reasons for this will, of course, be perfectly obvious to readers of Goffman (1952).

It took the dolphin craze about ten years to subside; the present chimp fad, which is as yet in the expansive stage, will take a little longer to ease off, since contemporary behaviorists are still in the firm grip of La Mettrie (Limber 1977:288). For a few notable exceptions besides Limber, see the prominent agnostic psychologists Brown and Herrnstein (1975:490–491) and Terrace and Bever (1976:583). A complication is that two delusions are almost inextricably entangled here: I already called attention to the Pathetic Fallacy in 1963 (Sebeok 1972:59); what I am after now are the background and broader implications of the Clever Hans Fallacy (idem 1978).

5. Looking in the Destination for What Should Have Been Sought in the Source

1. In view of the now hardly controvertible fact, underlined once again by Hediger (1974:27–28), that the Clever Hans effect in "animals is only explainable by the continually repressed fact that the animal—be it horse, monkey or planarian—is generally more capable of interpreting the signals emanating from humans than is conversely the case," it is irksome to repeatedly come across reports fatuously stating that "in order to avoid the results of suggestion [certain] investigators decided to use animals rather than humans as their experimental organisms" (this in reference to mice, in a test of "laying-on-of-hands" healing, as reported by Rhine [1970:316–317]).

2. Cf. Weizenbaum's (1977) telling remark about the "power of . . . [his] computer program [being] no more and no less than the power to deceive," and the constant, inevitable, yet apparently discounted intrusion of Clever Hans cues into the Lana experiment intended to be conducted by means of an "impersonal" computerized system—see, e.g., Rumbaugh (1977:159, 161), and the acerb comment on this project by Gardner and Gardner (1978:44), alleging that Rumbaugh's "results . . . presented thus far are more parsimoniously interpreted in terms of such classic factors as Clever Hans cues . . ." The Gardners claim that, to the contrary, testing procedures they themselves developed rule out this and kindred alternative interpretations. The procedures they refer to presumably involve the "double-blind" design, adapted from psychopharmacological researches. The objectivity of this method, however, though comforting, is altogether illusory; see, e.g., Tuteur 1957–1958. So what we have here is a blatant case of, paraphrasing Cervantes, the pot calling the kettle black.

3. As recently as 1975, one still finds books on communication between man and horse imbued with the Clever Hans Fallacy. Thus Blake (1975, Ch. 10) devotes an entire chaotic chapter to "telepathy in horse language." He describes, no doubt accurately, his experiences with a horse, Weeping Roger (Ch. 7), but goes on to imply an absurd explanation: "I discovered that I could direct [this stallion] where I wanted to go just by thinking it. I would steer him to the left or right or straight ahead simply by visualizing the road. This was the first time I had consciously experienced telepathy with a horse" (p. 126). Elsewhere (p. 94), he remarks, "I was always at one with him." Plainly,

all the constituents for a Clever Hans setup are present, but Blake still finds it necessary to resort to ESP instead of the correct semiotic explanation, which he apparently knows nothing of.

4. Perhaps echoing Upton Sinclair's (1930:4) technologically puerile yet by virtue of that very fact endearing simile, comparing ESP to "some kind of vibration, going out from the brain, like radio broadcasting." This imagery has its ultimate source in Democritus.

5. On "muscle reading" as explanation for other pseudo-occult phenomena, such as the movement of a Ouija board, table tipping, and automatic writing, see Gardner (1957:109), who speaks of the "unwitting translation of thoughts into muscular action . . ." See also Vogt and Hyman (1959, Ch. 5). Regarding the most flashy of contemporary "psychics," the Israeli stage-performer Uri Geller, see Marks and Kammann (1977:17), who similarly conclude that "parsimony dictates the choice of normal explanations for the phenomena described. . . . Geller's procedures allow him to use ordinary sensory channels and ordinary motor functions." Incidentally, James ("The Amazing") Randi, a top-flight Canadian conjurer, has publicly duplicated all of Geller's feats. Concerning Peirce's disapprobation of telepathy, "with its infrequency and usual deceptiveness" (Peirce 1935–1966:7.686), and of kindred psychic doctrines and claims, see his extended if apparently incomplete essay on "Telepathy and perception" (ibid.:597–686).

6. The incidents happened on Saturday, June 2, 1879. Peirce recovered his watch on the following Tuesday. The two culprits were committed for trial on Wednesday, June 25. Peirce's detectival procedure is compared in detail, in Sebeok and Umiker-Sebeok (1979), with the famous "method" of Sherlock Holmes, wherein the similarity is accounted for by virtue of their common roots in Natural Semiotics (including medical). Kreskin (1975:27–28) incidentally sketches a stage illusion, *Guilty*, which unfolds precisely according to the strategy devised by Peirce, in applying which, Kreskin claims, it is "impossible for the 'guilty' person not to give himself away . . ." For a flagrant case of real life abuse of "telepathy" in law enforcement, seemingly motivated by social prejudice, see Posinsky (1961).

7. See note 2, above; I intend to return in much more depth elsewhere to these complex semiotic topics, which I had occasion to discuss but briefly before (Ch. 4, this volume, and Sebeok 1978b).

8. Francis Huxley, who professes to believe in the existence of ESP (1967:282), and appears perversely unaware of Cannon's highly significant study of a quarter of a century earlier than his, nevertheless gropes toward an analysis of voodoo in semiotic terms: "Is it . . . possible that symbols," he asks, meaning icons, "by containing the field of relationships and providing the ground of consciousness, are responsible for what we call ESP?" (ibid.:302). Discussion of the etiology of voodoo death continues in anthropological and other circles; for a summary of the recent literature and latest interpretations, see Lex 1974.

9. See Umiker-Sebeok (1978) for a detailed treatment of the elaborate semiotic code for partial or total eye concealment by means of eyeglasses and other devices in American culture.

10. One side effect of this 1913 experiment was a decisive improvement in the training of police dogs and in their consequent accuracy in tracking. Katz's conclusion is, of course, equally applicable to any "muscle reading" act. The performer may have a spectator take hold of his hand believing that "he is

being led by the magician, but actually the performer permits the *spectator to lead him* by unconscious muscular tensions" (Gardner 1957:109). The best muscle readers, like the famous Eugen de Rubini (whose case I discussed in Ch. 4, this volume), may dispense with physical contact altogether, relying on far more elusive guiding cues, such as tremors of the floor, faint sounds of feet, movements of arms and clothing, and/or those made by changes in breathing (Rinn 1950:531). The workings of several variants of the Clever Hans theme were known to scientists of the stature of Michael Faraday (table turning) and Michel Eugene Chevreul (the magic pendulum) by at least the early 1850s (Hansel 1966:33–34).

11. Parents who act on the assumption that their child is bright appear to proceed in just this way. I recently observed an infant of seventeen months being fed beef. Her mother interrogated her, "What's this?" The daughter replied, "Chicken." The mother observed, "She loves to tease me!" She then followed this remark up with a further unsubstantiated general comment: "She enjoys making a game out of oppositions." Bingham (1971) has shown that preverbal children are addressed in a carefully accommodated register by mothers who judge that *their* infants have the capacity to understand quite a bit, but not by mothers who set a lower estimate on *their* infants' capacity.

12. In part no doubt inspired by Jules Romains, the French writer, who was obsessed with "paroptic" vision, or "eyeless sight." His book on this subject (Romains 1920; American version, 1924) was widely read in the postwar years here and throughout Europe.

13. Chauvin-Muckensturm (1974:207) explicitly compares the drumming code she imparted to her Greater Spotted Woodpecker to the man-monkey performances variously shaped by the Gardners and Premack, stressing that *"le bec est au moins l'égal de la main du chimpanzé."* This woodpecker is French. It will not have escaped notice, however, that the happily defunct myth of dolphin discourse, as well as the currently continuing promotion of primates to the status of a putatively (Limber 1977) productive *animal loquens*, have been confined, so far without a single exception, to the United States.

6. Iconicity

1. The inaugural discourse was delivered from memory at the formal opening of the Johns Hopkins University on September 12, 1876; it appeared in print the following year (J. Huxley 1877). For another version of Huxley's Baltimore misadventures, where his speech was said to have been given "under circumstances of peculiar difficulty," see the account by his son (Leonard Huxley 1900:465ff.).

2. I am aware—as some discussants of iconicity appear (or choose) not to be —that Peirce sometimes (as in 1935–1966:2.281) classifies photographs, "especially instantaneous photographs," as indices, because "their resemblance is due to the photographs having been produced under such circumstances that they were physically forced to correspond point by point to nature." (This is probably the main reason why a photographer is seldom identifiable from his pictures, whereas a painter usually is.) One may further surmise that he would have, *mutatis mutandis*, classified instantly trans-

mitted television images the same way. However, he is also careful to stress at once that such images belong to the second class of signs, that is, those by physical connection, "in that aspect" (2.281); hence, at other times, he also singles photographs out as a good example of a hypoicon, i.e., of an iconic representamen (2.320). Since any sign may—and more often than not does—exhibit a hierarchy of environment-sensitive aspects, and since, as Charles Morris (1971:273) succinctly put it, "Iconicity is...a matter of degree," all photographs must have an iconic aspect as well, however attenuated that aspect may be in this or that context. This is, moreover, a corollary of Peirce's claim that "The only way of directly communicating an idea is by means of an icon; and every indirect method of communicating an idea must depend for its establishment upon the use of an icon" (2.278).

In general, it is therefore inane to ask whether any given object "is," or is represented by, an icon, an index, or a symbol, for all signs are situated in a complex network of syntagmatic and paradigmatic contrasts and oppositions, i.e., simultaneously participate in a text as well as a system; it is their position at a particular moment that will determine the predominance of the aspect in focus. One illustration of this must suffice here. The flag of the United States is sometimes referred to as the Stars and Stripes to call attention to its iconic aspect, since its seven red horizontal stripes alternating with six white ones are understood to stand one for each founding colony, whereas its fifty white stars in the single blue canton are interpreted to correspond one to each state in the present Union (cf. Sebeok 1976:121). For Francis Scott Key, detained overnight (September 13–14, 1814) aboard a British ship, watching the bombardment of Fort McHenry, in Baltimore, the Star-Spangled Banner served an indexical function, signifying to him, "by dawn's early light," that "the flag was still there." As for the flag as a symbol, viz., an emblem, in some sense this is obvious to every schoolboy, but is under scientific scrutiny by a recently named and well-organized field of scholarship, vexillology; for a semiotic overview of the subject of how "national flags symbolize a set of sociological realities," see Weitman (1973:331).

3. An early Auden couplet also comes to mind: "Now tell me what your children are?/Pocket editions of their papa."

4. A dramatic example of the shattering efficacy of an effigy in modern times is told by India's former Prime Minister, Indira Gandhi. As related to a reporter of *The New Yorker* (March 22, 1976, p. 94), Mrs. Gandhi says that, when she was five, "she discovered that her doll was made in Britain. For days she pondered what she should do about it, and she struggled, in her words, 'between love of the doll—[along with] pride in the ownership of such a lovely thing—and...duty towards my country.' She continues, 'At last the decision was made and, quivering with tension, I took the doll up on the roof terrace and set fire to her. Then the tears came as if they could never stop. And for some days I was ill with a temperature! To this day I hate striking a match!'"

5. Still, one finds statements even recently like the following: "Iconic vehicles of meaning are poor things, which are not fit to carry most meaning. Human languages hardly use them: except for minor cases of onomatopoeia [they are] free of iconic cramps" (Bennett 1976:149).

6. For a particularly sophisticated discussion of metaphor and allied con-

cepts—although in the tradition of G. H. Mead rather than C. S. Peirce, from whom the author could have profited—see Fernandez (1974).

7. This seeming truism is actually subject to all sorts of constraints, especially if viewed in the light of Uexküll's semiotic model and his concept of *Auswahlfunktion*; for details, see Chapter 10.

8. Peirce, of course, saw nothing strange in a human being himself being a sign: "For . . . the fact that every thought is a sign, taken in conjunction with the fact that life is a train of thought, proves that man is a sign" (1935–1966:5.314; cf. 6.344); and ". . . the general answer to the question what is man? is that he is a symbol" (7.583). This last quotation is taken from a fragment of a truly stupefying essay, "Consciousness and Language" (7.579–596), in which Peirce compares man with verbal signs (I discuss this in more detail in Sebeok 1977b).

9. Which is to say, semiotic, for Peirce identified the whole of logic with semiotics: ". . . I extend logic to embrace all the necessary principles of semiotic, and I recognize a logic of icons . . ." (1935–1966:4.9); or ". . . logic may be regarded as the science of the general laws of signs" (1.191).

10. In some cultures, shadows are promoted to a high art form and complex religious rite, as in the Javanese *wajang*, or shadow puppet-play, which, as Professor Geertz reports (1973:137f.), "appears most directly in terms of an explicit iconography," although he adds that "neither icons, parables, nor moral analogies are the main means by which the Javanese synthesis is expressed in the *wajang* . . ."

11. "I would have you imagine . . . that there exists in the mind of man a block of wax . . . and that when we wish to remember anything which we have seen, or heard, or thought in our own minds, we hold the wax to the perceptions and thoughts, and in that material receive the impression of them as from the seal of a ring; and that we remember and know what is imprinted as long as the image lasts" (trans. B. Jowett).

12. The geometric property of "chirality," the subject of a fascinating Nobel lecture by Prelog (1976), is focally relevant to the overarching concept of iconicity. Many objects of one three-dimensional perceptual world are "enantiomorphs," meaning that they are not only chiral, but appear in nature in two versions, related, at least ideally, as an object and its mirror image. Incidentally, the terms *chiral* and *chirality* were coined by Lord Kelvin, in 1884, in his Baltimore lectures (echoes of John Bulwer's *chirologia*, "the Naturell Language of the Hand," and *chironomia*, "The Arte of Manuall Rhetoricke," are unmistakable).

7. Aboriginal Sign "Languages" from a Semiotic Point of View

1. See Chapter 6, note 12, of this volume, concerning the related pairs of terms *chiral* and *chirality*, *chirologia* and *chiromania*, and their relevance to a discussion of the concept of iconicity (cf. Fisch's [1977] mention of Peirce's "Art Chirography"). Stokoe (e.g., 1972) has introduced into studies of sign languages of the deaf the terms *cheremes* (patterned after spoken language *phonemes*), *cherology* (cf. *phonology*), and *cheremics* (cf. *phonemics*).

2. West's adoption of Birdwhistell's terminology brought to aboriginal sign

language studies a set of terms parallel to those given in note 1 above (cf. *kinesics/cheremics, kineme/chereme*). A third set of terms, *gestemics* and *gestemes*, was proposed by Ljung (1965) following the linguist Lamb's stratificational analysis. Meggitt (1954) suggested *finguistics* and *mimetics* as a sign language parallel to *linguistics* and *phonetics* (see the discussion in West 1963).

3. Stokoe (1974a:118) suggests the use of the term *gSign*, where *g* is "any gestural manifestation," and *Sign* " a sign vehicle in a semiotic system." Following Kendon (1972), Stokoe would restrict the term *gesticulation* to the flow of corporeal movement accompanying speech. See also the discussions of these as well as other terms frequently used to describe nonverbal communication systems in Sebeok 1976:158–162, and Chapter 3 of this volume.

4. Cf. the similar positions regarding the question of the existence of pure icons taken by Eco (1976) and Sebeok (Ch. 6, this volume).

5. However, in a recent personal communication (July 2, 1977), Max H. Fisch writes: "Peirce and Mallery must have known of each other and may have been personally acquainted. They were fellow members of The Philosophical Society of Washington. Peirce's active participation (presenting formal papers) was in the early years, 1871–1874. (Peirce's father was also a member during his superintendency of the Coast Survey.) So far as my notes show, Mallery was active at least from 1877. He was president around 1887–1888 and sketched the history of the Society at a meeting in January 1888. He seems to have been present at a meeting on October 23, 1888, at which resolutions memorializing Benjamin Peirce were presented, and several members recited their recollection of him."

8. The Two Sons of Croesus: A Myth about Communication in Herodotus

1. Cited in Evans 1968:11. This article contains an excellent discussion of the ups and down of Herodotus' reputation since the time of Thucydides (d. ca. 401 B.C.).

2. The English translation by Aubrey de Sélincourt (Herodotus 1954) was used throughout, compared as seemed advisable with the translations of A. D. Godley (Herodotus 1921) and George Rawlinson (Herodotus 1910).

3. The merest intimation of a construal along some such lines as will be suggested below may be found in a brief paragraph, set down in 1888, by the versatile writer Kleinpaul (1972:iv–v): "Krösus, des Besitzer unermesslicher Schätze, ist wie der reiche Menschengeist, der aller Sprache Vater heisst; seine beiden Söhne, der plötzlich der Sprache Zurückgegebenc und der plötzlich der Sprache und dem Leben verlorene können uns zu Typen für die zwei Arten der Rede dienen; für die Sprache mit Worten und für die Sprache ohne Worte."

4. The men adduced by Solon as more fortunate than Croesus represent ideal types within the three Indo-European religious and social conceptual categories, or functions, postulated by Dumézil (1953). The first function is characterized by sacerdotal and juridical sovereignty, the second by the power

and prowess of the warrior, and the third by aspects of physical health, wealth, and fecundity (ibid.:25). Dumézil regards Solon's speech as a reproach to Croesus, who has abandoned the virtues proper to a monarch and warrior for the allurements of the third function (ibid.:30): "... le prospère et fécond Tellos s'élève finalement au-dessus de cette condition par l'héroisme, et les vigoureux athlophores Cléobis et Biton s'élèvent de même, à leur dernier jour, par une conduite exemplairement religieuse, tandis que le roi Crésus, pourtant sage, dévot entre tous, cher aux dieux, et même brave, encourt la ruine pour avoir surestimé la richesse et pour avoir, lui si riche, attaqué et mis en appétit un peuple pauvre: seul un retour sincère et profond à la sagesse et à la dévotion lui sauvera la vie *in extremis*."

5. This innominate son would today more likely be described as an autistic child. Wing (1976:41) remarks: "Children with undiagnosed congenital deafness may show behaviour like that of autism as a consequence of their problems in communication." However, she continues, if they are able to discover for themselves, or are taught, "alternative methods of communication ... they rapidly lose their 'autism'." The severity of the impairment can also be affected by management crises according to, for instance, "situational peculiarities," according to Schopler (ibid.:243). On semiotic aspects of autism, see further Chapter 4 of this volume.

6. Thom (1974a, Ch. 10) took Heraclitus' gnome as the epigraph of one of his brilliant essays, "Topologie et signification," which shows the vivid pertinence of Heraclitus' *logos* for the contemporary sign science.

7. Lévi-Strauss speaks elegantly of "une question à laquelle on postule qu'il n'y aura pas de réponse," vs. the transform of this statement, "une réponse pour laquelle il n'y a pas eu de question" (1973:33).

8. Lévi-Strauss, in a personal communication to T. A. S., has remarked that, in order to be complete, our analysis "should unravel a link between, on the one hand, the twofold nature of Croesus' ascendants (one parent positive, the other one negative) and, on the other hand, the twofold nature of his progeny. Taking into account the fact that the positive son turns out to be negative, and the negative positive, one wonders if in Croesus' life history, a similar inversion could not be shown to exist at the parents' level."

To expand the analysis in this dimension, one can but cautiously extrapolate from a paucity of data, for instance, such as are set forth in Radet's (1893, Part 2, Ch. 5) distinguished history of Lydia and the Greek world from 687 to 546, which, in turn, relies on a multiplicity of sources that, of course, include Herodotus.

Croesus, who was born in 596, was the eldest son of Alyattes, who had succeeded his father, the despot Sadyattes, upon the latter's premature death. The career and public policies of Alyattes are quite well known. Of his personality, it was said: "... après quelques années d'humeur sauvage et orageuse, durant lesquelles il s'emportait jusqu'à maltraiter les personnages de distinction, jusqu'à déchirer leurs habits et jusqu'à leur cracher au visage, revint à une politique moins farouche. Assagi par le temps,—ou sûr d'être obéi sans conteste,—il se montra le plus sage et le plus juste des hommes" (Radet 1893:204–205), and thus eventually became a popular monarch. Croesus, by virtue of primogeniture, was entitled to the throne of the Mermnades, but apparently did not attain it without a struggle: "Des intrigues de harem, une compétition dynastique des plus âpres, les enterprises d'une faction sans scrupules inquiétèrent sa vie et compromirent son avènement" (ibid.: 206).

The anonymity of the harem veils the personal identity of Croesus' mother; we know only that he, the eldest son, was "né d'une Carienne," whereas his younger brother and factional rival, Pantaleon, was the son "d'une Ionienne" (ibid.). This Ionian woman tried to murder Croesus by getting his baker to poison the bread being prepared for his consumption. The loyal servant, however, revealed the plot to her master, who, as related by both Herodotus and Plutarch, upon his ascendance to the throne consecrated, in the temple at Delphi, an effigy to his female baker. According to Plutarch, he arranged to have served to the children of his stepmother the same deadly alimentation which she had intended for him.

Since little more is known about the familiar relations between Alyattes and his wives, and next to nothing about the filial relations of Croesus to his umbrous mother, it seems that the analysis can progress no further to achieve the ideal symmetry of design postulated by Lévi-Strauss.

9. The French Swiss Connection

1. Dana (1813–1895) was an important and prolific American geologist and mineralogist, professor at Yale University from 1850. The book referred to in Saussure's letter cited in this chapter was Dana's *Reports* of the Wilkes exploring expedition (1838–1842), mainly devoted to geology, corals, and crustaceans, published between 1846 and 1854.

2. Professor Fisch, who read a draft of this paper, responded in a letter on December 8, 1977, from which I should like to quote two paragraphs:

"It may be worth mention that Peirce had five sojourns in Europe: 1870, 1875–76, 1877, 1880, 1883. In 1875 he was at Geneva from about July 7 through September 17, and during the last three weeks he swung pendulums in the Observatory there, whose director at that time was Emile Plantamour (1815–1882). He might well have met some of the de Saussures at that time. He visited Geneva at least once again, in 1883, after Plantamour's death. He almost certainly gave offprints of some of his papers to Plantamour, and they may be in the library of the Observatory. He might conceivably have given other offprints to one or another of the de Saussures.

"Though the *Cours* did not appear until after Peirce's death, Peirce's interest in linguistics might well have put him on the track of Ferdinand de Saussure after the latter began to publish."

10. Neglected Figures in the History of Semiotic Inquiry: Jakob von Uexküll

1. Assume that a Greek and a Barbarian hear an identical speech signal designating an object with which both are familiar. The Greek understands it, the Barbarian doesn't. What feature is involved other than the signifier and the object? None, for the sound and the object remain the same. But the object,

in the brain of the Greek, has an attribute that it lacks in the Barbarian's, and it is this that the Stoics named *lektón*.

2. Jennings was well acquainted with the researches of his contemporary, von Uexküll. The methods as well as the results of the two independent investigators, of entirely different background and schooling, converged in essential details; especially, they shared a systems-oriented outlook later featured in holistic or organismic theories of J. C. Smuts, J. B. S. Haldane, L. von Bertalanffy, A. Meyer, and others in the 1920s and the 1930s (see Giuseppe Montalenti, in Ayala and Dobzhansky 1974:8-9, and Sebeok 1977b). Reciprocally, von Uexküll (e.g., 1926:205, 238) cites with admiration Jennings's results of his experiment made on *Paramecium*.

3. In psychology, another one of Lorenz's teachers (Lorenz 1977:8), K. Bühler, similarly anticipated a cybernetic model (Sebeok 1972:35). It is extremely interesting to note that, in 1934, Bühler (1965:27) remarked that von Uexküll "in seinen Grundbegriffen 'Merkzeichen' und 'Wirkzeichen' sematologisch [i.e., semiotically] orientiert ist."

4. Von Uexküll had a forerunner in the eccentric nineteenth-century American proto-primatologist, Garner, who wrote (1892:171) that the "speech" of monkeys "is capable of communicating the ideas that they are capable of conceiving, and measured by their mental, moral, and social status, [which] is as well developed as the speech of man measured by the same unit." According to Graven (1967:181 n. 1)—who, in turn, could be described as a forerunner of Griffin—Garner's interests were even wider: "My knowledge of the animal world has given me the firm belief that all mammals are capable of speaking to a degree proportionate to their experience." For a hilarious fictional account about a German naturalist, Dr. Johausen, who followed in Garner's footsteps in Central Africa, did much better than he but came to a curious end, see Verne (1901). Verne's scientist also held that cognition preceded language, from which he concluded: "La vérité, enfin, est que, si les bêtes ne parlent pas, c'est que la nature ne les a pas dotées d'une intelligence suffisante, car rien ne les en empêcherait" (p. 98).

11. Gyula Laziczius

1. Harmatta 1958; a German version appeared in the Hungarian periodical *Acta Linguistica* 7 (1958):211-216. I am indebted to Harmatta's account for the chronology of the principal events in Laziczius's biography, and to John Lotz for his helpful comments.

2. While characterizing him as "undoubtedly the most European, the most modern figure of his age" among Hungarian linguists, László Deme repeatedly stressed the domestic isolation of Laziczius in a challenging article concerning the influence of Saussure on linguistics in Hungary: see Deme 1959, esp. nn. 6-7 and p. 12. Deme's article has the signal merit of having evoked fresh appraisals of the role of Laziczius both in Hungary and abroad in a series of responses by István Fodor, Iván Fónagy, György Szépe, and Edith Vértes (Fodor et al. 1960). On the present state of "structuralism" in Hungary, see also Hajdú 1965.

3. Laziczius 1930a; 1930b. For the purposes of this chapter, the terms *phonology* and *phonemics* may be taken as roughly equivalent.

4. It strikes me as a bizarre oversimplification to bracket Laziczius with André Martinet as "adherents" of Trubetzkoy, as W. K. Matthews (1958) did.

5. Juilland's "Bibliography of Diachronic Phonemics" (1953) needs to be emended in regard to Uralic linguistics in general and the "important explicative contributions" of Laziczius in particular.

6. E.g., Harris 1941.

7. These ideas were worked out, in several somewhat differing forms, in Hungarian: 1935a; 1942a; in German: 1935b (reprinted, 1966:38–58); in English: 1936 (reprinted, 1966:59–63); in French: 1948:298–300 (reprinted, 1966:95–104). For Trubetzkoy's counter-statement, see Trubetzkoy 1939.

8. See, for example, Osgood and Sebeok 1965, Ch. 4; Sebeok, Hayes, and Bateson 1964. For a critique of Laziczius's view of the phoneme from the viewpoint of semiotic classification, see Jakobson 1962:292, 297f.

9. A part of this article is devoted to Twaddell's "splendid book," *On Defining the Phoneme*; while generally in agreement with him, Laziczius expresses some reservations in regard to Twaddell's doubts as to some views of the physical reality of the phoneme, certain ones of which—notably Bloomfield's—he regarded as soundly based.

10. *Fonétika* (Budapest, 1944); a second edition—with a Postscript by I. Fónagy—was published in 1963. A German edition—translated by W. Steinitz—appeared in Berlin in 1961.

11. *Language* 23 (1947):75–76.

12. "Dialect" from a Zoosemiotic Perspective

1. "... the more details we take into account when characterizing a dialect, the more faithful our depiction of it will prove. The more criteria we consider in our investigation, the more accurate the results of the research will be. In this respect there can be no doubt at all."

2. "Scientific research aims to continually uncover fresh data, strives to add them to the known store of facts, out of ever deeper mines, in order to insure further completeness and complexity."

3. "... if someone had asked him [Schleicher] at the end of his life which he deemed most important in his large-scale and in many respects valuable work, he would surely have replied: my transplantation of the methods of the natural sciences into linguistics."

13. Roman Jakobson's Teaching in America

1. Once I had to miss a class where he was to have dealt with Glossematics, and, the next time, I asked him to lend me his notes. He handed me a small stack of cards. The top card read: "The dog." The rest were equally uninformative. Plainly, the secrets of Glossematics were not concealed in that cache. Years afterward, the meaning of the legend on that card dawned on me—but that is another story, involving—to mention it only briefly—the various contextual meanings of the vocable "dog" in their relation to its general meaning.

2. "Beitrag zur allgemeinen Kasuslehre: Gesamtbedeutung der russichen Kasus," in Jakobson 1976:23–71.

3. Jakobson subscribed to a journal edited by this man, and told me that one of his checks was cashed with the erudite endorsement *Pecunia non olet*.

14. John Lotz: A Personal Memoir

1. Or, in conformity with a proposal prevalent in the Theoretical Division of Los Alamos, he was quintessentially a Martian, since the people of Hungary, according to this untested theory, are Martians. The reasoning goes like this: "The Martians left their own planet several aeons ago and came to Earth; they landed in what is now Hungary; the tribes of Europe were so primitive and barbarian that it was necessary for the Martians to conceal their evolutionary difference or be hacked to pieces. Through the years, the concealment had on the whole been successful, but the Martians had three characteristics too strong to hide: their wanderlust . . . ; their language . . . ; and their unearthly intelligence. One had only to look around to see the evidence: Teller, Wigner, Szilard, von Neumann—Hungarians all"—and so was Lotz (McPhee 1973).

2. Through the years, the numbering of the publications in this series, and items related to it, became muddled. For a complete, systematic report, see pp. 20ff. of the *Acta Universitatis Stockholmiensis, Studia Hungarica Stockholmiensia* I, published by Almqvist & Wiksell (Stockholm, 1965). In the text, I generally supply the year of publication only.

3. Robert Austerlitz, Lotz's student and *de facto* successor at Columbia, has been designated by Lotz's widow his literary executor. Plans are afoot to bring Lotz's published writings, which are rather scattered—as well as, hopefully, many of his unpublished papers—out in readily accessible form.

4. I am informed that Lotz had somehow managed to be infected by *Vibrio fetus*, which, nosologically, is closely related to *Vibrio cholera*. It is essentially a disease of cattle, sheep, and goats, but a few human infections have been reported beginning back in the 1950s. The disease in humans resembles brucellosis, or undulant fever. The infection is usually a generalized one, producing septicemia. (I am indebted for data on *Vibrio fetus* to William O. Umiker, M.D.)

5. It should be also recorded, for this is nowhere mentioned in the work itself, that the so-called Caucasian Area Handbook project upon which it was based had been sponsored by the Human Relations Area Files, i.e., ultimately financed by the U.S. Army's Psychological Warfare Branch. *Pecunia non olet* —or so it seemed in those days of our innocence!

6. Members of this congenial group included, besides Lotz and me, Samuel E. Martin, Nicholas N. Poppe, Andreas Tietze, and the late Lewis Thomas (for a short time, Omeljan Pritsak attended our meetings as well). On more than one occasion, I heard Lotz express his disdain for so-called Altaic specialists, and for the scholarly standards he alleged to prevail in Altaic studies, in contrast to those in Uralic studies; however, he had utmost respect and affection for Poppe, upon whose counsel he relied heavily. He surmised that the quality of Uralic scholarship was generally insured by communal criticism in such countries as Hungary and Finland, whereas Altaic scholarship was hardly anywhere responsible to any comparable national entity. This sour outlook did not endear him to such Columbia confreres as Karl Menges and Tibor Halasi-Kun, although they both grudgingly, if selectively, cooperated in his

well-financed projects. Odd as this may seem, I recently heard the "Lotz theory" of Altaic studies independently expounded by one of the most prominent Hungarian Turkologists.

7. Lotz held for example that the TG model of language, so overwhelmingly popular in the 1960s, did not, and *a priori* could not, yield the grammar of any natural language. That no Hungarian grammar of the TG-type was, in fact, ever produced—only fragments—led to the dissolution of a group working on this task, for a while, under the auspices of the Hungarian Academy of Sciences, and Lotz always cited this as evidence for his case. From 1967 onward, he labored on a revision of his own Hungarian grammar, but published only a few special studies resulting from these researches.

8. See, however, *The Linguistic Reporter* 16:1, 13 (1974).

15. Parasitic Formations and Kindred Semiotic Sets: Notes on the Legacy of John Lotz

1. This highly ingenious and seemingly exhaustive analysis of this variety of technical gestures was delivered (in my presence) at a small Conference on Sign Language, held, at the Center for Applied Linguistics, in December 1969. Regrettably, no record of that lengthy talk has yet been located.

2. Specific references to Lotz's publications are superfluous here, since I have mentioned practically all them in the original version of Chapter 14; see the footnote on page 231. However, direct quotations are dated. Lotz 1976 is, of course, a posthumous selection from his writings, translated mostly from the original English or German, postmortem, by Hungarian colleagues, and supplemented by a graceful Postface by the compiler, György Szépe.

3. The derivation of Lotz's use of the lexical shape *semiotics* is uncertain. My surmise is that he followed the 1947 usage of Greenberg (Ch. 16, this volume), who was the senior managing editor of *Word* at the time when the cited remark appeared in that journal.

4. See, for example, Naomi S. Baron's forthcoming article on "Independence and Interdependence in Spoken and Written Language," to appear in *Visible Language*, a journal dedicated to research on the visual media of language expression, and one in which Lotz himself had published one of his final pieces (1972) having to do with script.

16. Marginalia to Greenberg's Conception of Semiotics and Zoosemiotics

1. For some preliminary though suggestive, if already controversial, applications of studies of the lateralization of cerebral functions to cross-cultural differences in information processing, see Paredes and Hepburn 1976, with ensuing discussion.

In passing, it might be worth noting that the abundance and diversity of the means of human communication have found ample expression in mythology as well—as Lévi-Strauss continues to insist in his scintillating analyses of the Oedipus myths (characterized by excessive communication) and their opposite, the Percival cycle (dealing with interrupted communication). Particular mention should be made in this connection of the semilegendary narrative of Herodotus about the two sons of Croesus who were distinguished from one another by their respective semiotic competencies; one was gifted in the verbal arts to the highest degree, the other so bestial that he could make himself understood only by nonverbal devices. The fascinating resolution of this complicated relation, the central theme of which revolves around the mutual transformations prevailing between the worlds of verbal vs. nonverbal communication, is presented in another paper (Sebeok and Brady, Ch. 8 of this volume).

2. "That the meaning conveyed in a glossolalic utterance is emotional and social is clear in statements made by glossolalists" (Samarin 1972:164).

References

Aarsleff, Hans. 1967. *The Study of Language in England, 1780–1860*. Princeton: Princeton University Press.
Aldis, Owen. 1975. *Play Fighting*. New York: Academic Press.
Aly, Wolf. 1921. *Volksmärchen, Sage, und Novelle bei Herodot und seinen Zeitgenossen*. Göttingen: Vandenhoeck & Ruprecht.
Arbib, Michael. 1974. "The Likelihood of the Evolution of Communicating Intelligences on Other Planets." In *Interstellar Communication: Scientific Perspectives*, ed. by C. Ponnamperuma and A. G. W. Cameron, pp. 59–78. Boston: Houghton Mifflin.
Argyle, Michael. 1975. *Bodily Communication*. New York: International Universities Press.
Armstrong, Edward A. 1963. *A Study of Bird Song*. London: Oxford University Press.
Atz, James W. 1970. "The Application of the Idea of Homology to Behavior." In *Development and Evolution of Behavior: Essays in Memory of T. C. Schneirla*, ed. by L. R. Aronson et al., pp. 57–74. San Francisco: W. H. Freeman.
Audiat, Jean. 1940. "Apologie pour Herodot." *Revue des Etudes Anciennes* 42:3–8.
Axtell, Juliet L. 1891. *The Indian Sign Language and the Invention of Lewis F. Hadley, as Applied to the Speedy Christian Civilization and Education of the Wild Adult Indians*. Chicago: Western Label Co.
Ayala, Francisco José, and Theodosius Dobzhansky. 1974. (Eds.) *Studies in the Philosophy of Biology, Reduction and Related Problems*. Berkeley and Los Angeles: University of California Press.
Ayer, A. J. 1968. *The Origins of Pragmatism: Studies in the Philosophy of Charles Sanders Peirce and William James*. London: Macmillan.
Bally, Charles. 1939. "Qu'est-ce qu'un signe?" *Journal de Psychologie Normale et Pathologique*, April–June, pp. 161–174.
Barakat, Robert A. 1975. *The Cistercian Sign Language: A Study in Non-Verbal Communication*. Kalamazoo, Mich.: Cistercian Publications.
Barber, Theodore Xenophon, and David Smith Calverley. 1964. "Effect of E's Tone of Voice on 'Hypnotic-like' Suggestibility." *Psychological Reports* 15:139–144.
Barthes, Roland. 1964a. *Eléments de sémiologie*. Paris: Editions Gonthier.
———. 1964b. *Eléments de sémiologie*. Paris: Seuil.
———. 1967. *Elements of Semiology*. New York: Hill and Wang.
———. 1972. "Sémiologie et Médecine." In *Les Sciences de Folie*, ed. by Roger Bastide, pp. 37–46. Paris: Mouton.
Basedow, Herbert. 1925. *The Australian Aboriginal*, pp. 388–394. Adelaide: F. W. Preece and Sons.
Bateson, Gregory. 1966. "Problems in Cetacean and Other Mammalian Communication." In *Whales, Dolphins, and Porpoises*, Ch. 25. Berke-

ley and Los Angeles: University of California Press.
———. 1968. "Redundancy and Coding." In *Animal Communication: Techniques of Study and Results of Research*, ed. by Thomas A. Sebeok, pp. 614–626. Bloomington: Indiana University Press.
———. 1972. *Steps to an Ecology of Mind*. San Francisco: Chandler Publishing Co.
Bauman, Richard. 1974. "Speaking in the Light: The Role of the Quaker Minister." In *Explorations in the Ethnography of Speaking*, Joel Sherzer, pp. 144–160. Cambridge: Cambridge University Press.
Bäuml, Betty J., and Franz H. Bäuml. 1975. *A Dictionary of Gestures*. Metuchen, N.J.: Scarecrow Press.
Beard, Daniel Carter. 1918. *The American Boy's Book of Signs, Signals, and Symbols*. Philadelphia: J. B. Lippincott Co.
Beck, Henry. 1976. "Neuropsychological Servosystems, Consciousness, and the Problem of Embodiment." *Behavioral Science* 21:139–160.
Beecher, Henry K. 1955. "The Powerful Placebo." *Journal of the American Medical Association* 159:1602–1606.
Bennett, Jonathan. 1976. *Linguistic Behaviour*. Cambridge: Cambridge University Press.
Benthall, Jonathan, and Ted Polhemus. 1975. (Eds.) *The Body as a Medium of Expression*. London: Allen Lane.
Bentley, Arthur F. 1941. "The Human Skin: Philosophy's Last Line of Defense." *Philosophy of Science* 8:1–19.
Bernadete, Seth. 1969. *Herodotean Inquiries*. The Hague: Martinus Nijhoff.
Berndt, Ronald M. 1940. "Notes on the Sign-Language of the Jaralde Tribe of the Lower River Murray, South Australia" *Transactions of the Royal Society of South Australia* 64 (2):267–272.
Bertalanffy, Ludwig von. 1955. "An Essay on the Relativity of Categories." *Philosophy of Science* 22:243–263.
———. 1968. *General System Theory: Foundations, Development, Applications*. New York: George Braziller.
Bierman, Arthur K. 1962. "That There Are No Iconic Signs..." *Philosophy and Phenomenological Research* 23:243–249.
Bilz, Rudolf. 1940. *Pars pro toto: Ein Beitrag zur Pathologie menschlicher Affekte und Oranfunktionen*. Leipzig: Georg Thieme.
Bingham, N. E. 1971. "Maternal Speech to Pre-Linguistic Infants: Differences Related to Maternal Judgments of Infant Language Competence." Unpublished paper. Ithaca: Cornell University.
Birdwhistell, Ray L. 1975. "Background Considerations to the Study of the Body as a Medium of 'Expression.'" In *The Body as a Medium of Expression*, ed. by Jonathan Benthall and Ted Polhemus, pp. 36–58.
Blake, Henry N. 1975. *Talking with Horses: A Study of Communication between Man and Horse*. London: Souvenir Press.
Blest, A. D. 1961. "The Concept of 'Ritualisation.'" In *Current Problems in Animal Behaviour*, ed. by W. H. Thorpe and O. L. Zangwill, pp. 102–124. Cambridge: Cambridge University Press.
Bloomfield, Leonard. 1939. "Linguistic Aspects of Science." *International Encyclopedia of Unified Science* 1(4).
Blum, Harold F. 1951. *Time's Arrow and Evolution*. Princeton: Princeton University Press.

Blurton Jones, N., and Gill M. Leach. 1972. "Behaviour of Children and Their Mothers at Separation and Greeting." In *Ethological Studies of Child Behaviour*, ed. by N. Blurton Jones, Ch. 9. Cambridge: Cambridge University Press.
Boas, Franz. 1891. "Second General Report on the Indians of British Columbia." In "Sixth Report of the Committee... Appointed to Investigate the... North-Western Tribes of the Dominion of Canada." In *Report of the Sixtieth Meeting of the British Association for the Advancement of Science* (1890), pp. 638–641. London: John Murray.
———. 1966. "Gestures." *Kwakiutl Ethnography*, ed. by Helen Codere, pp. 372–376. Chicago: University of Chicago Press.
Bogatyrev, Petr. 1971. *The Functions of Folk Costume in Moravian Slovakia*. The Hague: Mouton.
Bogen, Joseph F. 1969. "The Other Side of the Brain II: An Appositional Mind." *Bulletin of the Los Angeles Neurological Societies* 34:135–162.
Bonfante, Giuliano, and Thomas A. Sebeok. 1944. "Linguistics and the Age and Area Hypothesis." *American Anthropologist* 46:382–386.
Bonner, John Tyler. 1963. "How Slime Molds Communicate." *Scientific American* 209(2):84–93.
Borbé, Tasso. 1978. *Semiotik III: Zeichentypologie*. Munich: Wilhelm Fink.
Bosmajian, Haig A. 1971. *The Rhetoric of Nonverbal Communication: Readings*. Glenview, Ill.: Scott, Foresman.
Bossu, Jean Bernard. 1771. *Travels in the Interior of North America, 1751–1762*. London: T. Davies. [Reprinted 1962, Norman: University of Oklahoma Press.]
Bouissac, Paul. 1973. *La Mesure des gestes: Prolegomènes à la sémiotique gestuelle*. The Hague: Mouton.
———. 1976. *Circus and Culture: A Semiotic Approach*. Bloomington: Indiana University Press.
Bourne, Geoffrey H. 1971. *The Ape People*. New York: G. P. Putnam's Sons.
Bower, Gordon H. 1970. "Analysis of a Mnemonic Device." *American Scientist* 58:496–510.
Brannigan, Christopher R., and David A. Humphries. 1972. "Human Non-Verbal Behaviour, a Means of Communication." In *Ethological Studies of Child Behaviour*, ed. by N. Blurton Jones, pp. 37–64. Cambridge: Cambridge University Press.
Bréhier, Emile. 1962. *La Théorie des incorporels dans l'ancien Stoicisme*. Paris: Librairie Philosophique J. Vrin.
Bronowski, Jacob. 1973. *The Ascent of Man*. Boston: Little, Brown.
Brothwell, Don R. 1976. (Ed.) *Beyond Aesthetics: Investigations into the Nature of Visual Art*. London: Thames and Hudson.
Broughton, W. B. 1963. "Method in Bio-Acoustic Terminology." In *Acoustic Behaviour of Animals*, ed. by R.-G. Busnel, pp. 3–24. Amsterdam: Elsevier.
Brown, Jerram L. 1975. *The Evolution of Behavior*. New York: W. W. Norton.
Brown, Roger. 1973. *A First Language: The Early Stages*. Cambridge: Harvard University Press.
Brown, Roger, and Richard J. Herrnstein. 1975. *Psychology*. Boston: Little, Brown.
Bruce, David J. 1956. "Effects of Context upon Intelligibility of Heard

Speech." In *Information Theory*, ed. by Colin Cherry, pp. 245–252. London: Butterworths Scientific Publications.
Bühler, Karl. 1965 [1934]. *Sprachtheorie: Die Darstellungfunktion der Sprache*. Stuttgart: Gustav Fischer.
Bullowa, Margaret. 1970. "The Start of the Language Process." *Actes du Xe Congrès International des Linguistes*, 3:191–198. Bucharest: Academy of the Romanian Socialist Republic.
Burks, Arthur W. 1949. "Icon, Index, and Symbol." *Philosophy and Phenomenological Research*. 9:673–689.
Burton, Richard F. 1862. *The City of Saints and Across the Rocky Mountains to California*, pp. 135–144. New York: Harper.
Butler, Colin G. 1970. "Chemical Communication in Insects: Behavioral and Ecological Aspects." In *Communication by Chemical Signals* 1:35–78. New York: Meredith Corporation.
Buyssens, Eric. 1967. "La Communication et l'articulation linguistique." In *Travaux de la Faculté de Philosophie et Lettres* 31. Brussels: Presses Universitaires de Bruxelles.
Callan, Hilary. 1970. *Ethology and Society: Towards an Anthropological View*. Oxford: Clarendon Press.
Cannon, Walter B. 1942. "'Voodoo' Death." *American Anthropologist* 44: 169–181.
Cassirer, Ernst A. 1945. "Structuralism in Modern Linguistics." *Word* 1: 99–120.
———. 1953 [1923] *The Philosophy of Symbolic Forms, Volume One: Language*. New Haven: Yale University Press.
Chance, Michael R. A. 1975. "Social Cohesion and the Structure of Attention." In *Biosocial Anthropology*. New York: John Wiley & Sons.
Charlesworth, William R., and Mary Anne Kreutzer. 1973. "Facial Expressions of Infants and Children." In *Darwin and Facial Expression: A Century of Research in Review*, ed. by Paul Ekman, pp. 91–168. New York: Academic Press.
Chauvin-Muckensturm, Bernadette. 1974. "Y a-t-il utilisation de signaux appris comme moyen de communication chez le pic epeiche?" *Revue du Comportement Animal* 9:185–207.
Cherry, Colin. 1966. *On Human Communication: A Review, a Survey, and a Criticism*, 2d ed. Cambridge: MIT Press.
Chomsky, Noam. 1959. Review. *Word* 15:202–218.
———. 1972. *Language and Mind*. New York: Harcourt Brace Jovanovich.
———. 1976. "On the Biological Basis of Language Capacities." In *The Neuropsychology of Language*, ed. by R. W. Rieber, pp. 1–24. New York: Plenum.
Christopher, Milbourne. 1970. *ESP, Seers & Psychics*. New York: Thomas Y. Crowell.
Clark, William Philo. 1885. *Indian Sign Language*. Philadelphia: L. R. Hamersly and Co.
Cody, Iron Eyes. 1952. *How: Sign Talk in Pictures*. Hollywood: H. H. Boelter Lithography.
———. 1970. *Indian Talk: Hand Signals of the American Indians*. Healdsburg, Calif.: Naturegraph Publishers.
Cortambert, Louise. 1833. *Le Langage des fleurs*. 4th ed. Paris: Audot.

Count, Earl W. 1973. *Being and Becoming Human: Essays on the Biogram*. New York: Van Nostrand Reinhold.
Critchley, Macdonald. 1975. *Silent Language*. London: Butterworths.
Cromer, Richard F. 1974. "Receptive Language in the Mentally Retarded: Processes and Diagnostic Distinctions." In *Language Perspectives—Acquisition, Retardation and Intervention*, ed. by Richard L. Schiefelbush and Lyle L. Lloyd, pp. 237–267. London: Macmillan.
Croneberg, Carl G. 1965. "Sign Language Dialects." In *A Dictionary of American Sign Language*, ed. by William C. Stokoe, Jr., et al., Appendix D. Washington: Gallaudet College Press.
Crookshank, F. G. 1938 [1923]. "The Importance of a Theory of Signs and a Critique of Language in the Study of Medicine." In *The Meaning of Meaning*, by C. K. Ogden and I. A. Richards, pp. 337–355. New York: Harcourt, Brace.
Crystal, David. 1969. *Prosodic Systems and Intonations in English*. Cambridge: Cambridge University Press.
Culler, Jonathan. 1976. *Saussure*. London: Fontana/Collins.
Culliton, Barbara J. 1975. "Edelin Trial: Jury Not Persuaded by Scientists for the Defense." *Science* 187:814–816.
Curtiss, Susan, et al. 1975. "An Update on the Linguistic Development of Genie." In *Georgetown University Round Table on Languages and Linguistics*, ed. by Daniel P. Dato, pp. 145–157. Washington, D.C.: Georgetown University Press.
Dampier, William Cecil. 1966. *A History of Science and Its Relations with Philosophy & Religion*. Cambridge: Cambridge University Press.
Darwin, Charles. 1871. *The Descent of Man and Selection in Relation to Sex*. New York: D. Appleton.
———. 1872. *The Expression of the Emotions in Man and Animals*. London: John Murray.
———. 1877. "A Biographical Sketch of an Infant." *Mind* 2:286–294.
Dascal, Marcelo. 1972. *Aspects de la sémiologie de Leibniz*. Jerusalem: Hebrew University.
Davis, Flora. 1971. *Inside Intuition: What We Know About Nonverbal Communication*. New York: McGraw-Hill.
De Mauro, Tullio. 1970. "Notizie biografiche e critiche su F. de Saussure." In Ferdinand de Saussure, *Corso di Linguistica generale*, ed. by Tullio de Mauro, pp. 283–363. Bari: Laterza.
Deme, László. 1959. "A saussure-i tanítások magyar visszhangjához." *Nyelvtudományi Közlemények* 61:3–27.
de Mille, Richard. 1976. *Castaneda's Journey: The Power and the Allegory*. Santa Barbara: Capra Press.
Dennis, Maureen, and Harry A. Whitaker. 1976. "Language Acquisition Following Hemidecortication: Linguistic Superiority of the Left over the Right Hemisphere." *Brain and Language* 3:404–433.
Dimond, Stuart. 1972. *The Double Brain*. Edinburgh: Churchill Livingstone.
Dingwall, William Orr. 1975. "The Species-Specificity of Speech." In *Georgetown University Round Table on Languages and Linguistics*, ed. by Daniel P. Dato, pp. 17–62. Washington, D.C.: Georgetown University Press.
Dodge, Richard Irving. 1882. *Our Wild Indians, or Thirty-Three Years'*

Personal Experience among the Red Men of the Great West. Hartford: A. D. Worthington; Chicago: A. G. Neggleton and Co. [Reprinted 1959, New York: Archer House.]

Dumas, R., and A. Morgan 1975. "EEG Asymmetry as a Function of Occupation, Task, and Task Difficulty." *Neuropsychologia* 13:219–228.

Dumézil, Georges. 1953. "Les Trois Fonctions dans quelques traditions grecques." In *Homage à Lucien Febvre: Eventail de l'histoire vivante*, 2:25–32.

Dunbar, William. 1809. "On the Language of Signs among Certain North American Indians." *Transactions of the American Philosophical Society* 6, pt. 1, no. 1:1–8.

Duncan, Starkey D., Jr. 1975. "Language, Paralanguage, and Body Motion in the Structure of Conversations." In *Socialization and Communication in Primary Groups*, ed. by Thomas R. Williams, pp. 283–311. The Hague: Mouton.

Eccles, John C. 1974. "Cerebral Activity and Consciousness." In *Studies in the Philosophy of Biology, Reduction and Related Problems,* ed. by Francisco J. Ayala and Theodore Dobzhansky. Berkeley: University of California Press.

Eco, Umberto. 1976. *A Theory of Semiotics.* Bloomington: Indiana University Press.

Eddy, Mary Baker. 1934 [1875]. *Science and Health with Key to the Scriptures.* Boston: Published by the Trustees under the Will of Mary Baker G. Eddy.

Efron, David. 1972 [1941]. *Gesture, Race and Culture.* The Hague: Mouton.

Egger, Victor. 1904. *La Parole intérieure.* Paris: Alcan.

Eibl-Eibesfeldt, Irenäus. 1970. *Ethology: The Biology of Behavior.* New York: Holt, Rinehart and Winston.

———. 1972. "Similarities and Differences between Cultures in Expressive Movements." In *Nonverbal Communication*, ed. by Robert A. Hinde, pp. 297–312. Cambridge: Cambridge University Press.

———. 1975. *Ethology: The Biology of Behavior.* New York: Holt, Rinehart and Winston.

Eimermacher, Karl. 1974. *Arbeiten sowjetischer Semiotiker der Moskauer und Tartuer Schule.* Kronberg: Scriptor.

Eisenberg, Abne N., and Ralph R. Smith, Jr. 1971. *Non-Verbal Communication.* Indianapolis: Bobbs-Merrill.

Eisenberg, John F., and Devra G. Kleiman. 1977. "Communication in Lagomorphs and Rodents." In *How Animals Communicate*, ed. by Thomas A. Sebeok, pp. 634–654. Bloomington: Indiana University Press.

Ekman, Paul. 1972. "Universals and Cultural Differences in Facial Expressions of Emotion." In *Nebraska Symposium on Motivation 1971*, ed. by James K. Cole, pp. 207–283. Lincoln: University of Nebraska Press.

———. 1973.(Ed.) *Darwin and Facial Expressions: A Century of Research in Review.* New York: Academic Press.

Ekman, Paul, and W. V. Friesen. 1969. "The Repertoire of Nonverbal Behavior: Categories, Origins, Usage, and Coding." *Semiotica* 1:49–98.

Emerson, Alfred E. 1938. "Termite Nests—A Study of the Phylogeny of Behavior." *Ecological Monographs* 8(2):247–284.

Eschbach, Achim, and Wendelin Rader. 1976. *Semiotik-Bibliographie I.* Frankfurt a/M: Syndikat.
Evans, James Allan Stewart. 1968. "Father of History or Father of Lies: The Reputation of Herodotus." *Classical Journal* 64:11–17.
Evans, Richard J. 1975. *Konrad Lorenz: The Man and His Ideas.* New York: Harcourt Brace Jovanovich.
Eylmann, Erhard. 1908. *Die Eingeborenen der Kolonie Südaustralien*, pp. 103–107. Berlin: Dietrich Riemer.
Fairbanks, Matthew J. 1976. "Peirce on Man as a Language: A Textual Interpretation." *Transactions of the Charles S. Peirce Society* 12:18–32.
Faye, J. P., J. Paris, and J. Roubaud. 1972. "Entretien de Roman Jakobson." In *Hypothèses: Trois entretiens et trois études sur la linguistique et la poétique*, pp. 33–49. Paris: Seghers/Laffont.
Ferguson, Charles A. 1976. "The Structure and Use of Politeness Formulas." *Language in Society* 5:137–151.
Fernandez, James. 1974. "The Mission of Metaphor in Expressive Culture." *Current Anthropology* 15:119–145.
Ferster, Charles B. 1964. "Psychotherapy by Machine Communication." In *Disorders of Communication: Proceedings of the Association for Research in Nervous and Mental Disease* 42:317–328.
Fine, Gary Alan, and Beverly J. Crane. 1977. "The Expectancy Effect in Anthropological Research: An Experimental Study of Riddle Collection." *American Ethnologist* 4:517–524.
Firth, John Rupert. 1949. "Atlantic Linguistics." *Archivum Linguisticum* 1:95–116.
Firth, Raymond. 1973. *Symbols Public and Private.* Ithaca: Cornell University Press.
Fisch, Max H. 1977. "Peirce's Place in American Thought." *Ars Semeiotica* 1:21–40.
———. 1978. "Peirce's General Theory of Signs." In *Sight, Sound, and Sense*, ed. by Thomas A. Sebeok. Bloomington: Indiana University Press.
Fisch, Max H., and Jackson I. Cope. 1952. "Peirce at the Johns Hopkins University." In *Studies in the Philosophy of Charles Sanders Peirce*, ed. by Philip P. Wiener and Frederic H. Young, pp. 277–311, 355–360. Cambridge: Harvard University Press.
Fisher, Seymour. 1965. "The Role of Expectancy in the Performance of Posthypnotic Behavior." In *The Nature of Hypnosis*, ed. by Ronald E. Shor and Martin T. Orne, pp. 80–88. New York: Holt, Rinehart and Winston.
Fodor, István, et al. 1960. "Vita a saussure-i tanítások magyar visszhangjáról." *Nyelvtudományi Közlemények* 62:134–149.
Foreman, Carolyn. 1949. "Lewis Hadley, the Long-haired Sign Talker." *Chronicles of Oklahoma* 27:41–55.
Fornara, Charles W. 1971. *Herodotus: An Interpretative Essay.* Oxford: Clarendon Press.
Fouts, Roger S. 1974. "Language: Origins, Definitions and Chimpanzees." *Journal of Human Evolution* 3:475–482.
———. Forthcoming. "Capacities for Language in Great Apes." In *Sociology*

and Psychology of Primates, ed. by R. H. Tuttle, pp. 371–390. The Hague: Mouton.

Fox, James J. 1975. "On Binary Categories and Primary Symbols: Some Rotinese Perspectives." In *The Interpretation of Symbolism*, ed. by Roy Willis, pp. 99–132. New York: John Wiley and Sons.

Frank, Jerome D. 1961. *Persuasion and Healing: A Comparative Study of Psychotherapy*. Baltimore: Johns Hopkins Press.

Frazer, James George. 1951 [1922]. *The Golden Bough: A Study in Magic and Religion*. New York: Macmillan Co.

Freud, Sigmund. 1933. *New Introductory Lectures in Psychoanalysis*. New York: Norton.

Friedmann, Herbert. 1955. "The Honey-Guides." *U.S. National Museum Bulletin 208*. Washington, D.C.: Smithsonian Institution.

Frings, Hubert, and Mabel Frings. 1977. *Animal Communication*. Norman: University of Oklahoma Press.

Frisch, Karl von. 1962. "Dialects in the Language of Bees." *Scientific American* 207:79–87.

———. 1967. *The Dance Language and Orientation of Bees*. Cambridge, Mass.: Belknap.

———. 1974. *Animal Architecture*. New York: Harcourt Brace Jovanovich.

Frisch, Peter. 1968. *Die Träume bei Herodot*. Meisenheim am Glan: Anton Hain.

Frishberg, Nancy. 1975. "Arbitrariness and Iconicity: Historical Change in American Sign Language." *Language* 51:696–719.

Frolov, Iurii P. 1938. *Pavlov and His School*. London: Paul, Trench, Trubner.

Galen. 1821–1833. *Claudii Galeni Opera omnia*, ed. by Carolus Gottlob Kühn, 22 vols. Leipzig: Cnobloch.

———. 1965. *Opera omnia 14*. Hildesheim: Georg Olms.

Gardner, Martin. 1957. *Fads and Fallacies in the Name of Science*. New York: Dover.

———. 1966. "Dermo-optical Perception: A Peek down the Nose" *Science* 151:654–657.

———. 1968 [1958]. *Logic Machines, Diagrams and Boolean Algebra*. New York: Dover Publications.

Gardner, R. Allen, and Beatrice T. Gardner. 1978. "Comparative Psychology and Language Acquisition." In *Psychology: The State of the Art*, ed. by Kurt Salzinger and F. Denmark. New York: Annals of the New York Academy of Sciences.

Garner, Richard L. 1892. *The Speech of Monkeys*. New York: Charles L. Webster.

Gazzaniga, Michael S. 1975. "Brain Mechanisms and Behavior." In *Handbook of Psychobiology*, ed. by M. S. Gazzaniga and C. Blakemore. New York: Academic Press.

Geertz, Clifford. 1973. *The Interpretation of Cultures*. New York: Basic Books.

Gerard, Ralph W. 1957. "Units and Concepts of Biology." *Science* 125:429–433.

———. 1960. "Becoming: The Residue of Change." In *Evolution after Darwin II*, ed. by Sol Tax, pp. 255–267. Chicago: University of Chicago Press.

Gilman, Daniel Coit. 1899. *The Life of James Dwight Dana: Scientific Ex-*

plorer, Mineralogist, Geologist, Zoologist, Professor at Yale University. New York: Harper & Brothers.
———. 1906. *The Launching of a University and Other Papers: A Sheaf of Remembrances*. New York: Dodd, Mead & Co.
Gipper, Helmut. 1969. *Bausteine zur Sprachinhaltsforschung: Neuere Sprachbetrachtung im Austausch mit Geistes- und Naturwissenschaft*. Düsseldorf: Schwann.
———. 1972. *Gibt es ein sprachliches Relativitätsprinzip?* Frankfurt am Main: S. Fischer.
Glasersfeld, Ernst von. 1974. "Signs, Communication, and Language." *Journal of Human Evolution* 3:465–474.
Goffman, Erving. 1952. "On Cooling the Mark Out." *Psychiatry* 15:451–463.
———. 1971. *Relations in Public: Microstudies of the Public Order*. New York: Basic Books.
———. 1975. *Replies and Responses*. Urbino: Centro Internazionale di Semiotica e di Linguistica.
Goldstein, Arnold P., et al. 1966. *Psychotherapy and the Psychology of Behavior Change*. New York: John Wiley & Sons.
Gombrich, Ernst H. 1951. "Meditations on a Hobby Horse or the Roots of Artistic Form." In *Aspects of Form: A Symposium on Form in Nature and Art*, ed. by Lancelot Law Whyte, pp. 209–228. Bloomington: Indiana University Press.
Goodman, Nelson. 1968. *Languages of Art: An Approach to a Theory of Symbols*. Indianapolis: Bobbs-Merrill Co.
Gould, Richard Allan. 1969. *Yiwara: Foragers of the Australian Desert*, pp. 69–70. New York: Charles Scribner's Sons.
Grace, George W. 1970. "Languages of Oceania." Paper prepared for presentation at the Center for Applied Linguistics World's Languages Conference, April 23–25, Washington, D.C.
Graven, Jacques, 1967. *Non-Human Thought: The Mysteries of the Animal Psyche*. New York: Stein and Day.
Greenberg, Joseph H. 1957. *Essays in Linguistics*. New York: Wenner-Gren Foundation for Anthropological Research.
———. 1961. Review, *American Anthropologist* 63:1140–1145.
———. 1971. "Linguistics and Ethnology." In *Language, Culture, and Communication*, ed. by Anwar S. Dil, pp. 1–10. Stanford: Stanford University Press.
Greimas, Algirdas Julien. 1976. *Sémiotique et sciences sociales*. Paris: Seuil.
Gribble, Charles E. 1968. (Ed.) *Studies Presented to Professor Roman Jakobson by His Students*. Cambridge: Slavica.
Griffin, Donald R. 1976. *The Question of Animal Awareness: Evolutionary Continuity of Mental Experience*. New York: Rockefeller University Press.
Grinker, Roy R. 1956. (Ed.) *Toward a Unified Theory of Human Behavior*. New York: Basic Books.
———. 1966. "The Psychosomatic Aspects of Anxiety." In *Anxiety and Behavior*, ed. by Charles D. Spielberger, Ch. 5. New York: Academic Press.
Gruenberg, Benjamin C. 1929. *The Story of Evolution: Facts and Theories on the Development of Life*. Garden City: Garden City Publishing Co.

Gump, Richard. 1962. *Jade: Stone of Heaven*. Garden City, N.Y.: Doubleday.
Guthrie, R. Dale. 1976. *Body Hot Spots: The Anatomy of Human Social Organs and Behavior*. New York: Van Nostrand Reinhold.
Hachet-Souplet, Pierre. 1897. *Le Dressage des animaux et les combats de bêtes, révélation des procédés employés par les professionels pour dresser le chien, le singe, l'éléphant, les bêtes féroces, etc.* Paris: Firmin Didot.
Haddon, A. C. 1908. "The Gesture Language of the Eastern Islanders." In *Reports of the Cambridge Anthropological Expedition to Torres Straits 3 (Linguistics)*, ed. by A. C. Haddon, pp. 261–262. London: Cambridge University Press.
Hadley, Louis F. 1890. *A Lesson in Sign Talk*. Fort Smith, Ark.: Hadley Pub.
———. 1893. *Indian Sign Talk*. Chicago: Baker and Co.
Hahn, Martin E., and Edward C. Simmel. 1976. (Eds.) *Communicative Behavior and Evolution*. New York: Academic Press.
Hailman, Jack P. 1977. *Optical Signals: Animal Communication and Light*. Bloomington: Indiana University Press.
Hajdú, Péter. 1965. "A mai Uráli nyelvészetröl." *Néprajz és Nyelvtudomány* 9:15–21.
Haldane, J. B. S. 1955. "Aristotle's Account of Bees' Dances." *Journal of Hellenic Studies* 75:24–25.
Hall, Edward T. 1959. *The Silent Language*. Garden City, N.Y.: Doubleday.
———. 1968. "Proxemics." *Current Anthropology* 9:83–108.
Hall, K. R. L., and Irven DeVore. 1965. "Baboon Social Behavior." In *Primate Behavior: Field Studies of Monkeys and Apes*, ed. by Irven DeVore, pp. 53–110. New York: Holt, Rinehart and Winston.
Hall, R. A., Jr. 1975. *Stormy Petrel in Linguistics*. Ithaca: Spoken Language Services, Inc.
Haller, Rudolf. 1959. "Des 'Zeichen' und die 'Zeichenlehre' in der Philosophie der Neuzeit." *Archiv für Begriffsgeschichte* 4:113–157.
Halliwell-Phillipps, James O. 1879. *Memoranda on Love's Labour's Lost, King John, Othello, and on Romeo and Juliet*. London: James Evan Adlard.
Hansel, Charles E. M. 1966. *ESP: A Scientific Evaluation*. New York: Charles Scribner's Sons.
Harmatta, János. 1958. *Nyelvtudományi Közlemények* 60:210–213.
Harrington, John Peabody. 1938. "American Indian Sign Languages." *Indians at Work* 5(7):8–15; 5(11):28–32; 5(12):25–30; 6(1):24–32; 6(3):24–29.
Harris, Zellig S. 1941. Review. *Language* 17:345–349.
Harrison, Randall P. 1974. *Beyond Words: An Introduction to Nonverbal Communication*. Englewood Cliffs, N.J.: Prentice-Hall.
Hartshorne, Charles. 1973. *Born to Sing: An Interpretation and World Survey of Bird Song*. Bloomington; Indiana University Press.
Hauvette-Besnault, Amédée. 1894. *Hérodot, historien des guerres médiques*. Paris: Hachette & Cie.
Hawkes, Terence. 1973. *Shakespeare's Talking Animals: Language and Drama in Society*. London: Edward Arnold.
Hediger, Heini. 1959. "Die Angst des Tieres." *Studien aus dem C. G. Jung-Institut* 10:7–34.

———. 1967. "Verstehens- und Verständigungsmöglichkeiten zwischen Mensch und Tier." *Schweizerische Zeitschrift für Psychologie und ihre Anwendungen* 26:234–255.
———. 1968. *The Psychology and Behaviour of Animals in Zoos and Circuses.* New York: Dover.
———. 1972. "Tierpsychologie." *Lexikon der Psychologie* 3:562–569.
———. 1973. "Ein verräterischer Vogel." *Tages Anzeiger Magazin* 23:24–31 (June 23).
———. 1974. "Communication between Man and Animal." *Image* 62:27–40.
———. 1976. "Der Kluge Hans: Möglichkeiten und Grenzen der Kommunikation zwischer Mensch und Tier." *Neue Zürcher Zeitung* 156:45–46 (July 7).
Heifitz, Milton D., and Charles Mangel. 1975. *The Right to Die: A Neurosurgeon Speaks of Death with Candor.* New York: Putnam & Sons.
Herodotus. 1910. *The History of Herodotus*, trans. by George Rawlinson. New York: E. P. Dutton & Co.
———. 1921. *Herodotus*, trans. by A. D. Godley. London: William Heineman.
———. *Herodotus: The Histories*, trans. by Aubrey de Sélincourt. Middlesex: Penguin Books.
Hess, Eckhard H. 1975. *The Tell-Tale Eye: How Your Eyes Reveal Hidden Thoughts and Emotions.* New York: Van Nostrand Reinhold.
Heyting, Arend. 1962. "After Thirty Years." In *Logic, Methodology and Philosophy of Science*, ed. by Ernest Nagel, Patrick Suppes, and Alfred Tarski. Stanford: Stanford University Press.
Hill, Jane H. Forthcoming. "Language Contact Systems and Human Adaptation."
Hinde, Robert A. 1969. (Ed.) *Bird Vocalizations.* Cambridge: Cambridge University Press.
———. 1972. (Ed.) *Non-Verbal Communication.* Cambridge: Cambridge University Press.
———. 1974. *Biological Bases of Human Social Behavior.* New York: McGraw Hill.
Hinton, H. E. 1973. "Natural Deception." In *Illusions in Nature and Art*, ed. by R. L. Gregory and E. H. Gombrich, pp. 97–159. London: Duckworth.
Hjelmslev, Louis. 1953. *Prolegomena to a Theory of Language.* Baltimore: Waverly Press.
Hofsinde, Robert (Gray-Wolf). 1941. "Talk-without-Talk." *Natural History* 47:32–39.
———. 1956. *Indian Sign Language.* New York: William Morrow & Co.
Holden, Constance. 1977. "Pain Control and Hypnosis." *Science* 198:808.
Hooff, J. A. R. A. M. van. 1971. *Aspects of the Social Behaviour and Communication in Human and Higher Non-Human Primates.* Rotterdam: Bronder-Offset.
Hopkins, Carl D. 1977. "Electric Communication." In *How Animals Communicate*, ed. by Thomas A. Sebeok, pp. 263–289. Bloomington: Indiana University Press.
Horányi, Özséb, and György Szépe. 1975. (Eds.) *A Jel tudománya.* Budapest: Gondolat.

Horowitz, Louise, Alex Ornstein, and Raphael Stern. 1979. (Eds.) *Languages and Psychotherapy*. New York: Haven Publishing Corp.
Hospers, John. 1967. "Aesthetics, Problems of." *The Encyclopedia of Philosophy* 1:35–56. New York: Macmillan Publishing Co.
How, W. W., and J. Wells. 1912. *A Commentary on Herodotus*. Oxford University Press.
Howitt, Alfred W. 1890. "Note on the Use of Gesture Language in Australian Tribes." *Report of the Australian and New Zealand Association for the Advancement of Science* 2:637–646.
———. 1904. *The Native Tribes of South-East Australia*, pp. 723–735. London: Macmillan and Co.
Huggins, W. H., and Doris Entwisle. 1974. *Iconic Communication: An Annotated Bibliography*. Baltimore: Johns Hopkins University Press.
Humfreville, James Lee. 1897. *Twenty Years among Our Savage Indians*. Hartford, Conn.: Hartford Publishing Co.
———. 1899. *Twenty Years among Our Hostile Indians*, pp. 108–111. New York: Hunter and Co.
Hutt, Corinne, and M. Jane Vaizey. 1966. "Differential Effects of Group Density on Social Behavior." *Nature* 209:1371–1372.
Huxley, Francis. 1967. "Anthropology and ESP." In *Science and ESP*, ed. by John R. Smythies, Ch. 13. New York: Humanities Press.
Huxley, Julian. 1966. (Ed.) *A Discussion on Ritualization of Behaviour in Animals and Man. Philosophical Transactions of the Royal Society of London* 251(B):249–526.
Huxley, Julian, and Ludwig Koch. 1964 [1938]. *Animal Language*. New York: Grosset & Dunlap.
Huxley, Leonard. 1900. *Life and Letters of Thomas Henry Huxley*. London: Macmillan.
Huxley, Thomas H. 1877. "Address on University Education." In *American Addresses*, pp. 97–127. New York: D. Appleton and Co.
Immerwahr, Henry R. 1966. *Form and Thought in Herodotus*. Cleveland: Western Reserve University Press.
Ivanov, Vjačeslav V. 1976. *Očerki po istorii semiotiki v SSR*. Moscow: Nauka.
Jacob, François. 1974. *The Logic of Living Systems: A History of Heredity*. London: Allen Lane.
Jakobson, Roman. 1962. *Selected Writings I*. The Hague: Mouton.
———. 1965. "Quest for the Essence of Language." *Diogenes* 51:21–37.
———. 1966. *Selected Writings IV: Slavic Epic Studies*. The Hague: Mouton.
———. 1968. "The Beginnings of National Self-Determination in Europe." In *Readings in the Sociology of Language*, ed. by Joshua Fishman, pp. 585–597. The Hague: Mouton.
———. 1970a. *Main Trends in the Science of Language*. New York: Harper.
———. 1970b. "Language in Relation to Other Communication Systems." In *Linguaggi nella società e nella tecnica*, pp. 3–17. Milan: Edizioni di Comunità.
———. 1971a. *Selected Writings II: Word and Language*. The Hague: Mouton.
———. 1971b. *Studies in Child Language and Aphasia*. The Hague: Mouton.

———. 1971c. "Concluding Note." *International Journal of Slavic Linguistics and Poetics* 14:209.
———. 1971d. "On Linguistic Aspects of Translation." In *Selected Writings II*, pp. 260-266. The Hague: Mouton.
———. 1971e. "The World Response to Whitney's Principles of Linguistic Science." In *Whitney on Language*, ed. by Michael Silverstein, pp. xxv-xlv. Cambridge: MIT Press.
———. 1972. "The Editor Interviews Roman Jakobson." *Modern Occasions*, Winter, pp. 14-20.
———. 1973. *Questions de poétique*. Paris: Seuil.
———. 1975. *Coup d'oeil sur le développement de la sémiotique*. Studies in Semiotics 3. The Hague: Mouton.
Janet, Pierre. 1925. *Psychological Healing: A Histological & Clinical Study*. New York: Macmillan.
Janisse, Michel Pierre. 1977. *Pupillometry: The Psychology of the Pupillary Response*. New York: Halsted Press.
Jaynes, Julian. 1969. "The Historical Origins of 'Ethology' and 'Comparative Psychology.'" *Animal Behavior* 17:601-606.
———. 1977. *The Origin of Consciousness in the Breakdown of the Bicameral Mind*. Boston: Houghton Mifflin.
Jennings, Herbert Spencer. 1906. *Behavior of the Lower Organisms*. New York: Columbia University Press.
Jervis, Robert. 1970. *The Logic of Images in International Relations*. Princeton: Princeton University Press.
Johnson, Harry Miles. 1912. "The Talking Dog." *Science* 35:749-751.
Juilland, A. G. 1953. "A Bibliography of Diachronic Phonemics." *Word* 9: 198-208.
Kainz, Friedrich. 1961. *Die "Sprache" der Tiere*. Stuttgart: Ferdinand Enke Verlag.
Kakumasu, Jim. 1968. "Urubu Sign Language." *International Journal of American Linguistics* 34:275-281.
Kantor, J. R. 1936. *An Objective Psychology of Grammar*. Bloomington: Indiana University Press.
Katz, David. 1937. *Animals and Men: Studies in Comparative Psychology*. London: Longmans, Green.
Kauffman, Lynn E. 1971. "Tacesics, the Study of Touch: A Model for Proxemic Analysis." *Semiotica* 4:149-161.
Kavanagh, James F., and Ignatius G. Mattingly. 1972. (Eds.) *Language by Ear and by Eye: The Relationship between Speech and Reading*. Cambridge: MIT Press.
Kelley, David L. 1971. *Kinesiology: Fundamentals of Motion Description*. Englewood Cliffs, N.J.: Prentice-Hall.
Kendon, Adam. 1972. "Time Relationships between Body Motion and Speech." In *Studies in Dyadic Communication*, ed. by Aron W. Seigman and Benjamin Pope, Ch. 9. New York: Pergamon Press.
———. 1977. *Studies in the Behavior of Social Interaction*. Lisse: Peter de Ridder Press.
Kessel, Edward L. 1955. "The Mating Activities of Balloon Flies." *Systematic Zoology* 4:96-104.

Ketner, Kenneth Laine, and James Edward Cook. 1975. (Eds.) *Charles Sanders Peirce: Contributions to "The Nation," Part One: 1862–1893.* Lubbock: Texas Tech Press.
Kinney, Arthur E. 1973. (Ed.) *Rogues, Vagabonds, & Sturdy Beggars.* Barre, Mass.: Imprint Society.
Kinsbourne, Marcel. 1975. "Minor Hemisphere Language and Cerebral Maturation." In *Foundations of Language Development: A Multidisciplinary Approach,* ed. by Eric H. Lenneberg and Elizabeth Lenneberg, 2, Ch. 7. New York: Academic Press.
Kirchberg, Jutta. 1965. *Die Funktion der Orakel im Werke Herodots.* Göttingen: Vandenhoeck & Ruprecht.
Kleinpaul, Rudolf. 1972 [1888]. *Sprache ohne Worte: Idee einer allgemeinen Wissenschaft der Sprache.* The Hague: Mouton.
Kloft, Werner. 1959. "Versuch einer Analyse der trophobiotischen Beziehungen von Ameisen zu Aphiden." *Biologisches Zentralblatt* 78:863–870.
Klopfer, Peter H., and Jack P. Hailman. 1967. *An Introduction to Animal Behavior: Ethology's First Century.* Englewood Cliffs, N.J.: Prentice-Hall.
Knapp, Mark L. 1972. *Nonverbal Communication in Human Interaction.* New York: Holt, Rinehart and Winston.
Knowlton, James Q. 1966. "On the Definition of 'Picture.'" *AV Communication Review* 14:157–183.
Koehler, Otto. 1956. "Thinking without Words." *Proceedings of the XIV International Congress of Zoology,* pp. 75–87. Copenhagen: Danish Science Press.
Koenig, O. 1970. *Kultur und Verhaltensforschung: Einführung in die Kulturethologie.* Munich.
Koestler, Arthur. 1967. *The Ghost in the Machine.* New York: Macmillan.
———. 1971. *The Case of the Midwife Toad.* New York: Random House.
Kohl, Johann G. 1860. *Kitchi-Gami: Wanderings round Lake Superior,* pp. 137–143. London: Chapman and Hall.
Kolata, Gina Bari. 1977a. "Catastrophe Theory: The Emperor Has No Clothes." *Science* 196:287, 350–351.
———. 1977b. "Mathematics and Magic: Illumination and Illusion." *Science* 198:282–283.
Krames, Lester, Patricia Pliner, and Thomas Alloway. 1974. (Eds.) *Nonverbal Communication.* New York: Plenum Press.
Krampen, Martin. 1978. *Meaning in the Urban Environment.* London: Pion.
Krashen, Stephen D. 1976. "Cerebral Asymmetry." In *Studies in Neurolinguistics* 2, ed. by Haiganoosh Whitaker and Harry A. Whitaker, Ch. 5. New York: Academic Press.
Kreskin [George Kresge, Jr.]. 1973. *The Amazing World of Kreskin.* New York: Random House.
Kroeber, Alfred Lewis. 1972. "Sign Language Inquiry." In *Sign Language among North American Indians Compared with That among Other Peoples and Deaf-Mutes,* by Garrick Mallery, pp. ix–xxxiv. The Hague: Mouton. [Original, 1958, *International Journal of American Linguistics* 24:1–19.]
Kummer, Hans. 1971. "Spacing Mechanisms in Social Behavior." In *Man and Beast: Comparative Social Behavior,* ed. by J. F. Eisenberg and W. S.

Dillon, pp. 219–234. Washington, D.C.: Smithsonian Institution Press.
Labov, William. 1973. "The Social Setting of Linguistic Change." In *Current Trends in Linguistics*, 12, ed. by Thomas A. Sebeok, pp. 195–251. The Hague: Mouton.
Lakó, György. 1958. "A VIII. nemzetközi nyelvészkongresszus." *Nyelvtudományi Közlemények* 60:197.
Lamb, Sydney M., and Adam Makkai. 1976. "Semiotics of Culture and Language." *Current Anthropology* 17:352–354.
Lausberg, Heinrich. 1960. *Handbuch der Literarischen Rhetorik: Eine Grundlegung der Literaturwissenschaft*. Munich: Max Huber Verlag.
Laver, John. 1976. "Language and Nonverbal Communication." In *Handbook of Perception 7: Language and Speech*, Ch. 10. New York: Academic Press.
Law, Helen. 1947–1948. "Croesus from Herodotus to Boccaccio." *Classical Journal* 43:456–462.
Lawick-Goodall, Jane van. 1971. *In the Shadow of Man*. Boston.
Laziczius, Gyula. 1930a. "A phonológiáról." *Magyar Nyelv* [Hungarian Language] 26:18–30.
———. 1930b. "Egy magyar mássalhangzóváltozás phonologiája." *Magyar Nyelv* 26:266–276.
———. 1932. *Bevezetés a fonológiába* [Introduction to Phonology]. Budapest: Magyar Nyelvtudományi Társaság.
———. 1933. "A finnugor idők kialakulásának kérdéséhez." *Magyar Nyelv* 29:18–25.
———. 1935a. "Jeltan, elemtan." *Nyelvtudományi Közlemények* [Linguistic Communications] 49:172–189.
———. 1935b. "Probleme der Phonologie. Zeichenlehre—Elementenlehre." *Ungarische Jahrbücher* 15:495–510.
———. 1936. "A New Category in Phonology." In *Proceedings of the Second International Congress of Phonetic Sciences*, pp. 57–60. Cambridge.
———. 1938. "On Hungarian Pronunciation." [English title of Hungarian article] *Magyar Nyelv* 34:307–316.
———. 1939. "Das sogenannte dritte Axiom der Sprachwissenschaft." *Acta Linguistica* 1:162–167.
———. 1940. "Egy cikk margójára." *Magyar Nyelv* 36:81–89.
———. 1942a. *Általános nyelvészet: Alapelvek és módszertani kérdések* [General Linguistics]. Budapest: Magyar Tudományos Akadémia.
———. 1942b. "A magyar szókészlet nagysága." *Magyar Nyelv* 38:65–73.
———. 1944. *Fonétika* [Phonetics]. Budapest.
———. 1945. "La Définition du mot." *Cahiers Ferdinand de Saussure* 5:32–37.
———. 1948. "Phonétique et phonologie." *Lingua* 1.
———. 1966. *Selected Writings of Gyula Laziczius*, ed. by Thomas A. Sebeok. The Hague: Mouton.
Le Boeuf, Burney J., and Richard S. Peterson. 1969. "Dialects in Elephant Seals." *Science* 166:1654–1656.
Lenneberg, Eric H. 1967. *Biological Foundations of Language*. New York: John Wiley & Sons.
Lenneberg, Eric H., and Elizabeth Lenneberg. 1975. (Eds.) *Foundations of Language Development: A Multidisciplinary Approach*. 2 vols. New York: Academic Press.

Levin, Donald Norman. 1960. "Croesus as an Ideal Tragic Hero." *Classical Bulletin* 36:33–34.
Lévi-Strauss, Claude. 1963. *Structural Anthropology*. New York: Basic Books.
———. 1971. *Mythologiques 4: L'Homme nu*. Paris: Plon.
———. 1973. *Anthropologie structurale deux*. Paris: Plon.
———. 1976. "The Waste Land or the Hot-House? Notes on a Lecture by Lévi-Strauss." *Royal Anthropological Institute News*, no. 12:1–2 (January–February).
Levy, Jerre. 1973. "Psychobiological Implications of Bilateral Asymmetry." In *Hemisphere Functions in the Human Brain*, ed. by Stuart J. Dimond and J. Graham Beaumont, pp. 121–183. London: Elek.
Lex, Barbara W. 1974. "Voodoo Death: New Thoughts on an Old Explanation." *American Anthropologist* 76:818–823.
Lieberman, Philip. 1975. *On the Origins of Language: An Introduction to the Evolution of Human Speech*. New York: Macmillan.
———. 1977. "The Phylogeny of Language." In *How Animals Communicate*, ed. by Thomas A. Sebeok, pp. 3–25. Bloomington: Indiana University Press.
Lilly, John Cunningham. 1963. "Productive and Creative Research with Man and Dolphin." *Archives of General Psychiatry* 8:111–116.
———. 1967. *The Mind of the Dolphin: A Nonhuman Intelligence*. Garden City, N.Y.: Doubleday.
Limber, John. 1977. "Language in Child and Chimp?" *American Psychologist* 32:280–295.
Lindauer, Martin. 1961. *Communication among Social Bees*. Cambridge: Harvard University Press.
Linden, Eugene. 1976. *Apes, Men, and Language*. New York: Penguin Books.
Ljung, Magnus. 1965. "Principles of a Stratificational Analysis of the Plains Sign Language." *International Journal of American Linguistics* 31:119–127. [Corrected version in D. J. Umiker-Sebeok and T. A. Sebeok (eds.) 1978.]
Locke, John. 1975 [1690]. *An Essay Concerning Human Understanding*, ed. by Peter H. Nidditch. Oxford: Clarendon.
Long, Stephen Harriman. 1823. *Account of an Expedition from Pittsburgh to the Rocky Mountains* 1:378–394. Ann Arbor: University Microfilms.
Lore, Richard, and Kevin Flannelly. 1977. "Rat Societies." *Scientific American* 236:106–116.
Lorenz, Konrad. 1965 [1935]. *Über tierisches und menschliches Verhalten: Aus dem Werdegang der Verhaltenslehre* 1. Munich: R. Piper.
———. 1966. "Evolution of Ritualization in the Biological and Cultural Spheres." *Philosophical Transactions of the Royal Society of London* 251:273–284.
———. 1971. *Studies in Animal and Human Behaviour* 2. Cambridge: Harvard University Press.
———. 1977. *Behind the Mirror: A Search for a Natural History of Human Knowledge*. New York: Harcourt Brace Jovanovich.
Lott, D. F., and R. Sommer. 1967. "Seating Arrangements and Status." *Journal of Personality and Social Psychology* 7:90–94.
Lotz, John. 1951. Review. *Word* 7:66–67.
———. 1956a. "Symbols Make Man." In *Frontiers of Knowledge in the Study*

of Man, ed. by Lynn White, Jr., pp. 207-231. New York: Harper & Brothers.
———. 1956b. "A Notation for the Germanic Verse Line." *Lingua* 6:1-7.
———. 1972. "A Select Bibliography on Script and Language." *Visible Speech* 6:79-80.
———. 1976. *Szonettkoszorú a nyelvről*. Budapest: Gondolat.
Love, J. R. B. 1941. "Worora Kinship Gestures." *Transactions of the Royal Society of South Australia* 65:108-109.
Lubbock, John [Lord Avebury]. 1886. "Note on the Intelligence of the Dog." *Report of the Fifty-Fifth Meeting of the British Association for the Advancement of Science*, pp. 1089-1091. London: John Murray.
Luria, Aleksandr R. 1972. *The Man with a Shattered World: The History of a Brain Wound*. New York: Basic Books.
———. 1973. "Two Kinds of Aphasic Disorders." *Linguistics* 115:57-66.
Macksey, Richard. 1970. "Lions and Squares: Opening Remarks." *The Languages of Criticism and the Sciences of Man: The Structuralist Controversy*, ed. by Richard Macksey and Eugenio Donato, pp. 1-14. Baltimore: Johns Hopkins University Press.
Maclean, John. 1896. *Canadian Savage Folk: The Native Tribes of Canada*, pp. 486-495. Toronto: William Briggs.
McCormack, William, and Stephen A. Wurm. 1976. (Eds.) *Language and Man: Anthropological Issues*. The Hague: Mouton.
McCulloch, Warren S. 1965. *Embodiments of Mind*. Cambridge: MIT Press.
McNeill, David. 1975. "Semiotic Extension." In *Information Processing and Cognition: The Loyola Symposium*, ed. by Robert L. Solso, Ch. 11. Hillsdale: Erlbaum Associates.
McPhee, John. 1973. "Theodore B. Taylor: The Curve of Binding Energy." *The New Yorker*, December 17, p. 52.
Máday, Stefan von. 1914. *Gibt es denkende Tiere?* Leipzig: Wilhelm Engelmann.
Majno, Guido. 1975. *The Healing Hand: Man and Wound in the Ancient World*. Cambridge: Harvard University Press.
Malinowski, Bronislaw. 1965 [1935]. *Coral Gardens and Their Magic II: The Language of Magic and Gardening*. Bloomington: Indiana University Press.
Mallery, Garrick. 1879. "The Sign Language of the North American Indians." *Proceedings of the American Association for the Advancement of Science* 28:493-519.
———. 1880a. "The Sign Language of the Indians of the Upper Missouri, in 1832." *American Antiquarian* 2(3):218-228.
———. 1880b. *Introduction to the Study of the Sign Language among the North American Indians as Illustrating the Gesture Speech of Mankind*. Introductions Series, 3. Washington, D.C.: U.S. Bureau of American Ethnology. [Reprinted in D. J. Umiker-Sebeok and T. A. Sebeok (eds.) 1978 1:1-76.]
———. 1880c. *A Collection of Gesture-Signs and Signals of the North American Indians with Some Comparisons*. Washington, D.C.: Bureau of American Ethnology. [Reprinted in D. J. Umiker-Sebeok and T. A. Sebeok (eds.) 1978 1:77-406.]
———. 1882. "The Gesture Speech of Man." In *Proceedings of the American*

Association for the Advancement of Science, 30th Meeting (August 1881), pp. 283–313. [Reprinted in D. J. Umiker-Sebeok and T. A. Sebeok (eds.) 1978 1:407–437.]
———. 1884. "Sign Language." *Internationale Zeitschrift für Allgemeine Sprachwissenschaft* 1:193–210.
———. 1972. *Sign Language among North American Indians Compared with That among Other Peoples and Deaf-Mutes*. The Hague: Mouton. [Original 1881, Washington, D.C.: Bureau of American Ethnology.]
Malson, Lucien. 1964. *Les Enfants sauvages: Mythe et réalité*. Paris: Union Generale d'Editions.
———. 1973. "Un entretien avec Claude Lévi-Strauss." *Le Monde*, December 8.
Marcus, Solomon. 1974. "Linguistic Structures and Generative Devices in Molecular Genetics." *Cahiers de Linguistique Théorique et Appliquée* 11:74–104.
Marcy, R. B. 1866. *Thirty Years of Army Life on the Border*, pp. 32–34. New York: Harper and Brothers, Publishers.
Marks, David, and Richard Kammann. 1977. "The Nonpsychic Powers of Uri Geller." *The Zetetic* 1(2):9–17.
Marler, Peter, and Miwako Tamura. 1962. "Song 'Dialects' in Three Populations of White-Crowned Sparrows." *The Condor* 64:368–377.
Marples, Mary J. 1965. *The Ecology of the Human Skin*. Springfield, Ill.: Charles C. Thomas.
Martin, Charles Beebe. 1931. *Herodotus: The Martin Classical Lectures I*. Cambridge: Harvard University Press.
Marx, Karl. 1961. *Capital*. Moscow: Foreign Languages Publishing House.
Matthews, W. K. 1958. "Phonetics and Phonology in Retrospect." *Lingua* 7:254–268.
Maurer, David W. 1949. *The Big Con*. New York: Pocket Books.
Mead, Margaret. 1972. "Vicissitudes of the Study of the Total Communication Process." In *Approaches to Semiotics*, ed. by Thomas A. Sebeok, et al., pp. 277–287. The Hague: Mouton.
Medawar, P. B., and J. S. Medawar. 1977. *The Life Science: Current Ideas of Biology*. New York: Harper & Row.
Meggitt, Mervyn. 1954. "Sign Language among the Walbiri of South Australia." *Oceania* 25(1/2):2–16.
Mehrabian, Albert. 1972. *Nonverbal Communication*. Chicago: Aldine, Atherton.
Mehta, V. 1971. *John Is Easy to Please: Encounters with the Written and the Spoken Word*. New York: Farrar, Straus & Giroux.
Merton, Robert K. 1948. "The Self-Fulfilling Prophecy." *Antioch Review* 8:193–210.
Meunier, J. 1968. "L'Episode d'Adraste." *Didaskalikon* 23:1–12.
Michener, C. D. 1974. *The Social Behavior of the Bees*. Cambridge: Belknap Press of Harvard University Press.
Miller, James G. 1975–1976. "The Nature of Living Systems." *Behavioral Science* 20:343–535; 21:295–468.
———. 1976. "Second Annual Ludwig von Bertalanffy Memorial Lecture." *Behavioral Science* 21:219–227.

Miller, Molly. 1963. "The Herodotean Croesus." *Klio* 41:58–94.
Miller, Wick R. 1978. "A Report on the Sign Language of the Western Desert (Australia)." In D. J. Umiker-Sebeok and T. A. Sebeok (eds.) 1978, 2:435–440.
Moertel, Charles G., William F. Taylor, Arthur Roth, and Francis A. J. Tyce. 1976. "Who Responds to Sugar Pills?" *Mayo Clinic Proceedings* 51: 96–100.
Moles, Abraham A. 1964. "Les Voies cutanées, compléments informationnels de la sensibilité de l'organisme." *Studium Generale* 17:589–595.
Montagu, Ashley. 1971. *Touching: The Human Significance of the Skin*. New York: Columbia University Press.
Montague, Richard. 1974. *Formal Philosophy*, ed. by Richmond H. Thomason. New Haven: Yale University Press.
Morris, Charles. 1946. *Signs, Language and Behavior*. New York: Prentice-Hall.

———. 1964. *Signification and Significance: A Study of the Relations of Signs and Values*. Cambridge: MIT Press.

———. 1971. *Writings on the General Theory of Signs*. The Hague: Mouton.

———. 1976. *Image*. New York: Vantage Press.
Morris, Desmond. 1962. *The Biology of Art*. London: Methuen.

———. 1977. *Manwatching: A Field Guide to Human Behavior*. New York: Harry N. Abrams.
Mounin, Georges. 1973. "Une analyse du langage par gestes des Indiens (1881)." *Semiotica* 7:154–162.
Mountford, Charles P. 1938. "Gesture Language of the Ngada Tribe of the Warburton Ranges, Western Australia." *Oceania* 9(2):152–155.

———. 1949. "Gesture Language of the Walpari Tribe, Central Australia." *Transactions of the Royal Society of South Australia* 73:100–101.
Moynihan, Martin. 1975. "Conservatism of Displays and Comparable Stereotyped Patterns among Cephalopods." In *Function and Evolution in Behaviour*, ed. by Gerard Baerends, Colin Beer, and Aubrey Manning, Ch. 13. Oxford: Clarendon Press.
Nagel, Ernest. 1959. Review. *Scientific American* 200:185–192.
Nattiez, Jean-Jacques. 1975. *Fondements d'une sémiologie de la musique*. Paris: Union Générale d'Editions.
Nelson, Keith. 1973. "Does the Holistic Study of Behavior Have a Future?" In *Perspectives in Ethology*, ed. by P. P. G. Bateson and Peter Klopfer, Ch. 8. New York: Plenum.
Neuburger, Max. 1906. *Geschichte der Medizin* I. Stuttgart: Ferdinand Enke.
Nöth, W. 1972. *Strukturen des Happenings*. Hildesheim: Olms.
Nottebohm, Fernando. 1970. "Ontogeny of Bird Song." *Science* 167:948–956.

———. 1975. "A Zoologist's View of Some Language Phenomena with Particular emphasis on Vocal Learning." In *Foundations of Language Development: A Multidisciplinary Approach*, ed. by E. H. Lenneberg and E. Lenneberg, 1:61–103.
Oléron, P. 1974. *Eléments de répertoire du langage gestuel des sourds-muets*. Paris: Centre National de la Recherche Scientifique.
Orne, Martin T. 1959. "The Nature of Hypnosis: Artifact and Essence." *Journal of Abnormal and Social Psychology* 58:277–299.

Ornstein, Robert E. 1972. *The Psychology of Consciousness.* New York: The Viking Press.
Osgood, C. E., and T. A. Sebeok. 1965 [1934]. (Eds.) *Psycholinguistics: A Survey of Theory and Research Problems.* Bloomington: Indiana University Press.
Osmond-Smith, David. 1975. "L'Iconisme formel: Pour une typologie des transformations musicales." *Semiotica* 15:33–47.
Oyer, Herbert J., and E. Jane Oyer. 1976. (Eds.) *Aging and Communication.* Baltimore: University Park Press.
Paredes, J. Anthony, and Marcus J. Hepburn. 1976. "The Split Brain and the Culture-and-Cognition Paradox." *Current Anthropology* 17:121–127. Discussion: ibid.: 318–326, 503–511.
Parker, William Riley. 1966. "'Introduction' to John Lotz." In *The Uralic and Altaic Program of the American Council of Learned Societies (1959–1965)*, pp. 8–9. I. U. Uralic and Altaic Series, vol. 63.
Partee, Barbara H. Forthcoming. "Montague Grammar and Issues of Psychological Reality." In *Language and Psychotherapy*, ed. Raphael Stern. New York: Haven Press.
Patterson, Francine G. 1977. "Linguistic Capabilities of a Young Lowland Gorilla." In *Sign Language and Language Acquisition in Man and Ape: New Dimensions in Comparative Pedolinguistics*, ed. Fred C. C. Peng. Boulder: Westview Press.
Payne, Roger S., and Scott McVay. 1971. "Songs of the Humpback Whales." *Science* 173:587–597.
Peirce, Charles Sanders. 1867. "On a New List of Categories." *Proceedings of the American Academy of Arts and Sciences* 7:287–298.
———. 1899. [Anonymous.] Review of Gilman 1899. *The Nation* 69:455 (December 14).
———. 1929. "Guessing." *The Hound and Horn* 2:267–282.
———. 1935–1966. *Collected Papers of Charles Sanders Peirce*, ed. by Charles Hartshorne, Paul Weiss, and Arthur W. Burks. Cambridge: Harvard University Press. [References are to volumes and paragraphs, not pages.]
———. 1976. *The New Elements of Mathematics*, ed. Carolyn Eisele. The Hague: Mouton.
Peng, Fred C. C. 1977. "Sign Language and Culture." *Sociolinguistics Newsletter* 8(1):28–29.
Perry, Ralph Barton. 1935. *The Thought and Character of William James* 2. Boston: Little, Brown.
Pfungst, Oskar. 1965 [1911]. *Clever Hans (The Horse of Mr. von Osten)*, ed. by Robert Rosenthal. New York: Holt, Rinehart and Winston.
Phillips, D. C. 1976. *Holistic Thought in Social Science.* Stanford: Stanford University Press.
Philodemus. 1941. *On Methods of Inference: A Study in Ancient Empiricism*, ed. by Phillip Howard De Lacy and Estelle Allen De Lacy. *Philological Monographs* 10. Philadelphia: American Philological Association.
Piaget, Jean. 1970. *The Place of the Sciences of Man in the System of Sciences.* New York: Harper & Row.
Pierce, John R., and Edward E. David, Jr. 1958. *Man's World of Sound.* Garden City, N.Y.: Doubleday.

Pike, Kenneth L. 1943. *Phonetics: A Critical Analysis of Phonetic Theory and Technic for the Practical Description of Sound.* Ann Arbor: University of Michigan Press.
——. 1967. *Language in Relation to a Unified Theory of the Structure of Human Behavior.* 2d ed. The Hague: Mouton.
Pilisuk, Mark, Barbara Brandes, and Didier van der Hove. 1976. "Deceptive Sounds: Illicit Communication in the Laboratory." *Behavioral Science* 21:515–523.
Pliner, Patricia, Lester Krames, and Thomas Alloway. 1975. (Eds.) *Nonverbal Communication of Aggression.* New York: Plenum Press.
Polanyi, Michael. 1958. *Personal Knowledge: Towards a Post-Critical Philosophy.* Chicago: University of Chicago Press.
Ponnamperuma, Cyril, and Alistair G. W. Cameron. 1974. (Eds.) *Interstellar Communication: Scientific Perspectives.* Boston: Houghton Mifflin.
Ponzio, Augusto. 1976. *La semiotica in Italia: Fondamenti teorici.* Bari: Dedalo Libri.
Popper, Karl. 1972. *Objective Knowledge: An Evolutionary Approach.* Oxford: Clarendon.
Posinsky, S. H. 1961. "The Case of John Tarmon: Telepathy and the Law." *Psychiatric Quarterly* 35:165–166.
Poyatos, Fernando. 1976. *Man beyond Words: Theory and Methodology of Nonverbal Communication.* Oswego: New York State English Council.
Pratt, J. Gaither. 1973. *ESP Research Today: A Study of Developments in Parapsychology since 1960.* Metuchen: Scarecrow Press.
Prelog, Vladimir. 1976. "Chirality in Chemistry." *Science* 193:17–24.
Premack, Ann J. 1976. *Why Chimps Can Read.* New York: Harper & Row.
Premack, David. 1971. "Language in Chimpanzee?" *Science* 172:808–822.
Pribram, Karl H. 1971. *Languages of the Brain.* Englewood Cliffs, N.J.: Prentice-Hall.
Prieto, Luis J. 1975. *Etudes de linguistique et de sémiologie générales.* Geneva: Librairie Droz.
Radet, Georges. 1893. *Lydie et le monde Grec au temps des Mermnades (687–546).* Paris: Thorin & Fils.
Ray, Verne F. 1933. *The Sanpoil and Nespelem: Salishan Peoples of N. E. Washington.* University of Washington Publications 5:122–123. Seattle: University of Washington Press.
Razran, Gregory. 1958. "Pavlov and Lamarck." *Science* 128:758–760.
——. 1959. "Pavlov the Empiricist." *Science* 130:916–917.
Rhine, Louisa E. 1970. *Mind over Matter: Psychokinesis.* New York: Macmillan.
Rinn, Joseph F. 1950. *Sixty Years of Psychical Research.* New York: Truth Seeker.
Roberts, Don. 1973. *The Existential Graphs of Charles S. Peirce.* The Hague: Mouton.
Romains, Jules. 1920. *La Vision: Extra-rétinienne et le sens paroptique; recherches de psychophysiologie expérimentale et de physiologie histologique.* Paris: Nouvelle Revue Française.
Romeo, Luigi. 1976. "Heraclitus and the Foundations of Semiotics." *VS: Quaderni di Studi Semiotici* 15:73–90.
Rose, Steven. 1973. *The Conscious Brain.* New York: Alfred A. Knopf.

Rosenthal, Robert. 1966. *Experimenter Effects in Behavioral Research.* New York: Appleton-Century-Crofts.
———. 1976. *Experimenter Effects in Behavioral Research.* New York: Halsted Press.
Rosenthal, Robert, and Lenore Jacobson. 1968. *Pygmalion in the Classroom: Teacher Expectation and Pupils' Intellectual Development.* New York: Holt, Rinehart, and Winston.
Roth, Walter E. 1897. "The Expression of Ideas by Manual Signs: A Sign-Language." *Ethnological Studies among the North-West-Central Queensland Aborigines,* pp. 71–90. London: Queensland Agent-General's Office.
———. 1908–1910. "Signals on the Road: Gesture Language." *North Queensland Ethnography. Australian Museum Records* 7:82–93.
Roussel, Philippe. 1927. "Hérodot et l'expédition des Perses contre Delphes." *Revue des Etudes Anciennes* 29:337–340.
Ruesch, Jurgen. 1972. *Semiotic Approaches to Human Relations.* The Hague: Mouton.
Ruesch, Jurgen, and Weldon Kees. 1956. *Nonverbal Communication: Notes on the Visual Perception of Human Relations.* Berkeley and Los Angeles: University of California Press.
Rumbaugh, Duane M. 1977. (Ed.) *Language Learning by a Chimpanzee: The Lana Project.* New York: Academic Press.
Rumbaugh, Duane M., and Timothy V. Gill. 1976a. "Language and the Acquisition of Language-Type Skills by a Chimpanzee (*Pan*)." *Annals of the New York Academy of Sciences* 270:90–123.
———. 1976b. "The Mastery of Language-Type Skills by the Chimpanzee (*Pan*)." *Annals of the New York Academy of Sciences* 280:562–578.
Russell, Edward S. 1916. *Form and Function: A Contribution to the History of Animal Morphology.* London: John Murray.
Sakitt, Barbara. 1975. "Locus of Short-Term Visual Storage." *Science* 190:1318–1319.
Samarin, W. J. 1972. *Tongues of Men and Angels: The Religious Language of Pentacostalism.* New York.
Sapir, Edward. 1931. "Communication." In *Encyclopedia of the Social Sciences* 4:78–81. New York: Macmillan.
Sarbin, Theodore R., and William C. Coe. 1972. *Hypnosis: A Social Psychological Analysis of Influence Communication.* New York: Holt, Rinehart and Winston.
Sarton, George. 1954. *Galen of Pergamon.* Lawrence: University of Kansas Press.
Saussure, Ferdinand de. 1967. *Cours de Linguistique Generale,* ed. by Rudolf Engler. Wiesbaden: Otto Harrassowitz.
Sayce, A. H. 1880. "Sign Language among the American Indians." *Nature* 22 (553):93–94.
Sayce, James. 1883. *Commentary on the Text of Herodotus.* Oxford: Oxford University Press.
Scharf, Joachim-Hermann. 1975. "Bemerkenswertes zur Geschichte der Biolinguistik und des sogenannten Sprach-DARWINismus als Einführung in das Thema 'Aspekte der Evolution menschlicher Kultur.'" In *Evolution,* ed. by Joachim-Hermann Scharf. *Nova Acta Leopoldina*

42(218):323–341. Halle/Saale: Deutsche Akademie der Naturforscher Leopoldina.
Scherer, Klaus R. 1970. *Non-verbale Kommunikation: Ansätze zur Beobachtung und Analyse der aussersprachlichen Aspekte von Interaktionsverhalten.* Hamburg: Helmut Buske.
Schmeck, Harold M., Jr. 1974. *Immunology: The Many-Edged Sword.* New York: Braziller.
Schneirla, Theodore C. 1965. "Aspects of Stimulation and Organization in Approach/Withdrawal Processes Underlying Vertebrate Behavioral Development." *Advances in the Study of Behavior* 1:1–74.
Schutz, Noel W., Jr. 1976. *Kinesiology: The Articulation of Movement.* Lisse: Peter de Ridder Press.
Schwabl, Hans. 1969. "Herodot als Historiker und Erzähler." *Gymnasium* 76:253–272.
Schwimmer, E. 1977. "Semiotics and Culture." In *A Perfusion of Signs*, ed. by Thomas A. Sebeok. Bloomington: Indiana University Press.
Scott, Hugh Lennox. 1898. "The Sign Language of the Plains Indians." *Archives of the International Folk-lore Association* 1:206–220.
———. 1934. *Film Dictionary of the North American Indian Sign Language.* National Archives, Washington, D.C.
Sebeok, Thomas A. 1943. Review of John Lotz, *Das Ungarische Sprachsystem*. *Language* 19:55–58.
———. 1947. Review of Laziczius 1944. *Language* 23:75–76.
———. 1960. (Ed.) *Style in Language.* New York: Wiley.
———. 1963. "Communication in Animals and Men." *Language* 39:448–466.
———. 1965a. "Animal Communication." *Science* 147:1006–1014.
———. 1965b. Review of Roman Jakobson, *Selected Writings I: Phonological Studies*. *Language* 41:77–88.
———. 1966a. *Portraits of Linguists: A Biographical Source Book for the History of Western Linguistics, 1746–1963.* Bloomington: Indiana University Press.
———. 1966b. (Ed.) *Selected Writings of Gyula Laziczius.* Janua Linguarum, Series Minor 55. The Hague: Mouton.
———. 1968. (Ed.) *Animal Communication: Techniques of Study and Results of Research.* Bloomington: Indiana University Press.
———. 1970. "Is a Comparative Semiotics Possible?" In *Exchange and Communications, in Honour of C. Lévi-Strauss' 60th Birthday*, ed. by Pierre Maranda and Jean Pouillon, pp. 614–627. The Hague: Mouton.
———. 1972. *Perspectives in Zoosemiotics.* The Hague: Mouton.
———. 1974a. *Structure and Texture.* The Hague: Mouton.
———. 1974b. (Ed.) *Current Trends in Linguistics 12: Linguistics and Adjacent Arts and Sciences.* The Hague: Mouton.
———. 1974c. "Az állati kommunikáció." In *A nyelv keletkezése*, ed. by Maria Papp, pp. 191–212. Budapest: Kossuth.
———. 1975a. (Ed.) *The Tell-Tale Sign: A Survey of Semiotics.* Lisse: Peter de Ridder Press.
———. 1975b. "The Pertinence of Peirce to Linguistics." Presidential Address delivered to the Linguistic Society of America, San Francisco, December 30.

———. 1975–1976. "The Semiotic Web: A Chronicle of Prejudices." *Bulletin of Literary Semiotics* 2:1–65; 3:25–28.
———. 1976. *Contributions to the Doctrine of Signs*. Lisse: Peter de Ridder Press.
———. 1977a. (Ed.) *How Animals Communicate*. Bloomington: Indiana University Press.
———. 1977b. (Ed.) *A Perfusion of Signs*. Bloomington: Indiana University Press.
———. 1977c. Reply. *Current Anthropology* 18:361–362.
———. 1978a. *Sight, Sound, and Sense*. Bloomington: Indiana University Press.
———. 1978b. "'Clever Hans' in a Semiotic Frame." *Diogenes* 28.
Sebeok, Thomas A., Alfred S. Hayes, and Mary Catherine Bateson. 1964. (Eds.) *Approaches to Semiotics*. The Hague: Mouton.
Sebeok, Thomas A., and Donna Jean Umiker-Sebeok. 1976. (Eds.) *Speech Surrogates: Drum and Whistle Systems*. The Hague: Mouton.
———. 1979. "'You Know My Method'—A Juxtaposition of Charles S. Peirce and Sherlock Holmes." *Semiotica* 29.
———. Forthcoming. *What the Speechless Creatures Say*. Bloomington: Indiana University Press.
Segal, Charles. 1971. "Croesus on the Pyre: Herodotus and Bacchylides." *Wiener Studien* 84:39–71.
Seligmann, C. G., and A. Wilkin. 1907. "The Gesture Language of the Western Islanders." *Reports of the Cambridge Anthropological Expedition to Torres Straits* 3 (*Linguistics*), ed. by A. C. Haddon, pp. 255–260. London: Cambridge University Press.
Seton, Ernest Thompson. 1918. *Sign Talk: A Universal Signal Code, without Apparatus, for Use in the Army, Navy, Camping, Hunting, and Daily Life: The Gesture Language of the Cheyenne Indians*. Garden City, N.Y.: Doubleday, Page, and Co.
Shands, Harley C. 1971. *The War with Words: Structure and Transcendence*. The Hague: Mouton.
———. 1976. "Malinowski's Mirror: Emily Dickinson as Narcissus." *Contemporary Psychoanalysis* 12:300–334.
Shands, Harley C., and James D. Meltzer. 1975. "Clinical Semiotics." *Language Sciences* 38:21–24.
———. 1977. "Unexpected Semiotic Implications of Medical Inquiry." In *A Perfusion of Signs*, ed. by Thomas A. Sebeok, pp. 77–89. Bloomington: Indiana University Press.
Shapiro, Arthur K. 1960. "A Contribution to a History of the Placebo Effect." *Behavioral Science* 5:109–135.
Shapiro, Gary. 1975. "Intention and Interpretation in Art: A Semiotic Analysis." *Journal of Aesthetics and Art Criticism* 33:33–42.
Shaumjan, Sebastian K. 1976. "Linguistics as a Part of Semiotics." *Forum Linguisticum* 1:60–66.
Sheehan, Peter W., and Campbell W. Perry. 1976. *Methodologies of Hypnosis: A Critical Appraisal of Contemporary Paradigms of Hypnosis*. Hillsdale, N.J.: Erlbaum.
Sigerist, Henry E. 1961. *A History of Medicine* 2. New York: Oxford University Press.

Simone, Raffaele. 1972. "Sémiologie augustinienne." *Semiotica* 6:1–31.
Simpson, George Gaylord. 1966. "The Biological Nature of Man." *Science* 152:472–478.
Sinclair, Upton. 1930. *Mental Radio*. Pasadena: Upton Sinclair.
Smith, W. John. 1977. *The Behavior of Communicating: An Ethological Approach*. Cambridge: Harvard University Press.
Smith, W. John, et al. 1974. "Tongue Showing: A Facial Display of Humans and Other Primate Species." *Semiotica* 11:201–246.
Snell, Bruno. 1973. "Gyges and Kroisos als Tragödien-Figuren." *Zeitschrift für Papyrologie und Epigraphik* 12:197–205.
Speigelberg, Wilhelm. 1927. *The Credibility of Herodotus' Account of Egypt in the Light of Egyptian Monuments*, trans. by A. M. Blackmann. Oxford: Blackwell.
Spencer, Baldwin, and F. J. Gillen. 1927. *The Arunta: A Study of a Stone Age People* 2:600–608. London: Macmillan and Co.
Stafford, Philip B. 1977. "The Semiotics of Old Age in a Small Midwestern Town: An Interactionist Approach." Ph.D. dissertation. Indiana University, Bloomington.
Stanislavsky, K. 1959. *My Life in Art*. Moscow: Foreign Languages Publishing House.
Steiner, George. 1971. *Extraterritorial: Papers on Literature and the Language Revolution*. New York: Atheneum.
———. 1975. *After Babel: Aspects of Language and Translation*. New York: Oxford University Press.
Stepanov, Yuri S. 1971. *Semiotika*. Moscow: Nauka.
Stern, Theodore. 1957. "Drum and Whistle 'Languages': An Analysis of Speech Surrogates." *American Anthropologist* 59:487–506.
Stewart, Ian. 1975. "The Seven Elementary Catastrophes." *New Scientist* 68:447–454.
Stirling, Edward C. 1896. "Gesture or Sign Language." *Report on the Work of the Horne Scientific Expedition* 4:111–125.
Stokoe, William C., Jr. 1972. *Semiotics and Human Sign Languages*. The Hague: Mouton.
———. 1974a. "Motor Signs as the First Form of Language." *Semiotica* 10:117–130.
———. 1974b. "Classification and Description of Sign Languages." In *Current Trends in Linguistics* 12, ed. by Thomas A. Sebeok, pp. 345–372. The Hague: Mouton.
———. 1977. "First Hand Reporting from the Field . . ." *Signs for Our Times* 46:1.
Stratton, George M. 1921. "The Control of Another Person by Obscure Signs." *Psychological Review* 28:301–314.
Strehlow, Carl. 1978. "The Sign Language of the Aranda." In D. J. Umiker-Sebeok and T. A. Sebeok (Eds.) 1978 2:349–370. [English translation by C. Chewings and D. J. Umiker-Sebeok of original German version, 1915. *Die Aranda- und Loritjastämme in Zentral-Australien* 4(2):54–78. Frankfurt am Main: Joseph Baer & Co.]
Strong, Herbert A., Willem S. Logeman, and Benjamin Ide Wheeler. 1891. *Introduction to the Study of Language*. London: Longmans, Green, & Co.

Szőke, Péter. 1963. "Ornitomuzikológia." *Magyar Tudomány* 9:592–607.
Taylor, Allan R. 1975. "Nonverbal Communications Systems in Native North America." *Semiotica* 13:329–374.
———. 1978. "Nonverbal Communication in Aboriginal North America: The Plains Sign Language." In D. J. Umiker-Sebeok and T. A. Sebeok (eds.) 1978, 2:223–244.
Teit, James A. 1930. *The Salishan Tribes of the Western Plateaus*. In Forty-Fifth Annual Report of the United States Bureau of American Ethnology, pp. 135–150, 261, 373, 396. Washington, D.C.: Smithsonian Institution.
Temerlin, Maurice K. 1975. *Lucy: Growing Up Human*. Palo Alto: Science and Behavior Books, Inc.
Temkin, Oswei. 1973. *Galenism: Rise and Decline of a Medical Philosophy*. Ithaca: Cornell University Press.
Terrace, H. S., and T. G. Bever. 1976. "What Might Be Learned from Studying Language in the Chimpanzee? The Importance of Symbolizing Oneself." In *Origins and Evolution of Language and Speech*, ed. by Stevan R. Harnad, Horst B. Steklis, and Jane Lancaster. *Annals of the New York Academy of Sciences* 280:579–588.
Thibaud, Pierre. 1975. *La Logique de Charles Sanders Peirce: De l'algèbre aux graphes*. Aix-en-Provence: Université de Provence.
Thielcke, Gerhard. 1969. "Geographic Variation in Bird Vocalizations." In *Bird Vocalizations: Their Relations to Current Problems in Biology and Psychology*, ed. by R. A. Hinde, pp. 311–339. Cambridge: Cambridge University Press.
Thom, René. 1968. "Topologie et signification." *Age de la Science* 4:219–242.
———. 1970. "Topologie et linguistique." In *Essays in Topology and Related Topics*, ed. by Andre Laefliger and Raghavan Narasimhan, pp. 226–247. New York: Springer-Verlag.
———. 1973. "De l'icone au symbole: Esquisse d'une théorie du symbolisme." *Cahiers Internationaux de Symbolisme* 22/23:85–106.
———. 1974a. *Modèles mathématiques de la morphogenèse: Recueil de textes sur la théorie des catastrophes et ses applications*. Paris: Union Générale d'Editions.
———. 1974b. "La Linguistique, discipline morphologique exemplaire." *Critique* 30:235–245.
———. 1975a. *Structural Stability and Morphogenesis: An Outline of a General Theory of Models*. Reading: W. A. Benjamin.
———. 1975b. "Les Mathématiques et l'intelligible." *Dialectica* 29:71–80.
Thomas, Lewis. 1974. *The Lives of a Cell: Notes of a Biology Watcher*. New York: Viking.
———. 1976. "Most Things Get Better by Themselves." *New York Times Magazine*, July 4.
Thomson, J. A. K. 1934. *The Art of the Logos*. Cambridge: Harvard University Press.
Thomson, J. Arthur. 1924. "Zoology (Animal Behaviour)." In *The Life-Work of Lord Avebury (Sir John Lubbock)*, pp. 115–156. London: Watt.
Timaeus, Ernst. 1973. "Some Non-Verbal and Paralinguistic Cues as Mediators of Experimenter Expectancy Effects." In *Social Communication*

and Movement: Studies of Interaction and Expression in Man and Chimpanzee, ed. by Mario von Cranach and Ian Vine, Ch. 11. New York: Academic Press.
Tinbergen, E. A., and N. Tinbergen. 1972. "Early Childhood Autism: An Ethological Approach." *Journal of Comparative Ethology*, Supplement 10. Berlin: Paul Parey.
Tinbergen, Niko. 1963. "On Aims and Methods of Ethology." *Zeitschrift für Tierpsychologie* 20:410–433.
Tomkins, Gordon M. 1975. "The Metabolic Code." *Science* 189:760–763.
Tomkins, William. 1929. *Universal Indian Sign Language of the Plains Indians of North America*. San Diego: William Tomkins. [Reprinted 1969, New York: Dover Press.]
Trubetzkoy, Nikolaj Sergeevič. 1939. "Phonologie und Lautstilistik." In *Grundzüge der Phonologie*, pp. 17–29. Prague.
Truzzi, Marcello. 1977. Review of de Mille 1976. *The Zetetic* 1/2:86–87.
Tunnell, Gary G. 1973. *Culture and Biology: Becoming Human*. Minneapolis: Burges Publishing Co.
Turner, Victor. 1975. "Symbolic Studies." *Annual Review of Anthropology* 4: 145–161.
Tuteur, Werner. 1957–1958. "The 'Double-Blind' Method: Its Pitfalls and Fallacies." *American Journal of Psychiatry* 114:921–922.
Uexküll, Gudrun von. 1964. *Jakob von Uexküll: Seine Welt und seine Umwelt*. Hamburg: Christian Wegner.
Uexküll, Jakob von. 1926. *Theoretical Biology*. New York: Harcourt, Brace & Co.
———. 1935. "Der Kampf um den Himmel." In *Neue Rundschau*, pp. 367–377. Frankfurt am Main: S. Fischer.
———. 1936. *Niegeschaute Welten: Die Umwelten meiner Freunde: Ein Errinerungsbuch*. Berlin: Suhrkamp.
———. 1940. "Bedeutungslehre." *Bios* 10.
———. 1957 [1934]. *A Stroll through the Worlds of Animals and Men: A Picture Book of Invisible Worlds*. In *Instinctive Behavior: The Development of a Modern Concept*, trans. and ed. by Claire H. Schiller. New York: International Universities Press.
———. 1970 [1934] [1940]. *Streifzüge durch die Umwelten von Tieren und Menschen: Ein Bilderbuch unsichtbaren Welten* (illustrated by Georg Kriszat); and *Bedeutungslehre*. Frankfurt am Main: S. Fischer. [The 1934 monograph appeared in English, in 1957, translated and edited by Claire H. Schiller, in *Instinctive Behavior: The Development of a Modern Concept* (New York: International Universities Press), pp. 5–80. The 1940 monograph also appeared in French, in 1956, titled *Théorie de la signification* (Paris: Gonthier).]
Uexküll, Thure von. 1978. "Terminological Problems of Medical Semiotics." In *Semiotik III: Zeichentypologie*, ed. by Tasso Borbé. Munich: Wilhelm Fink.
———. In press. "Krankheitsymptome als Übersetzungsfehler—Verbalisierung nonverbaler Kommunikationen als Problem einer Semiotik der Heilkunde." Paper presented at the II. Wiener Symposium über Semiotik, June 5, 1976.
Ullman, I. M. 1975. *Psycholinguistik—Psychosemiotik*. Göttingen.

Umiker-Sebeok, D. Jean. 1974. "Speech Surrogates: Drum and Whistle Systems." In *Current Trends in Linguistics 12: Linguistics and Adjacent Arts and Sciences*, ed. by Thomas A. Sebeok, pp. 497–536. The Hague: Mouton.
———. 1977a. "Semiotics of Culture: Great Britain and North America." *Annual Review of Anthropology* 6:121–135.
———. 1977b. "Nature's Way? Visual Representations of American Life Cycles." To appear in *Semiotica* 28 (1979).
———. 1978. "You're Only as Old as You Look: Age Displays in American Culture." Unpublished ms.
Umiker-Sebeok, D. Jean, and Thomas A. Sebeok. 1978. (Eds.) *Aboriginal Sign Languages of the Americas and Australia*. 2 vols. New York: Plenum Press.
Vachek, J. 1966. *The Linguistic School of Prague: An Introduction to Its Theory and Practice*. Bloomington: Indiana University Press.
Valesio, Paolo. 1969. "Icons and Patterns in the Structure of Language." *Actes du Xe Congrès International des Linguistes* 1:383–387.
Veltruský, Jiří. 1976 [1973]. "Some Aspects of the Pictorial Sign." In *Semiotics of Art: Prague School Contributions*, ed. by Ladislav Matejka and Irwin R. Titunik, pp. 245–264. Cambridge: MIT Press.
Verne, Jules. 1901. *Le Village aérien*. Paris: Collection Hetzel.
Voegelin, Carl F. 1960. "Subsystem Typology in Linguistics." In *Man and Cultures: Selected Papers*, ed. by Anthony F. C. Wallace, pp. 202–206. Philadelphia: University of Pennsylvania Press.
———. 1972. "Sign Language Analysis: On One Level or Two?" In *Sign Language among North American Indians . . .* , ed. by Garrick Mallery, pp. xxxv–xliii. [Original version, 1958, *International Journal of American Linguistics* 24:71–77.]
Voegelin, Charles F., and Zellig S. Harris. 1947. "The Scope of Linguistics." *American Anthropologist* 49:588–600.
Vogt, Evon A., and Ray Hyman. 1959. *Water Witching U. S. A.* Chicago: University of Chicago Press.
Voigt, Vilmos. 1977. *Bevezetés a szemiotikába*. Budapest: Gondolat.
Vološinov, Valentin N. 1973. *Marxism and the Philosophy of Language*. New York: Seminar Press.
Vygotsky, Lev Semenovich. 1962. *Thought and Language*. Ed. and trans. by E. Hanfmann and G. Vakar. Cambridge: MIT Press.
Wade, Nicholas. 1977. "Scandal in the Heavens: Renowned Astronomer Accused of Fraud." *Science* 198:707–709.
Wagoner, David. 1976. "The Literature of Legerdemain." *Times Literary Supplement*, no. 3, 902, December 24, pp. 1598–1599.
Walker, Jerell R. 1953–1954. "The Sign Language of the Plains Indians of North America." *Chronicles of Oklahoma* 31(2):168–177.
Wallis, Mieczysław. 1975. "On Iconic Signs." In *Arts and Signs. Studies in Semiotics* 2:1–19. Bloomington: Research Center for Language and Semiotic Studies.
Warner, W. Lloyd, 1937. *A Black Civilization*, pp. 515–518. New York: Harper and Row Publishers, Inc.
Washburn, Sherwood L. 1973. "The Promise of Primatology." *American Journal of Physical Anthropology* 38:177–182.

Wassell, William H. 1896. "The Indian Sign Language." *Chataquan* 23:581–585.
Watt, W. C. 1975. "What Is the Proper Characterization of the Alphabet? I. Desiderata." *Visible Language* 9:293–327.
Webb, Walter Prescott. 1931. "Preserving the Indian Sign Language." *New York Times Magazine* 8, July 5, 1931, Section 8.
Weil, Elsie. 1931. "Preserving the Indian Sign Language." *New York Times Magazine* 8 (July 5).
Weinreich, Uriel. 1968. "Semantics and Semiotics." *International Encyclopedia of the Social Sciences* 14:164–169.
Weitman, Sasha R. 1973. "National Flags: A Sociological Overview." *Semiotica* 8:328–367.
Weitz, Shirley. 1974. (Ed.) *Nonverbal Communication: Readings with Commentary*. New York: Oxford University Press.
Weizenbaum, Joseph. 1976. *Computer Power and Human Reason*. San Francisco: W. H. Freeman.
———. 1977. "Computers as 'Therapists.'" *Science* 198:354.
Wells, Rulon. 1971. "Distinctively Human Semiotics." In *Essays in Semiotics/Essais de sémiotique*, ed. by Julia Kristeva, Josette Rey-Debove, and Donna Jean Umiker, pp. 95–119. The Hague: Mouton.
Wenner, Adrian M. 1971. *The Bee Language Controversy: An Experience in Science*. Educational Program Improvement Corporation.
Wertheimer, Max. 1967 [1923]. "Laws of Organization in Perceptual Forms." In *A Source Book of Gestalt Psychology*, ed. by Willis D. Ellis, pp. 71–88. New York: Humanities Press.
Wescott, Roger W. 1969. *The Divine Animal: An Exploration of Human Potentiality*. New York: Funk & Wagnalls.
———. 1971. "Linguistic Iconism." *Language* 47:416–428.
———. 1974. (Ed.) *Language Origins*. Silver Spring, Md.: Linstock Press.
West, La Mont, Jr. 1960. "The Sign Language: An Analysis." Ph.D. dissertation, Indiana University, Bloomington.
———. 1963. "Aboriginal Sign Language: A Statement." In *Australian Aboriginal Studies*, ed. by W. E. H. Stanner and Helen Sheils, pp. 159–165. London: Oxford University Press.
White, M. E. 1969. "Herodotus' Starting Point." *Phoenix* 23:39–48.
Whitfield, Francis. 1969. "Glossematics." In *Linguistics Today*, ed. by Archibald A. Hill, pp. 250–258. New York: Basic Books.
Whitney, William Dwight. 1867. *Language and the Study of Language*. New York: Charles Scribner's Sons.
Wickler, Wolfgang. 1968. *Mimicry in Plants and Animals*. New York: McGraw-Hill.
———. 1973. *The Sexual Code*. Garden City, N.Y.: Anchor Press/Doubleday.
Wied-Neuweid, Prince Maximilian von. 1839–1841. *Reise in das Nordamerika in den Jahren 1832–1834* 2:645–653. [English version, 1906, *Travels in the Interior of North America*, 3:300–312. Cleveland: Arthur H. Clark Co.]
Wilson, Edward O. 1971. *The Insect Societies*. Cambridge: Harvard University Press.
———. 1975. *Sociobiology: The New Synthesis*. Cambridge: Harvard University Press.

Wimsatt, William R., Jr. 1954. *The Verbal Icon: Studies in the Meaning of Poetry*. New York: University of Kentucky Press.

Wing, Lorna. 1976. (Ed.) *Early Childhood Autism: Clinical, Educational and Social Aspects*. Oxford: Pergamon Press.

Winner, Irene Portis, and Thomas G. Winner. 1976. "The Semiotics of Cultural Texts." *Semiotica* 18:101–156.

Wittgenstein, Ludwig. 1953. *Philosophische Untersuchungen*. Oxford: Basil Blackwell.

Wolfe, John B. 1936. "Effectiveness of Token-Rewards for Chimpanzees." *Comparative Psychology Monograph* 12(5).

Wood, Forrest G. 1973. *Marine Mammals and Man: The Navy's Porpoises and Sea Lions*. Washington D.C.: Robert B. Luce.

Wormell, Donald Ernest Wilson. 1963. "Croesus and the Delphic Oracle." *Hermathena* 97:2–22.

Young, John Z. 1977. *What Squids and Octopuses Tell Us about Brains and Memories*. Forty-Sixth James Arthur Lecture on the Evolution of the Human Brain. New York: American Museum of Natural History.

Zangwill, Oliver L. 1975. "The Relation of Nonverbal Cognitive Functions to Aphasia." In *Foundations of Language Development: A Multidisciplinary Approach*, ed. by Eric H. Lenneberg and Elizabeth Lenneberg, 2, Ch. 6. New York: Academic Press.

Zeeman, E. Christopher. 1965. "Topology of the Brain." In *Mathematics and Computer Science in Biology and Medicine*, pp. 277–292. London: Her Majesty's Stationery Office.

Zeman, J. Jay. 1964. *The Graphical Logic of C. S. Peirce*. Ph.D. dissertation, University of Chicago.

Zirkle, Conway. 1958. "Pavlov's Beliefs." *Science* 128:1476.

Zorn, E. R. 1928. "Zeichensprache und Signalwesen bei den Prärieindianervölkern." *Erdball* 2:52–56.

Index of Names

Aarsleff, Hans, 32, 33, 297
Adam, 128
Aesculapius, 96
Aesop, 268
Aldis, Owen, 256, 297
Alexander, Richard D., 8, 29
Allen, Woody, 35, 52
Alloway, Thomas, 310, 317
Allwood, Martin S., 242
Alonso (character in *The Tempest*), 130
Altmann, Stuart A., 59
Aly, Wolf, 173, 297
Alyattes, 289, 290
Andrade, Manuel, 223
Angell, James R., xiv, 54
Apollo, 179
Apuleius, 90
Arbib, Michael, 60, 297
Argyle, Michael, 47, 48, 297
Aristotle, 110, 249
Armstrong, Daniel, 221n.
Armstrong, Edward A., 218, 219, 297
Arnauld, Antoine, ix–x
Aronson, Lester Ralph, 297
Atthis, 173, 174
Atys, 169, 170, 173, 174, 175, 176
Atz, James W., 32, 297
Auden, Wystan Hugh, 286
Audiat, Jean, 173, 297
Auerbach, Erich, 110
Augustine, Saint, ix, xiii, 63
Austerlitz, Robert, 293
Avebury, Lord. *See* Lubbock, John
Axtell, Juliet L., 143, 298
Ayala, Francisco José, 205, 291, 297, 302
Ayer, Alfred Jules, 111, 118, 120, 297

Baerends, Gerard, 315
Bally, Charles, 122, 297
Banks, John, 75, 76, 90
Barakat, Robert A., 38, 297
Barber, Theodore Xenophon, 98, 297
Bar-Hillel, Yehoshua, 229
Baron, Naomi S., 294
Barth, Fredrik, 61
Barth, John, 61
Barth, Karl, 61, 64
Barthes, Roland, 5, 8, 27, 52, 61, 63, 65, 259, 297
Basedow, Herbert, 141, 143, 152, 297
Bastide, Roger, 297
Bates, Henry, 116
Bateson, Gregory, 5, 41, 44, 63, 115, 200, 256, 257, 258, 297
Bateson, Mary Catherine, 292, 320
Bateson, Paul Patrick Gordon, 315
Baudoin de Courtenay, Jan, 211
Bauman, Richard, 42, 298
Bäuml, Betty J., 51, 298
Bäuml, Franz H., 51, 298
Beard, Daniel Carter, 130, 298
Beaumont, J. Graham, 312
Beck, Henry, 44, 298
Beecher, Henry K., 95, 298
Beer, Colin, 315
Beke, Ödön, 235
Bělinskij, Vissarion G., 210
Bell, Alexander Graham, 146
Bellour, Raymond, 278
Bender, Harold H., 226
Bennett, Jonathan, 286, 298
Benthall, Jonathan, 37, 41, 298
Bentley, Arthur F., 44, 265, 298
Berkeley, George, xi, xiii
Bernadete, Seth, 174, 298
Bernadette of Lourdes, 97
Berndt, Ronald M., 134, 145, 152, 298
Bernheim, Hippolyte, 191
Bertalanffy, Ludwig von, 66, 67, 68, 203, 291, 298
Berto (horse), 53
Bettetini, Gianfranco, 111
Bever, Thomas Gordon, 283, 322

Index of Names

Bierman, Arthur K., 111, 298
Bilz, Rudolf, 192, 195, 298
Bingham, N. E., 285, 298
Birdwhistell, Ray L., 4, 287, 298
Biton, 289
Blackmann, Aylward Manley, 321
Blake, Henry N., 283, 284, 298
Blakemore, Colin, 304
Blest, A. D., 9, 28, 298
Blondie (fictional character), 81
Bloomfield, Leonard, 37, 63, 75–76, 223, 224, 227, 253, 292, 298
Blum, Harold F., 119, 298
Blurton Jones, Nicholas G., 31, 58, 299
Boas, Franz, 221, 223, 227, 234, 299
Bogatyrev, Petr, 52, 229, 299
Bogen, Joseph F., 44, 56, 257, 299
Bonfante, Giuliano, 218, 299
Bonner, John Tyler, 23, 263, 299
Borbé, Tasso, 299, 323
Bosmajian, Haig A., 49, 299
Bossu, Jean Bernard, 299
Bouissac, Paul, vii–viii, 48, 52, 78, 277, 278, 282, 299
Bourne, Geoffrey H., 40, 299
Bower, Gordon H., 44, 56, 299
Brady, Erika, xvi, 168, 168n., 295
Brandes, Barbara, 317
Brannigan, Christopher R., 58, 299
Bréhier, Emile, 190, 299
Brøndal, Viggo, 226
Bronowski, Jacob, 25, 47, 299
Brothwell, Don R., 40, 299
Broughton, W. B., 256, 299
Brown, Jerram L., 217, 218, 299
Brown, Roger, 54, 58, 283, 299
Bruce, David J., 81, 299
Buffon, Georges Louis Leclerc, Comte de, 99
Bühler, Karl, 53, 187n., 210, 212, 214, 216, 217, 249, 281, 291, 300
Bullowa, Margaret, 58, 300
Bulwer, John, 287
Burghardt, Gordon M., 57
Burkhardt, Frederick, 241
Burks, Arthur W., 111, 300, 316
Burton, Richard F., 141, 300
Busnel, René-Guy, 299
Butler, Colin G., 116, 300

Butler, Samuel, xiii
Buyssens, Eric, 27, 122, 148, 149, 300
Buytendijk, Frederik J. J., 100

Caldwell, David K., 54
Caldwell, Jill, 276
Caldwell, Melba C., 54
Callan, Hilary, 31, 300
Calverley, David Smith, 98, 297
Calvet de Magalhaes, Theresa, 274, 275, 277
Cameron, Alistair G. W., 102, 297, 317
Cannon, Walter B., 96, 284, 300
Carnap, Rudolf, 36, 65, 255, 258
Casetti, Francesco, 111
Cassirer, Ernst A., 63, 67, 192, 193, 300
Cervantes, Miguel de, 283
Chambers, Robert, 76
Chance, Michael R. A., 300
Charlesworth, William R., 58, 300
Chauvin-Muckensturm, Bernadette, 81, 285, 300
Chee-Chee (dolphin), 99
Cherry, Colin, 36, 300
Chevreul, Michel Eugene, 285
Chewings, C., 321
Chomsky, Noam, xv, 32, 62, 253, 260, 261, 269, 300
Christopher, Milbourne, 54, 75, 78, 90, 95, 300
Chrysippus, ix, xiii, 187
Cicero, 168
Clair, Pierre, ix
Clark, William Philo, 130, 300
Cléobis, 289
Clever Hans. *See* Hans, Clever
Codere, Helen, 299
Cody, Iron Eyes, 130, 132, 300
Coe, William C., 96, 318
Cole, James K., 302
Columbus, Christopher, 230
Cook, James Edward, 184, 310
Cooper, Franklin S., 237, 238
Cope, Jackson I., 109, 303
Cortambert, Louise, 52, 300
Costabel, P., 79
Count, Earl W., 19, 301

Index of Names 329

Cowan, J Milton, 242
Cranach, Mario von, 323
Crane, Beverly J., 95, 303
Creak, M., 72
Critchley, Macdonald, 47, 48, 58, 301
Crito, 230
Croesus, 169–179 passim, 288, 289, 290, 295
Cromer, Richard F., 72, 301
Croneberg, Carl G., 218, 301
Crookshank, Francis Graham, 8, 190, 301
Crystal, David, 48, 50, 301
Culler, Jonathan, 27, 301
Culliton, Barbara J., 112, 301
cummings, e. e., 247
Curtiss, Susan, 37, 301
Cuvier, Georges, 8, 32, 33, 57, 269, 270
Cybele, 173
Cyrus, 171, 174, 176, 177, 179

Daisy (fictional dog), 81
Dampier, William Cecil, 6, 301
Dana, James Dwight, 184, 290
Dar (chimpanzee), 99
Darwin, Charles, 4, 31, 33, 58, 256, 269, 270, 282, 301
Dascal, Marcelo, 66, 301
Dato, Daniel P., 301
David, Edward E., Jr., 102, 316
da Vinci, Leonardo, 119
Davis, Flora, 49, 301
Dawkins, Richard, xiii
Deely, John N., vii, 274, 277
Degérando, Marie-Joseph, 122
De Lacy, Estelle Allen, 316
De Lacy, Phillip Howard, 316
De Mauro, Tullio, 185, 301
Deme, László, 291, 301
de Mille, Richard, 87, 301
Democritus, 284
Denmark, F., 304
Dennis, Maureen, 55, 301
de Quincey, Thomas, 172
DeVore, Irven, 118, 306
Diaconis, Persi, 93
Dickinson, Peter, 103
Dil, Anwar S., 305
Dillon, Wilton Sterling, 311

Dimond, Stuart J., 55, 301, 312
Dingwall, William Orr, 37, 48, 301
Disney, Walt, 268
Dobzhansky, Theodosius, 205, 291, 297, 302
Dodge, Richard Irving, 132, 140, 150, 301
Don (dog), 78, 80, 282
Donato, Eugenio, 312
Donne, John, 111
Dostoevski, Fedor, 210
Douglas, Mary, 261
Dumas, Roland, 258, 302
Dumézil, Georges, 288, 289, 302
Dunbar, William, 302
Duncan, Starkey D., Jr., 51, 302

Ebers, Hermann, 80
Ebers, Miss, 80
Eccles, John C., 54, 56, 204, 205, 206, 302
Eco, Umberto, 36, 48, 111, 112, 115, 118, 274, 275, 288, 302
Eddington, Arthur Stanley E., 119
Eddy, Mary Baker, 191, 302
Edelin, Kenneth, 112, 124
Efron, David, 51, 257, 302
Egger, Victor, 44, 302
Eibl-Eibesfeldt, Irenäus, 4, 31, 32, 60, 82, 302
Eilenberg, Samuel, 236
Eimermacher, Karl, 39, 302
Eisele, Carolyn, 122, 316
Eisenberg, Abne N., 49, 302
Eisenberg, John F., 101, 302, 310
Ekman, Paul, 4, 33, 41, 257, 275, 277, 300, 302
Eliot, Charles, 125
Ellis, Willis D., 325
Elvar (dolphin), 99, 100
Emerson, Alfred E., 124, 302
Engler, Rudolf, 318
Entwisle, Doris, 118, 308
Eschbach, Achim, 49, 303
Euthymos, 178
Evans, James Allan Stewart, 172, 288, 303
Evans, Richard J., 193, 303
Eve, 128
Eylmann, Erhard, 303

Index of Names

Fairbanks, Gordon, 240
Fairbanks, Matthew J., 62, 303
Fant, Gunnar, 237
Faraday, Michael, 285
Fay (cited by Henri de Saussure), 184
Faye, Jean Pierre, 224, 225, 226, 303
Fejos, Paul, 237, 238
Ferber, Andrew, 31
Ferguson, Charles A., 31, 60, 242, 303
Fernandez, James, 287, 303
Ferster, Charles B., 72, 303
Fichte, Johann Gottlieb, 200
Fine, Gary Alan, 95, 303
Firth, John Rupert, 223, 303
Firth, Raymond, 31, 261, 303
Fisch, Max H., 64, 94, 109, 183n., 274, 276, 277, 279, 287, 288, 290, 303
Fisher, Seymour, 96, 303
Fishman, Joshua, 308
Flanagan, Newman A., 112
Flannelly, Kevin, 82, 312
Fodor, István, 291, 303
Fónagy, Iván, 291, 292
Fonda, Claudia, 90
Foreman, Carolyn, 303
Fornara, Charles W., 168n., 169, 179, 303
Foucault, Michel, xi
Fouts, Roger S., 37, 40, 115, 303
Fox, James J., 111, 304
Frank, Jerome D., 77, 191, 304
Frazer, James George, 113, 304
Frege, Gottlob, 202, 204
Freud, Sigmund, ix, xiii, 263, 266, 304
Freudenthal, Hans, 38
Friedmann, Herbert, 14, 15, 304
Fries, Charles C., 228, 229
Friesen, Wallace V., 257, 302
Frings, Hubert, 270, 304
Frings, Mabel, 270, 304
Frisch, Karl von, 40, 124, 216, 217, 249, 304
Frisch, Peter, 175, 304
Frishberg, Nancy, 114, 304
Frolov, Iurii P., 86, 304

Galen, 7, 8, 26, 29, 71, 187, 190, 281, 304
Gandhi, Indira, 286
Gardner, Beatrice T., 81, 283, 285, 304
Gardner, Martin, 102, 122, 284, 285, 304
Gardner, Richard Allen, 81, 283, 285, 304
Garner, Richard L., 103, 268, 291, 304
Gazzaniga, Michael S., 257, 304
Geertz, Clifford, 261, 287, 304
Geller, Uri, 284
Geoffroy-Saint-Hilaire, Etienne, 8, 32, 269, 270
Gerard, Ralph W., 27, 28, 67, 304
Gill, Timothy V., 54, 200, 318
Gillen, Francis James, 141, 152, 321
Gilman, Daniel Coit, 107, 108, 109, 184, 304
Gilpatric, Chadbourne, 239
Gingerich, Owen, 87
Gipper, Helmut, 193, 203, 305
Girbal, François, ix
Glasersfeld, Ernst von, 270, 305
Gödel, Kurt, 205
Godel, Robert, 183n.
Godley, Alfred Denis, 288, 307
Goethe, Johann Wolfgang von, 201
Goffman, Erving, 31, 51, 68, 78, 266, 274, 283, 305
Goldstein, Arnold P., 192, 305
Golopenția-Eretescu, Sanda, vii, 38
Gombocz, Zoltán, 233, 252
Gombrich, Ernst H., 118, 305, 307
Gonzalo (character in *The Tempest*), 130
Good, Robert A., 264
Goodman, Nelson, 111, 305
Gordon, Paula, 275
Gould, Richard Allan, 305
Goulet, John, 103
Grace, George W., 219, 305
Graven, Jacques, 291, 305
Greenberg, Joseph H., 32, 253–261 passim, 294, 305
Gregory, Richard Langton, 307
Greimas, Algirdas Julien, 37, 305

Index of Names 331

Gribble, Charles E., 227, 230, 305
Griffin, Donald R., 40, 41, 43, 54, 200, 291, 305
Grimshaw, Polly, 275
Grinker, Roy R., 66, 263, 305
Gross, Maurice, 38
Gruenberg, Benjamin C., 73, 85, 86, 305
Gump, Richard, 98, 306
Guthrie, Russell Dale, 31, 47, 52, 306

Hachet-Souplet, Pierre, 99, 282, 306
Haddon, Alfred Cort, 152, 306, 320
Hadley, Louis F., 130, 306
Hahn, Martin E., 40, 57, 60, 306
Hailman, Jack P., 29, 134, 153, 193, 197, 306, 310
Hajdú, Péter, 208, 291, 306
Halasi-Kun, Tibor, 293
Haldane, John Burdon Sanderson, 124, 240, 291, 306
Hall, Edward T., 45, 47, 203, 306
Hall, Granville Stanley, 109
Hall, K. R. L., 118, 306
Hall, Robert Anderson, Jr., 227, 306
Hall-Craggs, Joan, 39
Halle, Morris, 237
Haller, Rudolf, 193, 306
Halliwell-Phillipps, James O., 75, 90, 306
Halporn, Barbara, 276
Hamilton, Alexander, 33
Hamilton, Allan McLane, 58, 71
Hanfmann, Eugenia, 324
Hans, Clever (horse), xiv, xv, 53, 54, 55, 74, 75, 78, 82, 83, 87, 88, 90, 91, 95, 100, 106, 192, 283, 284, 285
Hansel, Charles E. M., 285, 306
Harmatta, János, 291, 306
Harnad, Stevan R., 322
Harrington, John Peabody, 130, 135, 136, 138, 140, 143, 148, 154, 158, 159, 306
Harris, Zellig S., 49, 292, 306, 324
Harrison, Randall P., 49, 306
Hartshorne, Charles, 39, 306, 316
Haskins, Caryl P., 238
Haushalter, Dr. (cited by A. Shapiro), 191

Hauvette-Besnault, Amédée, 172, 306
Hawkes, Terence, 128, 306
Hayes, Alfred S., 292, 320
Hediger, Heini, xiv, 5, 14, 15, 17, 37, 45, 53, 55, 81, 82, 83, 99, 100, 101, 102, 203, 265, 266, 267, 270, 283, 306
Hegel, Georg Wilhelm Friedrich, 175, 210
Heifitz, Milton D., 112, 307
Heine, Heinrich, 85
Hellanicus, 168
Hepburn, Marcus J., 55, 294, 316
Heraclitus, 176, 289
Herodotus, xvi, 168, 169, 173, 174, 175, 178, 288, 290, 295, 307
Herrnstein, Richard J., 283, 299
Hess, Eckhard H., 52, 82, 307
Hewes, Gordon W., 39, 59
Heyting, Arend, 186, 307
Hill, Archibald A., 325
Hill, Jane H., 220, 307
Hinde, Robert A., 29, 32, 36, 39, 40, 41, 49, 50, 58, 59, 270, 302, 307, 322
Hinton, Howard Everest, 116, 307
Hippocrates, 6, 7, 8, 29, 53, 259
Hiż, Henry, 231
Hjelmslev, Louis, 38, 65, 166, 229, 235, 240, 253, 255, 256, 258, 307
Hockett, Charles F., 59
Hofsinde, Robert (Gray-Wolf), 130, 133, 134, 143, 307
Holden, Constance, 96, 307
Holmes, Sherlock, 183, 284
Hooff, J. A. R. A. M. van, 5, 32, 307
Hopkins, Carl D., 101, 307
Horányi, Özséb, 216, 274, 277, 307
Horowitz, Louise, 85n., 308
Hospers, John, 117, 308
How, Walter Wybergh, 174, 308
Howe, Margaret, 81
Howitt, Alfred W., 141, 143, 152, 308
Huggins, William H., 118, 308
Humboldt, Wilhelm von, 203, 204, 219
Hume, David, xi–xii
Humfreville, James Lee, 129, 131, 134, 141, 142, 152, 308

Index of Names

Humphrey, Nicholas, 40
Humphries, David A., 58, 299
Hutt, Corinne, 45, 308
Huxley, Aldous, 201
Huxley, Francis, 284, 308
Huxley, Julian, 9, 29, 31, 33, 41, 45, 47, 260, 270, 285, 308
Huxley, Leonard, 285, 308
Huxley, Thomas, 107, 108, 109, 308
Hyman, Ray, 102, 284, 324

Ice Cream (cat), 240, 249
Immerwahr, Henry R., 174, 308
Ingram, Thomas T. S., 72
Irvine, Betty Jo, 276
Ivanov, Vjačeslav V., 39, 308

Jackson, John Hughlings, 58, 59
Jackson, W. Carl, 275
Jacob, François, 42, 43, 67, 265, 308
Jacobson, Lenore, 73, 87, 318
Jakobson, Roman, viii, xiii, 6, 53, 66, 113, 114, 149, 183, 210, 221–231 passim, 234, 235, 237, 238, 240, 259, 261, 273, 275, 278, 292, 293, 308
Jakobson, Svatava Pírková, 228
James, William, 125, 259
Jancewicz, Zofia, 278
Janet, Pierre, 96, 309
Janisse, Michel Pierre, 98, 309
Jastrow, Joseph, xiv–xv
Jaynes, Julian, 8, 32, 98, 268, 309
Jennings, Herbert Spencer, 198, 291, 309
Jervis, Robert, 68, 309
Johausen, Dr. (fictional character), 103, 104, 268, 291
Johnson, Harry Miles, 78, 282, 309
Jones, Ernest, ix
Jones, Russell, xv
Jones, William, 32
Jonson, Ben, 90
Jowett, Benjamin, 221, 230, 287
József, Attila, 236
Juilland, Alphonse, 253n., 292, 309
Jung, Carl G., 192

Kainz, Friedrich, 269, 309
Kakumasu, Jim, 309

Kammann, Richard, 284, 314
Kammerer, Paul, 87, 282
Kant, Immanuel, xi, xiii, 193, 194, 195, 204
Kantor, Jacob Robert, 228, 309
Katz, David, 43, 53, 54, 98, 234, 284, 309
Kauffman, Lynn E., 45, 309
Kavanagh, James F., 38, 251, 309
Kees, Weldon, 49, 318
Kelley, David L., 48, 309
Kelvin, William Thomson, 287
Kendon, Adam, 31, 100, 259, 288, 309
Kessel, Edward L., 18, 19, 20, 21, 30, 309
Ketner, Kenneth Laine, 183n., 184, 310
Key, Francis Scott, 286
Kinney, Arthur E., 75, 310
Kinsbourne, Marcel, 56, 310
Kinzel, Augustus F., 46
Kiparsky, Valentin, 240
Kirchberg, Jutta, 171, 310
Kleiman, Devra, 101, 302
Kleinpaul, Rudolf, 6, 49, 69, 175, 259, 288, 310
Kloft, Werner, 13, 19, 116, 310
Klopfer, Peter H., 40, 193, 197, 310, 315
Knapp, Mark L., 49, 310
Knowlton, James Q., 112, 310
Koch, Ludwig, 45, 47, 308
Kodály, Zoltán, 214
Koehler, Otto, 33, 59, 310
Koenig, Otto, 260, 310
Koestler, Arthur, 67, 87, 282, 310
Kohl, Johann G., 134, 152, 310
Koko (gorilla), 81, 99
Kolata, Gina Bari, 67, 93, 310
Krames, Lester, 49, 50, 310, 317
Krampen, Martin, 193, 310
Krashen, Stephen D., 55, 310
Kresge, George, Jr. (Kreskin), 93, 284, 310
Kreutzer, Mary Anne, 58, 300
Kristeva, Julia, 325
Kriszat, Georg, 323
Kroeber, Alfred Lewis, 132, 134, 140, 149, 158, 159, 166, 310
Kroll, Karl, 74, 80, 88
Kruševskij, Nikolai V., 211

Kugelmass, O. F. (fictional character), 35, 52
Kühn, Carolus Gottlob, 304
Kuleshova, Rosa, 102
Kummer, Hans, 118, 310
Kunoff, Hugo, 279
Kuryłowicz, Jerzy, 229

Labov, William, 219, 311
Lady (horse), 90
Laefliger, Andre, 322
Laferrière, Daniel, 272n.
Lakó, György, 209, 311
Lamb, Sydney M., 65, 259, 288, 311
La Mettrie, Julien Offray de, 283
Lana (chimpanzee), 81, 283
Lancaster, Jane, 322
Lausberg, Heinrich, 110, 115, 311
Laver, John, 50, 51, 311
Law, Helen, 173, 311
Lawendowski, Bogusław, 274, 278
Lawick-Goodall, Jane van, 256, 311
Laziczius, Gyula, 208–217 passim, 220, 249, 291, 292, 311
Leach, Edmund, 261
Leach, Gill M., 31, 298
Le Boeuf, Burney J., 218, 311
Lees, Robert B., 22
Leffler, Béla, 233
Leibniz, Gottfried Wilhelm, xiii, xiv, 44, 66, 78, 79, 127, 195, 265, 271
Lenhart, Margot D., 278
Lenneberg, Elizabeth, 70, 72, 310, 311, 315, 326
Lenneberg, Eric H., 33, 40, 70, 72, 269, 310, 311, 315, 326
Lepschy, Giulio, viii
Levin, Donald Norman, 173, 312
Lévi-Strauss, Claude, viii, xiii, 3, 24, 43, 79, 168n., 169, 175, 176, 179, 191, 225, 229, 240, 261, 289, 290, 294, 312
Levy, Jerre, 56, 312
Lex, Barbara W., 284, 312
Lieberman, Philip, 40, 312
Lilly, John Cunningham, 81, 100, 312
Limber, John, 74, 201, 283, 285, 312
Lindauer, Martin, 250, 312
Linden, Eugene, 192, 312
Livingstone, Frank B., 39

Ljung, Magnus, 153, 166, 288, 312
Lloyd, Lyle L., 301
Locke, John, vii, x, xi, xiii, 36, 37, 253, 312
Logeman, Willem S., 321
Lomax, Alan, 39, 228
Lomax, John A., 228
Long, Stephen Harriman, 312
Lore, Richard, 82, 312
Lorenz, Konrad, 14, 57, 119, 192, 193, 196, 198, 199, 291, 312
Lott, D. F., 118, 312
Lotz, Ann, 233, 242
Lotz, C. Peter, 233
Lotz, Catherine, 233
Lotz, John, 47, 48, 226, 231–252 passim, 291, 293, 294, 312
Lotz, John Martin, 233
Lotz, Martin, 233
Love, J. R. B., 313
Lubbock, John (Lord Avebury), 91, 92, 95, 313
Lucy (chimpanzee), 115
Luria, Aleksandr R., 55, 58, 113, 313
Lyons, John, 59
Lysenko, Trofim Denisovich, 106

McCormack, William, 50, 58, 312
McCulloch, Warren S., 190, 313
McGuire, James P., 112
MacKay, Donald, 270
Macksey, Richard, 109, 310
Maclean, John, 140, 143, 152, 312
McNeill, David, 69, 313
McPhee, John, 293, 313
McVay, Scott, 39, 316
Máday, Stefan von, 53, 54, 313
Majno, Guido, 8, 313
Makkai, Adam, 65, 259, 311
Maldonado, Tomás, 111
Malinowski, Bronislaw, 50, 52, 313
Mallery, Garrick, 141, 146, 147, 148, 150, 151, 152, 153, 158, 159, 160, 166, 167, 288, 310, 313, 324
Malmberg, Bertil, 212, 235
Malson, Lucien, 37, 44, 314
Mangel, Charles, 112, 307
Manning, Aubrey, 315
Maranda, Pierre, 319
Marcus, Solomon, 19, 37, 42, 64, 314

Marcy, Randolph Barnes, 141, 314
Marks, David, 284, 314
Marler, Peter, 57, 219, 275, 314
Maroccus Extaticus. *See* Morocco
Marples, Mary J., 45, 314
Martin, Charles Beebe, 172, 314
Martin, Samuel E., 293
Martinet, André, 238, 292
Martínez, D. José A., 183n.
Marx, Karl, 282, 314
Matejka, Ladislav, 324
Mathesius, Vilém, 210
Matthews, William Kleesman, 292, 314
Mattingly, Ignatius G., 38, 252, 309
Maurer, David W., 77–78, 282, 314
Mead, George Herbert, 287
Mead, Margaret, 68, 258, 314
Medawar, Jean S., 187, 194, 195, 264, 265, 269, 314
Medawar, Peter Brian, 187, 194, 195, 264, 265, 269, 314
Meggitt, Mervyn, 134, 141, 143, 152, 288, 314
Mehrabian, Albert, 49, 50, 314
Mehta, Ved Parkash, 225, 227, 229, 314
Meillet, Antoine, 186
Meleager, 173
Meletus, 227
Meltzer, James D., 6, 71, 320
Mendel, Gregor, 201
Menges, Karl, 293
Merle, Robert, 103, 268
Merton, Robert K., 86, 314
Meunier, J., 173, 314
Meyer, A., 291
Michener, Charles Duncan, 256, 314
Miller, James G., 43, 66, 67, 314
Miller, Molly, 173, 315
Miller, Wick, 134, 141, 149, 152, 153, 166, 315
Moertel, Charles G., 96, 315
Moles, Abraham A., 45, 315
Mona Lisa, 119
Montagu, Ashley, 45, 315
Montague, Richard, 195, 196, 315
Montalenti, Giuseppe, 291
Montlyard, Jean de (Sieur de Melleray), 90

Moore, Edward C., 276
Morgan, Arlene, 258, 302
Morocco (horse), 75, 76, 87, 90
Morris, Charles, vii, xii, xiii, xv–xvi, 6, 12, 19, 36, 43, 63–67 passim, 69, 121, 223, 253, 255, 258, 259, 286, 315
Morris, Desmond, 40, 98, 315
Mounin, Georges, 141, 147, 159, 165, 315
Mountford, Charles P., 152, 315
Moynihan, Martin, 30, 315
Myson, 178

Nagel, Ernest, 109, 307, 315
Narasimhan, Raghavan, 322
Nattiez, Jean-Jacques, 52, 315
Naville, Adrien, 216
Nelson, Keith, 40, 315
Neuberger, Max, 281, 315
Neumann, John von, 25, 293
Newman, Stanley, 240
Newton, Isaac, 127
Newton, Robert R., 87
Nicole, Pierre, ix–x
Nidditch, Peter H., 312
Nietzsche, Friedrich Wilhelm, 130
Norsworthy, Ann M., *See* Lotz, Ann
Nöth, Winfried, 225, 315
Nottebohm, Fernando, 219, 220, 315

Oedipus, 177, 194
Ogden, Charles Kay, 301
Ogibenin, Boris, 278
Oléron, Pierre, 257, 315
Orne, Martin T., 96, 303, 315
Ornstein, Alex, 85n., 308
Ornstein, Robert E., 44, 55, 316
Osgood, Charles Egerton, 255, 260, 292, 316
Osmond-Smith, David, 117, 316
Osmundsen, Lita, 238
Osten, Wilhelm von, xiv, 74, 75, 90
Osten-Sacken, Carl Robert, 18
Oyer, E. Jane, 70, 316
Oyer, Herbert J., 70, 316

Pantaleon, 290
Papp, Maria, 319
Paredes, J. Anthony, 55, 294, 316

Paris, Jean, 224, 225, 303
Parker, William Riley, 241, 316
Parsifal. *See* Percival
Partee, Barbara H., 196, 316
Patterson, Francine G., 81, 98, 316
Paul, Hermann, 33
Pavlov, Ivan, 73, 74, 75, 78, 81, 83–87 passim, 95, 98, 101
Payne, Roger S., 39, 316
Pegasus (fictional horse), xv
Peirce, Benjamin, 186, 288
Peirce, Charles Sanders, vii–xiii passim, 3, 5, 6, 9, 10, 12, 13, 19, 22, 23, 25–28 passim, 36, 39, 43–47 passim, 53, 61, 62, 65, 66, 67, 69, 70, 77, 93, 94, 95, 109–122 passim, 125, 147, 150, 183, 184, 186, 191, 194, 195, 197, 200, 201, 203, 204, 205, 207, 229, 256, 257, 258, 259, 263, 266, 270, 273, 274, 275, 277, 279, 284–288 passim, 290, 316
Peng, Fred C. C., 153, 316
Pepys, Samuel, 90
Percival, 177, 294
Perry, Campbell W., 98, 320
Perry, Ralph Barton, 125, 316
Peter Dolphin (dolphin), 81
Peterson, Richard S., 218, 311
Petrarch, 172
Pfungst, Oskar, xiv, xv, 53, 54, 75, 78, 83, 90, 91, 95, 101, 316
Phillips, Dennis Charles, 67, 316
Philodemus, 63, 316
Piaget, Jean, 201, 316
Pictet, M. F. T., 184
Pierce, John R., 102, 316
Pignatari, Décio, 278
Pike, Kenneth L., 47, 65, 259, 317
Pilisuk, Mark, 82, 95, 317
Pitcairn, Thomas K., 60
Plantamour, Emile, 290
Plato, 3, 110, 120, 221, 228, 230, 268
Pliner, Patricia, 49, 50, 310, 317
Plutarch, 290
Pluto (fictional dog), 268
Poinsot, Jean, 274
Polanyi, Michael, 90, 317
Polhemus, Ted, 37, 41, 298
Polybius, 168
Ponnamperuma, Cyril, 102, 297, 317

Ponzio, Augusto, 111, 317
Pope, Alexander, 26
Pope, Benjamin, 309
Poppe, Nicholas N., 293
Popper, Karl, 203, 204, 205, 206, 317
Posinsky, Sollie Henry, 284, 317
Pouillon, Jean, 319
Poyatos, Fernando, 49, 51, 317
Pratt, Joseph Gaither, 102, 317
Prelog, Vladimir, 287, 317
Premack, Ann J., 54, 81, 317
Premack, David, 54, 81, 285, 317
Pribram, Karl H., 64, 317
Prieto, Luis J., 27, 36, 317
Pritsak, Omeljan, 293
Prospero (character in *The Tempest*), 130
Protagoras of Abdera, 3, 26
Ptolemy, Claudius, 87
Pumphrey, Richard Julius, 57
Pythagoras, 90

Quinlan, Karen Ann, 112, 125

Rader, Wendelin, 49, 303
Radet, Georges, 289, 317
Rahv, Philip, 228
Randi, James, 284
Rawlinson, George, 288, 307
Ray, Verne F., 317
Raymond, Dr. (cited by A. Shapiro), 190
Razran, Gregory, 73, 85, 86, 317
Rey, Alain, 277
Rey-Debove, Josette, 325
Rhine, Joseph Banks, 90
Rhine, Louisa E., 283, 317
Richards, Ivor Armstrong, 301
Rid, Samuel, 75, 90, 91, 95
Rieber, Robert W., 300
Rigby, Peter, 37
Rinn, Joseph F., 285, 317
Roberts, Don, 117, 317
Robertson, Anthony, 281
Robinson, N. H., 92
Romains, Jules, 285, 317
Romeo, Luigi, 176, 317
Rose, Steven, 64, 317
Rosenthal, Robert, xiv, 53, 54, 73, 75, 81, 82, 87, 95, 101, 316, 318

Roth, Arthur, 149, 315
Roth, Walter E., 141, 143, 152, 318
Roubaud, Jacques, 224, 225, 303
Rousseau, Jean-Jacques, 185
Roussel, Philippe, 172, 318
Roux, Georges, 104, 268
Rubini, Eugen de, 82–83, 285
Ruesch, Jurgen, 49, 66, 75, 318
Rumbaugh, Duane M., 54, 81, 200, 283, 318
Russell, Edward S., 32, 318

Sacerdote, Paul, 96
Sadyattes, 289
Saint Pierre (Leibniz's correspondent), 79
Sakitt, Barbara, 118, 123, 318
Sallust, 168
Salzinger, Kurt, 304
Samarin, William J., 295, 318
Sapir, Edward, 32, 37, 38, 43, 210, 318
Sarah (chimpanzee), 81
Sarbin, Theodore R., 96, 318
Sarton, George, 7, 318
Šaumjan, Sebastian, *See* Shaumjan, Sebastian K.
Saussure, Ferdinand de, vii, viii, xii, xiii, 5, 6, 8, 27, 36, 37, 63, 65, 113, 121, 122, 183–187 passim, 210, 216, 252, 253, 259, 273, 290, 291, 301, 318
Saussure, Henri de, 184, 185, 290
Saussure, Horace-Bénédict de, 184, 185
Saussure, Théodore de, 184, 186
Sayce, Archibald Henry, 143, 318
Sayce, James, 173, 318
Schapiro, Meyer, 231
Scharf, Joachim-Hermann, 33, 318
Scherer, Klaus R., 49, 319
Schiefelbush, Richard L., 301
Schiller, Claire H., 323
Schlegel, Friedrich von, 8, 32, 33, 57
Schleicher, August, 33, 220, 292
Schmeck, Harold M., Jr., 264, 319
Schneirla, Theodore C., 43, 123, 319
Schooneveld, Cornelis H. van, 221n.
Schopler, Eric, 289
Schroer, Sabine, 17

Schutz, Noel W., Jr., 48, 319
Schwabl, Hans, 174, 319
Schwimmer, Erik, 65, 261, 319
Scott, Hugh Lennox, 132, 134, 141, 143, 146, 153, 319
Sebeok, Thomas A., xvi, 4–9 passim, 12, 19, 22, 27, 28, 29, 31, 33, 35–42 passim, 44, 47–65 passim, 68, 71, 73, 74, 81, 86n., 100, 101, 102, 109, 111, 113, 115, 116, 118, 121, 122, 124, 128n., 134, 135, 149, 168n., 183, 186, 190, 192, 193, 195, 201, 204, 209n., 216, 217, 218, 221, 223, 225, 229, 235, 249, 250, 251, 255, 256, 258, 259, 260, 269, 274, 277, 281–292 passim, 295, 298, 299, 302, 303, 307, 311–316 passim, 319–322 passim, 324
Segal, Charles, 174, 175, 320
Seigman, Aron, 309
Seligman, Charles Gabriel, 149, 320
Sélincourt, Aubrey de, 288, 307
Seton, Ernest Thompson, 130, 320
Seurat, Georges, viii
Sextus Empiricus, 187
Shakespeare, William, 75, 128
Shands, Harley C., xiv, 6, 8, 44, 71, 128, 190, 265, 275, 277, 281, 320
Shanon, Benny, 22
Shapiro, Arthur K., 77, 190, 192, 320
Shapiro, Gary, 117, 320
Shaumjan, Sebastian K., 255, 256, 275, 320
Sheehan, Peter W., 98, 320
Sheils, Helen, 325
Sherzer, Joel, 298
Shor, Ronald E., 303
Shur, Max, ix
Sigerist, Henry E., 6, 320
Silverstein, Michael, 309
Simmel, Edward C., 40, 57, 60, 306
Simmons, Ernest J., 235, 236
Simone, Raffaele, 63, 321
Simpson, George Gaylord, 4, 321
Sinclair, Upton, 284, 321
Singer, Milton, 261, 275, 276
Smith, Ralph R., Jr., 49, 302
Smith, William John, 28, 29, 58, 193, 268–271 passim, 321
Smuts, Jan Christiaan, 291

Index of Names

Smythies, John R., 308
Snell, Bruno, 173, 321
Snoopy (fictional dog), 35
Socrates, 124, 221, 227
Soffietti, James Peter, 227
Solon, 169, 173–177 passim, 179, 288, 289
Solso, Robert L., 313
Sommer, Robert, 118, 312
Sommerfelt, Alf, 229
Šor, R. O., 211
Speigelberg, Wilhelm, 172, 321
Spencer, Baldwin, 141, 152, 321
Spielberger, Charles D., 305
Stafford, Philip B., 59, 70. 321
Stanislavsky, Konstantin S., 225, 321
Stanner, William E. H., 325
Stansbury, Howard, 141
Steiner, George, 128, 219, 220, 321
Steinitz, Wolfgang, 234, 292
Steinthal, Heymann von, 58, 71
Steklis, Horst B., 322
Stepanov, Yuri S., 9, 12, 193, 199, 321
Stern, Raphael, 85n., 308, 316
Stern, Theodore, 149, 321
Stewart, Ian, 24, 121, 125, 126, 127, 321
Stirling, Edward C., 143, 152, 321
Stokoe, William C., Jr., 38, 99, 100, 147, 148, 150, 153, 166, 275, 277, 287, 288, 301, 321
Stratton, George M., 83, 91, 321
Strehlow, Carl, 152, 321
Strong, Herbert A., 33, 321
Studentsov (Pavlov's assistant), 73, 81, 86, 87, 101
Stumpf, Carl, 53, 75, 95
Suppes, Patrick, 307
Swayzee, Cleon O., 244
Sweet, Henry, 212
Sybil, 177
Szépe, György, 216, 291, 294, 307
Szilard, Leo, 103, 293
Szöke, Péter, 39, 322

Tamura, Miwako, 219, 314
Tarnóczy, Tamás, 235
Tarski, Alfred, 307
Tatu (chimpanzee), 99
Tax, Sol, 304

Taylor, Allan R., 132, 134, 149, 150, 152, 166, 322
Taylor, William F., 315
Teit, James A., 322
Teller, Edward, 293
Tellos, 289
Temerlin, Maurice K., 115, 322
Temkin, Oswei, 71, 322
Terrace, Herbert S., 283, 322
Theaetetus, 124
Theopompus, 169
Thibaud, Pierre, 117, 322
Thielcke, Gerhard, 218, 322
Thom, René, viii, x, xi, xii, xiii, 5, 6, 22, 24, 25, 34, 44, 57, 62, 66, 67, 77, 111, 115, 120–127 passim, 201, 202, 207, 261, 266, 271, 281, 289, 322
Thomas, Lewis (M.D.), 8, 23, 71, 281, 322
Thomas, Lewis (Turkologist), 293
Thomason, Richmond H., 196, 315
Thompson, D'Arcy Wentworth, 25, 57
Thompson, Stith, 228
Thomson, James Alexander Kerr, 174, 322
Thomson, John Arthur, 91, 322
Thorpe, William Homan, 41, 298
Thucydides, 168, 169, 288
Tietze, Andreas, 293
Timaeus, Ernst, 54, 322
Tinbergen, Elisabeth A., 29, 72, 323
Tinbergen, Niko, 29, 32, 72, 323
Titunik, Irwin R., 324
Tolman, Edward C., 83, 91
Tolstoy, Leo, 210
Tomkins, Gordon M., 22, 23, 24, 43, 44, 64, 281, 323
Tomkins, William, 130, 323
Trubetzkoy, Nikolaj Sergeevič, 210–214 passim, 223, 292, 323
Truzzi, Marcello, 87, 323
Tunnell, Gary G., 56, 323
Turner, Richard L., 276, 277
Turner, Victor, 111, 261, 323
Tuteur, Werner, 283, 323
Tuttle, Russell H., 304
Twaddell, William Freeman, 210, 292
Tyce, Francis A. J., 315

Udin, S., 27n.
Uexküll, Gudrun von, 188, 192, 193, 323
Uexküll, Jakob von, viii, x–xi, xiii, 9, 10, 11, 12, 14, 22, 24, 26, 28, 37, 42, 66, 67, 83, 188, 192–205 passim, 207, 261, 281, 287, 291, 323
Uexküll, Thure von, x, 96, 188, 190, 265, 281, 323
Uldall, Hans, 166
Ullman, I. M., 260, 323
Umiker, William O., 293
Umiker-Sebeok, Donna Jean, xvi, 38, 47, 51, 61n., 65, 69, 71, 86n., 115, 128, 128n., 149, 168n., 284, 312–315 passim, 320, 321, 322, 324, 325

Vachek, Josef, 223, 324
Vaisey, M. Jane, 45, 308
Vakar, Gertrude, 324
Valesio, Paolo, 114, 324
Van (dog), 91
van der Hove, Didier, 317
van Hooff, J. A. R. A. M., 5, 32, 307
van Wijk, Nicolaas, 212
Vavilov, Sergeĭ Ivanovich, 12
Velten, Harry V., 228
Veltruský, Jiří, 117, 324
Verne, Jules, 103, 104, 268, 291, 324
Vértes, Edith, 291
Vine, Ian, 323
Vinokur, Grigoriĭ O., 211
Voegelin, Carl F., 49, 75, 141, 159, 164, 165, 228, 324
Vogt, Evon Z., 102, 284, 324
Voigt, Vilmos, 68, 324
Volli, Ugo, 111
Vološinov, Valentin N., 44, 324
Vygotsky, Lev Semenovich, 44, 324

Waddington, Conrad H., 25, 40, 57
Wade, Nicholas, 87, 324
Wagoner, David, 96, 324
Walker, Jerell R., 324
Wallace, Anthony F. C., 324
Wallis, Mieczysław, 111, 119, 324
Warner, William Lloyd, 152, 324
Washburn, Sherwood L., 43, 324
Washoe (chimpanzee), 81, 115

Wassell, William H., 134, 325
Watson, O. Michael, 45
Watt, W. C., xii, 118, 325
Webb, Walter Prescott, 134, 150, 152, 325
Weeping Roger (horse), 283
Weil, Elsie, 132, 143, 325
Weinreich, Uriel, 37, 63, 258, 325
Weiss, Paul, 316
Weitman, Sasha R., 286, 325
Weitz, Shirley, 49, 325
Weizenbaum, Joseph, 56, 283, 325
Welby, Victoria, 65, 122
Wells, Joseph, 174, 308
Wells, Rulon, 110, 258, 276, 325
Wenner, Adrian M., 249, 325
Wertheimer, Max, 113, 114, 325
Wescott, Roger W., 39, 40, 48, 59, 114, 325
West, La Mont, Jr., 132, 134, 135, 141, 143, 146, 147, 149–153 passim, 158, 164–167 passim, 287, 288, 325
Wheeler, Benjamin Ide, 321
Whitaker, Haiganoosh, 310
Whitaker, Harry A., 55, 301, 310
White, M. E., 174, 325
Whiten, Andrew, 40
Whitfield, Francis, 65, 325
Whitney, Josiah, 183, 184, 325
Whitney, William Dwight, 146, 183, 184
Whorf, Benjamin Lee, 203, 204
Whyte, Lancelot Law, 305
Wickler, Wolfgang, 116, 119, 325
Wied-Neuweid, Maximilian von, 325
Wiener, Philip P., 303
Wigner, Eugene Paul, 293
Wilkin, A., 149, 320
Williams, Thomas R., 302
Willis, Roy, 304
Wilson, Edward O., 117, 217, 325
Wimsatt, William R., Jr., 110, 326
Windelband, Wilhelm, 201
Wing, Lorna, 289, 326
Winner, Irene Portis, 39, 64, 69, 86n., 326
Winner, Thomas G., 39, 64, 69, 326
Winteler, Jost, 159
Wittgenstein, Ludwig, 200, 326

Wolfe, John B., 43, 326
Wood, Forrest G., 54, 100, 326
Wormell, Donald Ernest Wilson, 173, 326
Wurm, Stephen A., 50, 58, 312

Xenophon, 168

Young, Frederic H., 303
Young, John Z., 28, 43, 266, 326

Zangwill, Oliver L., 55, 57, 298, 326
Zasetsky, L., 58
Zeeman, E. Christopher, 281, 326
Zeman, J. Jay, 117, 326
Zirkle, Conway, 73, 74, 85, 326
Zorn, E. R., 326